ArcGIS Pro 2.x C

Create, manage, and share geographic maps, data, and analytical models using ArcGIS Pro

Tripp Corbin, GISP

BIRMINGHAM - MUMBAI

ArcGIS Pro 2.x Cookbook

Commissioning Editor: Arun Lazar
Acquisition Editor: Nitin Dasan
Content Development Editor: Nikhil Borkar
Technical Editor: Jash Bavishi
Copy Editor: Safis Editing
Project Coordinator: Ulhas Kambali
Proofreader: Safis Editing
Indexer: Pratik Shirodkar
Graphics: Tania Dutta
Production Coordinator: Aparna Bhagat

First published: February 2018

Production reference: 1260218

Published by Packt Publishing Ltd.
Livery Place
35 Livery Street
Birmingham
B3 2PB, UK.

ISBN 978-1-78829-903-9

www.packtpub.com

To my wife, Polly Corbin, for all her love and support, without which I would not be the successful GIS professional I am today.

About the reviewer

Timothy J. Gaunt, GISP, has over 10 years of experience in information technology with a focus on networking, communications, enterprise software deployment, and server maintenance. Over the years, he has installed and configured Windows Server, ArcGIS, Microsoft SQL Server, and APIs for customizing web and mobile GIS applications. He has also undertaken development with Windows PowerShell, Python, HTML, Visual Basic, security system configuration, order system overhauls, and website creation and design. Gaunt has been working with eGIS Associates as an Enterprise IT and GIS specialist since 2012.

The completion of this undertaking would not have been possible without the support and encouragement from my loving wife, Brittany. I would also like to thank Dr. J. B. Sharma of the University of North GA, my colleagues at JCWSA and eGIS Associates, and all my friends and family who have provided guidance and training over the years.

Packt is searching for authors like you

If you're interested in becoming an author for Packt, please visit `authors.packtpub.com` and apply today. We have worked with thousands of developers and tech professionals, just like you, to help them share their insight with the global tech community. You can make a general application, apply for a specific hot topic that we are recruiting an author for, or submit your own idea.

Table of Contents

Preface

ArcGIS Pro is Esri's newest desktop GIS application with powerful tools for visualizing, maintaining, and analyzing data. ArcGIS Pro makes use of the modern ribbon interface and 64-bit processing to increase the speed and efficiency of GIS. It allows users to create amazing maps in both 2D and 3D quickly and easily.

If you want to gain a thorough understanding of how ArcGIS Pro can be used to perform various types of geospatial analysis, how to work with various data formats, and how to share your ArcGIS Pro results via ArcGIS Online, then this book is for you.

Beginning with a refresher on ArcGIS Pro and how to work with projects, this book will quickly take you through recipes on using various data formats supported within the application. You will learn the limits of each format such as Shapefiles, Geodatabase, and CAD files, and see how to convert the data to the format that best suites your needs. Next, you will learn how to link tables from outside sources to existing GIS data to expand the amount of data that can be used in ArcGIS Pro. From there, you will dive into ways to edit 2D and 3D data using ArcGIS Pro and understand how topology can be used to ensure data integrity. We will explore different analysis tools that allow us to perform both 2D and 3D analysis. Lastly, the book will show how data and maps can be shared via ArcGIS Online and used with web and mobile applications. This book will also introduce you to ArcGIS Arcade, Esri's new expression language, which is supported across the entire ArcGIS platform.

Who this book is for

If you have limited experience with ArcGIS and want to learn more about how ArcGIS Pro works and the powerful tools for data maintenance, analysis, and sharing it contains, this is the book for you. It is also a great resource for those migrating from ArcGIS Desktop (ArcMap and ArcCatalog) to ArcGIS Pro.

What this book covers

Chapter 1, *ArcGIS Pro Capabilities and Terminology*, reviews basic ArcGIS Pro functionality and terms.

Chapter 2, *Creating and Storing Data*, examines ArcGIS Pro's ability to use different storage data formats.

Chapter 3, *Linking Data together*, explains how to link external data to your GIS for use in analysis and display.

Chapter 4, *Editing Spatial and Tabular Data*, explores various tools for creating and editing new features in your GIS databases.

Chapter 5, *Validating and Editing Data with Topologies*, shows how to use topologies to improve the accuracy of your data and increase editing efficiency.

Chapter 6, *Projections and Coordinate System Basics*, explains the importance of coordinate systems in GIS and how to move your data from one to another.

Chapter 7, *Converting Data*, steps you through various methods you can use to convert GIS data from one storage format to another.

Chapter 8, *Proximity Analysis*, explores different tools for determining how far or near features in a map are from one another.

Chapter 9, *Spatial Statistics and Hot Spots*, shows how you can locate clusters, spot patterns, and determine the spatial center of a collection of features.

Chapter 10, *3D Maps and 3D Analyst*, shows how you can use ArcGIS Pro and the 3D analyst extension to perform 3D analysis such as calculating sight lines and volumes.

Chapter 11, *Introducing Arcade*, shows how you can create labeling and symbology expressions using the new Arcade expression language.

Chapter 12, *Introducing ArcGIS Online*, steps you through connecting to your ArcGIS Online account and how to access content that others have published to create a web map.

Chapter 13, *Publishing Your Own Content to ArcGIS Online*, takes you through the process of publishing your own content to ArcGIS Online so that others in your organization can access it.

Chapter 14, *Creating Web Apps Using ArcGIS Online*, shows you how you can create your own web GIS applications without having to be a programmer.

To get the most out of this book

1. This book assumes that the reader has at least some knowledge of ArcGIS Pro. It is recommended that you have read and worked through the exercises in the *Learning ArcGIS Pro* book by Packt Publishing or have previous real-world experience using ArcGIS Pro or ArcMap.

2. You will need to have ArcGIS Pro 2.1 or later installed with a Standard or higher license along with a license for the 3D Analyst extension for ArcGIS Pro in order to complete all the recipes in this book. If you are limited to a basic license or don't have a 3D Analyst license, you will still be able to complete the majority of the recipes, just not all of them.

3. You will need a username and a login password for ArcGIS Online with at least Publisher-level permissions.

4. You will need to download and install the sample data files as instructed in the *Download the example code files* section.

5. If you do not have a license for ArcGIS Pro, 3D Analyst extension, or ArcGIS Online, you can request a trial license from Esri at http://www.esri.com/arcgis/trial.

Download the example code files

You can download the example code files for this book from your account at www.packtpub.com. If you purchased this book elsewhere, you can visit www.packtpub.com/support and register to have the files emailed directly to you.

You can download the code files by following these steps:

1. Log in or register at www.packtpub.com.
2. Select the **SUPPORT** tab.
3. Click on **Code Downloads & Errata**.
4. Enter the name of the book in the **Search** box and follow the onscreen instructions.

Once the file is downloaded, please make sure that you unzip or extract the folder using the latest version of:

- WinRAR/7-Zip for Windows
- Zipeg/iZip/UnRarX for Mac
- 7-Zip/PeaZip for Linux

The code bundle for the book is also hosted on GitHub at
`https://github.com/PacktPublishing/ArcGIS-Pro-2.x-Cookbook`. We also have other
code bundles from our rich catalog of books and videos available at `https://github.com/`
`PacktPublishing/`. Check them out!

Download the color images

We also provide a PDF file that has color images of the screenshots/diagrams used in this
book. You can download it here:
`http://www.packtpub.com/sites/default/files/downloads/ArcGISPro2.xCookbook_Colo`
`rImages.pdf`.

Conventions used

There are a number of text conventions used throughout this book.

`CodeInText`: Indicates code words in text, database table names, folder names, filenames,
file extensions, pathnames, dummy URLs, user input, and Twitter handles. Here is an
example: "Navigate to `C:\Student\ArcGISProCookbook\Chapter2\RasterVector` by
clicking on `C:\` in the area on the left."

A block of code is set as follows:

```
if (cond=="Good")
   {
   return "<CLR green='255'>"+name+"</CLR>"
   }
if (cond=="Fair")
   {
   return name
   }
else
   {
   return "<BOL><CLR red='255'>"+name+"</CLR></BOL>"
   }
```

Bold: Indicates a new term, an important word, or words that you see onscreen. For
example, words in menus or dialog boxes appear in the text like this. Here is an example:
"Select the **Map** tab in the ribbon and then click the small arrowhead located
under **Bookmarks**."

Warnings or important notes appear like this.

 Tips and tricks appear like this.

Sections

In this book, you will find several headings that appear frequently (*Getting ready*, *How to do it...*, *How it works...*, *There's more...*, and *See also*).

To give clear instructions on how to complete a recipe, use these sections as follows:

Getting ready

This section tells you what to expect in the recipe and describes how to set up any software or any preliminary settings required for the recipe.

How to do it...

This section contains the steps required to follow the recipe.

How it works...

This section usually consists of a detailed explanation of what happened in the previous section.

There's more...

This section consists of additional information about the recipe in order to make you more knowledgeable about the recipe.

See also

This section provides helpful links to other useful information for the recipe.

Get in touch

Feedback from our readers is always welcome.

General feedback: Email `feedback@packtpub.com` and mention the book title in the subject of your message. If you have questions about any aspect of this book, please email us at `questions@packtpub.com`.

Errata: Although we have taken every care to ensure the accuracy of our content, mistakes do happen. If you have found a mistake in this book, we would be grateful if you would report this to us. Please visit `www.packtpub.com/submit-errata`, selecting your book, clicking on the Errata Submission Form link, and entering the details.

Piracy: If you come across any illegal copies of our works in any form on the internet, we would be grateful if you would provide us with the location address or website name. Please contact us at `copyright@packtpub.com` with a link to the material.

If you are interested in becoming an author: If there is a topic that you have expertise in and you are interested in either writing or contributing to a book, please visit `authors.packtpub.com`.

Reviews

Please leave a review. Once you have read and used this book, why not leave a review on the site that you purchased it from? Potential readers can then see and use your unbiased opinion to make purchase decisions, we at Packt can understand what you think about our products, and our authors can see your feedback on their book. Thank you!

For more information about Packt, please visit `packtpub.com`.

1
ArcGIS Pro Capabilities and Terminology

In this chapter, we will cover the following recipes:

- Determining whether your computer can run ArcGIS Pro
- Determining your ArcGIS Pro license level
- Opening an existing ArcGIS Pro project
- Opening and navigating a map
- Adding and configuring layers
- Creating a project

Introduction

ArcGIS Pro represents a huge step forward in Desktop GIS. This new 64-bit solution allows GIS Professionals to take full advantage of modern computer hardware, which brings increased performance and capability that has not been available for the desktop. It also has a brand new modern ribbon interface. This is completely different from the toolbar-based interface we have become accustomed to in ArcMap or ArcCatalog. While more intuitive for completely new users, it can be a bit challenging for existing ArcGIS Desktop users.

In this chapter, you will begin exploring ArcGIS Pro. You will first determine whether your computer has the capability to run this powerful software. Then you will determine which license levels are available to you. This is important as it will impact your ability to complete some of the recipes in this book.

You will then move on to working in ArcGIS Pro. You will start by learning how to open an existing ArcGIS Pro project. Then you will open and navigate a map. From there, you will learn methods for adding new layers and configuring some of their properties.

Finally, you will learn how to create a new project from the beginning. This will include adding new maps, and importing ArcMap map documents.

Determining whether your computer can run ArcGIS Pro

Unlike the 32-bit ArcMap and ArcCatalog applications, ArcGIS Pro supports hyperthreading (use of multiple core processors), graphics processing units, and more than 4 GB of RAM. This also means ArcGIS Pro requires more computer resources to run properly.

The minimum requirements for ArcGIS Pro 2.1 are:

- Windows 64-bit OS:
    - Windows 7, 8.1, or 10
    - Windows Server 2008 R2, 2012, 2012 R2, or 2016
- Hyperthreaded dual core processor
- 4 GB RAM
- 32 GB hard drive space
- 2 GB video memory
- Microsoft .NET Framework 4.6.1
- Microsoft Internet Explorer 11
- DirectX 11
- OpenGL 3.3
- Shader Model 4.1
- Pixel Shader 4.0
- Vertex Shader 4.0

Keep in mind that these are the minimum requirements. The more hardware the better where ArcGIS Pro is concerned. In general, I would recommend at least 12 GB of RAM, an i5 dual core processor, and a separate video card with its own GPU and memory. For a complete set of recommended hardware specifications, you may want to look at my other book from Packt Publishing, *Learning ArcGIS Pro*.

In this recipe, you will learn how to use the system requirements tool to verify whether your computer can run ArcGIS Pro. This is a free tool provided by Esri.

Getting ready

To work through this recipe, you will need to make sure you have access to the internet and sufficient permissions to install software on your computer.

How to do it...

1. Open your favorite web browser, such as Google Chrome, Microsoft Internet Explorer, or Firefox.
2. Go to `http://pro.arcgis.com`.
3. Click the **Get Started**, tab as shown in the following screenshot:

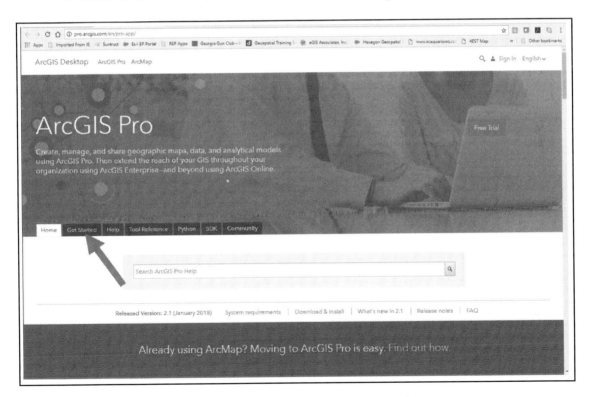

4. Click the link located in **Review the system requirements**.

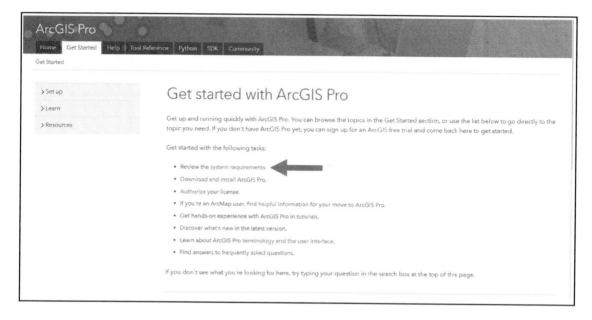

5. Click on the **Supported Operating Systems** link located on the right-hand side of the page in the **In this topic** box.

6. Click **Check your computer's ability to run ArcGIS Pro 2.1**:

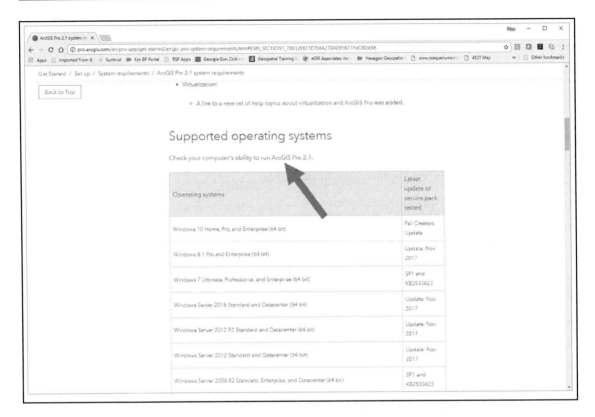

A new tab should open in your browser and take you to the **Can You RUN It** page powered by System Requirements Lab.

7. Click the **Can You RUN It** button, as shown here, to download the
`Detection.exe` file:

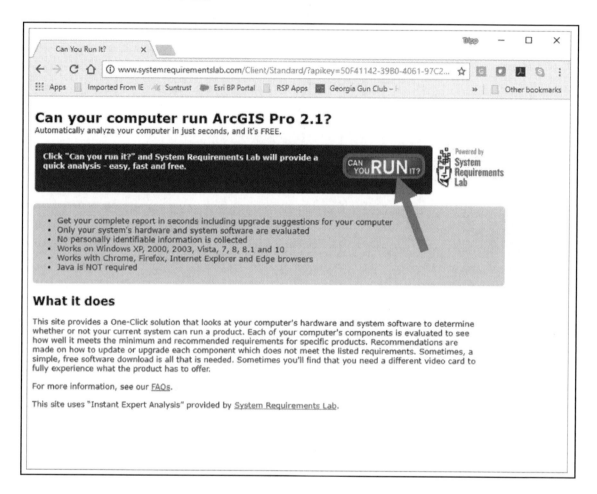

8. Once the `Detection.exe` file is downloaded, click it to run the file. This
executable will check the specifications of your computer and generate a report
indicating whether your computer is capable of running ArcGIS Pro.

9. When the hardware detection application is complete, return to your web
browser to see the results. It hopefully will indicate your system passed, similar
to the following screenshot:

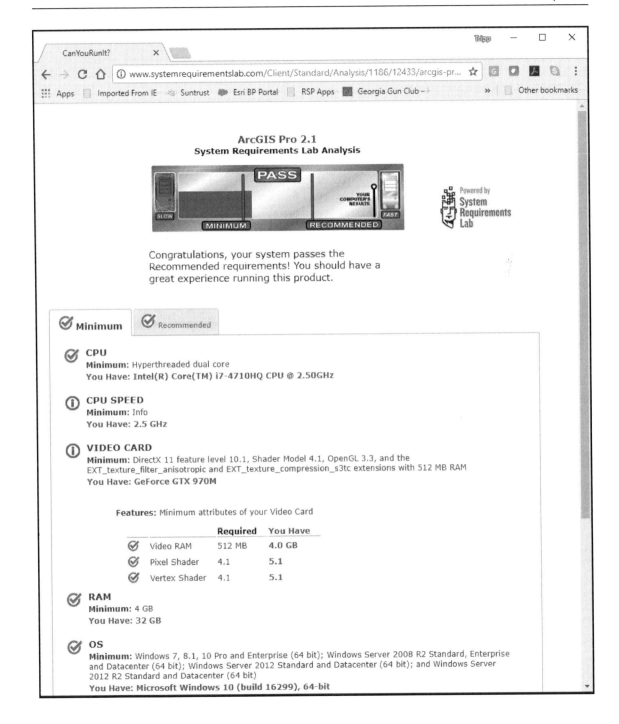

Notice that you can see whether your system meets the minimum and recommended specifications for running ArcGIS Pro. If your system just meets the minimum specifications, you can expect ArcGIS Pro to run slowly and require the application to be restarted much more frequently.

If your system failed, you will need to upgrade the components or software that the reports indicate are below the required specifications. This might be as simple as updating your drivers or Internet Explorer. It might require you to purchase new hardware if your CPU, RAM, or video card fail to meet the minimum requirements.

If your system meets or exceeds the system requirements, you may download and install ArcGIS Pro. Please refer to the installation instructions located at `http://pro.arcgis.com/en/pro-app/get-started/install-and-sign-in-to-arcgis-pro.htm`.

How it works...

ArcGIS Pro has very specific requirements that must be met in order to run effectively. In this recipe, you downloaded and used the tool provided by Esri to verify whether your system met or exceeded those requirements. This tool checks for both hardware and software dependencies needed to successfully run ArcGIS Pro, and provides you with a detailed report so you know without a doubt whether your computer has the horsepower required.

Determining your ArcGIS Pro license level

ArcGIS Pro has three different license levels: Basic, Standard, and Advanced. The license level determines the level of functionality available to the user. Basic has the least functionality, Advanced has the most, and Standard is somewhere in between.

In general, Basic allows you to visualize GIS data, produce maps, perform simple data edits, and perform basic GIS data analysis. Standard builds on the capabilities of the Basic level, with more advanced editing and data validation tools. Advanced expands the capabilities of both Basic and Standard by adding more data analysis tools. For a complete list of the capabilities of each license level of ArcGIS Pro, go to `http://pro.arcgis.com/en/pro-app/get-started/license-levels.htm`.

It important for you to know what license level you are using so you know what capabilities are available to you. Some recipes in this book will require a Standard or Advanced license. In this recipe, you will learn how you can determine your ArcGIS Pro license level.

Getting ready

You will need to make sure that you have successfully installed ArcGIS Pro 2.0 or higher. If you have not installed ArcGIS Pro yet, please refer to `http://pro.arcgis.com/en/pro-app/get-started/install-and-sign-in-to-arcgis-pro.htm` for installation instructions.

How to do it...

1. Go to the Windows Start button, which is normally located in the lower-left corner of your screen.
2. Scroll down to the **ArcGIS** program group and click **ArcGIS Pro**:

Depending on the version of Windows you are running, your Windows Start button and display might be a bit different. You may also need to click **All Programs** to see the **ArcGIS** program group. If you right click the **ArcGIS Pro** icon you can select to add it to your task bar at the bottom of your display. This makes starting ArcGIS Pro faster and easier.

3. The ArcGIS Pro start window will appear. Click **About ArcGIS Pro**, located in the lower-left corner of the start window.

4. In the **About ArcGIS Pro** window, select **Licensing**, located in the left side of the window. This will display your ArcGIS Pro licensing information:

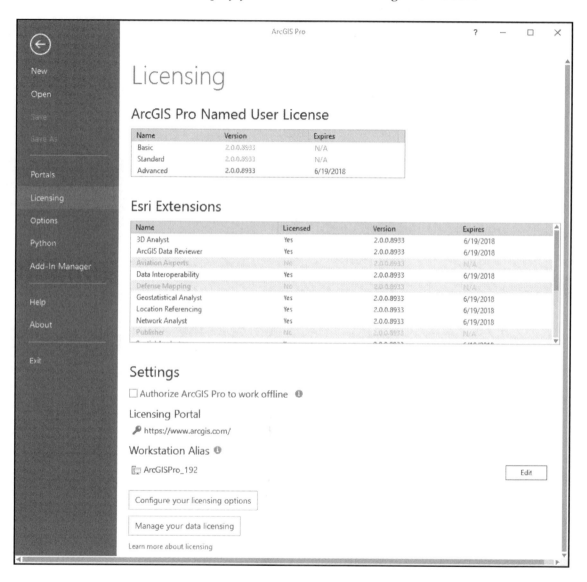

If you already have an ArcGIS Pro project open, you can access this same information from the project pane.

At the top of the **Licensing** window, you will see what license level you have been assigned. As you can see in the image, I have access to the **Advanced** license level. From here, you can also see which extensions you have access to. Extensions are add-ons for ArcGIS Pro, which provide additional functionality and are normally focused on a specific use, such as 3D analysis or network analysis. Again, in the image, you can see I have access to several extensions:

> **Question**: What license level have you been assigned, Basic, Standard or Advanced?

> **Answer**:
>
> **Question**: Do you have access to any extensions, and if so which ones?
>
> **Answer**:

5. Once you have determined the license level you have access to, you can close ArcGIS Pro if you are not continuing to the next recipe. If you are continuing, keep ArcGIS Pro open.

How it works...

In this recipe, you learned how to determine which license level of ArcGIS Pro you had access to. You did this by going to the **About ArcGIS Pro** window from the ArcGIS Pro start window. From there, you accessed your license level information by clicking the **Licensing** option located on the left side.

The license level is important, as it determines what functionality you have access to within the program. As you will see in this book, some recipes will require you to have access to higher license levels.

There's more...

The **Licensing** window allows you to do more than just see what license level and extensions have been assigned to you. It also allows you to determine what type of ArcGIS Pro licensing you want to use, check out a license for use in the field, and more.

ArcGIS Pro supports three basic types of licensing: single user, concurrent user, and named user. Named user is the default and requires you to have a username and password in your organization's ArcGIS Online or ArcGIS Portal. Single user licenses are the traditional software license, where the software is licensed to a single computer. Concurrent licenses are sometimes referred to as network licenses. These make use of a license manager that is typically installed on a server and controls how many users can be running the software at once. To learn more about the types of licenses supported in ArcGIS Pro, go to `http://pro.arcgis.com/en/pro-app/get-started/licensing-arcgis-pro.htm`.

Opening an existing ArcGIS Pro project

ArcGIS Pro makes use of project files that have a `.aprx` file extension. Projects store 2D maps, 3D scenes, database connections, folder connections, custom toolboxes, and more. When you start ArcGIS Pro, you must open a project.

In this recipe, you will learn how to open an existing project. Later in this chapter, you will learn how to create a new project.

Getting ready

To complete this recipe, you will need to make sure you have downloaded and installed the data associated with this book. If you followed the installation instructions, the data and projects should be located in `C:\Student\ArcGISProCookbook`. You will also need access to the internet. You will need to have ArcGIS Pro 2.1 or later installed as well. The recipe can be completed with any license level of ArcGIS Pro: Basic, Standard, or Advanced.

How to do it...

1. If you closed ArcGIS Pro at the end of the last recipe, open ArcGIS Pro. If you still have ArcGIS Pro open, click the back arrow located in the top-left corner of the **About ArcGIS Pro** window.

2. In the **ArcGIS Pro** start window, click **Open another project**, as shown in the following screenshot:

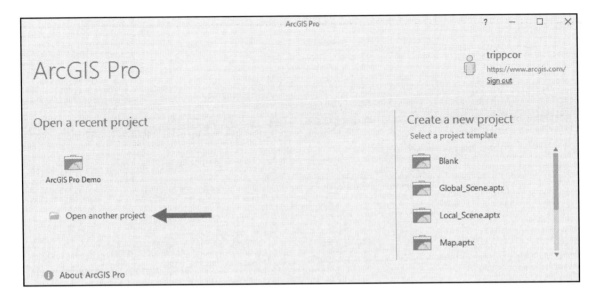

3. Click the **Browse** button, which looks like a file folder.
4. Under **Computer** in the left panel, select **C:**.

    If you do not see anything below **Computer** in the panel on the left, click the small arrow head. That will expand the contents of the computer, so you should see the **C:** drive.

    If you installed the book data to another drive, select the drive containing the book data.

5. In the panel on the right, scroll down until you see the **Student** folder and double click it.
6. Double click the **ArcGISProCookbook** folder.
7. Double click the **Chapter1** folder.
8. Select the **Chapter 1 Ex 1.aprx** folder and click **OK**.

You have now opened your first ArcGIS Pro project. If it opened successfully, ArcGIS Pro should look similar to this:

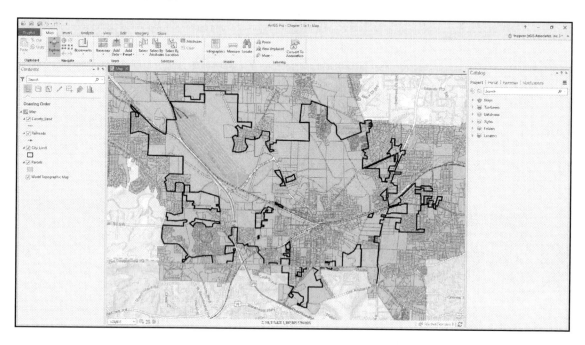

How it works...

Before you can start working in ArcGIS Pro, you must first open a project. To open a project, you must navigate to where it is stored. In this recipe, if you installed the data in the default location, the project was stored on your computer's `C:\` drive in a series of folders, so that the full path was `C:\Student\ArcGISProCookbook\Chapter1`. You were able to access this project by navigating to that location.

Projects can be saved to your local computer or on a network server. It is also possible to save projects to external and flash drives. You may encounter issues if you do save and try to access projects stored on these devices because of slow data transfer rates.

There's more...

You are not required to close ArcGIS Pro if you want to open another project. ArcGIS Pro doesn't allow you to open a project if you already have a project open. This will close the current project and open the one you select. To do this, follow these steps.

1. Click the **Open** button located on the Quick Access Toolbar at the top of the ArcGIS Pro interface, as indicated in the following image:

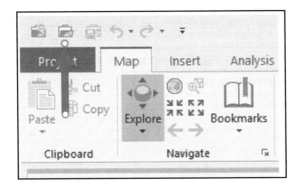

2. In the **Open Project** window that appears, navigate to
   C:\Student\ArcGISProCookbook\Chapter1 using the same method you did to open the current project.

3. Select the **Chapter 1 Ex 1A.aprx** file and click **OK**.

The project you originally opened should now be closed and a new project should be open, which looks similar to this:

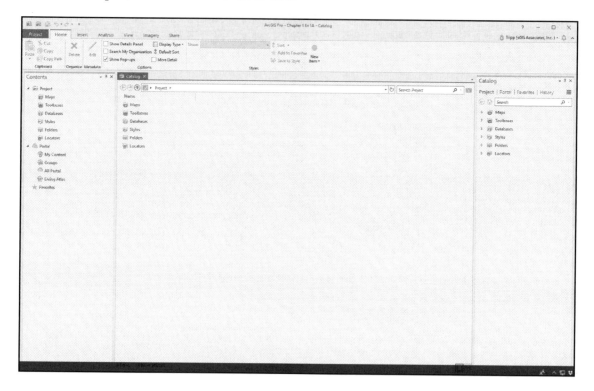

You have now opened two projects in ArcGIS Pro using two different methods. You will find, while using ArcGIS Pro, that there are usually at least two ways to accomplish any tasks. Often there are more.

4. If you are not continuing to the next recipe, close ArcGIS Pro without saving the project.

You can alternatively use *Ctrl + O* as a shortcut to open new projects. *Ctrl+S* works as a shortcut to save a project, and *Ctrl+N* as a shortcut to create a new project.

Opening and navigating a map

Now that you know how to open an existing project, it is time to learn how to open a map stored within the project. Projects can contain 2D maps, 3D scenes, data connections, layouts, styles, toolboxes, and more. However, 2D maps are still the primary canvas that GIS professionals work with.

In this recipe, you will learn how to open existing 2D maps. Once open, you will learn how to navigate within the map.

Getting ready

If you have successfully completed all the previous recipes, you should not need to do anything more to continue with this recipe. If you have not completed the other recipes in this chapter, you will need to do so before starting this one.

How to do it...

1. Start ArcGIS Pro if you closed it at the end of the last recipe and open the **Chapter 1 Ex 1A** project located in C:\Student\ArcGISProCookbook\Chapter1.

If you don't remember how, you should refer back to the previous recipe or click the project name in the list of recently opened projects.

2. In the **Catalog** pane located on the right of the ArcGIS Pro interface, expand the **Maps** folder by clicking the small arrowhead to the left of the word **Maps**.

If the **Catalog** pane is not open, check that it is not set to autohide. If it is, you will see a small tab located on the right side, named **Catalog**. Simply click the tab to make the **Catalog** pane open. If you have closed the **Catalog** pane, click the **View** tab in the ribbon. Then click the small arrowhead located below **Catalog** and select **Catalog Pane**.

3. Right-click on **Map** and select **Open**, as shown here:

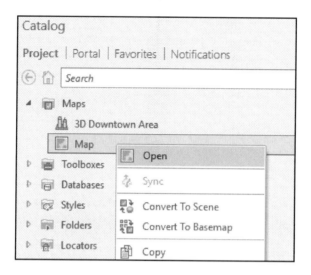

You have just opened an existing project map. A project can contain multiple maps that can be either 2D or 3D. 3D maps are referred to as scenes. Now you will learn how to navigate within the maps.

4. Click the **Map** tab in the ribbon.
5. Click the **Explore** tool located on the **Map** tab in the **Navigate** tool group.

The **Explore** tool is a jack of all trades. It allows you to pan, zoom, and access data about features in your map. For those that have used ArcMap, the Explore tool replaces the identify, zoom in, zoom out, and pan tools.

6. Move your mouse pointer into the map and roll the scroll wheel on your mouse away from you to zoom into the map. Stop whenever you are zoomed in to a desired scale.
7. Now roll the scroll wheel back toward you in the opposite direction to zoom out. Stop whenever you are zoomed out to a desired scale.
8. To return to the full extent of the map, click the **Full Extent** button located in the **Navigate** group on the **Map** tab in the ribbon, as shown here:

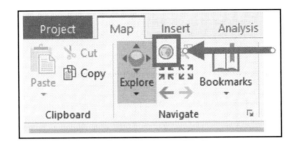

9. Click **Bookmarks** in the **Navigate** group on the **Map** tab in the ribbon.

10. Select **Washington Park** from the window that appears. This will zoom you to a predefined area in your map that focuses on Washington Park. Your map should now look similar to this:

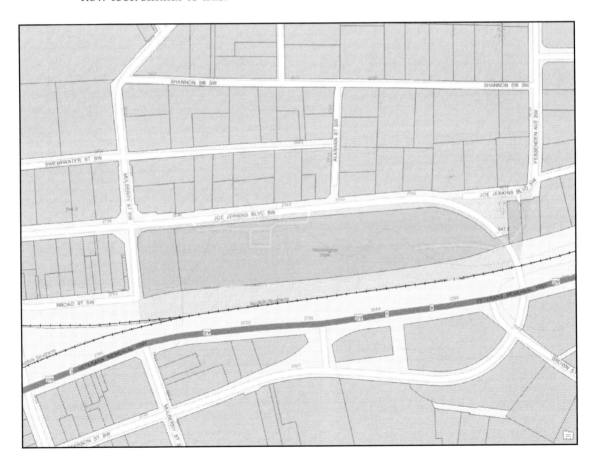

11. Now you want to zoom in closer to the block just to the north of Washington Park. Select the **Explore** tool again.

12. Hold your *Shift* key down and click near the intersection of **Mulberry ST SW** and **Sweetwater ST SW**. Continue holding down the *Shift* key and drag your mouse pointer to the southeast until you reach the intersection of **Alabama St SW** and **Joe Jerkins Blvd SW**. As you are dragging your mouse, you should see a dashed rectangular box appear in the map. This represents the area you want to zoom into. Once you have created a box that looks similar to the following image, release both the *Shift* key and your mouse button:

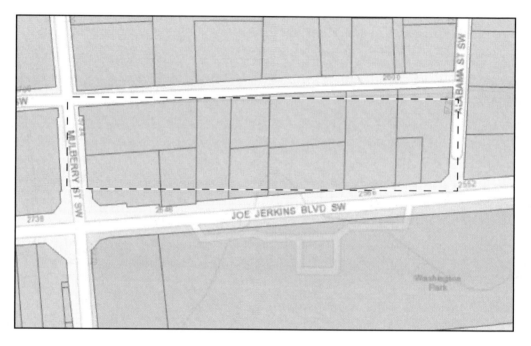

13. Ensure the **Explore** tool is still active in the **Map** tab.

14. In the map, click the northwesternmost parcel in the block you just zoomed into.

   Question: What happens when you click on this parcel?

   Answer:

If you look closely at the information window that appears, you will notice it shows the information for the **City Limits** and not the parcel. You need to adjust the settings for the **Explore** tool.

15. Close the information window by clicking the small **X** located in the upper right corner.
16. Click the arrowhead located below the **Explore** tool and select **Visible Layers**.
17. Click the same parcel once again.
18. On the bottom left of the information window, look at the number of features which are being identified. It should say 1 of 2.
19. Click the small arrowhead located next to the number 2. This will display the information for the parcel you clicked in place of the **City Limit**.
20. Close the information window once you are done.
21. Try clicking other features in the map and using some of the other options associated with the **Explore** tool to see how they work.
22. Click the **Full Extent** button to return to the full extents of the map.
23. Save your project by clicking the **Save Project** button located in the Quick Access toolbar.

How it works...

In this recipe, you began exploring the contents of a project by opening an existing map that was contained in a project that you opened in the last recipe. Once you opened the map from that **Catalog** pane, you began to navigate within it using the **Explore** tool. You used the Explore tool to first zoom in and out within the map. Then, you used the **Full Extent** button to return to the full extent of the map view. Next, you used a book mark to zoom to **Washington Park** in the map. From there, you zoomed into an even more specific area, using a combination of the **Explore** tool and the *Shift* key along with your mouse.

Once you zoomed into a block of parcels you were interested in, you used the **Explore** tool to retrieve information about a specific parcel.

Adding and configuring layers

Now you know how to start ArcGIS Pro and open a project so you can begin accessing functionality. You have learned how to open an existing map and navigate within the map. You can even see information about features displayed within the map using the Explore tool.

But how did those layers get added to the map? How did ArcGIS Pro know how to display the layers you saw within the map? That is your next step in your ArcGIS Pro journey.

In this recipe, you will learn various methods for adding new layers to a map. You will then discover how to configure various properties associated with a layer, such as its name and symbology.

Getting ready

If you have already completed the previous recipes, you should be ready for this one. If you have not completed them, you will need to do so. This recipe builds on the past ones.

How to do it...

1. Start ArcGIS Pro and open the `Chapter 1 Ex 1A.aprx` project if you closed ArcGIS Pro at the end of the last recipe.
2. Open the map named **Map** if it is not already open.

 If you are not sure how to open the map, you should refer back to the previous exercise.

As you can see, this is a very simple map. You will want to add some new layers to show additional information.

3. Click the **Add Data** button. Do not click the words **Add Data**. You want to click the icon located above the words.
4. In the left window in the **Add Data** dialog box, expand **Project** by clicking the small arrowhead located to the left of **Project** if you do not see the contents in the following image.

5. Double click **Databases** so you see two databases in the window to the right of the dialog box. You should see the **Chapter 1 Ex 1** and **Trippville_GIS** geodatabases:

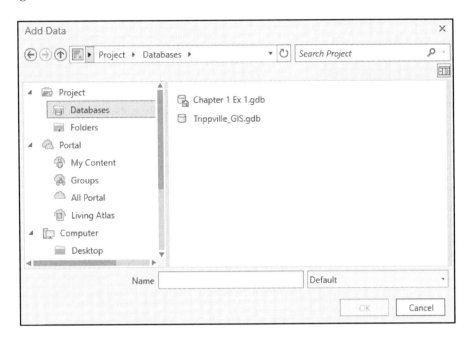

6. Double-click the **Trippville_GIS** geodatabase to reveal its contents.
7. Double click the **Base** feature dataset.
8. Select the **Buildings** feature class.
9. While holding down the *Ctrl* key, click the **Natwtr_Body** and **Natwtr_Stream** feature classes.
10. Once you have selected those three feature classes, click **UK** to add them as three new layers to your map.

You have just added three new layers to your map using the **Add Data** button. This is just one of several methods that you can use to add a new layer to a map. You will use some other methods later in this recipe. Now, you will adjust some of the properties associated with the layers you just added.

When you add a new layer to a map in ArcGIS Pro, the software will display the new layer using a random color. Also, it will automatically add the new layers to your map contents based on what type of layer it is. Point layers will be added to the top. Line layers will be added below points. Polygon layers will be added below the line layers. Raster layers are added below the polygons, and base maps are placed at the very bottom. In a map, the drawing order starts with the layers at the bottom of the list and draws each succeeding layer on top of the previous, so that the last layer drawn is the one on the top of the list.

11. Right-click the **Natwtr_Stream** layer you just added to your map and select **Properties**, located at the bottom of the menu that appears.

12. Click through the list of options located in the window on the left of the dialog box. Look at some of the properties of the layer that you can configure from this dialog box. You will make some adjustments to these as you work through the recipe.

13. In the **Layer Properties** dialog box, select **General** from the window on the left side.

14. In the cell located below **Name**, where it says **Natwtr_Stream**, replace that with **Streams and Creeks**.

15. Click **Metadata** in the left window.

16. Type the following values into the metadata as shown in the screenshot:
     - **Title**: Streams and Creeks
     - **Tags**: Natural Water, Streams, Creeks
     - **Summary**: Streams and Creeks located in the City of Trippville
     - **Description**: This layer shows the general location of most creeks and streams located in and around the City of Trippville.
     - **Credits**: eGIS Associates, Inc.
     - **Use Limitations**: This data is for training use only

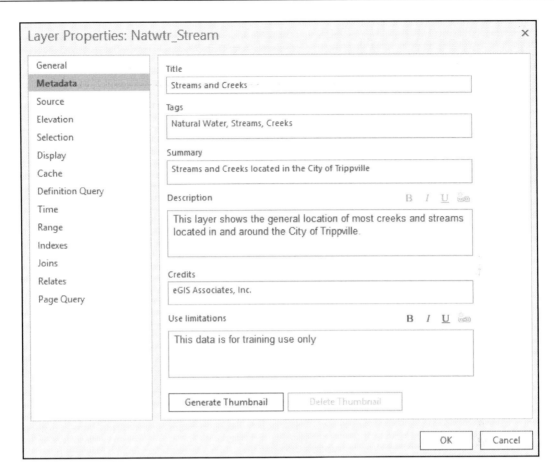

Your **Layer Properties** window should now look like the preceding screenshot.

17. Click **OK** to apply the changes you have just made to the properties of the **Natwtr_Stream** layer.

18. Repeat this process for the **Natwtr_Body** layer you added using the following values to update its properties. Remember to click **OK** when you're done:

- General: **Name**: Lakes and Ponds
- Metadata:
    - **Title**: Lakes and Ponds
    - **Tags**: Natural Water, lakes, ponds
    - **Summary**: Lakes and ponds located in the City of Trippville

- **Description**: This layer shows the general location of most lakes and ponds located in and around the City of Trippville.
- **Credits**: eGIS Associates, Inc.
- **Use Limitations**: This data is for training use only

Now you will move the **Streams and Creeks** layer so it is beneath the **Lakes and Ponds** layer.

19. Select the **Streams and Creeks** layer in the **Contents** pane.
20. Holding your left mouse button down, drag the layer so it is below the **Lakes and Ponds** layer. Your **Contents** pane should look similar to the following image when you are done. Remember, your colors may be different:

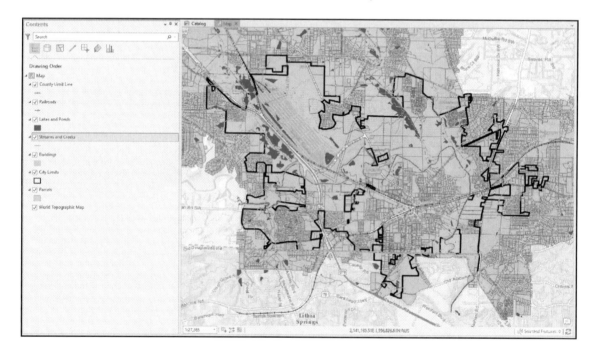

21. Click the symbol patch located beneath the **Lakes and Ponds** layer so you can adjust the **Symbology** settings.

22. The **Symbology** pane will open on the right side of the interface. Make sure you are viewing the **Gallery** and type **lake** into the search cell:

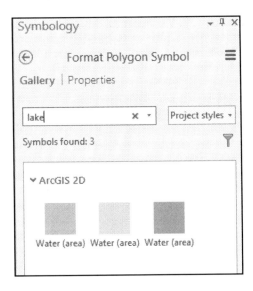

23. Select one of the presented symbols. Any will work.
24. Click the **Properties** tab located next to **Gallery** in the **Symbology** pane, as illustrated in the following screenshot:

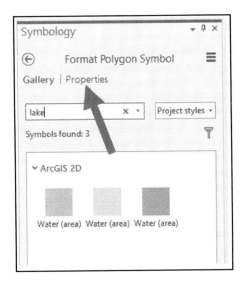

25. Click the drop-down arrow for the **Outline Color**, select Cretan Blue from the color palette that is presented.

26. Set the **Outline Width** to **1 pt**, as shown here:

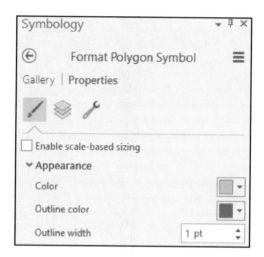

27. Click **Apply**, located at the bottom of the **Symbology** pane.

28. Following that same process, click the symbol patch for the **Streams and Creeks** layer.

29. Search **Stream** in the **Gallery** and select the **Water (Line)** symbol that should be presented.

Your map should now look like this. The color of the Buildings layer may be different, depending on what ArcGIS Pro assigned it when you added the layer:

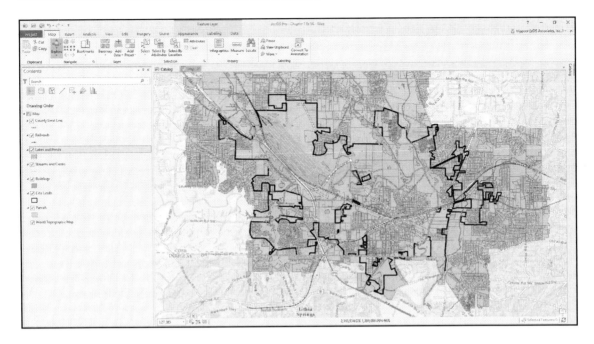

30. Now you will change the symbology for the buildings so that you can determine the type. Select the **Buildings** layer in the **Contents** pane.

31. Select the **Appearance** tab in the **Feature Layer contextual** menu in the ribbon.

32. Click the small arrowhead located below the **Symbology** button.

33. Select **Unique Values** from the presented menu.

34. The **Symbology** pane will open once again, though it will look a bit different. Next to **Field 1**, click the drop-down menu and select **Building Type**.

35. Click the **Color** scheme and select a desired color scheme, such as **Basic Random**. Notice the symbology for the **Buildings** layer has changed in the **Contents** pane to reflect your new symbology settings.

36. Close the **Symbology** pane.

37. Right-click the **Buildings** layer in the **Contents** pane and select **Zoom to Layer**. You can now see the type for each building, as shown in the following screenshot. Your buildings may be displayed with different colors depending on the color scheme you selected:

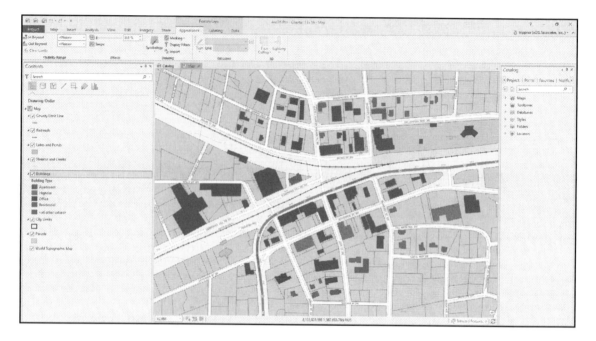

38. Save your project by clicking the **Project** tab in the ribbon and selecting **Save**.

It is recommended that you save your projects often. This will help to prevent you from losing work if ArcGIS Pro or your system experiences a problem.

39. In the **Catalog** pane, expand the **Databases** folder by clicking the small arrowhead located to the left.

If you accidentally close the **Catalog** pane or **Contents** pane, click on the **View** tab in the ribbon to reopen them.

40. Expand the contents of the **Trippville_GIS** geodatabase.

41. Right-click the **Power_Poles** feature class and select **Add to Current Map**:

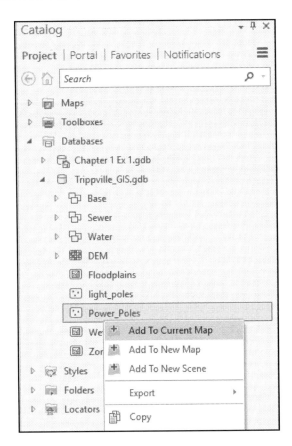

42. The **Power Poles** layer has been added to you map. Right-click the symbol under the layer name to display a color palette.

43. Select Mars Red from the color palette to change the color of the symbol for the **Power Poles** layer. Your map should now look similar to this one:

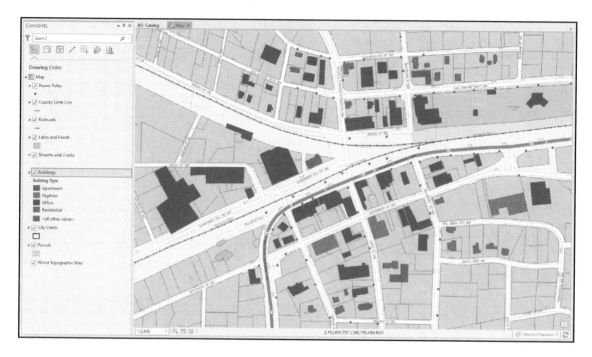

44. Click the **Share** tab in the ribbon.
45. Select **Map File** from the **Save As** group in the **Share** tab.
46. Select **C:** in the left side of the **Save Map AS MAPX File** window.
47. Scroll down if needed and double-click the **Student** folder.
48. Double-click the **ArcGISProCookbook** folder.
49. Double-click the **MyProjects** folder.
50. In the **Name** cell located at the bottom of the **Save Map AS MAPX File**, type **TrippvilleBuildingTypeMap** and click **Save**.

   You just created a **Map File** that will allow you to add this same map to other projects quickly and easily. You will use this file in the next recipe.

51. Close ArcGIS Pro and save your project if asked to.

How it works...

In this recipe, you started by adding new layers to a map. You added multiple layers at one time using the **Add Data** button. Once you added the new layers, you began to adjust their properties so that they would be more useful within the map. First, you renamed the layer using a more descriptive and understandable name than the one originally associated with the feature class in the geodatabase. Then, you updated the metadata for the layer so others using the map would have a better understanding of its purpose.

After you updated some of the basic properties of the layers you added, you worked on the symbology so that the map was easier to read. You made the **Streams**, **Creeks**, **Lakes**, and **Ponds** layers blue so they resembled the features they represent, also, people are accustomed to seeing them presented this way in a map. You made these adjustments by clicking the symbol patch located beneath each layer and then changing the symbol properties in the **Symbology** pane.

The **Buildings** layer required a little more effort, because you needed to change the symbology so that you could tell each building type from within the map. This required you to base the symbology on an attribute of the buildings that was stored in a field found in the attribute table of the **Buildings** layer. To do this, you went to the **Appearance** tab and selected the **Unique Values** symbology. Then, you configured this symbology type to use the **Building Type** field from the attribute table for the layer. Once you pointed the symbology type to that field, it automatically created a unique symbol for each building type it found. In this case, it created a unique symbol allowing you to determine the type of buildings (for example, houses or apartments).

You added the **Power Poles** layer from the **Catalog** pane by right-clicking the feature class within the geodatabase and selecting **Add to Current Map**. You then adjusted the color of the **Power Poles** symbol to red by right-clicking the symbol and selecting Mars Red from the presented color palette.

Finally, you created a **Map File** based on the map you made, so you will be able add the map to other projects quickly and easily. The map will be added with all the layer properties and settings that you just configured, so you will not need to go through that process again.

Creating a project

We have mentioned several times that you must first open a project before you are able to access the functionality included in ArcGIS Pro. You have begun to experience this in the previous recipes where you opened and worked with existing projects. These were already configured, and contained several project items including maps and database connections. How were these projects created?

In this recipe, you will create a new project using one of the four project templates included with ArcGIS Pro. You will see the structure created by ArcGIS Pro when a new project is created.

Getting ready

To complete this recipe, all you need to do is ensure that you have ArcGIS Pro installed, access to a license, and the data for the book downloaded and installed. This recipe does not even require you to have completed the previous recipes, though it might help provide a better understanding of what you are doing.

How to do it...

1. Start ArcGIS Pro.
2. When the **ArcGIS Pro** start window appears, select the **Blank** template from **Create a new project** on the right side:

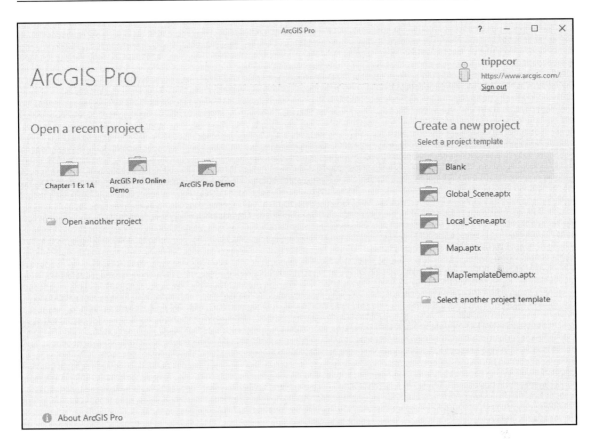

3. In the **Name** cell, name your new project `%your name%Chapter1NewProject` (for example `TrippChapter1Newproject`).

4. Click the **Browse** button located next to the **Location** cell. It looks like a small file folder with a blue arrow.

5. Under **Computer**, click the **C:** drive.

6. Scroll down and double-click the **Student** folder.

7. Double-click the **ArcGISProCookbook** folder.

8. Select the **MyProjects** folder and click **OK**. Do not double-click it.

9. Verify that your **Create a New Project** dialog window looks like this, except for the name which will include your name:

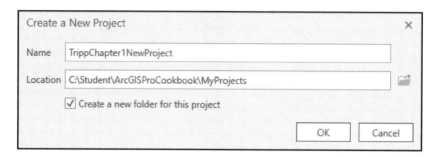

10. Once you have verified that you have entered everything properly, click **OK**.

You have just created your first new project in ArcGIS Pro using the **Blank** template. This created a new bare bones project. This project contains the minimum number of items you will find in a project. You can now begin to explore your new project.

11. Expand the **Toolboxes** folder in the **Catalog** pane.

Question: What do you see in this folder?

Answer:

12. Expand the **Databases** folder in the **Catalog** pane.

Question: What do you see in this folder?

Answer:

13. Expand the other folders within the project.

Question: What do you notice is missing from your new project?

Answer:

You should have noticed that your new project contains a single custom toolbox and file geodatabase that has the same name as your project. These were automatically created by ArcGIS Pro when you created the new project. You should have also noticed that several styles and locators were also automatically connected by default.

There are three basic types of geodatabase: personal, file, and SDE. ArcGIS Pro only supports file and SDE geodatabases. It does not support the personal geodatabase. To learn more about geodatabases, go to `http://pro.arcgis.com/en/pro-app/help/data/geodatabases/overview/what-is-a-geodatabase-.htm`.

This new project is missing several key elements that you will need to perform any GIS work. First, it is missing a map. Second, if you expand the geodatabase that is connected to the project, you will notice it is empty. So, you also need data. Now you will connect to an existing geodatabase and then add a map.

14. Right-click the **Databases** folder in the **Catalog** pane and select **Add Database**:

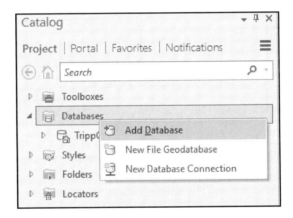

15. Click **C:** under **Computer** in the area located on the left of the **Select Existing Geodatabase** window that appears.
16. Scroll down and double-click the **Student** folder.
17. Then double-click **ArcGISProCookbook** and **Databases**.
18. Select the **Trippville_GIS.gdb** and click **OK**. Do not double-click the **Trippville_GIS** geodatabase.

19. Right click the **Trippville_GIS.gdb** you just added to your project and select **Add to New Projects**, as shown in the following image:

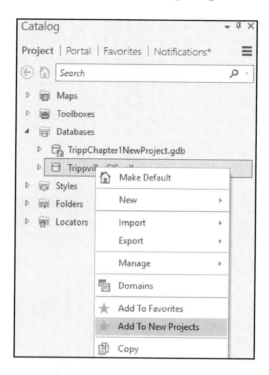

You just added a connection to the Trippville GIS geodatabase you have been using in the other recipes. In those, the database connection had already been established. Now you know how it was done. Once you added the connection, you then added it to your favorites and set it so it will automatically be added to any new projects you create.

You still need to add a map. You could do this the same way you did in the previous recipe. However, in this one you will import the **Map File** you created in the last recipe.

20. Click the **Insert** tab in the ribbon:

21. Click the **Import Map** tool in the **Project** group on the **Insert** tab in the ribbon:

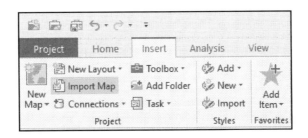

22. Using the same process you did to add the database connection, navigate to the
C:\Student\ArcGISProCookbook\MyProjects folder.

23. Select the **TrippvilleBuildingTypeMap.mapx** file and click **OK**.

> If you did not complete the previous recipe, you can instead navigate to
> C:\Student\ArcGISProCookbook\Chapter1 and select the
> **Chapter1Ex1AResults.mapx** file.

A familiar-looking map should now be added to your project. It contains all the layers that you created in the last recipe along with the symbology and properties you configured.

24. Save your project by using the *Ctrl+S* shortcut keys.

How it works...

In this recipe, you created your first new project. You used the **Blank** template, which creates a very basic project for ArcGIS Pro. Projects created with the **Blank** template include connections to a custom toolbox and geodatabase that have the same name as the project, along with several styles and locators. The toolbox and geodatabase are automatically created by ArcGIS Pro when you create the new project. They are both empty and are intended for you to save project-specific items to them. However, in most cases, your organization will already have an established GIS database.

Once you created your project, you added a connection to an existing geodatabase, **Trippville_GIS**. This database contains the GIS data for the City of Trippville that you used in other recipes. This is actually the primary database that you will use in the remainder of this book. So, you added it to your favorites and set it to automatically be added to all new projects you create.

After you established a connection to the primary geodatabase, you imported a new map. This new map was based on a Map file you created in a previous recipe. The new map was added with layers already added and their properties configured, saving you a lot of effort.

There's more...

In the last recipe, you created a new project using the **Blank** template. As you saw, this template automatically created the project structure including a project geodatabase, custom toolbox, and more. The blank template is not the only one included with ArcGIS Pro. There are several others you can use when creating a new project. Let's take a quick look at them.

ArcGIS Pro stock project templates

As you may have noticed when you created your new project, ArcGIS Pro includes three other project templates: Global Scene, Local Scene, and Map. Each of these will create slightly different projects:

Name	Description	Project items that are created
Map	Creates a new project that automatically includes a new 2D Map	• Project Toolbox • Project File Geodatabase • Project Map Geodatabase • 2D Map
Local Scene	Creates a new project that automatically includes a new local 3D Map	• Project Toolbox • Project File Geodatabase • Project Scene Geodatabase • 3D Local Scene
Global Scene	Creates a new project that automatically includes a new global 3D Map, similar to what you experience with Google Earth the first time you open it	• Project Toolbox • Project File Geodatabase • Project Scene Geodatabase • 3D Global Scene

In addition, connections to standard styles, locators, and any favorites that are set to add to new projects are also added to the items created, based on the selected new project template.

Using the skills that you have learned in the previous recipes, try creating a new project using a template other than Blank. See how they differ from one another.

2

Creating and Storing Data

In this chapter, we will cover the following recipes:

- Adding Raster and Vector data to a map
- Creating a new Geodatabase
- Creating a new Shapefile
- Adding CAD data to a map
- Plotting X,Y points from a table
- Geocoding addresses

Introduction

As you have begun to see, ArcGIS Pro is a powerful tool for visualizing data. However, you have only begun to scratch the surface. One of the things that makes ArcGIS Pro so powerful is its ability to make use of many different data types and formats.

Unlike other programs, such as Word, Excel, or even AutoCAD, ArcGIS Pro is not limited to a single file type. Based on your experience with previous recipes you have learned that ArcGIS Pro makes use of project with a `.aprx` file extension. In the projects, you accessed a file geodatabase to add new layers to a map and you were able to import a map file with a `.mapx` file extension. These are just three of the many different files you can bring into ArcGIS Pro. You will encounter many more the longer you use ArcGIS Pro.

In this chapter, you will begin to explore some of the various data formats you can use with ArcGIS Pro, and their limitations. You will start with the two basic data categories, Raster and Vector, to ensure you have a good foundational understanding of GIS data. From there, you will learn how to create Esri data storage types, such as a Geodatabase and shapefile. Next, you will see how to access non-Esri CAD formats so they can be added to your maps. Finally, you will explore the use of traditional tabular data in ArcGIS Pro.

Adding Raster and Vector data to a map

GIS data can generally be categorized as either being Raster or Vector. Within those categories, there are many specific formats. In an ArcGIS Pro project, you will often combine both raster and vector data together in order to create maps, edit data, and perform analyses. So, what is the difference between these two data categories? How do I make use of this data in ArcGIS Pro?

In this recipe, you will explore vector and raster data by adding them to a map. You will perform various steps to help you gain a better understanding of how they work within ArcGIS Pro.

Getting ready

For this recipe, you will need to ensure that you have installed both the book sample data and ArcGIS Pro software. An ArcGIS Pro Basic license level will be sufficient for this recipe. It is recommended that you complete Chapter 1 or have previous experience using ArcGIS Pro before beginning this recipe.

How to do it...

1. Start ArcGIS Pro.
2. In the **ArcGIS Pro** start window, click **Open another project**.

3. Select **Computer** from the **Open** window and then click **Browse** in the area on the right:

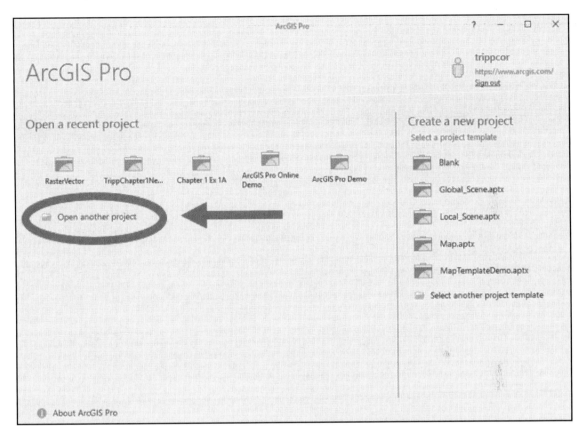

4. Navigate to `C:\Student\ArcGISProCookbook\Chapter2\RasterVector` by clicking on `C:\` in the area on the left of the **Open Project** window. Then double-click the **Student, ArcGISProCookbook, Chapter2,** and **RasterVector** folders.

5. Select the **RasterVector.aprx** project file and click **OK**.

The project will open with a single aerial photograph. An aerial photograph is one example of raster data and is one of the most common you will use.

6. Select the **Map** tab in the ribbon and then click the small arrowhead located under **Bookmarks**.

7. Select the **Raster 1** bookmark to zoom into to a specific location in the map.

Your map should now zoom in very closely to the aerial you were just viewing:

Pixelated Image due to zoom scale

The aerial now looks like a series of individual squares. These are called cells, though many people mistakenly refer to them as pixels.

All rasters consist of cells that are assigned a numeric value. You can think of them as being similar to a spreadsheet. The value assigned to each cell can represent different properties depending on the purpose of the raster. In the case of a color aerial photo, such as the one you have been working with in this recipe, the value assigned to the cell equals the color for each band to be displayed.

8. Activate the **Explore** tool on the **Map** tab in the **Navigate** group.

9. Click one of the cells in the Aerial Photo to see what information is linked to the cell you selected:

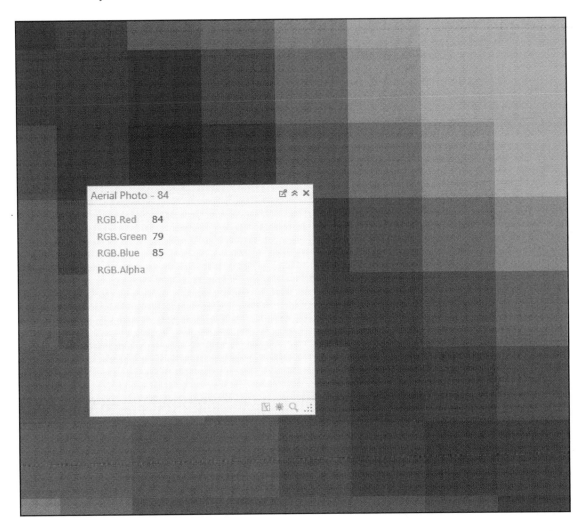

As you can see, the cells store information. In this case, it stores the values used to display the Red, Green, and Blue bands stored in the photo. When these three bands are overlapped, you are able to see the true color.

Rasters can have a single band or multiple bands. Bands are similar to layers. Most aerial photographs have three bands: Red, Green, and Blue. However, some will also have infrared bands if they are multispectral. Those additional bands allow you to extract information such as vegetation and impervious surfaces.

10. Close the information window by clicking the small **X** in the upper-right corner.
11. Right-click the **Aerial Photo** layer in the **Contents** pane and select **Properties**.
12. Click **Source** in the right-hand side of the **Layer Properties** window.
13. If needed, expand the **Data Source** option by clicking the small arrowhead.
14. Look at the **Dataset** cell in the presented table.

 Question: What is the dataset listed in the table for the Aerial Photo layer?

Answer:

15. Click **OK** when done.

 The source for the Aerial Photo layer was 152380.sid. This is what is commonly called a **Mr. SID** file. Rasters come in many formats, Mr. SID is just one. Other common raster formats include: **Joint Photographic Experts Group (JPEG/JPG)**, **Portable Network Graphic (PNG)**, **Tag Image File Format (TIFF)**, and **ERDAS Imagine (IMG)**.

16. Right-click the **Aerial Photo** layer in the **Contents** pane and select **Zoom to Layer**.
17. In the **Catalog** pane located on the right side of the **ArcGIS Pro** interface, click the **Portal** tab located at the top of the pane next to **Project**.
18. Click the Living Atlas button, as shown here:

19. In the Search cell, type DEM.

 Digital Elevation Model (DEM) is a raster format commonly used to represent changes of elevation along the ground.

20. Right-click **Terrain: Hillshade** and select **Add to Current Map**:

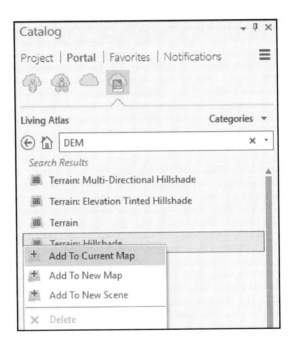

You have just added a raster layer that comes from a web service hosted in Esri's ArcGIS Online living atlas. Data in the Living Atlas is available to everyone for use in ArcGIS Pro and other GIS applications.

21. Click the Full Extent button located in the **Map** tab in the **Navigate** group. It looks like a small globe. This takes you to the full extent of the map. You will see more of the new **Terrain** layer you just added.

22. Now you will take a closer look. In the **Map** tab, click the arrowhead located under **Bookmarks** and select **DEM Zoomed**:

Zoomed in DEM

23. Look at the two raster layers now present in the map and compare the two.

    Question: How many bands does the Aerial Photo have?

    Answer:

    Question: How many bands does Terrain: Hillshade have?

    Answer:

24. Activate the **Explore** tool in the **Map** tab.
25. Click a cell in the **Terrain: Hillshade** layer to access the information linked to the cell.
26. Review the information presented. Compare it to the information you saw when you did the same thing for the Aerial Photo layer.

27. Close the information window when you are done.

As you can see, the Terrain layer you added was a good bit different than the Aerial Photo layer even though they are both rasters. The Aerial Photo layer has three bands, where the Terrain has a single band. The Terrain also has more information attached to each cell than the Aerial Photo. That is because the terrain was created to do more than just present a picture. It is designed so you can determine the elevation of an area and perform analysis based on the elevation. You will get a chance to do that later in this book.

Now, you will look more closely at vector data. The majority of the data you will work with will most likely be stored as a vector, meaning it will be either a point, line, or polygon.

28. Click the **Full Extent** button to see the entire map.
29. Turn off the **Terrain: Hillshade** layer by clicking the check box located next to the layer name.
30. In the **Catalog** pane, select the **Project** tab at the top of the pane.
31. Expand the **Databases** folder so you see the two geodatabases connected to the project.
32. Expand **Trippville_GIS.gdb** so you can see its contents.
33. Expand the **Base Feature Dataset** in the **Trippville_GIS** geodatabase.

 Feature Datasets are organizational units in a geodatabase. They act similarly to folders on your computer. They allow you to store related feature classes in a common container within the geodatabase so that you can easily find them. All feature classes stored within a feature dataset share the same coordinate system. This allows the feature classes stored in the feature dataset to take part in a topology and geometric network. Feature datasets only exist in geodatabases. You will not find them in other GIS data formats, such as shapefiles.

34. Select the **Parcels** feature class and then drag and drop it into the map view.
35. Click the arrowhead under **Bookmarks** on the **Map** tab and select **Parcels**.
36. Activate the **Explore** tool on the **Map** tab and click one of the parcels displayed in the map.

Question: What fields of information are linked to the parcels?

Answer:

37. Close the **Information** window.
38. Right-click the **Parcels** layer in the table of contents. Select **Attribute Table** from the menu that appears:

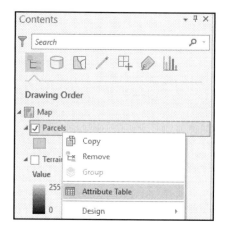

You should see **Attribute Table** open at the bottom. This is another way to view attributes associated with a vector layer.

Question: Is there a difference between the fields you saw when using the Explore tool and what you see in Attribute Table?

Answer:

You should see the same fields of information in both the Explore tool information window and the attribute table. However, how the information is presented is quite different. The attribute table presents data for all features in the layer in a tabular format. The information window only presents the information about one feature at a time.

All vector layers will have a database table of attributes attached to it. This attribute table will include a combination of Default fields and User Defined fields. Default fields are those created and maintained by the software. They will vary depending on the type of data and the format. User defined fields are those columns created by software users and must be manually maintained.

39. Activate the **Select** tool in the **Map** tab.
40. Double-click one of the **Parcels** in the map.
41. Look at the bottom of the **Parcels attribute table** you have opened. It should say **1 of 8,129 selected**.

If it still says **0 of 8,129 selected**, you did not select a parcel. This might be due to the Layer not being set as selectable. Try going to the **List by Selection** button in the **Contents** pane and verifying that the **Parcels** layer is set to be a selectable layer.

42. Click the Show selected records button located to the left:

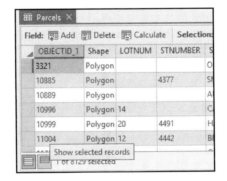

Only a single record should be displayed now because you only have a single parcel selected.

43. Click the **Select** tool again.

44. Click the upper-left side of the map and draw a rectangle similar to the following image:

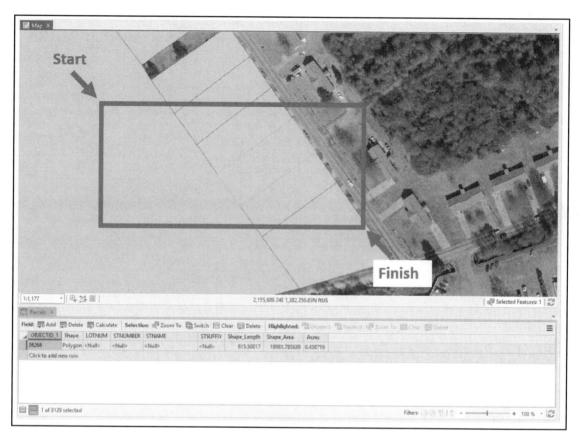

Selection window location

45. Look at the **Parcels attribute table** now. You should see an additional records appear in the table now that they are selected.

    When working with vector data there is a one-to-one relationship between features in the map and records in the attribute table.

46. Click the **Clear** button located on the **Map** tab in the **Selection** group to deselect all selected features.

47. Close the attribute table by clicking the small **X** located next to the word **Parcels** in the small tab at the top of the table.

48. Now click the **Edit** tab in the ribbon.

49. Activate the **Select** tool on the **Edit** tab.

50. Click one of the small parcels located along the road. The parcel should now be selected.

51. Click the **Vertices** button located in the **Tools** window on the **Edit** tab in the ribbon.

If the selection disappears when you click the **Vertices** button, then the parcels layer is most likely not set to be an editable layer. To verify, click the **List by Editing** button in the **Contents** pane.

52. Notice the change in the display of the parcel. You should now see the vertices that form the parcel polygon.

Vector data is stored using the x, y coordinates of the vertices that form the feature. As you have seen, each of those features is then linked to additional attributes that are stored in the attribute table. So, all vector data includes two components, geometry, and attributes. A group of vector data that shares the same geometry (point, line, or polygon) and the same attribute table is called a **feature class**.

Like rasters, there are several types of vector files that you may encounter while using ArcGIS Pro. Some of the most common are:

- **Geodatabase feature class**: Stored in one of several types of geodatabases. Displayed as a gray icon in the **Catalog** pane. Is the preferred storage format for ArcGIS Pro.
- **Shapefiles**: Esri format that stores a single feature class. Is made up of multiple files including SHP, DBF, SHX, and others. Displayed with a green icon in the **Catalog** pane
- **AutoCAD drawing**: Has a DWG file extension and stores multiple feature classes.
- **AutoCAD drawing exchange file**: Has a DXF file extension and stores multiple feature classes. Displayed with a blue icon with a compass in the **Catalog** pane.
- **Microstation drawing**: Has a DGN file extension and stores multiple feature classes. Displayed with a blue icon with a compass in the **Catalog** pane.

53. Zoom to the full extent and save your project.
54. If you are not continuing to the next recipe, close ArcGIS Pro.

How it works...

In this recipe, you learned how to add raster and vector data to a map. First, you opened an existing project that already contained a map with a single raster layer, this was the aerial color photograph. You then zoomed into that layer using a bookmark to examine it further. Bookmarks allow you to return to specific locations within a map by storing the extents and scale of your map view at the time you create the bookmark. This allows you to easily return to a specific location on the map. There is no limit on the number of bookmarks that are contained within a project.

Once you zoomed into the location using the bookmark, you used the Explore tool to access information linked to a cell within the aerial photo to discover it included three bands. A different numeric value was assigned to the cell for each band, allowing the true color to be displayed in ArcGIS Pro. The information is presented in an HTML window that displays the attributes associated with the cell, feature, or features being identified. This functionality also allowed you to access the information from the parcels layer, which was a vector dataset. From this, you were able to see that vector and raster datasets can have different attributes that can be customized based on their purpose.

In the recipe, you added a raster layer that represented the terrain or elevation. This came from the Esri Living Atlas as a web service which is hosted by Esri's ArcGIS Online. Rasters and vectors can both be published as web services. These are typically accessed through a REST point connection. **REST** stands for **Representational state transfer**. These types of connections provide interoperability across the web along with good performance.

Finally, you added the parcels vector layer to your map and explored it. When you added it to your map, the parcel polygons were displayed in the map view. ArcGIS Pro does this by reading the *x* and *y* coordinates for each vertex that makes up the boundary of each parcel. This was demonstrated when you selected a parcel and displayed its vertices using the **Vertices** button on the **Edit** tab.

These coordinates are typically stored in a real-world coordinate system that allows it to be displayed with other layers in the correct location on the Earth. The *x* and *y* coordinates for each vertex are referred to as a coordinate pair. Each pair describes a unique location. In the case of a polygon, no fewer than four coordinate pairs are required to fully describe the location and shape of a polygon. A line only requires a minimum of two, and a point only one. You will learn more about real-world coordinate systems later in this book.

In addition to the spatial component of the parcels layer, you were able to view the associated attribute table. You saw how selecting features in the map also changed what records were selected in the attribute table, demonstrating the one-to-one relationship between features shown in the map and records listed in the attribute table. This showed you that vector data includes two components: spatial/geometry and attributes.

The link between the spatial features and the records in the table is automatically done within the data itself using the **ObjectID** or **FeatureID** (sometimes called **FID**) for each feature.

Creating a new Geodatabase

As we have mentioned, there are many GIS data storage formats. However, the Geodatabase is the preferred storage format for ArcGIS Pro. It has many advantages over other formats such as shapefiles, coverages, or DWG files.

First, it can store tabular, raster, and vector data in a single database. This makes it easier to manage and access all your GIS data because it is in one place.

Second, it allows for data validation using topologies, geometric networks, domains, and subtypes. This allows you to find and correct errors in your data.

Third, geodatabases are scalable, so they can grow as your organization does. There are several types of geodatabases. Each is designed to support varying sizes of organizations. So, as you grow, so can your geodatabase.

In the previous recipes, you made use of existing geodatabases. You used the data contained in them to create various maps. In this recipe, you will learn the basics skills needed to create a new geodatabase.

Getting ready

If you have completed the previous recipes, you should be ready to begin.

How to do it...

1. If you closed ArcGIS Pro after completing the previous exercise, start ArcGIS Pro and click **Open another project**. If you still have ArcGIS Pro open, click the **Project** tab in the ribbon and select **Open** from the area on the left side of the pane.
2. Click the **Browse** button and navigate to `C:\Student\ArcGISProCookbook\Chapter2\Creating a Geodatabase`.
3. Select the **Creating a Geodatabase.aprx** and click **OK**:

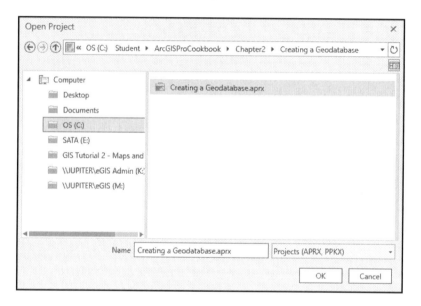

4. Right-click the **Databases** folder in either the **Contents** or **Catalog** pane, either will work:

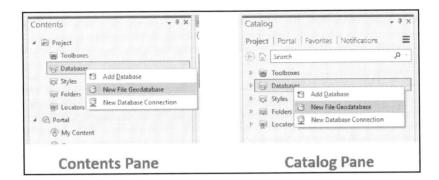

Contents Pane   **Catalog Pane**

5. Select **New File Geodatabase**.
6. In the panel located on the left side, double click **C:**, then navigate to C:\Student\ArcGISProCookbook\MyProjects.
7. Name your new geodatabase MyGeodatabase and click **Save**:

You just created your first geodatabase using ArcGIS Pro. It was a file geodatabase. If you remember from the previous chapter, a file geodatabase is one of three basic types of geodatabases that exist.

The file geodatabase is designed to be used by small organizations with only one or two primary users. It stores information within multiple files that are contained in a single folder with a .gdb extension. By default, a file geodatabase can store up to 1 TB per feature dataset, contained within the geodatabase plus at the root of the database. A feature dataset is similar to a folder on you computer used to store related files. A feature dataset is used to group related feature classes within the geodatabase. The total amount of data that can be stored per feature dataset can be changed to 4 or 256 TB using a configuration keyword. To learn more about configuration keywords for a geodatabase file, go to http://pro. arcgis.com/en/pro-app/help/data/geodatabases/overview/ configuration-keywords-for-file-geodatabases.htm.

Now that you have created a new database, you need to create items that will actually hold your data. This will include feature classes and feature data sets. We will start with a simple feature class.

8. Right-click the **MyGeodatabase.gdb** you just created. You can do this from the **Catalog** view or pane.

If you are trying to create the new feature class from the Catalog pane, you may need to expand the Databases folder so you can see the new file geodatabase you just created.

9. Go to the **New** option in the menu and select **Feature Class** from that:

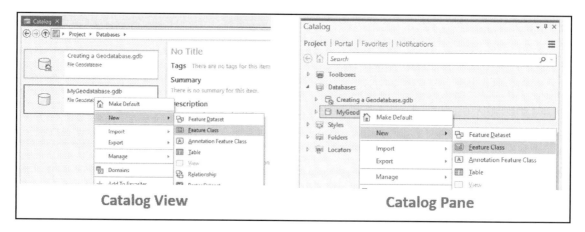

10. The **Geoprocessing** pane should appear on the right side, with the feature class location already filled in. Name the new feature class `Side_Walks`.

 Feature class names in a geodatabase have some limitations you should be aware of. They must start with a letter. Though the name can contain a number, it cannot start with one. Also, the name cannot contain spaces or special characters. The only exception is an underscore. The length of the name is limited by the operating system of the computer where you are storing the geodatabase file. However, I generally recommend keeping them as short as possible to avoid potential issues if you ever need to convert the database to another format.

11. Set the **Geometry** type by selecting **Polyline** from the drop-down menu.

12. Accept all the other defaults and verify that your **Create Feature Class** tool looks like the following image:

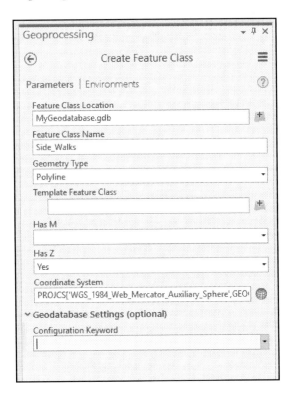

13. Once you have verified that you have the correct settings, click **Run**.

14. When the tool finishes, close the **Geoprocessing** pane.

15. In the **Catalog** pane, expand **MyGeodatabase.gdb** so you can see its contents.

    You should see the new feature class you just created. This is only the first part of creating a new feature class. The second part is defining the attributes you want to keep and associating it with the features you will store in the new feature class. So now you will create some attribute fields.

16. Right-click the **Side_Walks** feature class you just created. Go to **Design** and select **Fields**, as shown here:

17. The **Design** view will open in the middle of the interface. Notice that some fields have already been created. These are the default fields for a polyline geodatabase feature class.

Question: What default fields were automatically created when you created the new feature class?

Answer:

18. Click where it says **Click here to add a new field.**

19. In the **Field Name** cell, type Street.

20. Click in the **Alias** cell and type Street Sidewalk Follows.

21. Click in the **Data type** cell and choose **Text** from the drop-down menu.
22. Click in the **Length** cell and replace `255` with `50`.

 Database fields also have several limitations. The first is the name, it has the same limitations as the name of a feature class. Also, you must designate a data type. Field types typically include: Text or String, Long Integer, Short Integer, Single or Float, Double, Date, Blob, Guid, and Raster. To learn more about these different field types, go to `http://pro.arcgis.com/en/pro-app/help/data/geodatabases/overview/arcgis-field-data-types.htm`.

23. Click the **New Field** button located in the **Changes** group in the **Fields** tab in the ribbon. This is another way to add a new field.
24. Fill in the following properties:
    - **Field Name**: `Install_Date`
    - **Alias**: `Date Sidewalk was installed`
    - **Data Type**: `Date`
25. Using these skills, try adding another field for pavement type. It should be a text field that is limited to 15 characters:

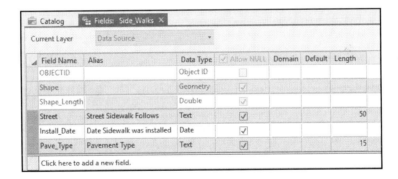

Your design view should look similar to this. Your field name for the pavement type and alias may be different, but that is acceptable as long as the length is the same.

26. Click the **Save** button, located in the ribbon on the **Fields** tab, to save the new fields you have created to the feature class.
27. Close the **Design view** by clicking the small **X** located on the tab above the view with **Fields: Side_Walks**.

28. Use the skills you learned in previous recipes to add a new map, and then add the new feature class you just created to the map.

    The new feature class should appear in the **Contents** pane. However, nothing is displayed because it is empty. Later in this book, you will learn how to edit the layer to create new features in it. Now you will learn how to add a new feature dataset to your geodatabase.

29. In the **Catalog** pane, right-click **MyGeodatabase.gdb**. Go to **New** and select **Feature Dataset**:

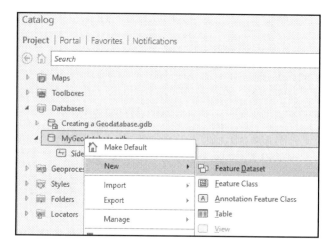

30. In the **Geoprocessing** pane, the **Create Feature Dataset** tool should appear. The output should already be defined as MyGeodatabase. Name your new feature dataset Property.

31. Accept the default for the **Coordinate System**. It should be set to WGS_84_Web_Mercator_Auxilary_Sphere. This is the coordinate system used by most online mapping systems, including Google Earth, ArcGIS Online, and Bing Maps.

32. Click **Run** to create the new feature dataset.

33. Close the **Geoprocessing** pane when complete.

    You should now see the new feature dataset appear in your MyGeodatabase database. It is identified in the geodatabase with three squares that overlap one another. This is the common icon for a feature dataset.

It is empty, so you will create a couple new feature classes in it that you will populate with some features later in the book:

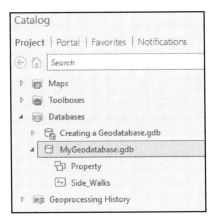

34. Right-click the new feature dataset you just created and, using the same methods you did to create the Side_Walks feature class, create a new feature class with the following properties:
    - **Feature Class Name**: Property_Lines
    - **Feature Class Type**: Polyline

35. Using the same method you did for the Side_Walks feature class, add the following attribute fields:
    - Field 1:
        - **Field Name**: Type
        - **Alias**: Property Line Type
        - **Data Type**: Text
        - **Length**: 10
    - Field 2:
        - **Field Name**: Length_FT
        - **Alias**: Length in Feet
        - **Data Type**: Float

Challenge your skill
Using the skills you have learned, create another new feature class in the same feature dataset, called Parcels. It should be a polygon feature class. Once you create the new feature class, add the fields for Mapped Acres and Square Feet. Both should be float field types.

How it works...

In this recipe, you learned how to create a new file geodatabase. You then created a new feature class within the geodatabase you created. Once you created the new feature class, you added several attribute fields to the attribute table associated with the feature class you created.

You then learned how to create a new feature dataset in your geodatabase. As you may recall from the previous recipe, feature datasets are an organizational unit in a geodatabase. They allow you to group related feature classes together so they are easier to find and so they can take part in a topology. Remember, all feature classes stored in the same feature dataset will have the same coordinate system. You will learn more about coordinate systems later in this book.

Once you created the new feature dataset, you added new feature classes within it using the skills you learned earlier in the recipe, this included creating several attribute fields.

Creating a new Shapefile

While geodatabases are the primary format for ArcGIS Pro, Shapefiles are probably the most common GIS data format you will encounter. It has become the default data sharing format because so many GIS applications are able to make use of them. This includes QGIS, AutoCAD Map 3D, MapInfo, Map Window, and Manifold. In addition, most high-grade GPS/GNSS units are also able to input or export shapefiles. This makes them very versatile when you need to share data between different platforms.

They do, however, have some limits. First, shapefiles can only store a single feature class. This means a shapefile will only contain either points, lines, or polygons. It is not able to contain a mix of feature types. Second, shapefiles are built on old technology. They were developed in the 1990s for use with Esri's now-discontinued ArcView GIS application. A shapefile uses dBase tables to store its attributes. This greatly limits the amount of data that can be stored, as well as the number of fields and field names. Lastly, shapefiles do not have the native ability to validate the data they contain, unlike the geodatabase.

But due to their popularity and versatility, you may often need to create new shapefiles. In this recipe, you will learn how to create a new shapefile.

Getting ready

You need to have completed the previous recipes in this chapter before you can begin this one. You will also need to have ArcGIS Pro and the sample data installed. An ArcGIS Pro Basic license should be sufficient for completing this recipe.

How to do it...

1. If you closed ArcGIS Pro at the end of the last recipe, open ArcGIS Pro. If you still have ArcGIS Pro open, click the back arrow, located in the top-left corner of the About **ArcGIS Pro** window.

2. In the **ArcGIS Pro** start window, click **Open another project**, as shown in the following image:

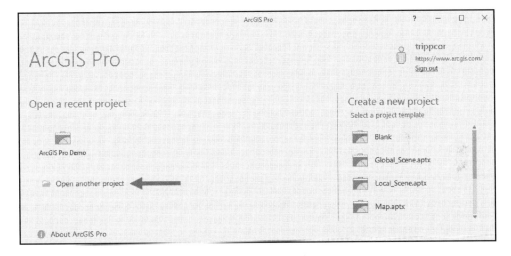

3. Click the Browse button, which looks like a file folder.

4. Using the skills you have learned, navigate to
   `C:\Student\ArcGISProCookbook\Chapter2`. Select **Creating a Shapefile.aprx** and click **OK**.

   The project should open with a map that contains the layers that reference the three feature classes you created in the last recipe. They are still empty. Next, you will create a new shapefile to store street signs that will be inventoried by a field crew using a GPS unit that can make use of shapefiles.

5. In the ribbon, click the **Analysis** tab.

6. Select the **Tools** button in the **Geoprocessing** group to open the **Geoprocessing** pane.

 Geoprocessing means to perform operations on geospatial data. This includes analysis, data conversion, projecting coordinate systems, creating new feature classes, and adding data fields. The tools you use to perform these functions are called **geoprocessing tools**.

7. In the **Geoprocessing** pane, click the **Toolboxes** tab located between **Favorites** and **Portal**:

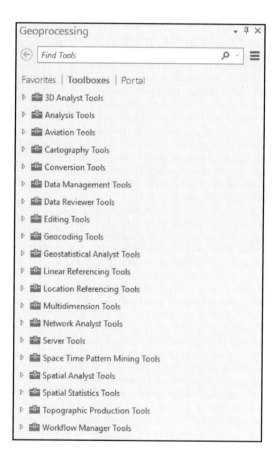

8. Click the small arrowhead located next to **Data Management Tools** to expand its contents.

9. Click the small arrowhead located next to the **Feature Class** toolset to expand its contents:

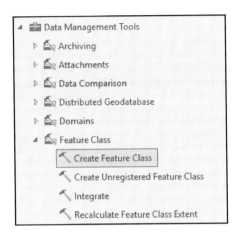

10. Double-click the **Create Feature Class** tool.

11. Click the **Browse** button, located to the right of the **Feature Class Location** cell.

12. In the area on the left of the **Feature Class Location** dialog window, scroll down to **Computer** and select **C:**.

13. In the area on the right, scroll down and double-click the **Student** folder.

14. Double-click the **ArcGISProCookbook** folder.

15. Select the **MyProjects** folder. Do not double-click it:

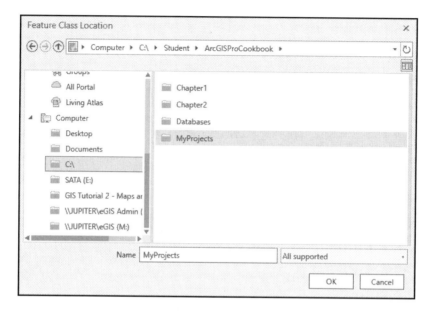

16. Click **OK**.
17. In the **Feature Class Name** cell, type ST_Signs.
18. You will use the same coordinate system you used for the geodatabase feature classes you created in the last recipe. So click the drop-down arrow in the **Coordinate System** cell.
19. Select **Side_Walks** from the list that is presented. This should set the coordinate system to be **WGS_1984_Web_Mercator_Auxillery_Sphere**.

20. Verify that the tool looks like the following graphic. If it does, click **Run**:

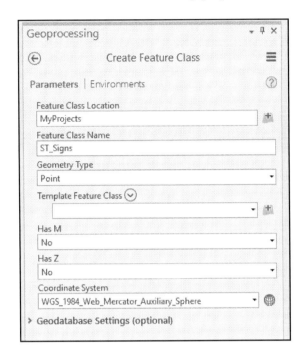

21. Close the **Geoprocessing** pane once it is complete.

This same tool can also be used to create geodatabase feature classes. All you need to do is ensure the **Feature Class Location** is set to a geodatabase or a feature dataset within a geodatabase.

Now that you have created the new shapefile, you will verify that it was created correctly. To do this, you will need to connect to the folder where you created the shapefile.

22. Right-click **Folders** in the **Catalog** pane and select **Add Folder Connection**.
23. In the area located on the left of the **Add Folder Connection** dialog window, select **C:**.
24. Scroll down in the area on the right and double-click the **Student** folder.

25. Double-click the **ArcGISProCookbook** folder.

26. Select **MyProjects** and click **OK**. Do not double-click the folder.

27. If needed, expand the contents of **Folders** in the **Catalog** pane. Then expand the contents of the **MyProjects** folder connection you just added.

28. If your shapefile was created successfully, you should see an **ST_Signs.shp** file listed in the folder:

29. Look at the **Contents** pane located on the left side of the interface. The new shapefile should have automatically been added as a new layer to your map. If it has not been, then drag and drop the shapefile from the **Catalog** pane into the map view to add it as a layer to your map.

30. Right-click the **ST_Signs** layer in the **Contents** pane. Select **Design** and then **Fields** from the menus that appear:

31. Using the same process you used for the geodatabase feature classes, add the following attribute fields. For any properties not specified, accept defaults:
    - Field 1:
        - **Field Name:** Date_Inst
        - **Field Alias:** Date of Install
        - **Data Type:** Date
    - Field 2:
        - **Field Name:** Type
        - **Field Alias:** Sign Type
        - **Data Type:** Text
        - **Length:** 15
    - Field 3:
        - **Field Name:** Cond
        - **Field Alias:** Condition
        - **Data Type:** Text
        - **Length:** 5

- Field 4:

    - **Field Name:** Date_Col
    - **Field Alias:** Data Collected
    - **Data Type:** Date

Remember field names cannot have spaces or special characters (except an underscore) and must start with a letter. Also, because this is a shapefile, the length of the name is limited to 10 characters.

32. Verify that your attribute table looks like the following image and click the **Save** button in the **Fields** tab in the ribbon:

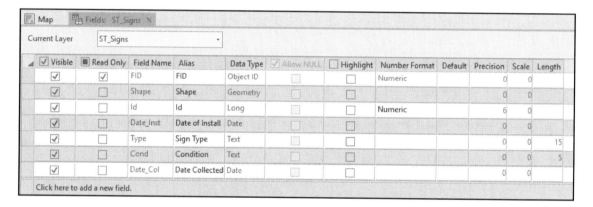

You may get a warning indicating the **Date data type is invalid**. Ignore this warning as it is incorrect and may be a bug in ArcGIS Pro 2.0. It was fixed in ArcGIS 2.1.

33. If you are not continuing to the next recipe, save your project and close ArcGIS Pro.

How it works...

In this recipe, you created a new shapefile that will be used to store information about street signs. You used the Create Feature Class geoprocessing tool to generate the new shapefile. After you created the new shapefile, you added attribute fields to the table that will store additional information about the street signs.

Adding CAD data to a map

A lot of data that ends up in GIS is often created first by engineers, surveyors, and landscape architects. They will often use a computer-aided drafting or design software, commonly referred to as CAD. There are two major CAD applications, AutoCAD and Microstation, with several smaller competitors. These will generally produce files that are referred to as drawings.

ArcGIS Pro does allow you to add these drawings to your map. Once added, you can adjust display properties, perform queries, and even import the CAD data into your GIS data.

In this recipe, you will learn how to add a CAD file to a map. Once added, you will learn how to adjust some display properties. Later in Chapter 7, *Converting Data*, you will learn how to import CAD data into GIS.

Getting ready

You will need to ensure that both ArcGIS Pro and the book sample data are installed. This recipe can be completed with an ArcGIS Pro Basic license.

This recipe is not based on previous recipes. So, you are not required to have completed any previous recipes before starting this one.

How to do it...

1. Start ArcGIS Pro if you closed it at the end of the last recipe, and open the Using CAD Data.aprx project located in C:\Student\ArcGISProCookbook\Chapter2\Using CAD Data.
2. In the **Catalog** pane, located on the right of the ArcGIS Pro interface, expand **Folders** by clicking the small arrowhead to the left of the word **Folders**.
3. Expand the **Chapter 2** folder so you can see its contents.

4. Locate the **Subdivision_NAD83.dwg** file. It should have a blue icon with a compass on it.

> CAD files will have one of three file extensions: DWG, DXF, or DGN. Like shapefiles and geodatabase feature classes, they too are vector data.
>
> DWG is the native format for Autodesk's AutoCAD-based product line. This includes AutoCAD, Map 3D, and Civil 3D. DWG files can also be created using other competitor applications, such as IntelliCAD or TurboCAD.
>
> DXF files are also an AutoCAD format. They are used to share data with other CAD applications that do not natively use the DWG format.
>
> DGN is the native format for Bentley's Microstation product line. Microstation is the primary competitor to AutoCAD. In the United States, Microstation is used by the Department of Transportation and the Department of Defense.
>
> As far as ArcGIS Pro is concerned, these files all work the same. So the workflow you will examine using a DWG file will also apply to DXF and DGN files.

5. Expand the **Subdivsion_NAD83.dwg** file.
6. Notice that the drawing file contains multiple feature classes, including **Annotation**, **MultiPatch**, **Point**, **Polyline**, and **Polygon**.
7. Select the **Subdivision_NAD83.dwg** file. Drag and drop it into the **Trippville** map view.

8. Right-click the **Subdivision_NAD83-Polygon Group** and select **Zoom to Layer**.

Your map should now look like the following image:

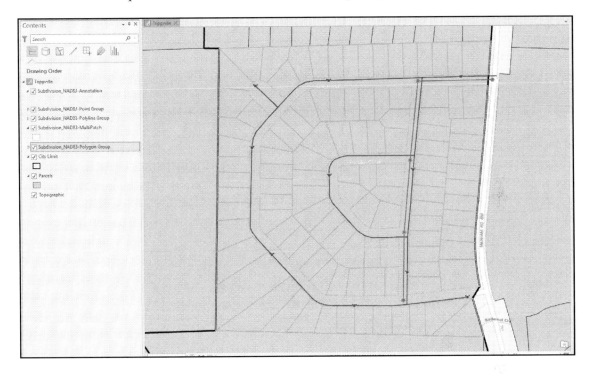

Map zoomed to Subdivision_NAD83-Polygon Group

You have just added an entire AutoCAD drawing file to your map. The drawing file shows a new subdivision that is going to be built in the City of Trippville. Now you will explore the drawing you just added to the map.

You could have added the individual feature classes instead of the entire drawing. In general, it is best to only add the data you need to your map. Otherwise you can become overloaded with information.

9. Expand the **Subdivision_NAD83 – Polyline Group** layer in the **Contents** pane.

Question: What layers are included in the group Polyline Group layer?

Answer:

10. Click the symbol located beneath the **Parcels** layer in the **Polyline Group** layer to open the **Symbology** pane.
11. Make sure the **Properties** tab is selected in the **Symbology** pane.
12. Click the drop-down arrow located next to **Color** and select Black. Then click **Apply**.
13. Now change the line width from 1.5 to 1, and click **Apply**.

Even though DWG files are not native to ArcGIS Pro, you can still display them and adjust some of their properties.

14. Close the **Symbology** pane.
15. Click the **Map** tab in the ribbon and activate the **Explore** tool.
16. Make sure the **Parcels** layer in the **Polyline Group** layer is still selected.
17. Click the drop-down arrow below the **Explore** tool and select **Selected in Contents**:

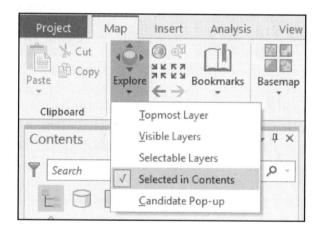

18. Click one of the lines in the **Parcels** layer in the map to open the informational window that displays information about the line you clicked:

As you can see, even though a drawing file is not in an Esri format, it also includes attribute data just like a shapefile or geodatabase feature class. In ArcGIS Pro, you can use these attributes just as you can those associated with data stored in an Esri format.

19. If you are planning to continue on to the next recipe, save your project and keep ArcGIS Pro open. If you are not continuing, you should save your project and close ArcGIS Pro.

How it works...

In this recipe, you added an entire AutoCAD drawing file to your map by dragging and dropping it from the Catalog map into your map view. Once you added the drawing file to your map, you explored some of the layers that were added in the Contents pane by zooming to one of the newly added layers and expanding the contents of the group layers.

You then changed the symbology of one of the newly added drawing file layers by clicking on the symbology beneath the layer and making adjustments to the color and width in the Symbology pane.

Lastly, you used the Explore tool to access attribute information about one of the parcel lines. You saw that even though the drawing file was created in another application, AutoCAD, it still has attributes just like a shapefile or Geodatabase feature class.

Plotting X,Y points from a table

It is not unusual to get data from outside sources that is nothing more than a table with some information that includes *X* and *Y* data. This may come from a surveyor, someone that collected data with their smartphone, or some other source. The data might be a spreadsheet, a text file, CSV file, or even a database table.

If the data includes coordinates for the location, you can turn these into points within a map. This is called an event layer. The coordinates can be in any known coordinate system as long as they are all the same, meaning that all coordinates for all the records in the table must be listed in the same coordinate system.

In this recipe, you will plot the locations of crimes from a standalone database table. This table has several records, each of which has a latitude and longitude coordinate. You will use that information to plot the location.

Getting ready

If you have already completed the previous recipes, you should be ready for this one. This recipe does not require the previous recipes to have been completed. You will need to ensure ArcGIS Pro and the sample data are installed. This recipe can be completed with an ArcGIS Pro Basic license.

How to do it...

1. Start ArcGIS Pro and open the `Plot XY from Table.aprx` project located in `C:\Student\ArcGISProCookbook\Chapter2\`.

2. In the **Catalog** pane, expand the **Databases** folder.

3. Expand the **Trippville_GIS** database so you can see the contents.

4. You should see a **Crimes_2014** database table. Right-click the table and select **Add to Current Map**:

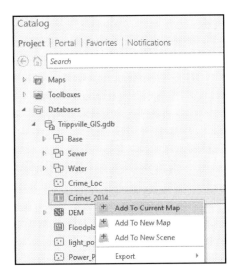

5. The **Crimes_2014** table should appear in the **Contents** pane. Right-click the table and click **Open**.

Question: What fields do you see in the table?

Answer:

You should see six different fields. Most important are the two at the end, Lat and Long. These are the coordinates that identify the location of each crime. You will now use those to create points in your map that show the location.

6. Close the table by clicking the small **X** in the tab at the top if the table.

7. Right-click the table in the **Contents** pane and select **Display XY Data**:

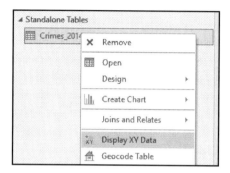

8. The **Geoprocessing** pane should open with the **Make XY Event Layer** tool. It should automatically populate with the required variables. Verify that yours looks like the following image. If it does, click **Run**. If not, make the appropriate adjustments:

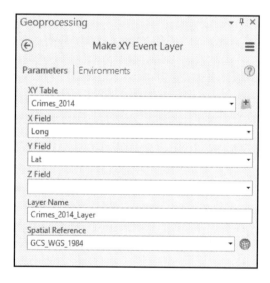

9. A new layer named `Crimes_2014_Layer` should appear in the **Contents** pane. If it does, close the **Geoprocessing** pane.

If the **Spatial Reference** is not set to GCS_WGS_1984, click the small globe to set it correctly. You will need to go to **Geographic Coordinate System** and **World**.

The US GPS system reports positions using the WGS 1984 geographic coordinate system. You will learn more about coordinate systems and how they work in ArcGIS Pro later in this book.

10. Right-click on **Crimes_2014_Layer** in the **Contents** pane. Select **Attribute Table**.
11. Compare what you see in the attribute table to what you saw when you opened the **Crimes_2014** table. They should be the same, with one exception.

Question: What is the one exception?

Answer:

12. Save your project and close ArcGIS Pro.

The layer you created is still linked to the original table. So, if the table changes, so does the layer. This same process works with spreadsheets, CSV files, and text files, as long as they are formatted similarly. The coordinates do not have to be latitude and longitude. They can be in any real-world coordinate system, such as State Plane, UTM, or WGS 84 Web Mercator Auxiliary Sphere, as long as you know what it is.

How it works...

In this recipe, you created points in a map showing the location of crimes using a standalone database table. You did this by first adding the table into your map by right-clicking it in the database and selecting **Add to Current Map**.

Once you added the table to the map, you viewed the table to ensure it included the coordinate values for each record. This was as simple as opening the table and looking at the data it contained.

Lastly, you right-clicked the table in the **Contents** pane and selected **Display XY Data**. This opened the **Geoprocessing** pane with the **Make XY Event Layer** tool. Because your table used several default fields, it automatically populated the required variables. Once this tool ran, a new point layer appeared in the map showing the actual location of the crimes from the table.

Geocoding addresses

In the previous recipe, you saw how data can be in something other than a traditional GIS format. It can be a standalone table which contains X and Y coordinates along with other information. That can then be turned into points on a map. X and Y coordinates are not the only way we identify a location.

Another even more common way to show a location is with an address. This is how postal carriers knew where the mail needed to be delivered well before the days of GPS. ArcGIS Pro can also use an address to identify a location. This is called geocoding.

Simply put, geocoding is the process of converting an address or series of addresses into a location on a map or in a GIS. In this recipe, you will learn how to geocode addresses within ArcGIS Pro. This will include determining reference data in your GIS, creating an address locator, and finally geocoding an inspections spreadsheet.

Getting ready

In addition to having ArcGIS Pro and the book data installed, you will need Microsoft Excel or a similar application installed in order to complete this recipe.

How to do it...

1. Before you start ArcGIS Pro, you will need to examine the spreadsheet of inspections you will be geocoding. Open Windows File Explorer.

You should see an icon that resembles a file folder in a folder on your task bar at the bottom of your display. This will open File Explorer.

2. In **File Explorer**, expand **Desktop** and **This PC** or **My Computer**, depending on the version of Windows you are using, located in the area on the left side of **File Explorer**.

3. Click the **C:** Drive so you can see its contents in the area on the right. It may be labeled as **OS** or **Local Drive**:

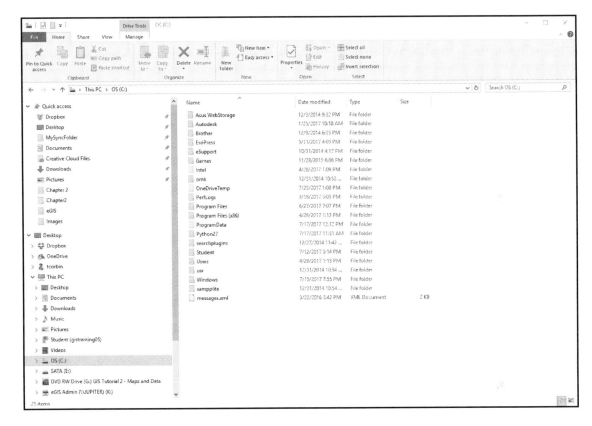

File Explorer looking at C: Drive

4. In the area on the right that displays the contents of the c:\ drive, scroll down until you see the **Student** folder and double-click it.

5. Continue using that same process to navigate to C:\Student\ArcGISProCookbook\Chapter2. Once you get to the **Chapter2** folder, you should see several files. One of them is **Inspections.xls**.

6. Double-click the **Inspections.xls** file to open it.

7. Review the spreadsheet you just opened. Note what information it contains:

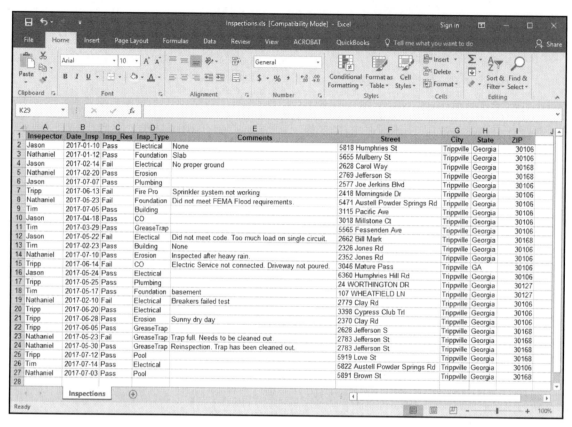

This spreadsheet represents an export from a permitting and inspections system that is outside of your GIS. That system does not have the ability to display data on a map, but the City Manager wants to see where inspections have been completed within the city. As you can see, the spreadsheet does include the address where the inspection took place. You will use that to geocode the location of each inspection on to a map.

8. Start ArcGIS Pro and open the `Geocoding.aprx` project located in `C:\Student\ArcGISProCookbook\Chapter2`.

9. Expand **Folders** in the **Catalog** pane.

10. Expand the **Chapter2** folder.

11. Expand the **Inspections.xls** spreadsheet and right-click the **Inspections$** table. Select **Add to Current Map**, as shown in the following image:

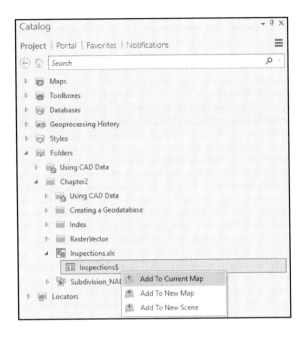

You have just added the spreadsheet you examined to your map so that you can geocode it. Before you geocode the data in the spreadsheet, you will first need to create a locator. Geocoding in ArcGIS Pro requires three components if you are using all your own data. You will need the table you want to geocode, reference data in your GIS that has address information, and a Locator.

Reference data is typically road centerlines, address points, or parcel polygons. Address points typically provide the greatest level of accuracy. This is followed by parcel polygons. The least accurate is road centerlines.

The **Locator** is the translator between your source data and the data you are trying to geocode. It provides basic settings and options required to geocode. There are several styles of locators that are dependent on your reference data and how the address information is formatted.

So, before you can create your locator, you must first identify your source data. This will be a GIS layer that already contains address information.

12. Since there is no address point layer in the Trippville geodatabase, you know that will not be your reference data. You do have parcel polygons, so right-click the **Parcels** layer in the **Contents** pane and select **Attribute Table**.

13. Examine the attribute table for the **Parcels** layer to determine whether it has address data.

Question: Does the Parcels layer contain address information?

Answer:

The Parcels layer does include some address information. It has a street name, street number, and street suffix. However, not all parcels have complete information. Also, it is missing other information that is included in an address, such as zip code, city, and state. Since the information attached to the parcels is incomplete, it is not well-suited to be your reference layer. It's time to look at the street centerlines to see whether they have more complete address information.

14. Close the **Parcels attribute table**.

15. Right-click the **Street Centerline** layer and select **Attribute Table**.

16. Review the **Attribute Table** for the **Street Centerline** layer. You may need to scroll over to see all the data fields.

Question: Is the Street Centerline address data more complete than the Parcels layer?

Answer:

The Street Centerline layer does have more complete address information. It has address ranges for both the left and right sides of the road. It also has fields for the road name and type. In addition, it has fields for the zip code and city on the left and right sides of each road. This is enough information to create complete addresses. So the Street Centerlines layer is the best choice as your reference layer, even if it might not produce the most accurate data points. Now you are ready to create your locator.

17. Close the **Attribute Table** for the **Street Centerlines** layer.

18. Click the **Analysis** tab in the ribbon.

19. Click the **Tools** button to open the **Geoprocessing** window.

20. Click the **Toolboxes** tab at the top of the **Geoprocessing** pane.

21. Expand the **Geocoding Tools** toolbox and click the **Create Address Locator** tool:

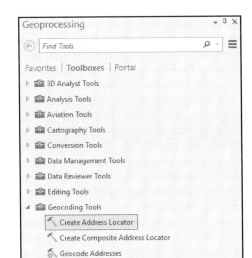

22. In the **Create Address Locator** tool, set the **Address Locator Style** to **US Addresses – Dual Ranges** by selecting it from the drop-down list.

The style you select is dependent on the geometry of the reference data and how the address information is formatted in the table. For example, the US Address Dual Range style only works with reference data that is a line or polyline feature class, and requires fields that identify starting and ending addresses for the right and left sides of the road. Other styles have other requirements. To learn more about Address Locator Styles, go to `http://pro.arcgis.com/en/pro-app/help/data/geocoding/understand-locator-styles.htm`.

23. Under **Reference data**, select **Street Centerlines** from the drop-down list. It should automatically be set as your primary table.

24. The field map should automatically populate. Scroll through the list and verify that all those with a "*" next to the field name are associated with an **Alias Name**. The **Alias Name** is the name of an attribute field in the **Street Centerlines** table.

25. Click the **Browse** button to the right of the **Output Address Locator**.

26. In the area on the left of the **Output Address Locator** window, scroll down to **C:** under **Computer**.

27. Select **C:**.

28. Scroll down and double-click the **Student** folder in the area on the right of the

window.

29. Double-click the **ArcGISProCookbook** folder.

30. Double-click the **MyProjects** folder.

31. In the **Name** cell, type `Trippville_Locator` and click **Save**.

32. Verify that your **Create Address Locator** tool looks like the following image. If it does, click **Run**:

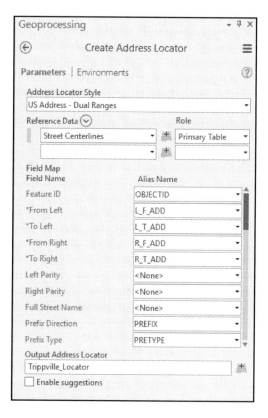

33. Close the **Geoprocessing** pane once the tool completes.

The locator you just created should appear in the **Catalog** pane in the **Locators** folder. That lets you know it was successfully created.

34. Right-click the **Trippville_Locator** you created in the **Catalog** pane. Select **Locator Properties**.

35. Select **Geocoding** options in the area on the left of the **Locator Property** window.

36. Scroll down to **Side Offset** and set it to 35. The side offset is how far off the centerline the geocoding process will create a new point. Since we know most of the street rights-of-way are between 50 and 60 feet, 35 should put the point on or close to the parcel it belongs on.

37. Set the **Side Offset** units to **Feet** from the drop-down list and click **OK**.

38. Right-click on the **Inspections$** table in the **Contents** pane and select **Geocode Table**:

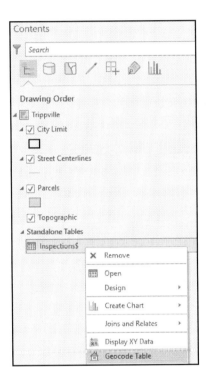

39. The **Geoprocessing** pane will open with the **Geocode Addresses** tool. The **Input Table** will automatically be set to the **Inspections$ table**. Set the **Input Address Locator** to Trippville_Locator.

40. Accept all other defaults and click **Run**:

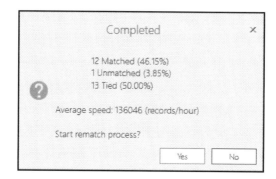

41. When the **Geocode Addresses** tool is complete, a window will appear and a new layer will be added to the **Contents** pane with the result. Click **Yes** to start the rematch process.

42. You were lucky to only have one address that did not match.

43. In the **Rematch Addresses** pane, make sure **Unmatched** is selected at the top. In the **Street or Intersection** cell, you can see that **Nature Pass** has been misspelled. Click in the cell and correct the name to **Nature Pass**.

44. The map should automatically zoom to the best match, and a grid will appear at the bottom of the **Rematch Addresses** pane with the best match at the top. Other close matches will also be presented.

45. Select the top match, labeled **A**.

46. Click the small green check mark located at the top of the grid to match it to the selected match.

47. Close the **Rematch Addresses** and **Geoprocessing** panes.

48. Right-click the **Inspections_GeocodeAddresses** layer in the **Contents** pane and select **Zoom to Layer**:

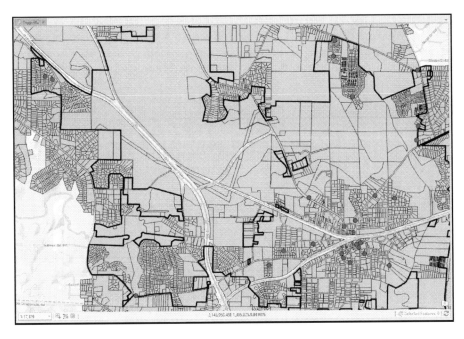

Map zoomed to Inspections_GeocodeAddresses layer

49. Using the skills you have learned, open the **Attribute Table** for the **Inspections_GeocodeAddresses** layer.
50. Examine the table to see the fields that were created by the geocoding process.
51. Save your project and close ArcGIS Pro.

How it works...

In this recipe, you geocoded a spreadsheet of inspections that had been exported from a Permitting and Inspections system which was external to your GIS. To do this, you first had to determine a reference layer. The reference layer is a GIS layer that contains address data. You examined your parcels and street centerline layers to determine which one would be the best reference layer. You determined that the street centerlines layer was best due to the completeness of the address information.

You then created a new locator that allowed you to use the centerlines as your reference. You used the **Create Address Locator** geoprocessing tool found in the **Geocoding** toolbox.

Once the locator was created, you were able to geocode the inspections spreadsheet. This created a new point layer in your map showing the locations of the inspections. One of the inspections did not match when you ran the initial geocoding. This was due to a misspelled name. You corrected this in the **Rematch Addresses** window, matching it to the correct location.

3
Linking Data together

In this chapter, we will cover the following recipes:

- Joining two tables
- Labeling features using a joined table
- Querying data in a joined table
- Creating and using a Relate
- Joining features spatially
- Creating and using a relationship class using existing data

Introduction

You now know that GIS data includes more than just what you may see in a map. Each layer has additional information linked to it which is stored in an Attribute Table. Also, not all data you display in a map is stored in a traditional GIS format. Some may be stored in standalone tables or even spreadsheets. These can also be displayed in a map if they include an address or x and y coordinates.

However, there is a lot data out there in various databases which may not have x and y coordinates, or an address, or even be part of our GIS, but we need to be able to use that information to perform queries, display information, or conduct analysis in the GIS. This data may come from other systems, such as tax appraisal, permitting, inspections, work order, and asset management systems. If we want to use data stored in these systems we must be able to link it to our GIS data. ArcGIS Pro provides a couple of methods to do this, Join and Relate.

At other times, we may need to transfer or link data together that is in our GIS. ArcGIS Pro supports several tools which allow you to do this, including a Spatial Join and creating relationship classes within a geodatabase.

In this chapter, you will learn the steps needed to link data in ArcGIS Pro to increase the capabilities of your datasets. You will learn how to create and use joins and relates. You will perform a spatial join to combine attributes between two layers based on a spatial relationship. Lastly, you will learn how to create and configure a relationship class within a geodatabase. You will start with a simple relationship class by creating an annotation feature class which is linked to another layer. Then you will create a relationship class manually, which will link two feature classes together.

Joining two tables

Join is one of two basic methods which can be used to link data in ArcGIS Pro. Joins link two datasets together to create a single virtual dataset within a single map in a project. This allows you to use the joined data to query, label, and symbolize using the information from both joined datasets.

In this recipe, you will join the Parcel layer to a table which contains a list of owner names. You will learn the requirements needed to join two tables and how to complete the join.

Getting ready

For this recipe, you will need to ensure that you have installed the book data and have ArcGIS Pro installed. An ArcGIS Pro Basic license level will be sufficient for this recipe.

How to do it...

1. To begin, you will need to start ArcGIS Pro.
2. In the **ArcGIS Pro** start window, click on **Open another project**.
3. Select **Computer** from the **Open** window and then click **Browse** in the area on the right:

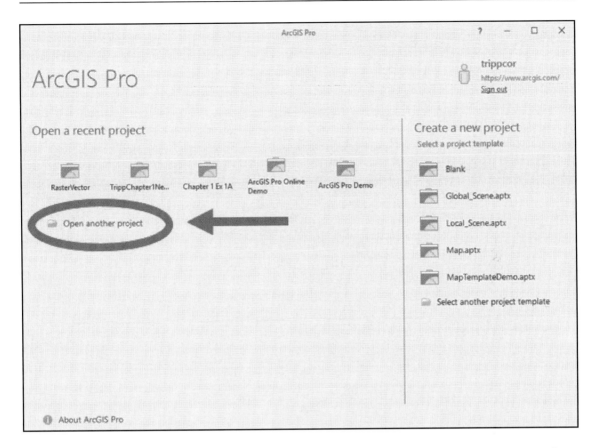

4. Navigate to C:\Student\ArcGISProCookbook\Chapter3\Joining Data by clicking on **C:** in the area on the left of the **Open Project** window. Then double-click on **Student**, **ArcGISProCookbook**, **Chapter3**, and **Joining Data** folders.

5. Select the **Joining Data.aprx** project file and click **OK**.

The project will open with a single map named City of Thomasville. The map contains two layers, City Limits and Parcels, plus the Topographic basemap. First you will review the information contained in the Attribute Table for the Parcel layer.

6. In the **Contents** pane, right click on the **Parcels** layer and select **Attribute Table** from the menu that appears. The **Attribute Table** for the **Parcels** layer should open in a window located at the bottom of the map view.

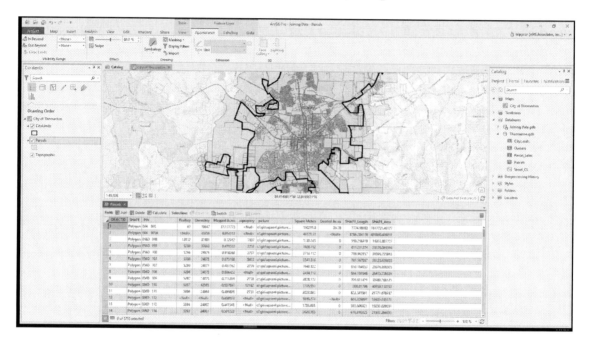

7. Take a moment to look at the fields the **Attribute Table** contains, and answer the following question:

Question: What fields does the Parcels Attribute Table contain?

Answer:

As you can see, the table contains information about the parcel, such as the **Parcel Identification Number** (**PIN**), RealKey, OwnerKey, and more. It does not, however, contain any information about who owns the parcels. However, you do know that information is available in the **Computer Aided Mass Appraisal** (**CAMA**) system located in the Tax Appraisal Office for the County.

They have provided you with a table of all the land owners in the County. You now need to join it to your Parcels layer.

8. In the **Catalog** pane, normally located on the right side of the interface, expand the **Databases** folder by clicking on the small arrowhead to the left.

9. Expand the **Thomaston.gbd** so that you can see its contents. You should see at least three feature classes (**CityLimits**, **Parcels**, and **Street_CL**) and a couple of stand-alone tables (**Owners** and **Parcels_Sales**).

10. Right-click on the **Owners** table and select **Add to Current Map**.

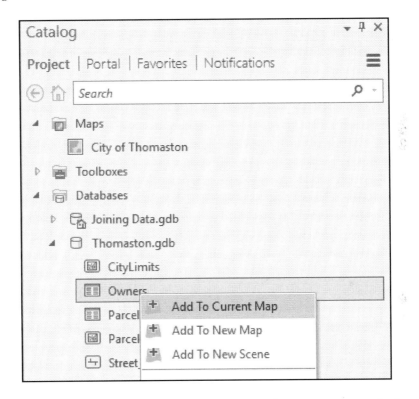

The newly added table should appear in your **Contents** pane at the bottom of the list. Now you will look at the data contained within this newly added table.

11. In the **Contents** pane, right click on the **Owner** table you just added and select **Open**. The **Owners** table should open in the same area as the **Parcels Attribute Table**.

12. Review the **Owners** table, paying close attention to what fields it contains. Then answer the following question:

    Question: What fields does the Owner table contain?

    Answer:

As you can see, this table does have information about all the land owners in the County. However, it does not have any information about the parcels they own. In order to join the Owner information to the Parcels, you must identify a **key field**. A key field is a field in each table which contains data common to the two tables you are attempting to link. Now you will identify a key field in each table, which you will use to link them together.

Key fields are not required to have the same names in both tables. The names can be different. However, they must be the same data type and contain the same data values. By the same data values, that means they must be exactly the same. This includes capitalization and the number of spaces if the key fields contain text. This why it is often best to use numeric values if possible.

13. In the table view area, click on the tab at the top of the table which says **Owners**. Hold your mouse button down and begin to drag it downward. A series of icons should appear in the middle of the table view. Drag your mouse to the icon which has the filled beige area located on the right side as shown ahead. Then release your mouse:

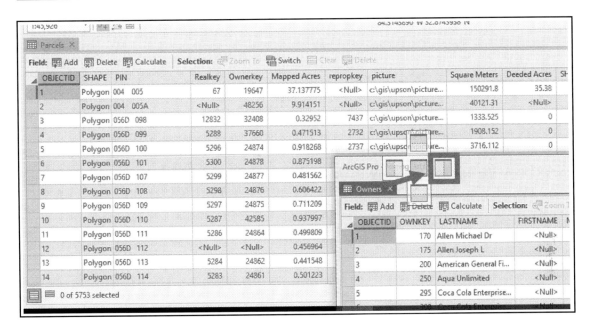

Click on Owners tab and drag to docking icon

You should now see the two tables side by side, as shown in the following image. This allows you to see data in both tables at the same time.

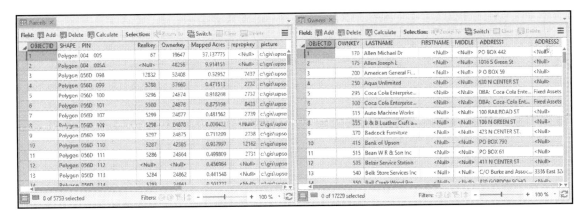

Two tables docked side by side

In ArcGIS Pro, you can actually drag the tables out so that they are viewable individually in their own window. These individual windows can then be positioned anywhere in your display, including on other monitors. They can also be sized individually as well. This can make it easier to view the multiple tables at one time.

14. In the **Parcels** table, right click on the **Ownerkey** field and select **Sort Descending**.

15. In the **Owners** table, right click on the **OwnKey** field and select **Sort Descending**.

16. Review and compare the values for these fields in each table, then answer the following question:

Question: These two fields appear to contain the same values?

Answer:

Now that you have verified the two fields contain like values, you need to verify the field types are the same.

17. Right-click on the **OwnerKey** field in the **Parcels** table and select **Fields** from the menu that appears:

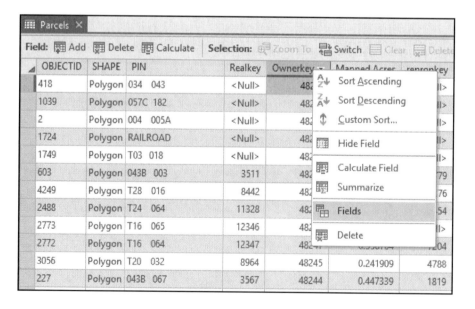

18. Perform the same operation on the **OwnKey** in the **Owners** table.

    Your table view should now look like this:

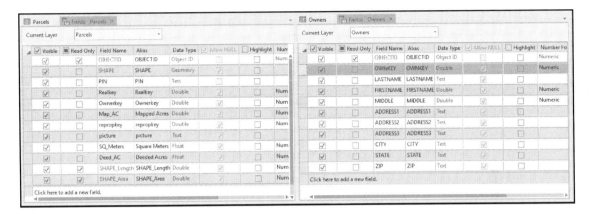

Table design views side by side

19. Verify that the **Data Type** is the same for the **Ownerkey** field in the **Parcels** table and the **OwnKey** in the **Owners** table.

    As you can see, the fields are both a Double data type. Since the fields contain the same data values and the field types are the same, these fields can be used to link the two tables. Now, it is time to link them.

20. Close the **Tables** and the **Fields** tab by clicking on the small **X**.

    It is not required to close the tables before joining them. You can leave them open if desired. It is just cleaner to close them before you join, to reduce screen clutter.

21. In the **Contents** pane, right click on the **Parcels** layer. Go to **Joins and Relates** and select **Add Join**.

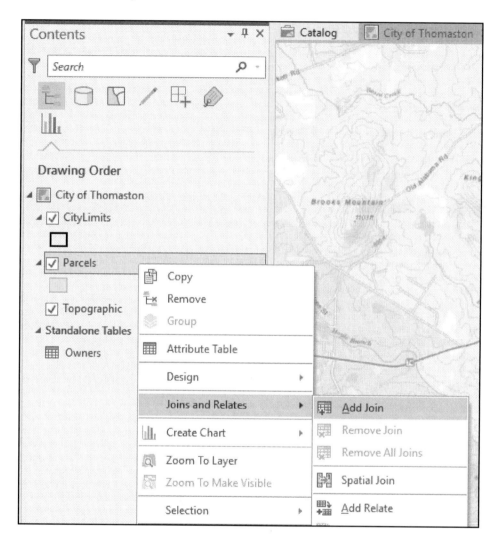

The **Geoprocessing** pane should open with the **Add Join** tool.

22. Verify that the **Layer Name or Table View** in the **Add Join** tool is set to **Parcels**.

23. For the **Input Join Field**, select **OwnerKey**.

24. For the **Join Table**, select **Owners** by clicking on the small drop-down arrow in the cell. The **Owners** table may automatically be populated into the cell. If so, you do not need to change it.

25. Set the **Output Join Field** to **OwnKey** using the drop-down arrow if needed. It may be automatically set.

26. Verify that the **Add Join** tool looks like the following screenshot. If it does, click **Run**:

27. Close the **Geoprocessing** pane once the **Add Join** tool has completed successfully by clicking on the small **X** in the upper-right corner of the pane.

28. Right-click on the **Parcels** layer in the **Contents** pane and select **Attribute Table**.

29. Using the scroll bar at the bottom of the **Parcels** table, scroll through the table fields.

Question: What do you see now that you have joined the Parcel and Owners table?

Answer:

As you can see, the fields that were on the Owners table have now been added to the Parcels Attribute Table. Now that those fields have been added, you can use that information to locate all parcels owned by a specific owner, or label parcels with the owner. Let's put that to the test. You will start with labeling the parcels with fields from the joined table in the next recipe.

30. Close the **Parcels** table by clicking on the small **X** in the tab which shows the table name.
31. Click on the **Project** tab in the ribbon, and click on **Save**, located in the panel on the left side.
32. If you are continuing to the next recipe, keep ArcGIS Pro open. If you are not you may close ArcGIS Pro.

How it works...

In this recipe, you joined the **Owners** table to the **Parcels** table. ArcGIS Pro links these two tables together, based on a key field in each table. The key fields are not required to have the same name, but must have the exact same values and be the same data type. ArcGIS Pro then compares the two tables and where the values are identical, it adds those fields and values to the primary table in the map. Where the values are not identical, it leaves the field values for the joined fields blank or null.

The **Join** only exists in the map in which you create it. It will not be applied to other maps within the ArcGIS Pro project. It is also not permanently applied to the feature class or table. **Join** works best when you want to link data which comes from other systems or datasets which will not be maintained in your GIS directly, such as the **Owners** table, which is maintained in the County's CAMA system. You just get an updated download of the data on a regular basis and replace the old table with the new one, so that when you open the map which contains the join, you always see the most current available information.

Labeling features using a joined table

Now that you have learned how to join tables, and seen how it links them to provide more information, what can you do with that information? In short, you can do anything with the joined information that you can do with the normal attributes in the layers Attribute Table.

In this recipe, you will learn how you label features using the data from the joined table. You will label each parcel with its PIN and Owner Name. You will use the new Arcade language to do this. You will learn more about Arcade in `Chapter 11`, *Introducing Arcade*.

Getting ready

You will need to have completed the previous recipe before you can begin this one.

How to do it...

1. If you closed ArcGIS Pro after completing the previous recipe, open the `Joining Data.aprx` project by following the same instructions as shown in the beginning of the previous recipe.
2. Click on **Bookmarks** on the **Map** tab in the ribbon. Select the **Labeling** bookmark. This will zoom you in to an area located in the center of the City.
3. Select the **Parcels** layer in the **Contents** pane so that the **Feature Layer Contextual** menu appears with three new tabs.
4. Click on the **Labeling** tab in the ribbon.

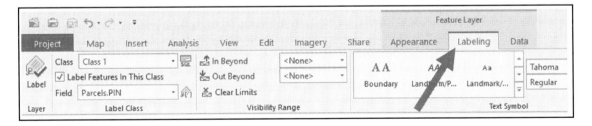

5. Click on the **Label** button located in the **Layer** group on the **Labeling** tab. It should be the located on the far-left side of the ribbon.

Text will appear in the map showing the PIN for each parcel. The values being displayed are being pulled from the **Attribute Table** for the **Parcels** layer. If you look in the **Label Class** group on the **Labeling** tab, you will see a setting for **Field**. It is set to **Parcels.PIN**. This means that the values being displayed are those found in the **PIN** field from the original **Parcels** table. You will now build an expression using the Arcade language, which will label each parcel with its **PIN** from the **Parcels** table and with its owner from the joined **Owners** table.

6. Click on the Expression button located to the right of the **Field** cell in the **Label Class** group. The **Label Class** pane should appear on the right of the interface. This is where you will build your labeling expression:

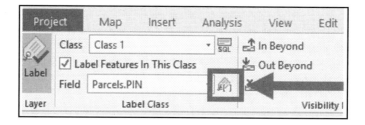

7. Click in form of $feature['Parcels.Pin'], the expression area in the **Label Class** pane. Type "PIN: "+ in the expression area, as shown ahead:

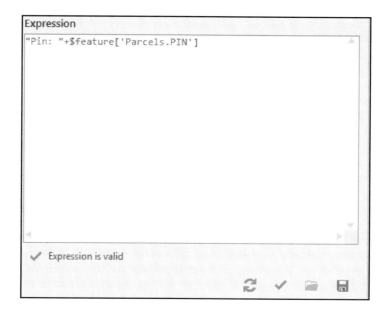

8. Click on the **Validate** button located at the bottom of the expression area. It looks like a green check mark. If it says **Expression is valid**, continue. If it does not, double check your expression against the previous graphic to make sure you typed in the correct syntax.

9. In the expression area, add the following to the end of the expression you have already created: `+Textformatting.Newline+"Owner: "`.

10. In the **Fields** window in the **Labeling Class** pane, scroll down until you see **Owners.LASTNAME**. Double click on **Owners.LASTNAME** to add it to the expression.

   Your full labeling expression should now say:

```
"PIN: "+$feature['Parcels.PIN']+Textformatting.Newline+"Owner:
"+$feature['Owners.LASTNAME']
```

11. Click on the **Validate** button once again to verify your syntax. If it says, **Your expression is valid**, click **Apply**. If it does not, verify your expression. If you continue to have issues, read the following tip:

   If you are having issues creating the expression, you can load one that has already been created. Just click on the Import button located next to the validate button and navigate to `C:\Student\ArcGISProCookbook\Chapter3\Joining Data`. Select the `PIN_Owner_Label_Expression.lxp`. Then click **OK** to import the expression.

12. Save your project.

   You have just labeled each parcel using the **PIN** field found in the original **Parcels Attribute Table** and the **LastName** field from the **Owners** table. You also added descriptive text to the label to make it easier to know what the labels were. Now you will clean up your labels so they are easier to read.

   ArcGIS Pro supports several languages for writing labeling expressions. In addition to Arcade, you can write expressions using Python, VBScript, and Jscript. Labeling expressions written for ArcMap and saved to expression files (`.exp`) are not compatible with ArcGIS Pro.

13. Click on the **Position** tab in the **Label Class** pane, as shown in the following screenshot:

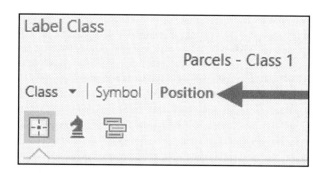

14. Click on the **Position** button in the **Position** tab in the **Label Class** pane.
15. If required, expand the **Placement** option and select **Land Parcel placement** from the drop-down menu.
16. Locate where it says **Horizontal in polygon** and click on the drop-down arrow. Select **Straight in polygon**.
17. Click on the Fitting Strategy button located at the top of the **Labeling Class** pane. It looks like a Knight chess piece.
18. Expand **Reduce size** by clicking on the small arrowhead.
19. Click on the box next to **Reduce font size** to enable this function.
20. Set the following parameters:
    - Font size reduction:
        - **Lower limit**: 4.0
        - **Step interval**: 1.0
    - Font width compression:
        - **Lower limit**: 60
        - **Step interval**: 5.0

The **Label Class** pane should now look like the following screenshot:

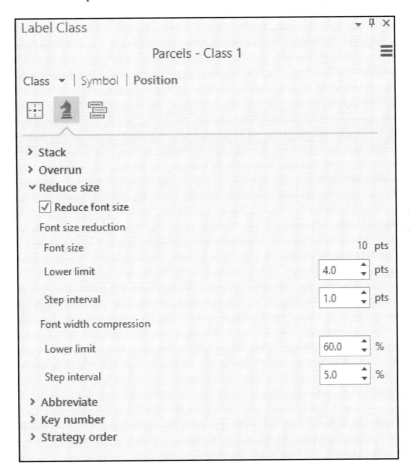

21. Click on the **Labeling** tab in the ribbon.

22. In the **Visibility Range** group, click on the drop-down arrow for **Out Beyond** and select **<Current>**. This will mean that the labels you just configured will only appear when you zoom in to the current scale of your map. If you zoom out to show a larger area, the labels will not be displayed.

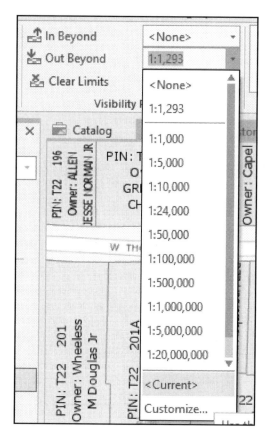

23. Save your project.

In this recipe, you labeled the parcels in the map with values from the **PIN** field in the **Parcels Attribute Table** and the **LASTNAME** field in the **Owners** table which you had joined to the parcels in the last recipe. You did this using Esri's new Arcade expression language.

In the first part of your expression, you added descriptive text which allowed users to know what the labeled values were. You did this in Arcade by using double quotes. This tells ArcGIS Pro to simply display the text values found inside the double quotes. For example, your expression contained "PIN: ". This produced a label which showed up in the map a PIN: .

This was then followed up with a reference to a database field. In Arcade, you did this using the + to indicate another part of the expression, followed by $feature['Parcels.PIN]. This displays the value found in the **PIN** field within the **Parcels Attribute Table**. The + sign must be used between each part of the expression. You then displayed the owner name on another line in the label using Textformatting.Newline in your expression. Once you set the owner name to be displayed on a separate line, you add more descriptive text by including "Owner: " in your expression. Lastly, you displayed the owners name by calling to the **LASTNAME** field in the joined **Owners** table by including $feature['Owners.LASTNAME'] at the end of your expression. This produced a label for each parcel that looked like this in the map:

- **PIN**: T22 028
- **Owner**: Unknown

You then adjusted several configuration settings for the labels in the **Label Class** pane to make the labels fit in the parcels better and to be easier to read. You did this by setting the placement option to Land parcel placement. This automatically applies some settings that are preconfigured in ArcGIS Pro for placing text within a parcel. This cleaned up several of the overlapping labels, but left many parcels without a label.

So, next you set the positioning to be **Straight in a polygon** as opposed to the default **Horizontal in a polygon**. This allows ArcGIS Pro to fit labels diagonally within the polygon if needed, first adjusting the size of the font. This allowed ArcGIS Pro to label a few more parcels, but still not all of them.

Next, you moved over to the Fitting Strategy to adjust the font size for your labels. You enabled **Reduce font size**. This allowed ArcGIS Pro to automatically resize the font within the parameters you designated to help fit the label within the parcels. By making this adjustment you were able to get all the parcels in the view labeled.

Querying data in a joined table

Labeling is not the only thing you can do with a joined table. You can also use the joined information to perform queries and analysis. In this recipe, you will perform a query to locate all the parcels owned by the City of Thomaston. You will then export that information to a spreadsheet using a geoprocessing tool.

Getting ready

You must have completed the recipe titled *Joining two tables* from this chapter before you can perform this recipe. You will also need to have Microsoft Excel or a similar application installed which will open a spreadsheet.

How to do it...

1. If you closed ArcGIS Pro after completing the previous recipe, open the `Joining Data.aprx` project by following the same instructions as shown in the beginning of the previous recipe. Otherwise continue with this recipe.
2. Click on the **Map** tab in the ribbon.
3. Click on the Full Extent button in the **Navigate** group on the **Map** tab. It looks like a small globe.
4. Click on the **Select by Attributes** tool in the **Selection** group on the **Map** tab in the ribbon. This will open the **Select Layer by Attribute** tool in the **Geoprocessing** pane.
5. Set the **Layer Name or Table View** to **Parcels** using the drop-down arrow.
6. Ensure the **Selection type** is set to **New selection**.
7. Under **Expression**, click on the **Add Clause** button.

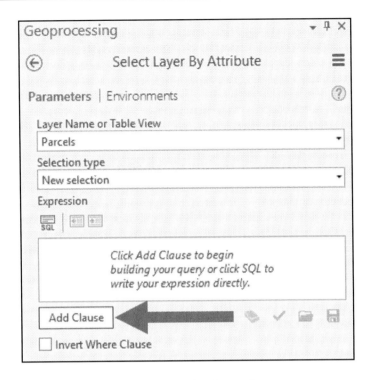

8. Set the **Field** to **LASTNAME** using the drop-down arrow.

9. Ensure the operator is set to **is Equal to**.

10. In the last cell, either type City of Thomaston, or pick it from the list of values shown with the drop-down arrow.

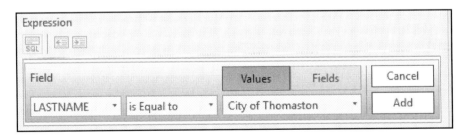

11. Verify that your clause looks like the preceding screenshot and click **Add**.
12. Click the Verify button located below the Expression to make sure your syntax is correct. The Verify button looks like a green check mark.
13. If your SQL expression is valid, click **Run**.
14. Click on the List by Selection button located at the top of the **Contents** pane. The button is three polygons, one blue and two white. Look at the number to the right of **Parcels**. Verify that you have selected **84 parcels**.

You have just selected all the parcels owned by the City of Thomaston using a **Select by Attributes** query. You were able to do that using data from the joined **Owners** table.

If you are already familiar with writing SQL where clauses, you can click on the small **SQL** button located under **Expression** and manually type the query you just built. The proper syntax would be `Owners.LASTNAME = 'City of Thomaston'`.

15. Click on the small arrow in a circle located at the top of the **Geoprocessing** pane.

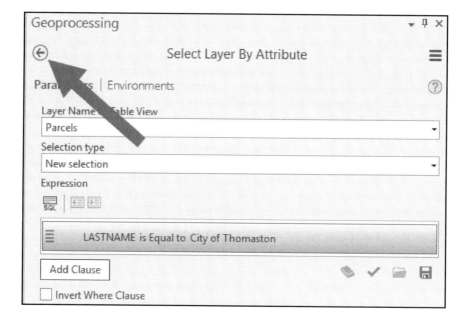

16. Click on the **Toolboxes** tab located near the top of the **Geoprocessing** pane.
17. Expand the **Conversion Tools** toolbox by clicking on the small arrowhead.
18. Expand the **Excel** toolset using the same method.
19. Double-click on the **Table to Excel python script**.

In the toolboxes, different icons indicate different types of tools. Hammers indicate system tools. Scrolls indicate python scripts. Series of connected squares indicate models created with ModelBuilder.

20. Set the **Input Table** to **Parcels** using the drop-down arrow.
21. For the **Output Excel File**, click on the **Browse** button located at the end of the cell.
22. In the **Save As** window that appears, navigate to the **MyProjects** folder located in `C:\Student\ArcGISProCookbook\`.
23. Type `Parcels owned by Thomaston` into the **File Name** cell.
24. Verify that your **Save As** window looks similar to the following screenshot and click **Save**. The folders you see in the **MyProject** folder will be different.

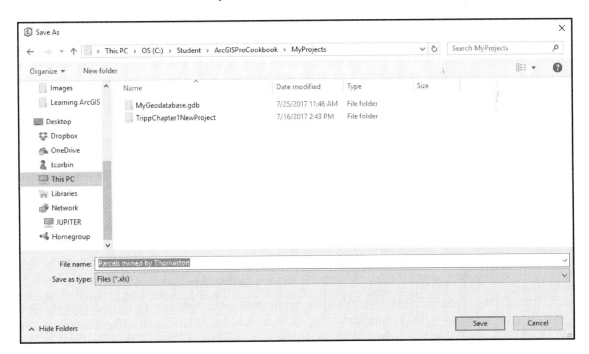

25. Your **Table to Excel** tool should look like the following. If it does, click **Run**.

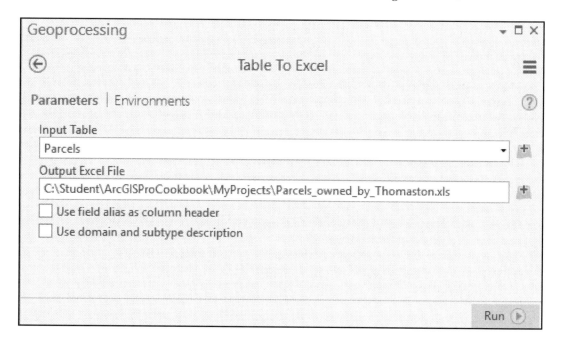

 When you run a geoprocessing tool with features selected, the tool only works on the selected features. So, in this case, you only exported the parcels which are owned by the City of Thomaston to a spreadsheet.

26. Open **File Explorer**. It is normally located on your taskbar near the Start button, and looks like a file folder in a holder.

27. In the tree on the left, select **This PC** or **My Computer** depending on what operating system you are running.

28. Double-click on your **C:** drive.

29. Navigate to C:\Student\ArcGISProCookbook\MyProjects. You should see the spreadsheet you just created from ArcGIS Pro.

30. Double-click on the **Parcels_owned_by_Thomaston.xls** file to open it. Take a moment to explore the spreadsheet to see what you have created.

31. When you are done reviewing the spreadsheet, close it and return to ArcGIS Pro.

32. Click back on the **Map** tab in ArcGIS Pro.

33. Click on the **Clear** button in the **Selection** group on the **Map** tab in the ribbon. This deselects all selected features.

34. Close the **Geoprocessing** pane.
35. Save your project and close ArcGIS Pro.

In this recipe, you queried all the parcels owned by the City of Thomaston and then exported the selected list to a spreadsheet. To query the parcels owned by the City, you created an SQL where clause using the query builder. This allows you to create SQL expressions without having to know SQL.

SQL stands for **Structured Query Language**. SQL is the standard language used by databases to communicate. It allows you to perform many functions within a relational database. Where clauses allow you to select records (or features within a GIS) which meet specific criteria. In the recipe you just completed, the criteria was where the Parcels owner equaled the City of Thomaston, thus why it is called a where clause. Like all languages, SQL has a specific syntax which must be followed to work. The ArcGIS Pro query builder you used knows the syntax and automatically creates the proper expression based on the parameters you provide. You used the **Create Feature Class** geoprocessing tool to generate the new shapefile. After you created the new shapefile, you added attribute fields to the table, which will store additional information about the street signs.

After you selected the parcels owned by the City of Thomaston, you exported them to a spreadsheet using the **Table to Excel** python script tool found in the **Conversion** toolbox and **Excel** toolset. Python is a scripting language which has been heavily integrated in to the ArcGIS platform. Python scripts can be created to assist with automating and streamlining workflows. To learn more about using Python with ArcGIS, we recommend *Programming ArcGIS with Python Cookbook, 2nd Edition* by Eric Pimpler from Packt Publishing.

Creating and using a Relate

A Join is just one of the basic methods you can use in ArcGIS Pro to link data together. Another method is a Relate. A Relate links two tables together, but unlike a Join, which adds information to the primary table, the two tables remain separate when related. This allows you to see all the related records in the linked table.

A Relate works best when you have one record in your primary table which matches to multiple records in the linked table, or when you have multiple records in the primary that match multiple records in the linked table. In these situations, a Join would not work as well because it would have multiple records which match.

In this recipe, you will create a Relate between the Parcels and a land sales table. The land sales table contains all parcels sales which have occurred over the last several years. This table also comes from the County's CAMA system, like the Owners table did. Once you relate the two tables, you will see how you can view all the sales for a selected parcel.

Getting ready

You will need to ensure that ArcGIS Pro and the book data is installed. This recipe is not based on previous recipes, so, you are not required to have completed any previous recipes before starting this one.

How to do it...

1. Start ArcGIS Pro and open the `Creating and using a Relate.aprx` project, located in `C:\Student\ArcGISProCookbook\Chapter3\Creating and using a Relate`.
2. In the **Catalog** pane located on the right of the ArcGIS Pro interface, expand **Databases** by clicking on the small arrowhead.
3. Expand the **Thomaston.gdb** geodatabase so you can see its contents.
4. Right-click on the **Parcels_Sales table** and select **Add to Current Map**. The table should then appear at the bottom of the list in the **Contents** pane.
5. Right-click on the **Parcels** layer and select **Attribute Table**.
6. Right-click on the **Parcels_Sales** table and select **Open**.
7. Using the skills you learned in the previous recipe, try to determine the key field in each table which you will use to link the two tables together. Remember the key fields must contain the same data values and be the same field data type. The field names do not need to be the same.

Question: What is the key field in each table?

Answer:

After reviewing each table, the key field should be fairly easy to pick out. The Realkey is the only field in each table which has the same data values and the same data type.

8. In the **Parcels Attribute Table**, right-click on the **Realkey** field and select **Sort Descending**.

9. In the **Parcels Attribute Table**, locate the records with a Realkey value of **15812**.

You could also use the **Select by Attribute** tool to create a query which would select all parcels with a Realkey value of **15812**.

Question: How many rows in the table contain a Realkey value of 15812?

Answer:

10. In the **Parcels_Sales** table, right-click on the **REALKEY** field and select **Sort Descending**.

11. In the **Parcels_Sales** table, locate the rows with a REALKEY value of **15812**. You will need to scroll down until you see that value, or you could use the **Select by Attribute** tool to select the records.

Question: How many records in the Parcels_Sales table have a REALKEY value of 15812?

Answer:

You should now know that there is one parcel and two sales records which have a realkey value of 15812. This means that you have a one to many cardinality, which works well with a Relate. Now you need to configure the Relate to link the Parcels to the Parcels_Sales table.

Cardinality refers to how many records in one table match to records in another table, based on a comparison of values found in a key field. There are four types of cardinality, one to one, one to many, many to one, and many to many. This relationship between records in the two tables can impact how you are able to work with them. Traditionally, with older Esri software such as ArcMap, if you had a one to one or a many to many, you would always want to use a Join. If you had a one to many or a many to many, you would always want to use a Relate. This is not the case with ArcGIS Pro. ArcGIS Pro offers more flexibility so you can choose either a Join or a Relate depending on how you need to use the data.

12. Right-click on the **Parcels** layer in the **Contents** pane. Go to **Joins and Relates** and select **Add Relate**. The **Add Relate** tool should open the **Geoprocessing** pane on the right-hand side of the ArcGIS Pro interface.

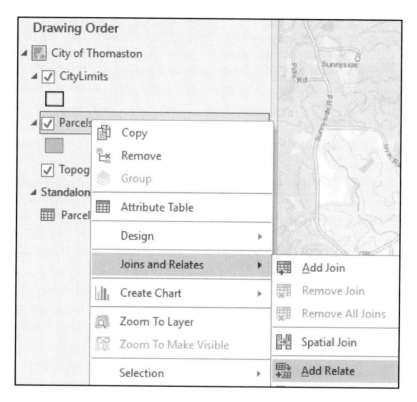

13. Ensure the **Layer Name or Table View** is set to **Parcels**. Since you right-clicked on the **Parcels** layer to add the Relate, this should be automatically populated.
14. Set the **Input Relate Field** to **Realkey** using the drop-down arrow.
15. The **Relate Table** and **Output Relate Field** should automatically populate because you have no other standalone tables in your map.
16. Change the **Relate Name** to `Parcel Sales`
17. Verify that your **Add Relate** tool looks like the following image. If it does click **Run**.

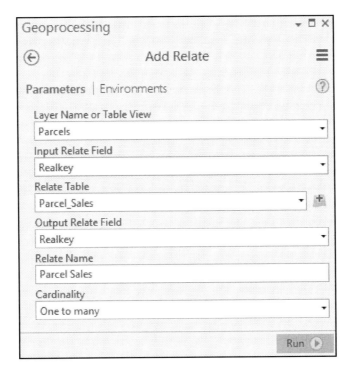

18. Once the **Add Relate** tool has completed successfully, close the **Geoprocessing** pane.
19. Save your project.
20. Select the **Map** tab in the ribbon.

21. Activate the **Explore** tool by clicking on it. Move your mouse point to the approximate center of the City and zoom in by pushing your scroll wheel away from you until your map looks similar in scale to the following.

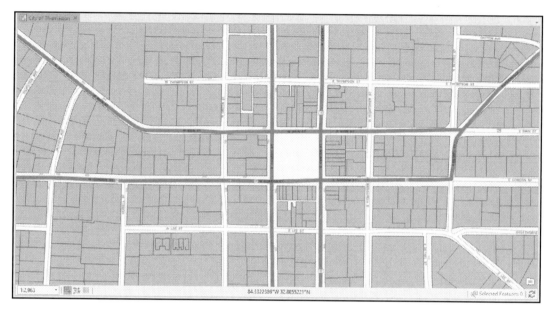

Center on town square and zoom to 1:2,900 +/-

22. Click on the **Parcels Attribute Table** in the table view.
23. Click on the **List by Selection** button near the top of the **Contents** pane.
24. If it is checked, click on the small box located next to the **CityLimits** layer to make it not selectable.
25. Select the **Parcels** layer in the **Contents** pane.
26. On the **Map** tab in the ribbon, select the **Select** tool.

27. Click on the parcel indicated in the following screenshot:

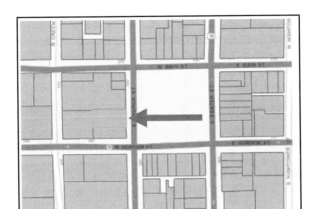

Select parcel due west of town square

28. Click on the **Data** tab in the ribbon.

29. Click on the **Related Data** button and select **Parcel_Sales:Parcel_Sales** as shown ahead:

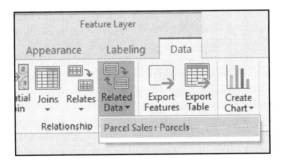

The records which show the two times that the selected parcel has been sold should be displayed in the **Parcels_Sales** table. So, as you can see, the two tables are linked but still remain separate.

30. Try selecting a few other Parcels and see if they have been sold multiple times. Some parcels may not have been sold even once. You may need to click the **Related Data** button with each selection to see the related records.

31. Save your project.

There is more....

As was mentioned earlier in this recipe, the cardinality was a major consideration when choosing whether you should use a Join or a Relate to link tables when using older Esri applications such as ArcMap. In ArcMap, you should always use a Join if you have a one to one or a many to one cardinality. However, if you have a one to many or many to many, you should use a relate in ArcMap otherwise you will miss data because the result would be a joined table that contained Null values or just the values from the first record it finds that matches.

ArcGIS Pro does not work that way. You can Join two tables regardless of the cardinality as long as they are in the same database. If you join two tables in ArcGIS Pro that have a one to many or a many to many cardinality, you see all the matched records. ArcGIS Pro does this by creating virtual records in the table view for each match, as shown ahead:

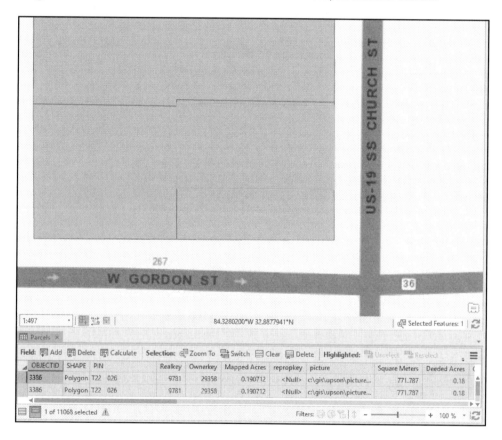

Single parcel selected but two records displayed in Attribute Table

As you can see, you have a single parcel selected but two records are shown in the table view for the layer. This is because the Parcels_Sales table was joined to the Parcels Attribute Table. As you saw in the recipe, there is a one to many cardinality between these tables. So, there are two sales associated with the selected parcel in the Parcel_Sales table, and both are displayed.

In ArcGIS Pro, this method of joining tables with one to many and many to many has other advantages. You are able to label features with values from each record in the joined table. This is something ArcMap users are unable to do. However, remember this only works with tables in the same database. If the tables are in two different databases or are different formats such as linking a spreadsheet to a geodatabase feature class, then the normal rules about when to use a join and when to use a relate still apply.

If you wish, use the skills you have learned in this and the previous recipe to join the Parcel_Sales table to the Parcels layer. Then explore how this join works by selecting several parcels while looking at the Attribute Table.

Joining features spatially

So in the previous recipes, you have seen how you can link external data to layers or other tables using a Join or a Relate. However, what if you want to transfer data from one layer to another but there is no key field to use to link the data. Maybe the two layers in question overlap one another, or are next to one another, or share some other spatial relationship, surely there should be some way to link or join the two layers together based on a spatial relationship.

You can join two layers together based on a spatial relationship. This is called a **Spatial Join**. A Spatial Join creates a new feature class which adds the attributes from the joined feature class to the target feature class based on a spatial relationship you define when you run the tool. It is not required that the target and joined feature classes be the same type. You can spatially join lines with polygons, or points with lines, or points with polygons, as well as those of the same feature type.

When you run the Spatial Join tool you can specify the Join Operation. This determines how joins between the target features and join features will be handled in the output feature class if multiple join features are found that have the same spatial relationship with a single target feature. The options for this include:

- **JOIN_ONE_TO_ONE**: When this option is chosen, if a single feature in the target layer matches to multiple features in the join layer because they have the same spatial relationship, the attributes from all the matched join features will be aggregated based on the field map merger rule you configure. For example, if you set the target layer to be the road centerlines and a road centerline crosses two wetland polygons which are in your join layer, the attributes from the two wetland polygons will be aggregated before being transferred to the output line feature class. If one wetland polygon has an area value of 2 acres and the other has an area value of 5 acres, and a Mean merge rule is specified, the aggregated value in the output feature class will be 3.5.

- **JOIN_ONE_TO_MANY**: When this option is chosen, if a single feature in the target layer is found to match with multiple features in the join layer because they have same spatial relationship, the resulting output feature class will contain multiple records representing the single target feature and each match it has with features in the join layer. Using the same example as previous, if a single road centerline crosses two wetland polygons, the output feature class will contain two road centerlines: one will have the attributes from one of the wetland polygons it crossed and the second will have the attributes from the other.

In this recipe, you have been asked to assign each sewer line and sewer manhole the name of the watershed it is located within. This is for an annual report the sewer superintendent must submit to the state every year. You have the boundary of the existing watersheds in your area and you have layers for the sewer lines and sewer manholes, so you will use the Spatial Join geoprocessing tool to assign the name of each watershed to the sewer features that are inside it.

Getting ready

This recipe can be completed with any license level of ArcGIS Pro. Completion of any other recipes is not required, though it is recommend that you complete the recipes in Chapter 1, *ArcGIS Pro Capabilities and Terminology*. This will ensure that you have the basic skills required to successfully complete this recipe. Of course, you must install the sample data before you begin.

How to do it...

1. Start ArcGIS Pro and open the Spatial Join.aprx project located in C:\Student\ArcGISProCookbook\Chapter3\Spatial Join\.

2. Right-click on the **Sewer Manholes** layer in the **Contents** pane and click **Attribute Table**.

3. Explore the **Attribute Table** for the **Sewer Manholes** layer and answer the following question:

Question: What fields do you see in the Attribute Table for the Sewer Manholes?

Answer:

You will notice that it does not indicate which watershed each manhole is located in. So, you need to add this attribute to each manhole. Luckily you do have a watershed layer which shows the boundary of each watershed and its name. You will be able to use the Spatial Join to add this information to the manholes. First you will explore the Attribute Table for the Watersheds layer. Then you will use the Spatial Join tool.

4. Right-click on the **Watersheds** layer and select **Attribute Table**.

5. Explore the fields contained in the **Attribute Table** for the **Watersheds** layer.

Question: What fields do you see in the Attribute Table for the Watersheds layer?

Answer:

6. Click on the **Analysis** tab in the ribbon.

7. Select the **Spatial Join** tool from the **Tools** group on the **Analysis** tab in the ribbon. This will open the **Geoprocessing** pane with the **Spatial Join** tool.

Select Spatial Join tool

8. Set the **Target Features** to **Sewer Manholes** using the drop-down arrow.
9. Set the **Join Features** to **Watersheds** using the drop-down arrow.
10. For the **Output Feature Class**, click the **Browse** button. Then select the **Databases** folder located under **Project** in the tree on the left side of the **Output Feature Class** dialog window.
11. Double-click on the **Spatial Join.gdb**.
12. In the **Name** cell, type Sewer_Manholes_Watersheds and click **Save**.
13. Set the **Join Operation** to **Join one to one** using the drop-down arrow.
14. Set the **Match Option** to **Within**. This is the spatial relationship which will join the watershed name to each manhole that is inside the watershed.

15. Verify that your **Spatial Join** tool looks like the following and click **Run**.

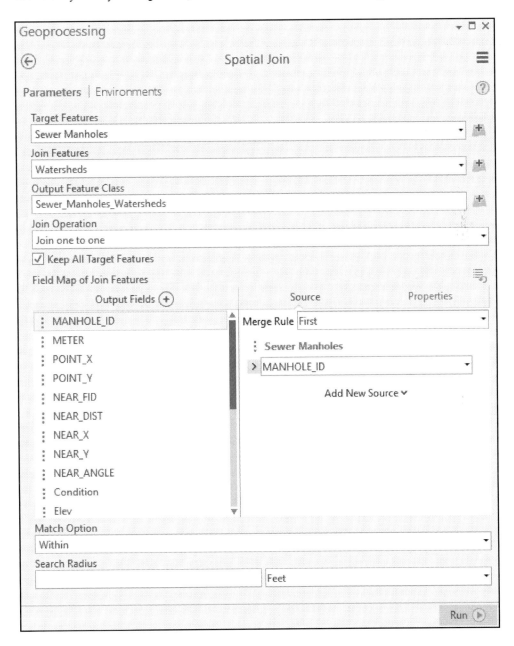

16. When the **Spatial Join** tool is complete, close the **Geoprocessing** pane.

17. A new layer should have been added to your map, called
    Sewer_Manhole_Watersheds. Right-click on this new layer and select **Attribute Table**.

    Question: What fields does the Attribute Table for this new layer contain?

    Answer:

    Question: How does the new table compare to the Attribute Table for the Sewer Manhole and the Watersheds layers?

    Answer:

    As you should hopefully see, the new layer contains the combined attributes of both the sewer manholes and watersheds layers. The output was a new point layer because the target was the sewer manholes, which was a point layer.

18. Close the **Attribute Table** and save your project.

19. Now, using the same process perform a spatial join between the sewer lines and the watersheds. However, this time set the **Match Option** to **Intersect** and the **Output Feature Class** to `Sewer_Lines_Watersheds`.

20. Your **Spatial Join** tool should look like this. If it does, click **Run**.

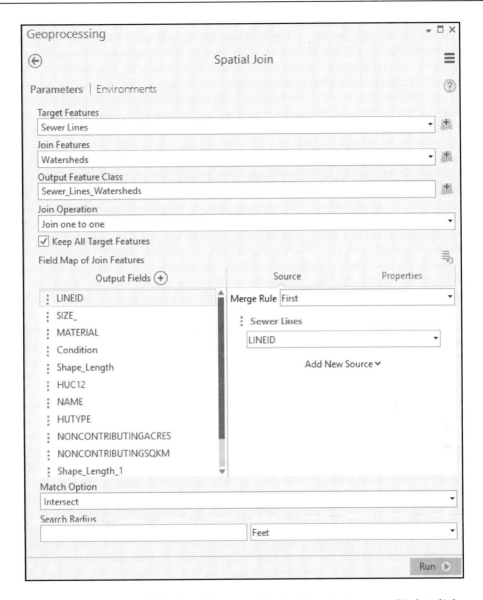

21. The **Crimes_2014** table should appear in the **Contents** pane. Right-click on the table and click **Open**.

22. Once the tool is complete, close the **Geoprocessing** pane and save your project.

When the tool completes, the new layer you created should be added to the map. If you open the Attribute Table you will see it too contains the combined attributes from both the inputs. This time, the output was a line layer instead of a point because the target layer was the sewer lines layer, which, as the name indicates, is a line layer.

23. Close ArcGIS Pro.

You have now seen how a spatial join can be used to merge data in two different layers into a single layer or feature class. This can increase the types of analysis you can perform on the data or how you can display it. Remember, when you perform a spatial join, it does create a new data layer. This means that your original data is still intact for you to use as well.

Creating feature linked annotation

You have now seen how to link data together based on a common key field using a Join or Relate, based on a spatial relationship. These methods are extremely useful. However, they do have limitations. Joins and Relates only exist in a single map and do not transfer easily to other maps or projects. Spatial Joins create new feature classes or tables while still leaving the original data unaltered. So, is there a way to permanently link two tables or two feature classes together?

The answer is yes, if the data is all in the same geodatabase. In a geodatabase, you can create a relationship class. A relationship class permanently links data together and the link carries over into any map, scene, or project you use the data in. You can create a relationship class between two feature classes, two standalone tables, or a feature class and a standalone table.

Relationship classes provide greater flexibility than the other methods we have looked at in previous recipes. Not only can you link data together so you can access the additional information, the related data can also impact the behavior or contents. For example, if I relate a sewer line feature class to a manhole feature class, the relationship class can be configured to allow information such as an attribute value from one feature class to also pass to another, or if I delete a feature in one feature class it deletes the connected feature in the other feature class.

One of the easiest relationship classes to create is called **Feature Linked Annotation**. In this recipe, you will create feature linked annotation and then explore its behavior.

Getting ready

To complete this recipe, you will need a Standard or Advanced license of ArcGIS Pro. A Basic license does not support this level of functionality. If you are not sure what license you have, you can check it by doing the following. Open ArcGIS Pro, and on the bottom left of the start window, where you would normally select a project to open, click on **About ArcGIS Pro**. Then select **Licensing** from the list on the left. This will display the license level available to you and any extensions you may have access to as well.

If you only have a Basic license, check with your account administrator to see if they can assign you a Standard or Advanced license at least temporarily. If a higher license is not available, you can request a trial license from Esri by going to their website, at `http://www.esri.com/arcgis/trial`. This will provide you with access to an Advanced license for ArcGIS Pro and more.

How to do it...

1. You will begin by starting ArcGIS Pro. Then open the `FeatureLinkedAnno.aprx` located in `C:\Student\ArcGISProCookbook\Chapter3\FeatureLinkedAnno`.

2. The project should open with a single map called `Trippville`. Click on the **Bookmarks** button located in the **Navigate** group on the **Map** tab. Select **Labeling Area** to zoom to the middle of Trippville.

3. In the **Contents** pane, select the **Street Centerline** layer.

4. From the ribbon, select the **Labeling** tab, which appears in the **Feature Layer** contextual tab.

5. In the **Map** group on the **Labeling** tab, select the **More** drop-down.

6. Click on the **Label** button located on the far-left side of the **Labeling** tab to turn on the labels for the **Street Centerlines** layer. Ensure **Use Maplex Labeling Engine** is not checked. If it is, click on it to deactivate. If you get a warning about switching the labeling engine, click **Yes**.

Select Label button on far left

7. Set the **Field** locate in the **Label Class** group on the **Labeling** tab to **ST_NAME** using the drop-down arrow to scroll to the field.

8. In the **Label Placement** group on the **Labeling** tab, select **Curved Line**.

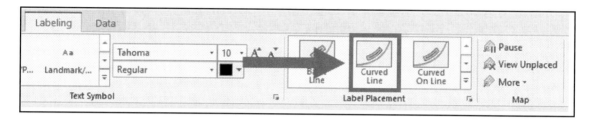

9. Verify that your font is set to **Tahoma**, size **10**, and color is black in the **Text Symbol** group on the **Labeling** tab.

You have added labels for the street names to the map. If you configured everything, your map should now look very similar to the following image. Yours may not be an exact match due to the size of your monitor being different or you may have other panes open.

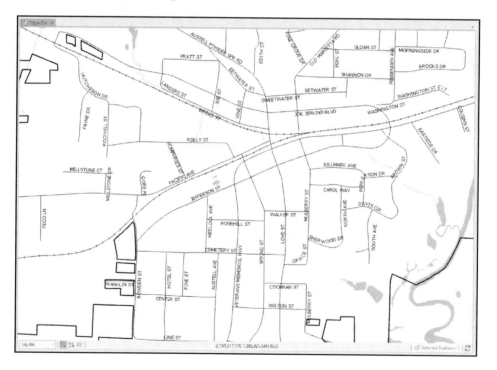

10. Click on the **Map** tab in the ribbon.

11. At the far-right end of the **Map** tab, click on the **Convert To Annotation** button. This will open the **Convert Labels to Annotation** tool in the **Geoprocessing** pane.

ArcGIS Pro supports two types of text display in a map or scene. The first is labels. Labels are dynamic text which is tied to a specific layer and attributes associated with that layer. The user can configure some settings which the computer will use when trying to determine where to place the label or if one will be placed at all. However, users are not able to individually place a label and guarantee it will always appear or be in a consistent location. The computer makes the final decision. Labels are extremely useful because they do automatically adjust as your map view changes in size or location. Annotation is the other method for displaying text. Annotation is fixed text, which can be individually placed and modified. This provides much greater control over the text, allowing you to put it exactly where and how you want it. Its big disadvantage is that it is more labor intensive to maintain and will not work at all scales. Feature Linked Annotation is the best of both worlds. It provides the control of annotation with some of the dynamic behavior of labels, as you will see in this recipe.

12. Verify that the **Input Map** is set to **Trippville**.

13. Click on the **Browse** button located to the right of the **Output Geodatabase**. Click on the **Databases** folder in the panel on the left side of the **Output Geodatabase** window that appears. Double-click on the **Trippville_GIS.gdb**. Select the **Base feature** dataset and click **OK**.

14. For the **Extent**, select the **Street Centerlines** layer from the list using the drop-down arrow.

15. Enable **Create Feature Linked Annotation** by clicking on the box next to it. Two other options will appear, **Create Annotation** when new features are added and Update annotation when features shape is modified. Ensure they are both enabled.

16. Change the **Output Layer** to **StreetNames**.

17. Verify that your **Convert Labels to Annotation** looks like the following graphic, and click **Run**:

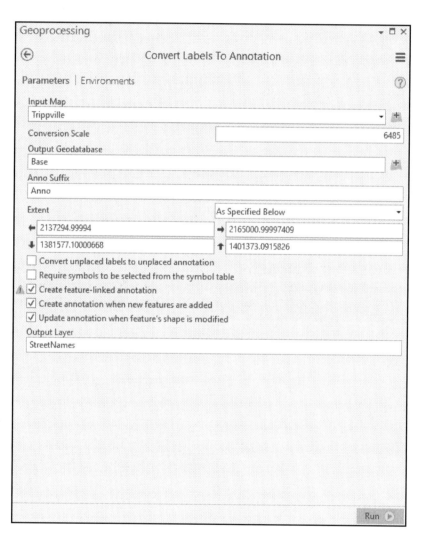

18. The new **StreetNames** layer you just created should appear in the **Contents** pane if the tool runs successfully. If the new layer does appear, close the **Geoprocessing** pane.

19. Now, let's look at what you created. In the **Contents** pane, expand the **StreetNames** layer by clicking on the small arrow located next to the layer name.

20. Select the **Street_CenterlinesAnno** layer. Right-click on it and select **Properties** from the bottom of the context menu that appears.

21. Select the **Source** option from the list on the left panel in the **Layer Properties** window, then answer the following questions:

    Question: What is the data type and feature type for the new layer?

    Answer:

    Question: What database is the feature class that the layer references named and where is it located?

    Answer:

    Question: What is the name of the feature class you created which is referenced by the new layer?

    Answer:

As you can see when you answer the preceding questions, the **Convert to Annotation** tool created not only a new layer in your map, but also a new feature class within the geodatabase. It is an annotation feature class which is a specialized version of a standard Polygon feature class; basically it acts like a text box. Like all feature classes, an annotation feature class is another form of vector data. As such, it has both the spatial component as well as an attribute component.

22. Click **OK** to close the **Layer Properties** window.

23. Right-click on the **Street_CenterlinesAnno** layer in the **Contents** pane. Select **Attribute Table** from the context menu which appears.

24. Take a moment to explore the **Attribute Table** for the new layer you just created, then answer the following question:

Question: What attribute fields are in the table for the Street_CenterlineAnno layer?

Answer:

25. Click on the List by Selection button located near the top of the **Contents** pane. It looks like three polygons, one of which has a blue fill.

26. Set the **Street Centerlines** and **Street_CenterlinesAnno** layers as selectable and all others as not selectable. Those with a check mark in the box are selectable layers and those without a check mark are not. To change the status from selectable or not selectable simply click on the box next to the layer name.

27. Click on the **Select** tool in the **Map** tab in the ribbon. If you click on the drop-down arrow, select **Rectangle**.

28. Click just to the southeast of Pine St, in the map. Continue to hold your mouse button down and move your pointer just to the northwest of Pine St as shown in the following screenshot, so you select both the street centerline and the road name.

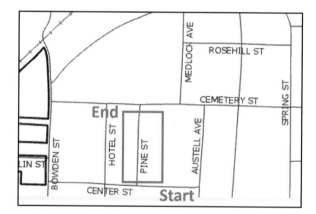

29. Right-click on the **Street Centerline** layer in the **Contents** pane and select **Attribute Table** from the context menu that appears.

30. At the bottom of the table view, click on the **Show Selected Records** button to only display the attributes for the street centerline you have selected.

31. Look at the attribute values for the selected street. Pay special attention to the value for the ObjectID.

32. Ensure the **Street Centerlines** layer is still selected in the **Content** pane, then click on the **Data** tab in the **Feature Layer** contextual menu in the ribbon.

33. Select the **Related Data** button in the **Relationship** group on the **Data** tab in the ribbon. Choose the **Anno_80_85:Street_CenterlinesAnno** option that appears. The numbers identifying the relationship may be different. This should open the **Attribute Table** for the **Street_CenterlinesAnno** layer and select the **related annotation record**.

34. Review the attribute values for the selected record, then answer the following question:

Question: Which fields for the Street_CenterlinesAnno layer contain similar values as those for the street centerline you have selected?

Answer:

Your comparison of the values for the selected street centerline and the related annotation should have revealed that the Object ID for the street centerline matched the FeatureID value for the annotation, and the ST_NAME value for the street centerline matched the TextString value for the annotation.

The two feature classes are linked to one another in the relationship class using the ObjectID of the Street Centerlines and the FeatureID of the Annotation as the key field, similar to how you used a key field to create both a join and a relate in previous recipes. As you will see next, the ST_NAME field and TextString fields are also linked as part of the relationship class.

35. Ensure that you still have the **Pine St centerline** selected, and then click on the **Edit** tab in the ribbon.

36. Click on the **Attributes** button located in the **Selection** group on the **Edit** tab.

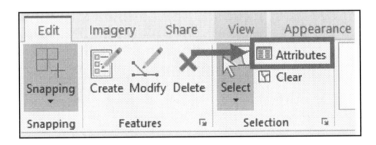

37. In the window at the top of the **Attributes** pane, select the **Street Centerlines** layer. This should display a list of all attributes associated with Pine St in the area below where you selected the layer.

38. Click in the cell located next to **ST_NAME**, which currently contains the value PINE ST and type OAK AVE. Hit your *Enter* key when done.

Notice what happens to the annotation for the street name in the map. It should have also changed because the ST_NAME field is linked to the TextString field for the annotation layer. Changing the ST_NAME value in the Street Centerlines layer automatically updates the value for the annotation layer because of the relationship class you created. For feature linked annotation, this is a one way relationship. This means the change is only pushed from the Street Centerlines layer to the Street_CenterlinesAnno layer, but not from the Street_CenterlinesAnno layer to the Street Centerlines.

39. While on the **Edit** tab, click the **Clear** button in the **Selection** group to clear your selection.

40. In the **Contents** pane, right-click on the **Street Centerlines** layer and select **Make this the only selectable layer**.

You may need to make sure you are still looking at the List by Selection option in the Contents pane.

41. Choose the **Selection** tool from the **Selection** group in the **Edit** tab on the ribbon.

42. Click on the street centerline for the newly renamed Oak Ave, which was formerly Pine St.

43. With **Oak Ave** selected and **only Oak Ave** selected, press your *Delete* key or click on the *Delete* button in the **Features** group on the **Edit** tab in the ribbon.

Notice that the annotation is also deleted when you delete the street centerline for Oak Ave. The relationship class not only links fields together, but also creates a link between the features in each feature class, so that by deleting the centerline it also deletes all related annotation features. Like the field relationship you explored earlier, this is only a one-way relationship. This means that if you were to delete the annotation it would not delete the related street centerline.

Not all relationship classes are a one-way relationship. Feature linked annotation is just one example of how a relationship class works. They can be configured in several different ways, depending on what you wish to accomplish.

44. On the **Edit** tab in the **Manage Edits** group, select **Discard** to discard all edits you have made.
45. In the **Catalog** pane, expand the **Databases** folder so you see the two geodatabases connected to the project.
46. Expand the **Trippville_GIS.gdb** geodatabase to see its contents.
47. Now expand the **Base feature dataset** and examine its contents. You should see the two feature classes which were referenced by the two layers you have been working with, **Street_Centerlines** and **Street_CenterlinesAnno**. You should also see the relationship class which you created when you created the feature linked annotation layer, **Anno_80_85**. Again, the name of your relationship class may have different numbers.

Because the feature classes and relationship classes exist as objects in your geodatabase, they may be used in other maps, scenes, or projects. This provides much greater flexibility than the joins and relates you performed in past recipes.

How it works...

As you saw in this recipe, feature linked annotation links text in one layer to the features in another layer. It does this using a relationship class. Like joins and relates, the relationship class relies on a key field from the Attribute Tables for both feature classes to establish a basic link between the text features in the annotation layer and the feature that the text references in the other feature class. In the case of feature linked annotation, the key field was automatically determined and the relationship class configured when you converted the labels for the street centerlines to annotation using the Convert to Annotation tool.

Feature Linked annotation takes advantage of the additional functionality the relationship class allows. In addition to relating the two features classes together so you can located related features or records, it also allows you to push changes from the feature to the annotation. This is called a **composite relationship**. In a composite relationship, the existence or values of the origin feature controls or changes the existence or values of the destination feature or record. You saw this demonstrated when you changed the street name for the centerline and deleted the centerline, which caused changes to the street annotation layer.

Creating and using a relationship class using existing data

You have seen the power of a relationship class in the previous recipe. You saw how linking two feature classes together allowed you to not only access information about the linked features but also control some behavior. However, this was all automatically set up by the Convert to Annotation tool. In many cases, the data you wish to link together already exists. So how do you create a relationship class which would link that existing data together?

In this recipe, you will create a relationship class between a feature class and a standalone table. This will be between the same parcel layer and sales table you related in the *Creating and using a Relate* recipe earlier in this chapter. However, once you establish the relationship class, the link becomes permanent, unlike the relate which is limited to the map in which it was created.

Getting ready

To complete this recipe, you will need a Standard or Advanced license of ArcGIS Pro. A Basic license does not support this level of functionality. If you are not sure what license you have, you can check it by doing the following. Open ArcGIS Pro, and on the bottom left of the start window, where you would normally select a project to open, click on **About ArcGIS Pro**. Then select **Licensing** from the list on the left. This will display the license level available, to you and any extensions you may have access to as well.

If you only have a Basic license, check with your account administrator to see if they can assign you a Standard or Advanced license at least temporarily. If a higher license is not available you can request a trial license from Esri by going to their website, at `http://www.esri.com/arcgis/trial`. This will provide you with access to an Advanced license for ArcGIS Pro and more.

How to do it...

1. As normal, you will need to start ArcGIS Pro and then open the `RelationshipClass.aprx` located in `C:\Student\ArcGISProCookbook\Chapter3\RelationshipClass\`. The project should open with a single map called Thomaston. If you completed the previous *Creating and using Relates* recipe it should look familiar.

2. In the **Contents** pane, you need to verify that you see the **Parcels** layer and the **Parcels_Sales** table. If not, use skills you have learned to add them to the map from the **Thomaston.gdb** geodatabase which is connected to the project.

3. In order to create a relationship class between the **Parcels** layer and the **Parcels_Sales** table, you need to determine two things: a key field in each table and the cardinality. If you completed the *Creating and using a Relate* recipe, you will be using the same key field and should already know the cardinality, so you can skip to *step 12* and continue from there. If you did not complete that recipe, continue to the next step.

4. Right-click on the **Parcels** layer and select **Attribute Table**.

5. Right-click on the **Parcels_Sales** table and select **Open**.

6. Click on the name of the **Parcels_Sales** located at the top of the table view, and drag it until your mouse point is over the docking icon, as shown ahead:

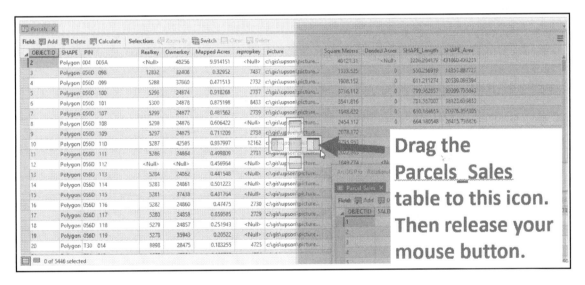

Drag and dock the tables so they can be seen side by side

The two tables should now appear side by side so you can more easily assess each one:

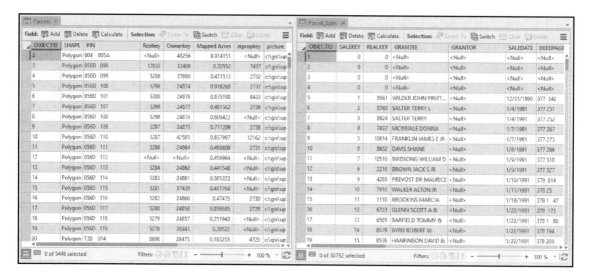

Tables viewed side by side

7. Review each table to determine the key field in each table that you will use to link the two tables together. Remember the key fields must contain the same data values and be the same field data type. The field names do not need to be the same.

Question: What is the key field in each table?

Answer:

After reviewing each table, the key field should be easy to pick out. The **Realkey** is the only field in each table which has the same data values and the same data type.

8. In the **Parcels Attribute Table**, right-click on the **Realkey** field and select **Sort Descending**.
9. In the **Parcels Attribute Table**, locate the records with a Realkey value of **15812**.

Question: How many rows in the table contain a Realkey value of 15812?

Answer:

10. In the **Parcels_Sales** table, right-click on the **REALKEY** field and select **Sort Descending**.

11. In the **Parcels_Sales** table, locate the rows with a REALKEY value of **15812**. You will need to scroll down until you see that value or you could use the **Select by Attribute** tool to select the records.

 Question: How many records in the Parcels_Sales table have a REALKEY value of 15812?

Answer:

12. Close both tables by clicking on the small **X** next to their name in the table view.

13. Click the **Clear** button located in the **Selection** group on the **Map** tab if you selected any records in either table.

You should now know that there is one parcel and two sales records which have a realkey value of 15812. This means you have a one to many cardinality. So, you know the key field and the cardinality you will need to create the relationship class which will link the Parcels layer to the Parcels_Sales table.

14. In the **Catalog** pane, expand the **Database** folder so you can see the two databases which are connected to the project.

15. Expand the **Thomaston.gdb** geodatabase, then right-click on it and select **Relationship**. The **Create Relationship** tool should open in the **Geoprocessing** pane.

16. Set the **Origin Table** to **Parcels** using the drop-down arrow. This establishes the Parcels as the primary table for the relationship.

17. Set the **Destination Table** to **Parcels_Sales** using the drop-down arrow. This establishes it as the secondary or child table for the relationship.

18. The **Output Relationship Class** should be automatically populated with **Parcels_Parcels_Sales**. You can change the name if you desire, or accept the default.

19. Both the **Forward Path Label** and **Backward Path Label** should be automatically populated as well. Accept these default values.

20. Set the **Message Direction** to **None** using the drop-down arrow, since we just want to be able to view related records between the tables. We are not trying to have one table control the information in the other.

21. Using the drop-down arrow, set the **Cardinality** to **One to Many (1:M)**, since this was what you determined the cardinality to be previously.

22. Set the **Origin Primary Key** to **Realkey** and set the **Origin Foreign Key** to **REALKEY**.

23. Verify that your **Create Relationship Class** looks like the following image. If it does, click **Run**.

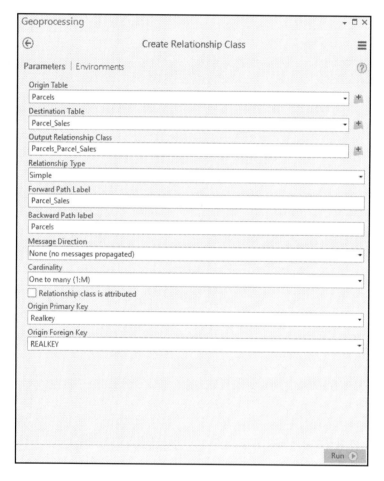

Create Relationship Class window in Geoprocessing pane

24. Once the tool has completed successfully, close the **Geoprocessing** pane.

25. In the **Catalog** pane, look at the contents of the **Thomaston.gdb** geodatabase. You should see the new relationship class you just created.

26. Right-click on the **Relationship** class in the **Catalog** pane and select **Properties**.

27. Take a moment to review the properties. They should reflect the settings you defined in the **Create Relationship Class** tool.

28. Click **OK** when done reviewing the properties.

29. Now to see if the new **Relationship** class you create works. Select the **Parcels** layer in the **Contents** pane.

30. Using the **Explore** tool, zoom into the center of the City of Thomaston. Zoom in so you can easily see the boundary of the individual parcels. This should be somewhere close to a scale of 1:4800.

31. On the **Map** tab in the ribbon, activate the **Select** tool and click on a single parcel in the map. The selected parcel should have a blue highlighted boarder around it.

32. Click on the **Data** tab in the **Feature Layer** contextual menu in the ribbon.

33. Select the **Related Data** button and the **Parcels_Parcels_Sales: Parcels** option that is displayed. The **Parcels_Sales** table should open, displaying any sales associated with the parcel you selected. If no sales are displayed, try selecting another parcel.

You will need to click on the **Related Data** button each time you select a new parcel to refresh the table view.

34. Once you have verified that the relationship class is working, close the table view.

35. Save your project and close ArcGIS Pro.

In this recipe, you created a Relationship class which linked the Parcels feature class to the Parcels_Sales standalone table. This permanently linked these two objects in the geodatabase so that you were able to select a parcel in the map and easily see each time it had been sold from the Parcels_Sales table.

This link was established using a key field you identified in each table. The key field used by a Relationship class, like a Relate or a Join, must contain the same exact values and be the same field type (text, long integer, short integer, and others). However, the field names are not required to be the same. ArcGIS Pro is then able to find records in both tables that have the same value and link those together, as you saw demonstrated in this recipe.

Unlike a Join or a Relate, a relationship class is part of your geodatabase. This means that anytime you add the Parcels feature class to a map in any project, you will have access to the data in the Parcels_Sales table automatically through the Related Data function.

Once you create a relationship class, you are not able to change how it is configured. If you wanted to change a simple relationship to a composite for example, you would have to create a completely new relationship class.

4
Editing Spatial and Tabular Data

In this chapter, we will cover the following recipes:

- Configuring editing options
- Reshaping an existing feature
- Splitting a line feature
- Merging features
- Aligning features
- Creating new point features
- Creating new line features
- Creating new polygon features
- Creating a new polygon feature using autocomplete
- Editing attributes using the Attribute Pane
- Editing attributes in the table view

Introduction

We live in an ever-changing world. New infrastructure is added, old infrastructure is removed, regulations change, new needs are discovered, and so on. Our GIS must be able to keep up with these changes so that it accurately reflects the world we live in as closely as possible. This means we must be able to quickly and easily make changes to our GIS data, both spatial and tabular.

ArcGIS Pro provides a wealth of tools and methods you can use to make updates to your data. The tools available to you and the types of data you can edit or update will largely depend on the license level you have. For example, if you only have a Basic license, you are not able to edit data in an SDE geodatabase. However, you can edit a shapefile or feature classes in a file geodatabase. Here is a quick list of the data formats you can edit and at which license level:

	Basic	**Standard or Advanced**
Personal Geodatabase	No	No
File Geodatabase	Yes, as long as not in Topology or Geometric Network	Yes
SDE/Enterprise Geodatabase	No (View Only with Basic)	Yes
Shapefile	Yes	Yes
DBF file	Yes	Yes
CAD Files (DWG, DXF, DGN)	No	No
Spreadsheets	No	No

ArcGIS Pro does not support the personal geodatabase at all and most likely never will. Esri has decided to replace the personal geodatabase with the file geodatabase because it provides much better performance. ArcGIS Pro Basic will allow you to edit data stored in a file geodatabase as long as it is not part of a topology or geometric network.

ArcGIS Pro cannot edit any data that is included in a Geometric Network. However, ArcGIS Pro 2.1 does support the newer Utility Network which was just released in its initial version in December 2017. The Utility Network provides similar functionality to the Geometric Network but is designed to be used in conjunction with the Utility Network Management extension for ArcGIS Enterprise. So it appears that the Utility Network will completely replace the older Geometric Network model. You can learn more about the Utility Network and the Management extension by going to https://www.esri.com/en-us/arcgis/products/arcgis-utility-network-management/overview.

An ArcGIS Pro Basic license will not allow you to edit data stored in an SDE Geodatabase either. SDE stands for Spatial Database Engine and provides multiple user capability for a Geodatabase. SDE Geodatabases require you to have ArcGIS Enterprise (formerly known as ArcGIS Server). With a Basic license, you can only view data in an SDE Geodatabase but not edit it. For more information about the different types of geodatabases, go to `http://desktop.arcgis.com/en/arcmap/latest/manage-data/geodatabases/types-of-geodatabases.htm`.

Shapefiles and DBF tables can be edited without any restrictions at all license levels. CAD files and spreadsheets can only be viewed in ArcGIS Pro and cannot be edited without converting them to a different format.

In this chapter, you will learn how to configure various editing options and use multiple tools. You will get to experience workflows for editing existing features as well as creating new features. Lastly, you will learn different methods for editing attributes and tables.

Configuring editing options

Before you start trying to edit data in ArcGIS Pro, there are several options you need to configure and verify. This will help ensure your edits are done smoothly and saved correctly. This will include setting your units, verifying tolerances, and more.

In this recipe, you will configure and verify several editing options, including how and when to save, setting your units of measure, making newly added layers editable by default, and configuring snapping.

Getting ready

For this recipe, you will need to ensure you have installed the book data and have ArcGIS Pro installed. The ArcGIS Pro Basic license level will be sufficient for this recipe.

How to do it...

1. To get started, launch ArcGIS Pro.
2. In the **ArcGIS Pro** start window, click on **Open another project**.

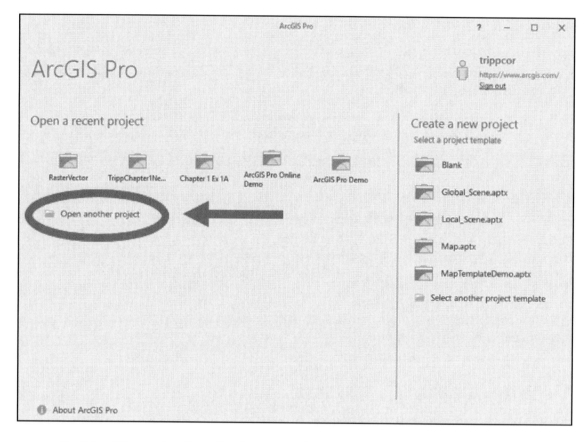

3. Select **Computer** from the **Open** window and then click **Browse** in the area on the right.
4. Navigate to `C:\Student\ArcGISProCookbook\Chapter4\Editing` by clicking on `C:\` in the area on the left of the **Open Project** window. Then double-click on **Student**, **ArcGISProCookbook**, **Chapter4**, and **Editing** folders.

5. Select the **Editing.aprx** project file and click **OK**.

The project will open with a single map named City of Trippville. The map contains three layers, City Limits, Parcels, and Railroads plus the Topographic basemap. Now that you have a project open, you will begin setting various options that can impact how you edit data. You will start with the Application and Project options:

6. Click on the **Project** tab in the ribbon
7. Select **Options** from the panel on the left side of the **Project** pane, as shown:

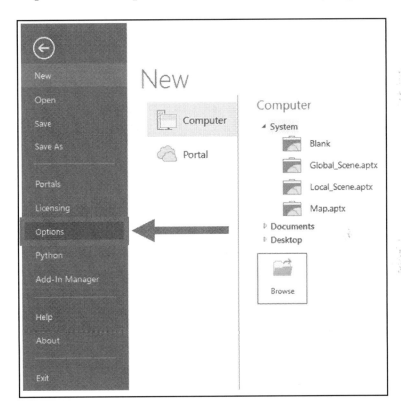

8. Select **Units** located under **Project** in the panel on the left of the **Options** window. You should see several items appear in the right-hand panel, including **Distance**, **Angular**, **Area**, **Location**, **Direction**, and **Page Units**, along with others.
9. Click on the small arrowhead located to the left of **Distance Units** to expand the options settings.

10. Since Trippville is located in the United States, select **Foot_US** as your distance units.

There is a difference between the US survey foot and the international foot. The difference starts after the sixth decimal place. Most places in the United States use the US survey foot as the standard for most measurements and local coordinate systems such as state plane. While only being slightly different, that difference does add up and can cause alignment and accuracy issues if not taken into account. For more information about the difference between the US survey foot and the international foot go to https://geodesy.noaa.gov/corbin/class_ description/NGS_Survey_Foot/.

11. Click on the small arrowhead located to the left of **Area Units** to expand those options.
12. Select **Square_Feet_US** from the list that is presented.
13. Select the **Editing** option from the panel on the left-hand side of the **Options** window.
14. If necessary, expand the **General** options by clicking on the small arrowhead.
15. Enable the **Show dynamic constraints in the map** option by clicking on the box next to it.
16. Ensure **Enable double-click as a shortcut for the Finish** button is checked.
17. Ensure both **Show feature symbology in the sketch** and **Show the editing toolbar on the map** are enabled.
18. If required, expand the **Session** options in the right-hand panel of the **Options** window.
19. Ensure **Show dialog to confirm save edits** and **Show dialog to confirm discard edits** are both enabled. Feel free to explore other options.
20. Verify that your **Options** window looks like the following screenshot. If it does, click **OK**:

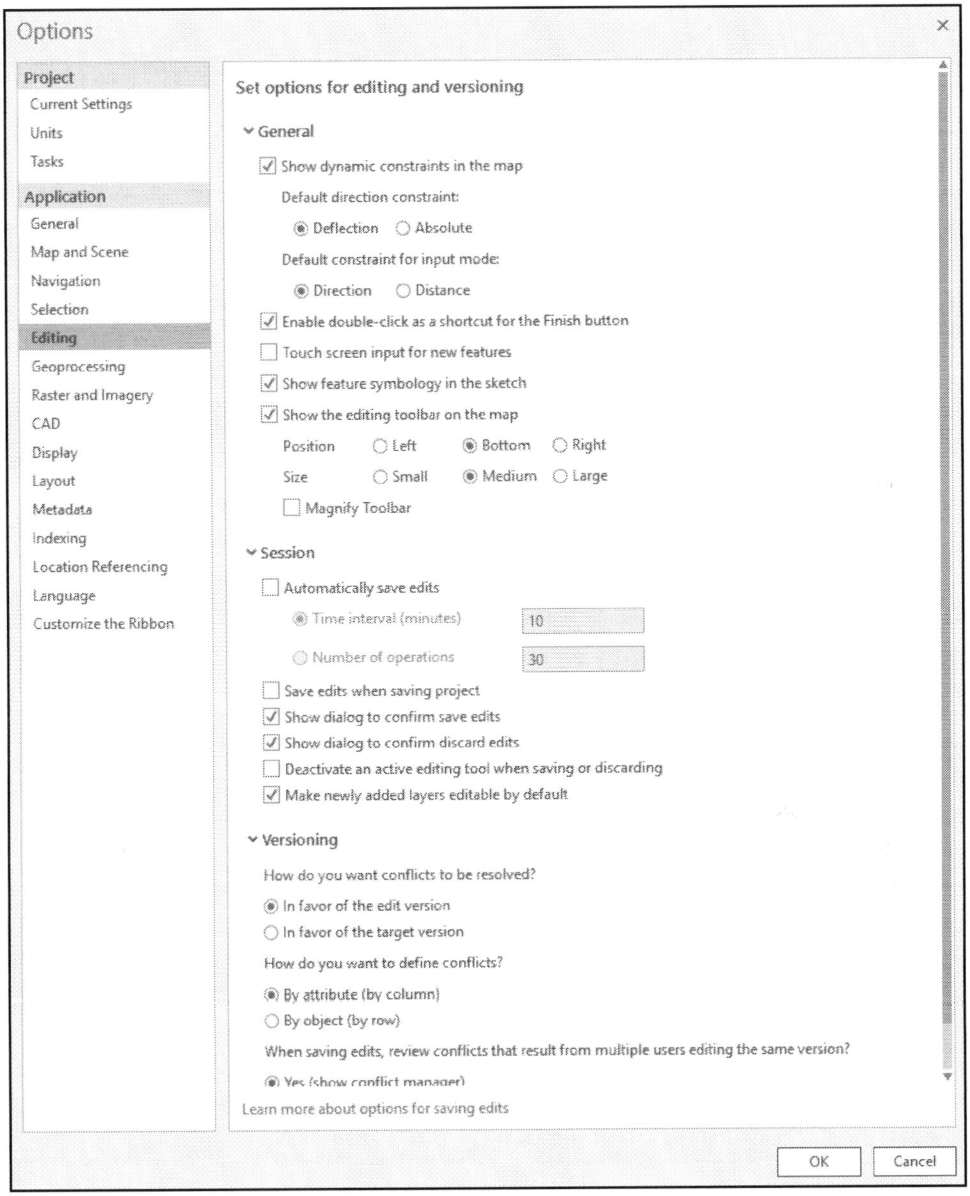

ArcGIS Pro editing options

You may have noticed that ArcGIS Pro has an autosave feature for edits. This is something new in ArcGIS Pro and if enabled can reduce the need to remember to manually save.

When editing, you need to ensure you save your edits frequently to avoid losing work if your computer crashes, locks up, or loses power. Unlike other applications, ArcGIS Pro does not create a restorable copy of your edits. The only way to ensure your edits are persistent is to save them.

The reason for this is ArcGIS Pro never really works directly with the data you see in a map or table. Instead, ArcGIS Pro determines what features are visible and loads those into your computer memory. This will change as you move within a map or table. This allows ArcGIS to work with large datasets which would cause other applications to slow or crash. You never open or load the entire database at one time. You only see what you need. This also means your edits are only stored in your computer's memory. They are not actually committed back to the source data until you save your edits. **So make sure to save often!**

Now that you have configured the application and project options, you will configure your snapping options.

21. Click on the back arrow, which looks like an arrow inside a circle, in the **Project** pane to return to the project view, as shown in the following screenshot:

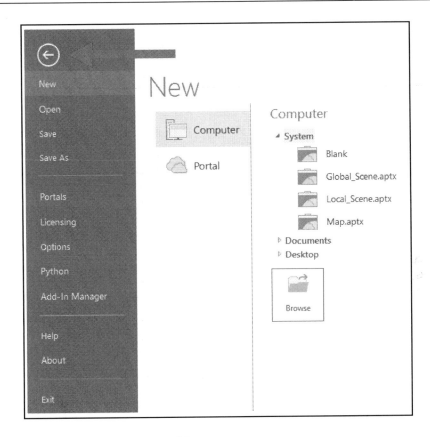

22. Click on the **Edit** tab in the ribbon.
23. Click on the drop-down arrow located below the **Snapping on the Edit** tab in the **Snapping** group.

24. Select **Snapping Settings...** as shown in the screenshot:

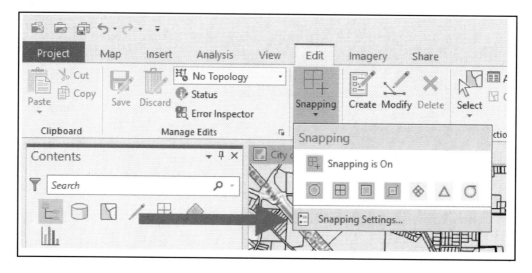

25. For the **XY Tolerance**, set the value number to 10 and change the units from **Pixels** to **Map units**. To change from **Pixels** to **Map units** simply click on the drop-down arrow located to the right of the word **Pixels** and select **Map units** from the list that appears.

26. Set the **Snap tip color** to red by clicking on the drop-down arrow located to the right of the color block. You can choose any shade of red you like.

27. Verify that your **Snapping Settings** window looks like the following screenshot and click **OK**:

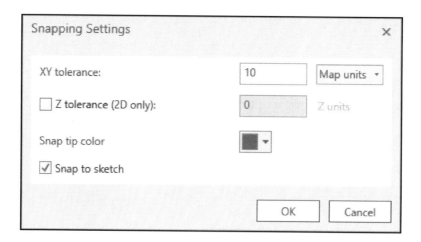

28. Save your project by clicking on the **Save Project** button located on the Quick Access toolbar on the top left of the ArcGIS Pro interface.

Reshaping an existing feature

Now that you have the various editing options set, it is time to start actually editing data. Unlike the older ArcMap application that preceded ArcGIS Pro, there is no need to start and stop editing. You can start editing data at any time.

In this recipe, you will reshape the City Limit boundary to reflect a recent annexation. You will need to ensure the City Limits layer is editable, snappable, and selectable. You will then draw a sketch using various construction tools that will represent a change to the City Limits boundary.

Getting ready

To complete this recipe, you need to have completed the previous *Configuring editing options* recipe. You will also need to start with the `Editing.aprx` project open. If you closed ArcGIS Pro after completing the previous recipe, follow *steps 1-5* in the previous recipe to open the `Editing.aprx` project.

How to do it...

1. To begin, ensure the **Map** tab is active in the ribbon, then click on **Bookmarks** and select the **Reshape City Limits** bookmark. This will zoom you in to the parcel which is being annexed into the City.
2. Click on the List by Selection button located at the top of the **Contents** pane. It should be the third button from the left and includes three polygons: one is blue and the other two are white.

3. Right-click on the **City Limits** layer and select **Make this the only selectable layer**, as illustrated in the following screenshot:

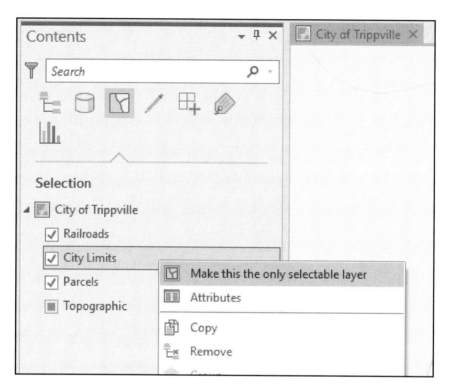

4. Click on the List by Snapping button in the **Contents** pane. It looks like four squares with a blue plus sign in the lower-right corner.
5. Disable snapping to the **Railroads** layer by clicking on the checkbox to the left of the layer name.
6. Ensure snapping is enabled for the **City Limits** and **Parcels** layer. Snapping is enabled when the box next to the layer is checked.
7. Click on the List by Editing button in the **Contents** pane. The icon looks like a pencil.
8. Right-click on the **City Limits** layer and select **Make this the only editable layer** in the menu that appears, as shown in the following screenshot:

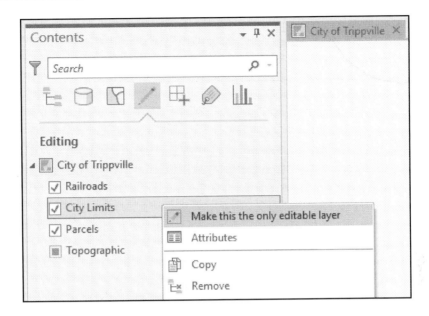

9. Select the **Edit** tab in the ribbon.

> Unlike the older ArcMap application, ArcGIS Pro does not require you to start an edit session in order to edit data. In ArcGIS Pro, you are basically always in an edit session. However, to access most editing tools to edit data, you need to select the **Edit** tab.

 Another difference between ArcMap and ArcGIS Pro when editing is the number of workspaces you can edit at one time. A workspace is a location that stores data such as a geodatabase, folder, or web service. In ArcGIS Pro, you are not limited to editing data in a single workspace at a time. It allows you to edit all editable layers at one time regardless of what workspace they are in.

10. Click on the drop-down arrow located below the **Snapping** button on the **Edit** tab in the **Snapping** group.

11. Enable snapping on the End, Vertex, and Edge, and disable all other snapping as indicated in the screenshot. To enable or disable a snapping option, simply click on it. If the icon is highlighted in blue, it is enabled. If it is not highlighted, it is disabled:

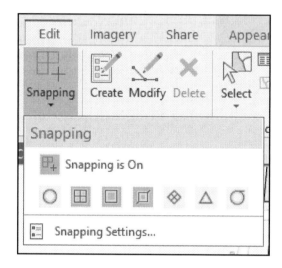

12. Click on the **Select** tool on the **Edit** tab in the **Selection** group.
13. Click inside the City Limit boundary to select it, as shown:

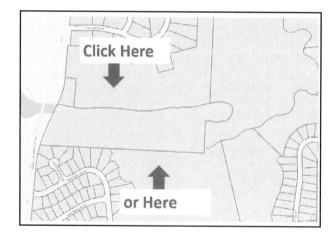

14. Click on the **Reshape** tool in the **Tools** group on the **Edit** tab.

15. Click on the south-western corner of the parcel being annexed into the city, as identified in the following diagram:

16. Select the Trace tool from the **Edit** toolbar located at the bottom of the map view area, as indicated here:

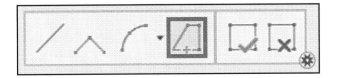

17. Click on the line that forms the western boundary of the parcel being annexed into the City. Then, move your mouse pointer along the boundary of the parcel, as shown in the diagram. Double-click when you reach the intersection of the parcel's northern boundary with the existing City Limits:

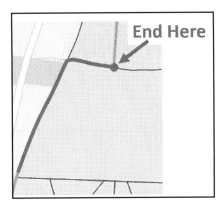

18. Click on the **Clear** button located in the **Selection** group in the **Edit** tab to deselect the **City Limits** you were just editing.

When you double-clicked to end your sketch, your City Limit boundary should have been reshaped to include the newly annexed parcel, as shown in the following diagram. Using the Trace tool, ensure you followed the boundary of the existing parcel exactly. This means your data is clean and does not have gaps between the City Limit boundary and the parcel:

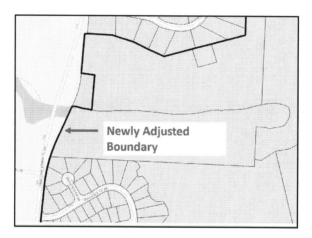

19. Click the Save Edits button in the **Manage Edits** group on the **Edit** tab. The icon looks like a floppy disk with a pencil. When asked to confirm saving your edits, click **Yes**.

Remember that, by default, ArcGIS Pro does not autosave data edits. You must do that manually. Also, saving your project does not save your data edits by default. You can enable an autosave for edits as well as have your edits save when you save the project in the **Options** in the **Project** pane.

If you don't enable the autosave feature in ArcGIS Pro, you will want to make sure you save often, otherwise you will lose any edits you have not saved if ArcGIS Pro or your computer crashes.

20. Save your project. If you are continuing to the next recipe, keep ArcGIS Pro open. If not, you may close ArcGIS Pro.

How it works...

In this recipe, you reshaped the City Limits boundary for the City of Trippville so that it included a newly annexed parcel. The first thing you needed to do in order to perform this edit was to set which layer you wanted to have as selectable and editable. You did this through the lists in the **Contents** tab.

When editing data, remember that data can be selectable but not editable, editable but not selectable, both, or neither. If you need to edit a feature by first selecting it from the map, as you did in this recipe, you need the layer to be both selectable and editable. If you select the feature for editing using an **Attribute** query, the layer does not need to be selectable. Setting a layer as selectable in the **Contents** pane only applies when performing an interactive selection in the map.

Using the Trace tool allowed you to edit the City Limit boundary so that it followed the parcel boundary exactly. The Trace tool automatically copies the geometry of the feature you are tracing to the new shape so it is an exact duplicate. This ensures your data is clean and accurate. It reduces errors such as overlaps and gaps which can impact the results of analysis and measurements.

Splitting a line feature

Polygons are not the only type of feature you may need to split. Lines often need to be split as you add other features to the same layer to maintain the correct connections. Lines often form a network used to travel across, such as roads, railroads, sidewalks, and trails. Travel is not limited to transportation. Utilities also use linear features to move water, sewer, electricity, and communications from one point to another. Other systems such as emergency dispatch systems rely on linear data from GIS as well. So, it is extremely important that we maintain these layers correctly.

As mentioned earlier, ArcGIS Pro 2.0 and earlier versions do not currently support geometric networks that are commonly used by utilities. If you have the Network Analyst extension, ArcGIS Pro will allow you to use, create, and maintain a Network Dataset. Esri has indicated that support for geometric networks will not be added in a future release of ArcGIS Pro. In ArcGIS Pro 2.1, they added support for the new Utility Network. In this recipe, you will draw new sewer lines based on a scanned and georeferenced plot. Once you draw the new sewer lines, you will split them where they connect to manholes, as shown on the plot, so you can get accurate measurements of each section of sewer line between the manholes.

Getting ready

You will need to have completed the first recipe in this chapter, *Configuring editing options*, before you are able to complete this recipe.

How to do it...

1. If you closed ArcGIS Pro before starting this recipe, you will need to start ArcGIS Pro and open the `Editing.aprx` project located in `C:\Student\ArcGISProCookbook\Chapter4\Editing` using the skills you learned in previous recipes.

2. In order to add the scanned plot, which will serve as the source data for adding the new sewer lines, you will need to add a folder connection to your project. In the **Catalog** pane, right-click on the **Folders** folder and select **Add Folder Connection**, as shown in the following screenshot:

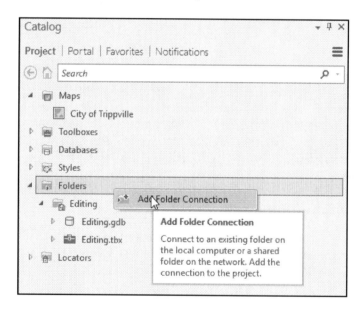

3. If needed, expand **Computer** in the panel located on the left-hand side of the **Add Folder Connection** window by clicking on the small arrowhead.

4. Select the **C:** drive from the list presented.

5. In the panel on the right, scroll down to the **Student** folder and double-click on it.

6. Select the **ArcGISProCookbook** folder and click **OK**.

Do not double-click on the folder name. Double-clicking will just select the folder, which you are trying to connect to. Double-clicking on it will open it instead of selecting it for a connection. If you do double-click on it, simply click on the **Back** button located near the top of the window. It too is a horizontal arrow in a circle. It will take you back one folder and allow you to select the correct folder.

The new folder connection should appear in your list. You should now have at least two folder connections, **Editing** and **ArcGISProCookbook**.

7. Expand the **ArcGISProCookbook** folder connection by clicking on the small arrowhead located to the left of the connection name.

8. Expand the **Chapter4** folder using the same method. You should see a **Forrest Park Subdivision.jpg** file, as shown here:

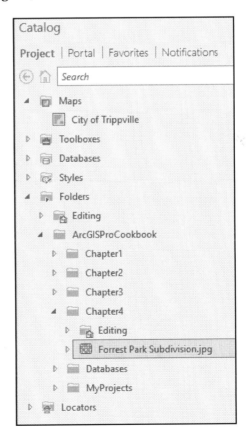

9. Right-click on the **Forrest Park Subdivision.jpg** file and select **Add to Current Map**. The file should now appear in the **Content** pane as a layer in the map.

10. Right-click on the newly added **Forrest Park Subdivision** layer and select **Zoom to Layer** from the context menu that appears, as shown in the following screenshot:

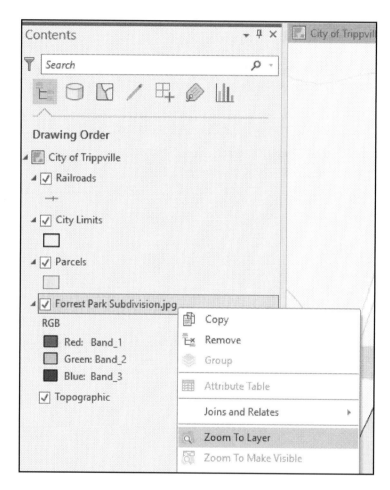

You are now zoomed in to the location of the subdivision. However, you are not able to see it because the **Parcels** layer is obscuring it. You will need to make a quick adjustment to the **Parcels** layer so you can see it.

10. Select the **Parcels** layer in the **Contents** pane.
11. Select the **Appearance** tab from the **Feature Layer** contextual menu, which appeared when you selected the **Parcels** layer.
12. Click on the **Symbology** button in the **Drawing** group on the **Appearance** tab to open the **Symbology** pane.

If you click on the drop-down arrow under the **Symbology** button, select **Single Symbol** from the list of symbology options. If you want to learn more about how to set the symbology for a layer, refer to Packt Publishing's *Learning ArcGIS Pro* in *Chapter 4, Creating 2D Maps*.

14. Click on the small square symbol patch located next to the work symbol in the **Symbology** pane, as shown in the following screenshot:

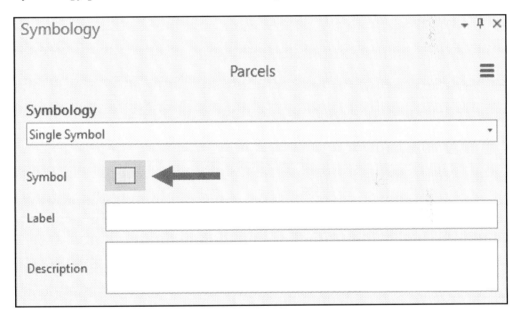

15. Near the top of the **Symbology** pane, select the **Properties** tab.

16. Click on the drop-down arrow located next to the Color symbol patch and select **No color**, as shown in the following screenshot:

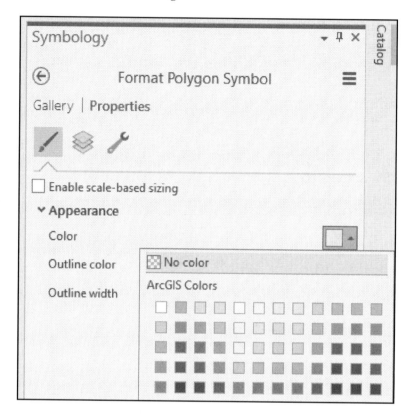

17. Click **Apply** at the bottom of the **Symbology** pane to apply the change to the **Parcels** symbology.

18. Close the **Symbology** pane by clicking on the small **X** located in the upper-right corner of the pane.

I find it helpful to close panes such as the **Symbology** pane when I am done using them. This limits the number you have open and the amount of screen space they take up. It also helps keep them from becoming lost in a stack of panes, which often happens if you don't manage the number of panes you have open. Another way to manage panes is to undock them and place them on a secondary monitor. This frees up screen space on your primary display while still making items easy to locate. I recommend that you keep the **Contents** and **Catalog** panes open at all times.

You should now see the scanned plot you added to your map. It should appear in the location where a new subdivision is being built. Next, you will draw the new sewer lines by tracing the ones shown on the new plot. Before you can draw the new sewer lines, you will need to add the sewer line layer.

19. Click on the **Map** tab in the ribbon to activate it.

20. Click on the **Add Data** button in the **Layer** group on the **Map** tab. Make sure to click the button and not the drop-down arrow below the button.

21. In the panel on the left of the **Add Data** window, select **Folders**. You should see the folder connections appear in the right-hand panel of the window. This should include at least the **Editing** and **ArcGISProCookbook** connections.

22. Double-click on the **ArcGISProCookbook** connection.

23. Double-click on the **Chapter4** folder in the right-hand panel.

24. Select the **Sewerlines.lyrx** file from the right-hand panel and click **OK**. The new **Sewer Lines** layer should appear in the map and the **Contents** pane as a thick green line, as shown here:

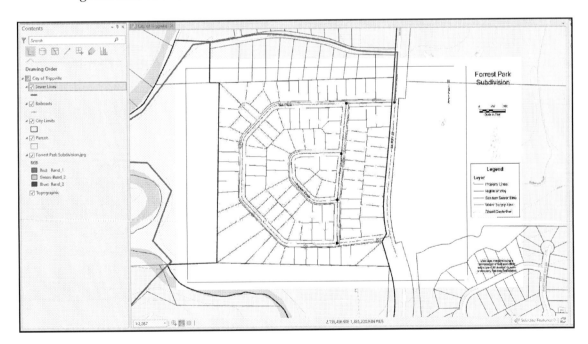

Sewer lines added to the map

Layer files allow you to add layers to a map, that already have their properties predefined. This includes properties such as symbology, labels, scale ranges, definition queries, and others. Layer files allow you to establish consistent display settings for layers so they look and behave the same way in multiple maps.

Layer files created in ArcGIS Pro have a `.lyrx` file extension. Those created in ArcMap have a `.lyr` file extension. ArcGIS Pro can make use of both. However, layer files created with ArcGIS Pro are version dependent. This means layer files created with ArcGIS Pro 2.0 are not compatible with previous versions but new versions of ArcGIS Pro can make use of layer files created with earlier versions. To learn how to create your own layer files, go to `http://pro.arcgis.com/en/pro-app/help/sharing/overview/save-a-layer-file.htm` or read *Chapter 12, Sharing* from Packt Publishing's *Learning ArcGIS Pro* book.

Now that you have made the subdivision plot visible and added the **Sewer Lines** layer to the map, you are ready to start adding the new sewer line.

25. Click on the **Edit** tab in the ribbon.
26. Click on the **Create** button in the **Features** group on the **Edit** tab. This should open the **Create Features** pane on the right-hand side of the ArcGIS Pro interface.
27. Verify that you see a feature template for the **Sewer Lines** layer in the **Create Features** pane. You may also see others but your primary concern for this recipe is the sewer lines.

If you do not see a feature template for the **Sewer Lines** layer you just added, check to ensure it is visible in the map. If it's not, go to the **Contents** pane. Make sure you are looking at **List by Drawing Order**, which is the first button at the top of the **Contents** pane. Then, click on the empty box next to the layer name to make the layer visible.

If the layer is visible but you still do not see a feature template in the **Create Feature** pane, then the **Sewer Line** layer may not be set as editable. To enable editing on the **Sewer Line** layer, click on the **List by Editing** button at the top of the **Contents** pane. Then, click on the checkbox located to the left of the layer name to enable editing for that layer.

Feature templates are directly linked to the **Contents** pane. If a layer is not visible or editable, you will not see a feature template for the layer in the **Create Features** pane.

28. Ensure **Snapping** is turned on. Look at the **Snapping** button in the **Snapping** group on the **Edit** tab in the ribbon. If it is highlighted in blue it is enabled, as shown in the screenshot. If it is not highlighted, it is not. To enable snapping, if it is not enabled, simply click on the button:

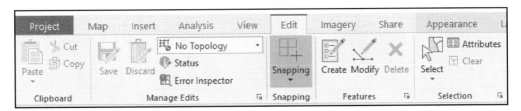

29. Click on the drop-down arrow located below the **Snapping** button and set the snapping location to End. Disable all others. Similar to enabling and disabling the snapping functionality, those locations that are highlighted in blue are enabled, as shown in the following screenshot:

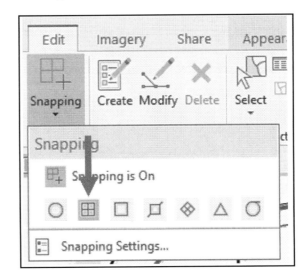

30. In the **Create Features** pane, click on the **Sewer Lines** feature template so that you can create a new sewer line feature. The template is located below the layer name and includes the symbol and feature name.

31. If required, zoom in to the new subdivision so you can easily see the location of all sewer lines shown as a red line on the plot. You should be able to use the scroll wheel on your mouse to zoom in or out as needed.

32. Move your mouse pointer to the end of the existing sewer line located on the north-eastern side of the new subdivision. When you see the snapping indicator appear, click at the end of the existing line to start creating the new sewer line, as shown in the following diagram:

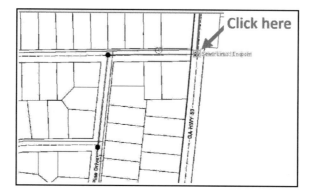

33. Continue drawing the new sewer line by clicking on the location of each manhole (shown on the plot as a large black dot), as shown in the diagram. To finish drawing the new sewer line, you can either double-click on the last point or single click and press the *F2* button:

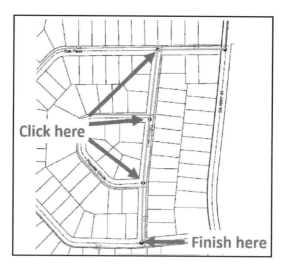

So now you have drawn the new sewer line as shown on the plot. Next, you need to split it at the manhole locations indicated on the plat. This will allow you to determine the pipe distance between manholes and provide a more accurate data model of the pipes. First, though, save your edits to ensure you do not lose the work you have completed so far.

34. Click on the **Save** button located in the **Manage Edits** group on the **Edit** tab in the ribbon. Click **Yes** when asked to confirm the saving of your edits.

 Remember that saving your project does not necessarily save edits to your data. Saving your project only saves changes to the project such as the addition of new layers, the creation of a new map, the addition of a layout, and so on. Data edits are saved separately unless you have adjusted the **Editing** options so that saving the project also saves data edits.

35. Click on the drop-down arrow located below the **Snapping** button in the **Snapping** group on the **Edit** tab in the ribbon.

36. Enable Vertex Snapping and disable End snapping using the same method you employed in *step 29* of this recipe, as shown here:

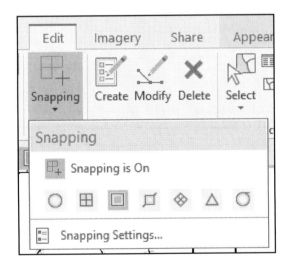

37. Ensure the new sewer line you drew is still selected. If it is not, click on the **Select** button and then click on the sewer line you drew.

38. Select the **Split Line** tool in the **Tools** group on the **Edit** tab. The **Modify Features** tab should open on the right-hand side of the interface.

39. Click on the sewer line of each manhole, as shown in the following diagram, to split the line at each manhole:

In the **Modify Features** pane, you should now see four features listed; you saw only one prior to using the Split Line tool. This indicates that you created three new features using the tool. Now you will verify that new features were created.

40. Click on the **Clear** button located in the **Selection** group on the **Edit** tab in the ribbon to deselect the sewer lines.

41. Activate the **Select** tool in the **Selection** group on the **Edit** tab in the ribbon.

42. Click on the southernmost sewer line segment to select it.

43. If you split the sewer line correctly, only the segment of the line from the last manhole to the manhole located at the intersection of Popular Circle and Pine Drive should be selected, as indicated in the following diagram:

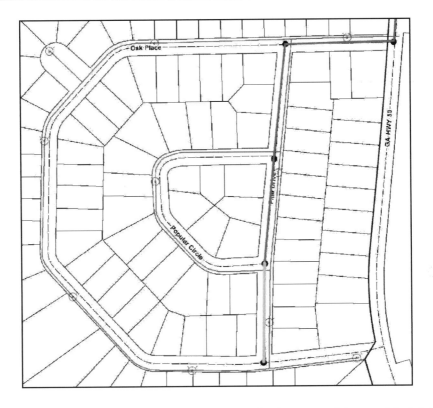

44. Once again, save your edits using the same method you used in *step 34* of this recipe.

45. Save your project using the skills you have learned in previous recipes.

46. If you are not continuing to the next recipe, you may close ArcGIS Pro. If you are, leave it open as you will continue to use this same project.

Merging features

You now know how to split and reshape features, but not all edits you may need to make will be limited to these. Sometimes you need to combine two or more existing features together. This might be done to simplify a layer for easier analysis or to reflect a change to the real-world features, such as someone buying two adjacent parcels to combine them into a single parcel.

In this recipe, you have found a road centerline, which is split into many unnecessary segments. This is causing issues when trying to calculate the total length of each road. You need to merge these segments together.

Getting ready

You can complete this recipe without completing any of the previous ones. This recipe can be completed with any license level.

How to do it...

1. If you closed ArcGIS Pro before starting this recipe, you will need to start ArcGIS Pro and open the `Editing.aprx` project located in `C:\Student\ArcGISProCookbook\Chapter4\Editing` using the skills you learned in previous recipes.
2. Click on **Bookmarks** in the **Navigate** group on the **Map** tab in the ribbon. Select the **Merge Street Centerlines** to zoom to the location of the street centerline segments that need to be combined.
3. In the **Catalog** pane, expand the **Databases** folder, if necessary, by clicking on the small arrowhead next to the folder name. You should see two file geodatabases connected in the project, **Editing.gdb** and **Trippville_GIS.gdb**.
4. Expand the **Trippville_GIS** geodatabase by clicking on the small arrowhead located to the left of the name.
5. Expand the **Base** feature dataset using the same method.

A feature dataset is an item inside a geodatabase that can be used to group related feature classes for better organization and to make use of advanced geodatabase functionality such as topologies. All feature classes in a feature dataset share the same coordinate system.

6. Right-click on the **Street_Centerlines** feature class and select **Add to Current Map** from the context menu presented.

7. Click on the List by Selection button in the **Contents** pane. The icon for the button looks like three polygons, with one of them being blue.

8. Right-click on the **Street_Centerlines** layer you just added and select **Make this the only selectable layer**, as shown in the following screenshot:

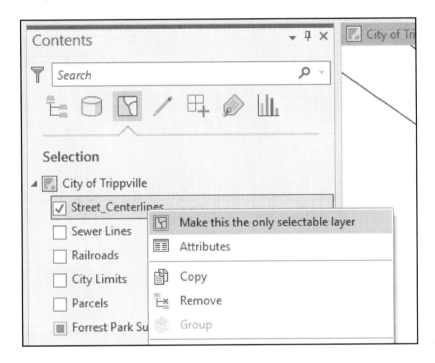

9. In the **Contents** pane, click on the List by Editing button. The icon looks like a pencil and is located next to the List by Selection button.

10. Right-click on the **Street_Centerlines** layer and select **Make this the only editable layer**, as shown:

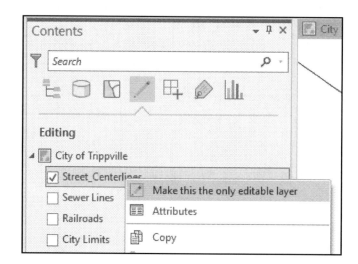

11. Click on the **Edit** tab in the ribbon.
12. Click on the **Select** tool in the **Selection** group on the **Edit** tab.
13. Click on the street centerline, as shown here, using the **Select** tool:

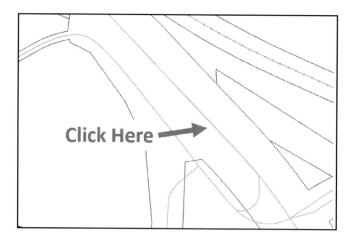

14. Hold your *Shift* key down and click on the other two street centerline segments, as shown here:

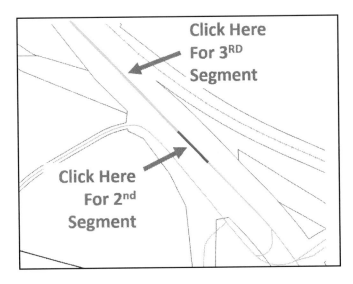

You should now have three segments selected. You can verify this by clicking on the List by Selection button in the **Contents** pane. This will tell you how many features in each layer are selected. Now you will merge the three selected features into a single feature.

15. Click on the **Merge** tool located in the **Tools** group on the **Edit** toolbar, as shown in the following screenshot. This opens the **Modify Features** pane on the right-hand side of the interface:

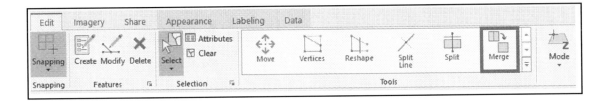

16. The layer should automatically be set to **Street_Centerlines** because you have features in that layer selected. In the **Features to Merge** grid, select the one listed as **278**, as shown in the next screenshot:

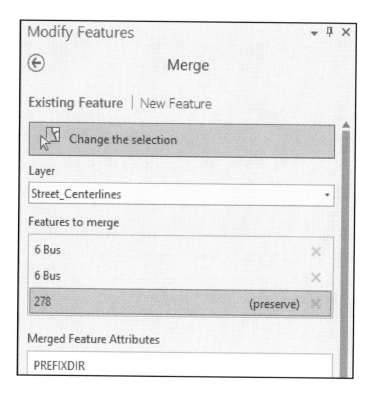

17. Click the **Merge** button located at the bottom of the **Modify Features** pane to actually merge the features.

    You have just merged three line segments into one single one. Now you will verify that this is what happened.

18. Click on the List by Selection button in the **Contents** pane. Then answer the following question:

Question: How many features are now selected?

Answer:

If the merge was successful, you should only have one feature selected. This is the new single feature you created using the **Merge** tool.

19. Click on the **Save** button in the **Manage Edits** group on the **Edit** tab to save the edit you just made. Click **Yes** to confirm your edit saving when asked.
20. You can save your project by clicking on the **Project** tab in the Ribbon, then clicking on the **Save** option that is shown.
21. If you are not continuing on to the next recipe, close ArcGIS Pro. If you are continuing to the next recipe, leave ArcGIS Pro and the project open.

How it works...

As you saw in this recipe, you merged three center line segments into one single segment. This simplifies the layer by reducing the total number of features, which makes it easier to analyze and maintain. The merge tool allows you to replace existing features or create a new feature while leaving the existing features in place. This option is accessed by clicking on one of the two tabs located at the top of the tool, Existing Feature or New Feature. The Existing Feature option replaces the selected features with a new feature that has the attributes of one of the selected features. The New Feature option creates a brand new feature and leaves the selected features in place as well. You can merge any type of feature as long as the features are in the same layer.

When using the Existing Feature option, as you did in this recipe, you get to select which selected feature the newly created feature will inherit. This is done by clicking on the feature in the Features to merge grid. The feature that is listed as preserved is the one that the new feature will inherit.

Aligning features

ArcGIS Pro can be a very valuable tool for performing analysis. But the results of any analysis is only as good as the quality of the data used. The adage of garbage in, garbage out certainly applies.

So, it is extremely important that our data is as clean as possible. This means we need to remove unwanted gaps or overlaps within our data. ArcGIS Pro has several tools to help you clean up your data. One of those is the Align Features tool. This tool is available with all license levels.

In the previous recipe, you located an area where two parcels overlap and where the City Limits are supposed to follow their common boundary. You will use the Align Features tool to fix this error in your data.

Getting ready

You will need to have completed the first recipe in this chapter, *Configuring editing options*, before you are able to complete this recipe. This recipe works at all licensing levels of ArcGIS Pro.

How to do it...

1. If you closed ArcGIS Pro before starting this recipe, you will need to start ArcGIS Pro and open the `Editing.aprx` project located in `C:\Student\ArcGISProCookbook\Chapter4\Editing` using the skills you learned in previous recipes.
2. Activate the **Map** tab and click on the **Bookmarks** button. Select the **Align Features** bookmark to zoom into the area where the data error exists.
3. You should see the City Limits and a parcel boundary, which appear to create a sliver or gap. Turn off the **City Limits** so you can see the parcel boundaries by clicking on the checkbox next to the **City Limits** layer, as shown here:

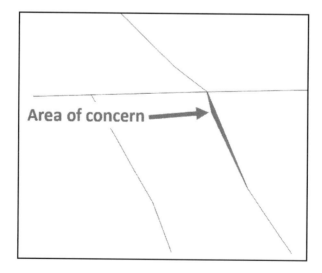

4. Now you need to determine whether this is a gap or overlap. In the **Contents** pane, click on the List by Selection button located near the top of the pane. The icon looks like three polygons, with one of them being blue.

5. Right-click on the **Parcels** layer and select **Make this the only selectable layer** from the menu that appears.

6. Choose the **Select** tool in the **Selection** group on the **Map** tab in the ribbon.

7. Click on the western parcel, as indicated in the following diagram:

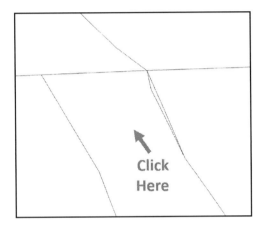

8. Next, click on the adjoining parcel to the west.

 Question: Do the two parcels overlap or have a gap between them?

Answer:

After clicking on both parcels, you should see that they overlap one another. Parcels should not overlap one another. Land owners tend to get upset if this happens. So you need to remove this overlap so that your data provides a more realistic representation of the parcel boundaries. The City Limits boundary should also follow the common boundary formed between the two parcels, so you will need to ensure it is adjusted as well:

9. Click on the **Clear** button located in the **Selection** group on the **Map** tab in the ribbon. This will deselect all selected features.

10. Turn the **City Limits** layer back on so you can see it on the map. To do this, click on the **List by Drawing Order** button at the top of the **Contents** pane. It is the first button on the left. Then, click on the box located to the left of the layer name.

11. Click on the List by Selection button at the top of the **Contents** pane.

12. Click on the box next to the **City Limits Layer** so that the **Parcels** and **City Limits** layer are both selectable, as shown in the following screenshot:

13. Click on the List by Editing button at the top of the **Contents** pane. It looks like a pencil and is next to the List by Selection button.

14. Ensure only the **Parcels** and **City Limits** layers are checked as editable, as shown here:

 You may see red exclamation points to the right of the two layers. These exclamation points indicate those layers are not editable. Layers may not be editable for several reasons. They might not be in an editable format or you might not have permission to edit the layers. In the case of this recipe, the two non-editable layers are stored as raster data, which is not editable by ArcGIS Pro.

15. Click on the **Edit** tab on the ribbon.

16. Click on the drop-down arrow located below the **Snapping** button and set End, Edge, and Vertex as the snapping locations, as shown in the following screenshot:

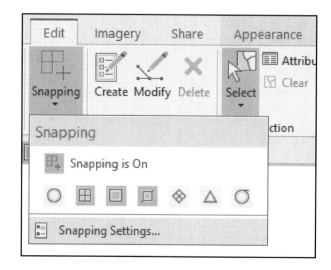

17. Click on the **Select** tool in the **Selection** group on the **Edit** tab in the ribbon.

18. In the **City of Trippville** map view, click on the starting location shown in the following diagram. While holding your mouse button down, drag your mouse to the south-west until you reach the approximate location of the stopping point, as shown in the following diagram. This creates a selection box that should select the two parcels and the City Limits:

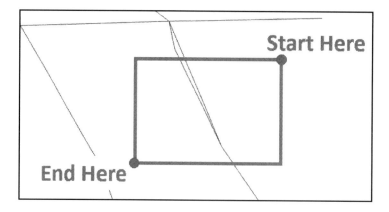

You should see that both parcels and the City Limits are selected. If you are not sure, you can go back to the **List by Selection** option in the **Contents** pane to verify. It will show you how many features in each layer you have selected.

When editing, it is recommended to keep the **Contents** pane on the List by **Selection** option as much as possible. This allows you to track how many features are on the layers you have selected. This information can stop you from accidentally editing or deleting features you do not intend to. This is a lesson I have learned the hard way. Remember, you cannot undo an edit once you have saved the edits you have performed.

19. Click on the arrowhead with a small line above it, located in the lower-right corner of the **Tools** group on the **Edit** tab, as shown in the following screenshot:

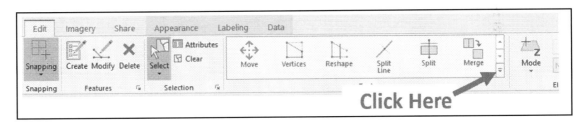

20. Select **More Tools** to open the **Modify Features** pane. You can also click on the **Modify** button in the **Features** group on the **Edit** tab.
21. Select the **Align Features** tool from the list of tools presented in the **Modify Features** pane.

22. The **Align Features** tool options will appear in the **Modify Features** pane. Set 5 as the value for **Alignment Tolerance**, select **ftUS** as the unit and select **Insert Vertices**, as shown here:

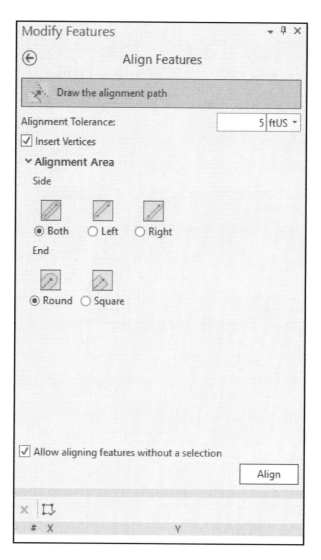

23. Click on the northernmost intersection of the two parcels in question and the City Limit, as shown in the following screenshot shown after *step 24*. You should automatically snap to the intersection if you set your snapping locations properly.

24. Then click on each location, as shown in the following screenshot. When you get to the Endpoint, you may either double-click to finish the sketch or single click and press the *F2* key:

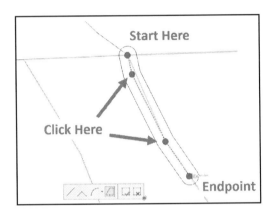

If you traced the alignment line correctly, all three features should have been edited so that they all now line up properly and there is no longer any overlap. So, this single tool allowed you to correct and edit three features on two different layers at one time. This is much more efficient than editing each one individually:

25. Click on the **Clear** button in the **Selection** group on the **Edit** tab to deselect all the features you have selected.

26. Using the **Select** tool on the **Edit** tab, click on one of the two parcels you selected earlier. You should notice it now aligns with the adjacent parcel and no longer has an overlap. To verify the overlap is gone, click on the other parcel.

27. Clear your selection again using the same method as in *step 25*.

28. Click on the **Save** button in the **Manage Edits** group on the **Edit** tab in the ribbon to save the edits you just completed. When asked to confirm the save, click **Yes**.

29. If you are not continuing to the next recipe, save your project and close ArcGIS Pro. If you are continuing, leave ArcGIS Pro and the editing project open.

How it works...

Now that you have seen the Align Features tool in action, how does it work? It will adjust line and polygon features so that they share coincident locations. This means the vertices of the lines and polygons that are adjusted end up being in the same exact locations.

Selecting the features tells the tool which ones will be adjusted. Alignment Tolerance provides a value to account for the distance difference between the features you wish to adjust. It will only adjust the portions of the features that are within the tolerance distance you specify. This prevents you from making undesired changes to your data.

Then you can start drawing a sketch that represents the stitch line to which all selected items are adjusted. You can choose which side of the stitch line you wish to adjust and how to handle the end of the stitch line.

The Align Feature tool automatically defaults to using the Trace construction tool. This allows you to easily follow an existing feature exactly, because you are tracing its form. This is what you did in the recipe. However, you can use any of the construction tools, such as Line, Perpendicular, or any of the Curve tools to create the stitch line.

Once you create the stitch line, ArcGIS Pro will automatically adjust the selected features to match the stitch line. It will either extend or trim line features and subtract or add to polygon features.

Creating new point features

So far, you have been editing existing features. You have realigned, reshaped, merged, and split them. Now it is time to look at how these features were created to begin with. We will start with the simplest of features, a point.

A point identifies an object at a single location. It is stored and located using a single coordinate pair. A coordinate pair consists of one x and one y coordinate. It is also possible for a point to have a z coordinate that normally represents its elevation.

In this recipe, you will create several new point features. You will start by adding the manholes that are in the new subdivision you were looking at in the recipe on splitting lines earlier in this chapter.

Getting ready

Before starting this recipe, you will need to have completed the *Configuring editing options* and *Splitting a line feature* recipes from earlier in this chapter. This recipe can be completed with all licensing levels of ArcGIS Pro.

How to do it...

1. If you closed ArcGIS Pro before starting this recipe, you will need to start ArcGIS Pro and open the `Editing.aprx` project located in `C:\Student\ArcGISProCookbook\Chapter4\Editing` using the skills you learned in previous recipes.

2. Activate the **Map** tab and click on **Bookmarks** located in the **Navigate** group on the **Map** tab. Select the **Create Manholes** bookmark to zoom back to the area from the other subdivision.

3. If needed, turn the **Sewer Line** layer back on, and the **Forrest Park Subdivision.jpg** in the **List by Drawing Order** in the **Contents** pane. If you do not see these layers in your project, refer to *steps 7-9* and *steps 20-24* of the *Splitting a line feature* recipe earlier in this chapter. Your map should now look like the following screenshot:

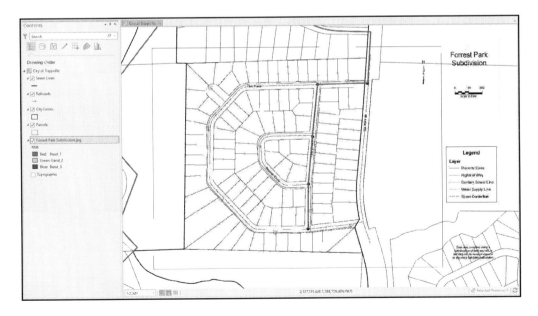

Next, you need to add the manholes layer to your map so you can create the new manholes.

4. In the **Catalog** pane, expand the **Databases** folder in the project. Then expand the **Trippville_GIS.gdb** geodatabase.

5. Expand the **Sewer** feature dataset and right-click on the manhole feature class. Select **Add to current map** from the list that is presented.

6. Click on the symbol located below the manhole layer that was just added to the **Contents** pane. This should open the **Symbology** pane.

7. Near the top of the **Symbology** pane, click on **Properties**.

8. Click on the small arrowhead located next to the color block and select Mars Red from the list of colors.

9. Set the **Size** to 12 and click **Apply**.

10. Close the **Symbology** pane once you have applied the new symbology settings for the manhole layer.

11. Click on the **Edit** tab in the ribbon.

12. Click on the drop-down arrow below the **Snapping** button in the **Snapping** group on the **Edit** tab. Set the snapping option to End Snapping, as shown in the following screenshot:

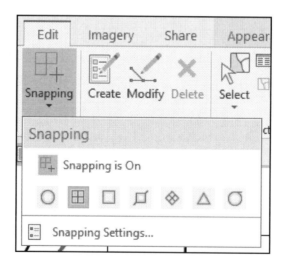

13. Click on the List by Snapping button in the **Contents** pane. It has an icon that looks like four squares with a blue plus sign in the lower-right corner.
14. Right-click on the **Sewer Lines** layer and select **Make this the only snappable layer** for the menu that appears.
15. Click on the List by Editing button in the **Contents** pane. Its icon looks like a pencil.
16. Ensure editing is enabled for the manhole layer you recently added. If the box next to the layer name is checked, editing is enabled. If it is empty, editing is not enabled. Click on the box to enable editing for the layer.
17. Click on the **Create** button located in the **Features** group on the **Editing** tab in the ribbon. This will open the **Create Features** pane on the right-hand side of the interface.
18. Select the manhole feature template. The feature template is located below the layer name and includes the symbol and the feature name.
19. Ensure the Point tool is selected below the feature template, as illustrated in the following screenshot:

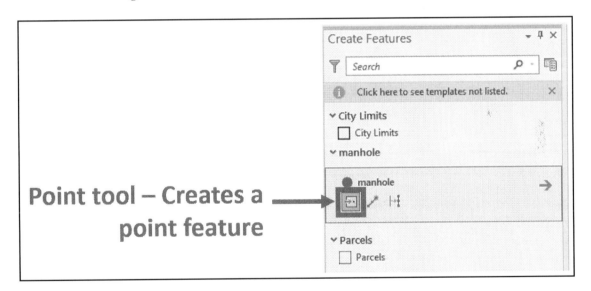

20. Move your mouse into the map until you reach the first sewer line intersection located near the intersection of Oak Place and Pine Drive, shown in the Forrest Park Subdivision plat. Your mouse should automatically snap to the correct location once you get close. Once you see the indicator showing that you are snapping to the end point of those intersecting sewer lines, click the location with your mouse to create the new manhole at that location. The new manhole should appear at the location, as shown in the following diagram:

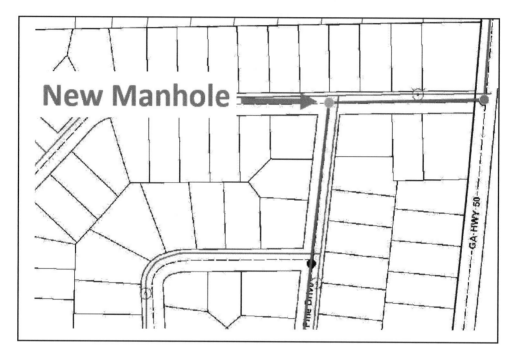

21. Now click on the **Attributes** tool in the **Selection** group in the **Editing** Tab. This will open the **Attribute** pane next to the **Create Features** pane.
22. In the grid located at the bottom of the **Attribute** pane, click on the cell located next to **MANHOLE_ID**, which should say **<NULL>**, type 101.
23. Go down to the **Condition** field in the grid and click in the cell that says **<NULL>**. A drop-down menu should appear; select **Good** from the list.

 The condition field has a domain assigned to it. A domain defines acceptable values that may be stored in the field. This can be a list of values, as you just saw, or a range of values if the field stores numbers.

24. Use the same process to add new manholes at the locations indicated in the following diagram. Increment the **MANHOLE_ID** value by one so that the next one will be `102`. The condition for all new manholes you create should be **Good**:

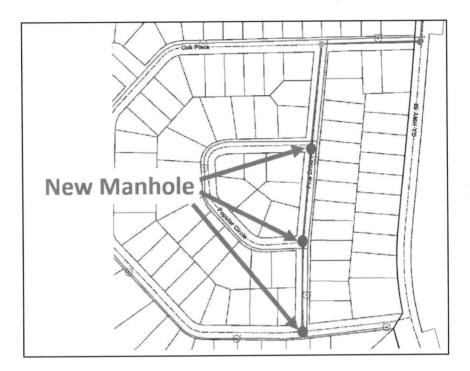

You should have added three more new manholes by the time you are done.

25. Click on the **Save** button located in the **Manage Edits** group on the **Edit** tab in the ribbon to save the new manholes you just created. Click **Yes** when asked to confirm the save.

26. If you are not continuing to the next recipe, save your project and close ArcGIS Pro. If you are continuing, just save your project.

Creating new line features

Now we will move onto creating Line features. These are more complicated because they require multiple vertices. At minimum, a line requires two vertices: a beginning and an ending. It is not uncommon for a Line feature to have multiple vertices. This is called a polyline.

As far as ArcGIS is concerned, a line and polyline are the same thing. They are stored together in the same feature classes and the tools used to create them are the same. So you will see the term line and polyline used interchangeably within ArcGIS. This is not true of all applications, such as AutoCAD.

Line features stored in a geodatabase feature class can also include curved segments. These segments are stored and created as arcs. Not all data storage formats support arcs. Shapefile is a good example of one that does not support arcs. Instead of using arcs, shapefile typically uses multiple very short straight segments to simulate the arc. When displayed to scale, these short straight segments appear to be a curve. Geodatabases and CAD formats (DWG, DXF, and DGN) do support true arcs.

There are many construction techniques for creating line features. You can simply digitize the vertices by clicking with your mouse, you can specify exact measurements, or enter coordinates. Which method will work best will depend on the source data you have and its quality.

In this recipe, you will create several new Line features that represent the street centerlines for the new Forrest Park Subdivision. You will use various construction techniques to do this.

Getting ready

Before starting this recipe, you will need to have completed the *Configuring editing options* and *Splitting a line feature* recipes from earlier in this chapter. This recipe can be completed with all licensing levels of ArcGIS Pro.

How to do it...

1. If you closed ArcGIS Pro before starting this recipe, you will need to start ArcGIS Pro and open the Editing.aprx project located in C:\Student\ArcGISProCookbook\Chapter4\Editing using the skills you learned in previous recipes.

2. If you have continued from the previous recipe, you can skip to the next step. Otherwise, activate the **Map** tab and click on **Bookmarks** located in the **Navigate** group on the **Map** tab. Select the **Create Manholes** bookmark to zoom back to the area from the other subdivision.

3. Select the List by Draw Order button in the **Contents** pane. It is the first button at the top left of the pane.

4. Turn off the **Sewer Line** and **manhole** layers.
5. If needed, turn on the **Forrest Park Subdivision.jpg** layer.
6. Activate the **Map** tab in the ribbon. Then, click on the **Add Data** button in the **Layer** group.
7. Select the **Databases** folder under **Project** in the panel on the left-hand side of the **Add Data** window.
8. Double-click on the **Trippville_GIS.gdb** geodatabase in the panel on the right-hand side of the **Add Data** window.
9. Double-click on the **Base feature** dataset. Feature datasets are symbolized by an icon that looks like three overlapping squares.
10. Scroll down and select **Street_Centerlines** from the list of feature classes, then click **OK** to add the **Street_Centerlines** as a layer to your map.
11. Click on the **Appearance** tab in the **Feature Layer** contextual tab in the ribbon.

 ArcGIS Pro makes use of a smart ribbon interface. The ribbon options will change based on what you have open and selected. Tabs or groups of tabs which appear when a specific item is selected are called contextual tabs or menus. The **Feature Layer** contextual menu is one example of these.

12. Ensure the **Street_Centerlines** layer is selected in the **Contents** pane, then click on the **Symbology** button in the **Drawing** group on the **Appearance** tab in the ribbon. This should open the **Symbology** pane.
13. Click on the small line patch located to the right of the word **Symbol** in the **Symbology** pane, as shown in the screenshot:

The color for your **Street_Centerline** layer may be different than what is displayed in the image. ArcGIS Pro assigns random colors to newly added layers. The same is true of the older ArcMap application.

14. The **Format Line Symbol** tool should appear in the **Symbology** pane. This allows you to adjust the display properties of the layer. Click on the **Properties** tab in the **Symbology** pane if needed. It is located next to the **Gallery** tab in the pane.

15. Ensure the Symbology button is selected in the **Symbology** pane. It looks like a paintbrush.

16. Click the drop-down arrow located next to the color patch. Select Ultra Blue from the color pallet that is presented. It is the tenth column and fourth row. If you would prefer to use a different color, then feel free to do so.

17. Set the **Line width** to 3.0 and click **Apply** at the bottom of the pane.

18. Click on the symbol located below the manhole layer that was just added to the **Contents** pane. This should open the **Symbology** pane.

You map should now look similar to the map shown here. The newly added **Street_Centerline** features should be visible and easy to see over the **Forrest Park Subdivision** image. This will help you when creating the new centerline features:

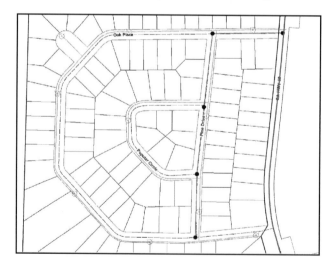

19. Click on the **Edit** tab in the ribbon.

20. Click on the **List by Editing** button in the **Contents** pane and verify that the **Street_Centerlines** layer is set to be editable. If it is not, make it so by clicking in the box.

21. Click on the **List by Snapping** button in the **Contents** pane. Set the **Street_Centerline** layer as the only snappable layer.

22. Click on the **List by Selection** button in the **Contents** pane. Set the **Street_Centerlines** layer as the only selectable layer.

   You have configured your map so you can successfully create the new street centerline features. You have ensured that the **Street_Centerline** layer is selectable, snappable, and editable. Now you are ready to begin creating the new centerlines using the Forrest Park Subdivision image as a guide. The street centerline is shown as a dashed black line. You will use various methods to trace this line.

23. Click on the **Create** button in the **Features** group on the **Edit** tab in the ribbon. This will open the **Create Features** pane so you can access the feature template for the **Street_Centerlines**.

24. Select the **Street_Centerline** feature template in the **Create Features** pane. The feature template is located below the layer name and has the symbol along with the name.

25. Using the scroll wheel on your mouse, zoom and pan to the southern intersection of Oak Place and GA HWY 50 until your map looks similar to the following diagram:

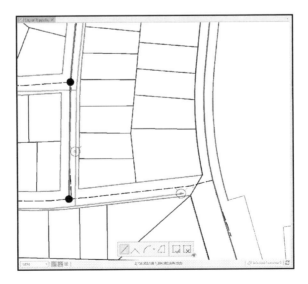

26. Click on the approximate intersection between Oak Place and GA HWY 50 to start drawing the new line. Your mouse should snap to the location when you get close.

27. Now trace the centerline shown on the scanned image by clicking on the locations, illustrated in the following diagram:

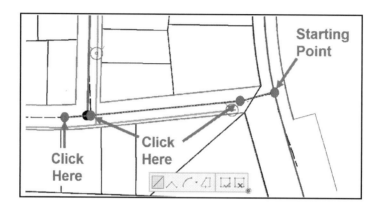

28. Press and hold the scroll wheel down on your mouse to pan to the right so you can see more of the centerline to trace while still being able to see your last vertex.

29. Click a point along the street centerline just before it starts to curve to the northwest, as shown in the following diagram:

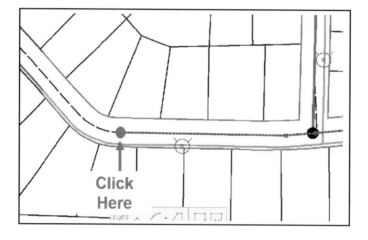

30. Click on the Arc Segment tool from the **Edit** toolbar located at the bottom of the map view, as illustrated in the diagram:

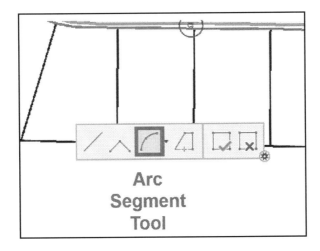

31. Using the Arc Segment tool, click on the locations indicated in the diagram. The starting point is the same as the last point you clicked on before changing to the Arc Segment tool. Then, click on the remaining two locations. The location in the middle of the arc sets the radius. The third point sets the end of the arc:

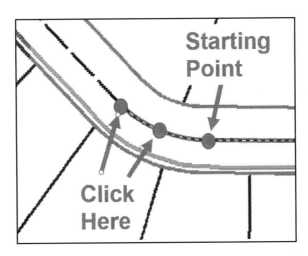

When using the Arc Segment tool, you can specify a radius by pressing the R. This will open a window that allows you to enter the radius measurement.

32. Select the Line tool from the **Edit** toolbar. It is the first tool on the left of the **Edit** toolbar.

33. If needed, press down on your scroll wheel on your mouse and pan your map until you can see the next curve in the road. Click the location where you believe the road starts to curve.

34. Using the same method you used for the previous curve, trace the arc of the road centerline as it turns toward the north. The following diagram illustrates the approximate locations of the start, midpoint, and end of the curve:

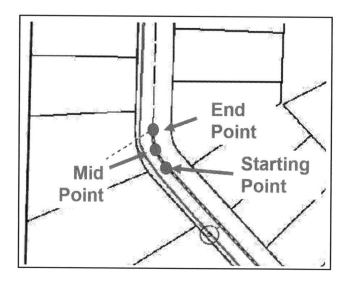

35. Continue this same process until you have completely traced the centerline of Oak Place until it intersects again with GA HWY 50 on the north side of the subdivision. When completed, your centerline should look similar to the following:

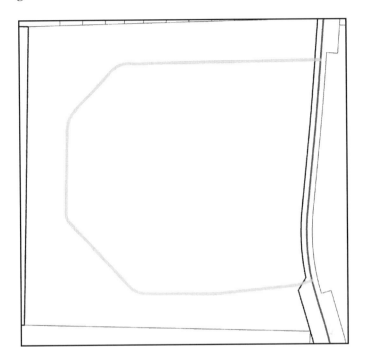

36. Click the **Save** button in the **Manage Edits** group on the **Edit** tab. Click **Yes** when asked to confirm your edits.

    You have just created a complex polyline feature. It includes straight segments and arcs, so it represents real-world features accurately. You created this feature by tracing the shape of the line from the scanned subdivision plat. Now we will use measurements to create some of the other centerlines shown in the plat.

37. Click on the drop-down arrow located below the **Snapping** button in the **Snapping** group on the **Edit** tab in the ribbon.

38. Set the **Snapping** location options to vertex, edge, and intersection, as shown:

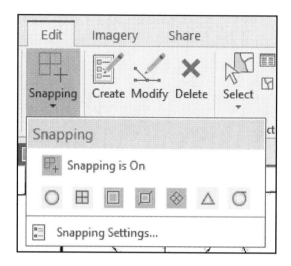

39. Activate the **Map** tab in the ribbon and select the **Explore** tool.

40. Hold down your *Shift* key and draw a box around the short cul-de-sac located on the northwestern side of the subdivision. Your map should zoom to the area of the box you drew and should look similar to the following:

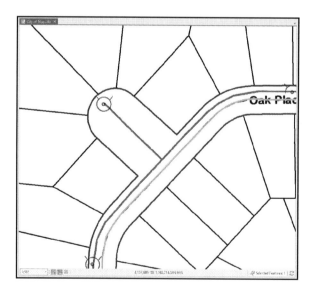

41. Click on the **Edit** tab in the ribbon.
42. Select the **Street_Centerlines** feature template from the **Create Features** pane.
43. You are about to draw the centerline for the cul-de-sac. This centerline is not shown on the plat so you will be provided with its measurements. Click on the centerline you drew earlier at the location you approximate the centerline of the cul-de-sac will intersect it.
44. Move your mouse in the general direction of the approximate centerline of the cul-de-sac. Right-click once you are near the end of the waterline, which is shown as a blue line on the scanned plat.
45. Select **Direction/Distance** from the context menu that appears, as shown in the following screenshot:

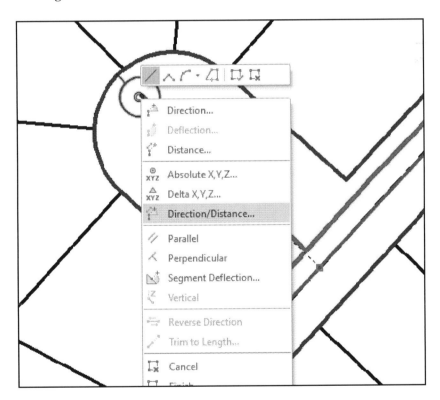

46. Set the **Direction** to N47-06-50W and **Distance** to 125 ftUS, as shown in the screenshot, and then press your *Enter* key to apply the measurements:

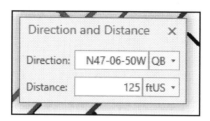

47. Press your *F2* key to finish the feature.

The QB next to the direction stands for **Quadrant Bearing**. This is a type of measurement commonly used by surveyors and engineers to identify direction. Quadrant Bearings divide the compass into four quadrants, north-east, south-east, south-west, and north-west. Then, the direction within that quadrant is measured based on the angle from either due north or due south to a maximum of 90 degrees. So, a feature heading directly due east could be identified as either north 90 east or south 90 east. Typically, the measurements are shown using degrees, minutes, and seconds as opposed to decimal degrees. In the example used in this recipe, 47 is the degrees, 6 is the minutes, and 50 is the seconds within the north-west quadrant.

48. Click on the **Save** button in the **Manage Edits** group on the **Edit** tab in the ribbon. Click **Yes** when asked to confirm your save.

49. Using the skills you have learned, zoom back so you can see the entire subdivision area once more. Then, zoom in so you can see **Pine Drive**, which is shown on the **Forrest Park Subdivision** plat. This will be the next centerline you draw.

50. Once again, click on the **Street_Centerline** feature template in the **Create Features** pane.

51. Click on the northern intersection of Pine Drive and Oak Place, as indicated on the plat. It should be very close to the location of the manhole.

52. Move your mouse along the centerline of Pine Drive, as shown on the plat, until you reach the intersection with Popular Circle. Then, right-click and select **Distance** from the **Context** menu.

53. Enter a distance of 350 ftUS and press your *Enter* key. This will lock the length of the line segment to 350 feet but still allow you to control the direction.

54. Move your mouse until the new line segment is in line with the centerline shown on the plat. You may need to zoom in using the scroll wheel on your mouse to see the location clearly. Once you are happy with the alignment, click with your mouse to set the direction of the new segment.

55. Use the same process to draw the next segment, which goes to the southern intersection of Pine Drive and Popular Circle. Set the **Distance** to 342 ftUS.

56. Lastly, click on the intersection of Pine Drive and Oak Place so your new centerline looks like the following:

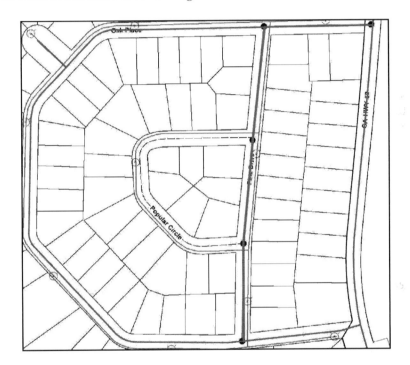

57. Click on the **Save** button in the **Manage Edits** group on the **Edit** tab in the ribbon. Click **Yes** to confirm the save when asked.

58. Using the skills you have learned, draw the centerline for Popular Circle. Make sure you save your edits once you are done.

Once you have drawn all the street centerlines in the new subdivision, they should look similar to the following:

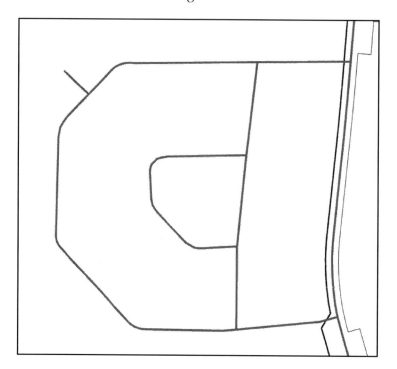

Next, you will use the **Buffer edit** tool to create the road rights of way based on the centerlines you just drew. This is yet another method you can use to create line features.

59. Close the **Create Features** pane.
60. In the **Catalog** pane, expand the **Databases** folder, then expand the **Trippville_GIS.gdb** geodatabase.

61. Next, expand the **Base feature** dataset and right-click on the RW feature class. Select **Add to current map** from the menu that appears. This should add the layer to the map. This layer represents the street rights of way boundary.

62. On the **Edit** tab in the ribbon, click on the **Select** tool.

63. Select the centerlines you created for Oak Place, Pine Drive, and Popular Circle. Do not select the cul-de-sac center line.

> You can select multiple features using several methods. The first is to click on each individual feature while holding down your *Shift* key. The other is to draw a rectangle by clicking in one location and dragging a box while holding down your mouse button. This will normally select all features that are either inside or touched by the rectangle you create. If you click on the drop-down arrow located below the **Select** tool, you can choose to create other shapes including, a polygon, circle, line, or lasso (free hand), or trace existing features.

64. Click on the Modify button in the **Features** group on the **Edit** tab in the ribbon. It has an icon which includes a pencil that appears to be drawing three lines and multiple points. This will open the **Modify Features** pane.

65. In the **Modify Features** pane, scroll down to the **Construct** toolset. If needed, expand it by clicking on the small arrowhead located to the left.

66. Click on the **Buffer edit** tool located at the bottom of the list. This will open the **Buffer edit** tool. It should show that three street centerline features are selected at the top of the pane.

67. Set the **Template** to the **RW (or Road Rights of Way)** by clicking on the drop-down arrow and selecting it from the presented list.

68. Set the **Buffer Distance** to 25 ftUS. If you measure the distance between the rights of way lines on the plat, you will find that they are 50 feet apart. Since the centerline runs down the center, the 25 foot buffer will place the rights of way lines in the correct location.

69. Expand the **Options** by clicking on the small arrowhead located to the left.

70. Ensure **Rings** are set to 1 and **Dissolve** is enabled. **Show Preview** is optional.

71. **Side** should be set to **Both** and **End** to **Round**.

72. Once you verify your **Buffer** tool is set, as in the following screenshot, click on the **Buffer** button at the bottom of the pane:

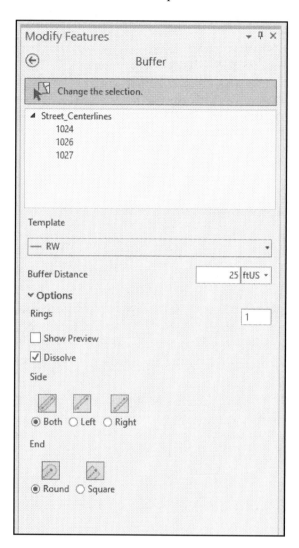

Once you click on the **Buffer** button, you should see a new set of lines appear in the map that represent the rights of way of the road centerlines you created earlier. The new rights of way should look like the following:

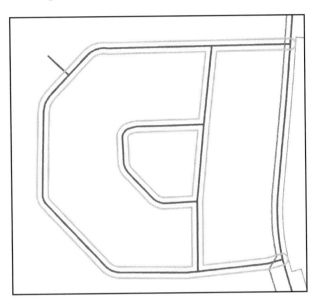

ArcGIS Pro contains several buffer tools. The one you have just used is the edit Buffer tool. It will create new polygon or line features depending on which template is selected. This tool only creates new features on existing layers. In addition to the edit Buffer tool, there are several buffer geoprocessing tools, which are most often used when performing spatial analysis. These include Buffer, Multi-ring Buffer, and Graphic Buffer. The Buffer and Multi-ring Buffer create completely new polygon feature classes and do not actually edit any existing layers.

Now you will perform some cleanup of the rights of ways you just created. If you look at the intersections with GA HWY 50, you will notice the rights of way overlap. This needs to be fixed.

73. Save your edits by clicking on the **Save** button and confirming your save.
74. Zoom in to the northern intersection of Oak Place with GA HWY 50 using your scroll wheel.
75. Turn off the **Parcels, City Limits**, and **Forrest Park Subdivision** layers in the **Contents** pane. Click on the **List by Draw Order** button to do this.

76. Disable snapping by clicking on the **Snapping** button on the **Edit** tab. If it is no longer highlighted in blue, snapping is disabled.

77. In the **Modify Features** pane, scroll to the **Reshape** toolset. Expand it if needed.

78. Select the **Extend or Trim** tool.

79. Click on the locations shown in the following diagram to trim unnecessary parts of the rights of way features. They should take on a dashed appearance when your mouse pointer is on them:

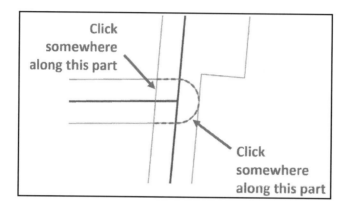

The rights of way at this intersection should now look like the following diagram. You have removed the overlap using the Extend or Trim tool:

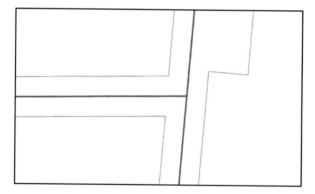

80. If your data looks like the previous diagram, save your edits. If not, click **Discard** and try again.

81. Zoom back to the extents of the subdivision. Then, zoom in to the southern intersection of Oak Place with GA HWY 50. If necessary, repeat the same process to clean up the overlapping rights of way lines. You may not need to because the previous steps may have also cleaned up this intersection.

82. If additional cleanup was required, save your edits and zoom in to the extents of the subdivision once again.

Your map should now look similar to the following diagram. You should see the centerlines and rights of way features you created. They should be clean with no overlaps and properly connected:

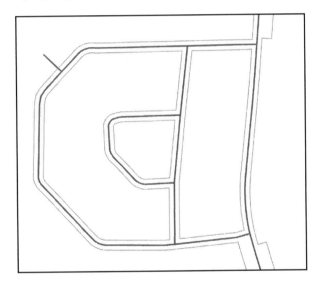

You still need to add the rights of way for the cul-de-sac. You will do that now.

83. Zoom in to the cul-de-sac located on the northeastern side of the subdivision.

84. Using the skills you have learned, buffer this centerline for the cul-de-sac by 50 ftUS.

85. Trim the rights of way for the cul-de-sac and Oak Place so they look like the following diagram:

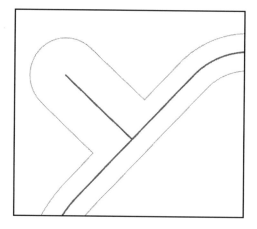

 Sometimes, the Extend or Trim tool will not trim the sections needed. If this happens, try splitting the lines at the intersections and then deleting the undesired segments.

86. Save your edits once again.
87. If you are not continuing to the next recipe, save your project and close ArcGIS Pro. Otherwise, continue to the next recipe.

Creating new polygon features

You've learned how to create point and line features using ArcGIS Pro. It is now time to learn how to create polygon features. Polygons are very similar to polylines in that they consist of multiple vertices. The big difference is that a polygon must form a closed figure and a polyline does not.

A polygon is constructed with a minimum of four vertices. This may seem confusing, as a triangle is a polygon but only has three sides. So why are four vertices required? Well, that is because the polygon must be closed. So, the first and last vertices are in the exact same location. When creating new polygons in ArcGIS Pro, the software automatically does this. So, you never have to worry about whether your polygon is closed or not.

In this recipe, you will create polygons that represent building footprints. You will use several different methods to do this. Many will be similar to the methods you used to create lines.

Getting ready

Before starting this recipe, you will need to have completed the *Configuring editing options* recipe. It is recommended that you complete the *Creating new line features* recipe as well, though it is not required. However, completing that recipe will help teach you some of the tools and skills you will also need to create new polygons. This recipe can be completed with all licensing levels of ArcGIS Pro. You will also need to ensure you have internet access in order to make use of the Esri provided basemaps.

How to do it...

1. If you closed ArcGIS Pro before starting this recipe, you will need to start ArcGIS Pro and open the `Editing.aprx` project located in `C:\Student\ArcGISProCookbook\Chapter4\Editing` using the skills you learned in previous recipes.

2. Click on the **Map** tab in the ribbon. Then, click on the **Basemap** button and select the **Imagery** basemap, as shown in the following screenshot:

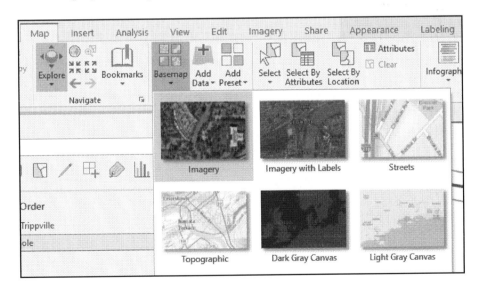

3. Turn off the following layers if they are currently visible in the map: Forrest Park Subdivision, Parcels, Sewer lines, and Manholes. You will do this in the **Contents** pane with the **List by Draw Order**, as you have in previous recipes.

4. Click on the **Bookmarks** button in the **Layer** group on the **Map** tab in the ribbon. Select the **Building 1** bookmark to zoom into the first building footprint you will create. You map view should now look similar to the following screenshot:

5. Using the skills you have learned from past recipes, add the **Buildings** feature class to your map from the **Trippville_GIS** geodatabase and the **Base feature** dataset.

6. In the **Contents** pane, click on the **List by Selection** button. Then, right-click on the **Buildings** layer you just added and select **Make this the only selectable layer**.

7. Next, click on the **List by Editing** button in the **Contents** pane and make sure the **Buildings** layer is marked as editable. It will have a check mark in the box located next to the layer name if it is. If it is not, click on the box to enable editing of that layer.

8. Click on the **Edit** tab in the ribbon.

9. Disable snapping by clicking on the **Snapping** button. If the **Snapping** button is highlighted in blue, snapping is enabled. If it is not highlighted, snapping is not enabled.
10. Click on the **Create** button in the **Feature** group on the **Edit** tab to open the **Create Features** pane.
11. Select the feature template for the **Buildings** layer. It is located below the layer name and includes the symbol patch and description.
12. Click on the southwestern corner of the building, as shown here:

13. Move your mouse to the southeastern corner of the building, as shown in the aerial screenshot. Then, click to create the next vertex.
14. Select the Right Angle Line tool from the **Edit** toolbar located at the bottom of the map view, as indicated here:

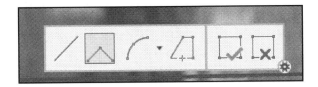

15. Click on the northeastern corner of the building, as shown in the aerial screenshot. Notice your line is locked so that it is perpendicular to the line you created, which represents the southern side of the building.

16. Then, move to the northwestern corner of the building, as shown in the aerial screenshot. Double-click to finish creating the polygon. If you single-click instead, press the *F2* button to finish. Your new building should look similar to the following:

You have just created your first polygon using a very simple method. You first constructed one side by tracing it from the aerial photo. Then, you used the right angle line tool to ensure the polygon had right-angled corners. This generated an accurate representation of the building.

17. Save your edits by clicking on the **Save** button in the **Manage Edits** group on the **Edit** tab.

18. Click on the **Map** tab in the ribbon. Then, select the **Bookmark** button and select the **Building 2** bookmark.

19. Click on the **Edit** tab again.
20. In the **Create Features** pane, click on the **Buildings** feature template to expose the construction tools associated with the template. So far, you have used the default polygon tool.
21. Select the Rectangle tool, as shown here:

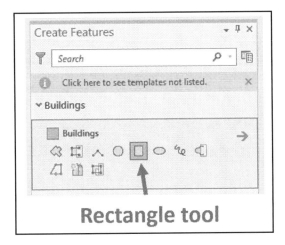

22. Click on the southwestern corner of the building. Then, click on the southeastern corner, as shown:

23. Drag your mouse toward the northeastern corner of the building. When you get to the corner and the rectangle matches the shape and size of the building, as shown in the aerial screenshot, click to create the polygon.

   Your building should look similar to the screenshot that follows. This rectangle tool created a building polygon like the first one you created. This was a faster and easier method though:

24. Save your edits by clicking on the **Save** button in the **Manage Edits** group on the **Edit** tab. Confirm your save when asked.
25. Activate the **Map** tab in the ribbon and click on the **Bookmarks** button. Select **Building 3**.
26. Click on the **Edit** tab in the ribbon.
27. Select the **Building feature** template in the **Create Features** pane.

28. Select the Polygon tool located below the template, as shown:

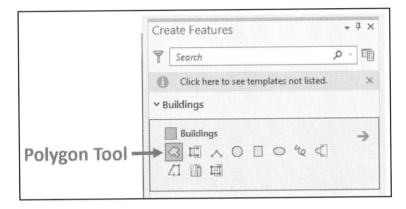

29. Using the skills you have learned in this recipe and those in the *Creating line features* recipe, draw the building footprint for the building you have zoomed in to. When completed, your building should look like this:

30. Save your edits by clicking on the **Save** button in the **Manage Edits** group on the **Edit** tab in the ribbon.

31. If you are not continuing to the next recipe, save your project and close ArcGIS Pro. If you are continuing to the next recipe, you do not need to do anything more in this recipe.

Creating a new polygon feature using autocomplete

You now know how to create new polygon features that are not connected or adjacent to other polygons. How do you create new polygon features that are adjacent to other existing polygon features? You would want to construct these in a way that would not create gaps or overlaps between the new polygon and existing ones. Using the Autocomplete tool is one way to successfully do this.

In this recipe, you will create a new parcel polygon located just outside the City Limits of Trippville. The City Council is considering annexing this parcel and wants to see how it relates to the existing city limits. You will create the new parcel using the Autocomplete tool.

Getting ready

Before starting this recipe, you will need to have completed the *Configuring editing options* recipe. It is recommended that you complete the *Creating new line features* and *Creating new Polygon Features* recipes as well, though it is not required. Completing those recipes will help teach you some of the tools and skills that will help you complete this recipe.

This recipe can be completed with all licensing levels of ArcGIS Pro. You will also need to ensure you have internet access in order to make use of the Esri provided basemaps.

How to do it...

1. If you closed ArcGIS Pro before starting this recipe, you will need to start ArcGIS Pro and open the `Editing.aprx` project located in `C:\Student\ArcGISProCookbook\Chapter4\Editing` using the skills you learned in previous recipes.

2. Click on the **Map** tab in the ribbon. Then, click on **Bookmarks** and select the **Autocomplete Polygon** bookmark.

3. In the **Contents** pane, turn on the **Parcels** and **City Limits** layers if needed. Remember, you will need to select **List by Draw Order** to do this.

4. Click on the **Edit** tab in the ribbon.

5. Enable snapping by clicking on the **Snapping** button on the **Edit** tab. If the button is highlighted in blue, snapping is enabled.

6. Click on the drop-down arrow below the **Snapping** button and ensure the snapping locations are set, as shown in the following screenshot:

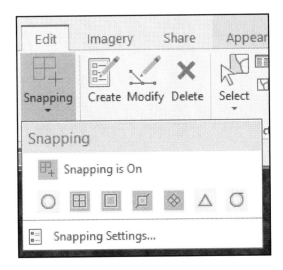

7. Click on the **List by Snapping** button located near the top of the **Contents** pane. Ensure the **Parcels** and **City Limits** layers are set to be snappable.

8. Click on the **List by Editing** button in the **Contents** pane. Ensure the **Parcels** layer is set to be editable.

9. Click on the **Create** button in the **Features** group on the **Edit** tab in the ribbon to open the **Create features** window.

10. Click on the **Parcels feature** template located below the layer name in the **Create Features** window.

11. Select the Autocomplete Polygon tool located below the feature template, as shown in the following screenshot:

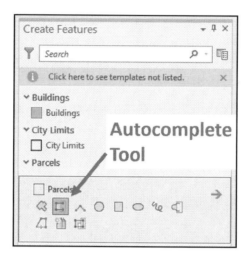

12. In the map, click on the intersection of the City Limits and the Rights of Way line, as illustrated in the following screenshot:

13. Click on the **Trace** tool on the **Edit** toolbar located on the bottom of the map view. Then click on the location, as shown in the previous screenshot.

14. Press the *O* key to open the **Trace Options** window. Click on the box located to the left of **Limit Trace Length** and enter a value of 125 ftUS, as shown in the following screenshot. Click **OK** once you verify you have configured things successfully:

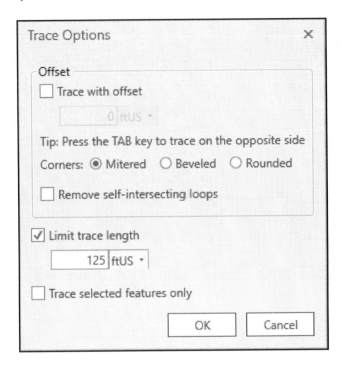

15. Move your mouse pointer along the road rights of way until the Trace tool stops drawing a boundary. That means you have reached the 125 foot limit. Once the trace stops, click on the road right of way where the trace stops, as indicated here:

16. Select the **Line** tool from the **Edit** toolbar.
17. Move your mouse pointer toward the north/north-west and right-click. Select the **Direction/Distance** tool from the menu that appears.
18. Set the **Direction** value to N33-34-03W QB and **Distance** to 290.00 ftUS. You may need to press your *Enter* key to apply the values.
19. Move your mouse to the east toward the existing parcel and right-click. Select **Direction** from the menu that appears.
20. Set the **Direction** value to N60-03-45E QB. You may need to press the *Enter* key to apply the value. The boundary you are drawing should now be locked into the set direction.

21. Move your mouse pointer so it is inside the existing parcel located to the east of the boundary you are drawing. Once you are inside the existing parcel, double-click to finish drawing the boundary for the new parcel. The new parcel should look like the following:

22. Save your edits by clicking on the **Save** button in the **Manage Edits** group on the **Edit** tab.
23. If you are not continuing to the next recipe, save your project and close ArcGIS Pro. If you are continuing to the next recipe, you do not need to do anything more in this recipe.

How it works...

When creating polygons that represent features such as parcels, political boundaries, emergency response boundaries, and others, it is important to create them in such a way to ensure they do not have overlaps and gaps. The Autocomplete tool is a great way to ensure the new polygons you create follow existing boundaries exactly. This means they do not have gaps or overlaps.

In this recipe, you created a new parcel polygon by defining three of four sides using traditional methods you learned in other recipes in this chapter. The fourth side was automatically created because the Autocomplete tool traces the boundary of the adjoining existing parcel automatically.

When using the Autocomplete tool, you need to ensure the sketch you create starts and ends by touching or crossing the boundary of the existing adjacent polygon. If your sketch does not touch or cross the existing adjacent boundary, the tool will fail to create a new polygon.

Editing attributes using the Attribute pane

In the previous recipes in this chapter, you learned how to edit and create new spatial features. However, that is only half of the data. Each feature also has attribute information linked to it. It is equally important to ensure you keep the attributes up to date.

ArcGIS Pro provides multiple methods you can use to update the attributes associated with features in your GIS. In this recipe, you will learn how to us the Attribute pane to update the values associated with features. You will update the attributes for the road centerlines you added in previous recipes.

Getting ready

Before starting this recipe, you will need to have completed the *Configuring editing options*, *Splitting line features* and *Creating new line features* recipes. This recipe can be completed with all licensing levels of ArcGIS Pro. You will also need to ensure you have internet access in order to make use of the Esri provided basemaps.

How to do it...

1. If you closed ArcGIS Pro before starting this recipe, you will need to start ArcGIS Pro and open the `Editing.aprx` project located in `C:\Student\ArcGISProCookbook\Chapter4\Editing` using the skills you learned in previous recipes.

2. Click on the **Map** tab in the ribbon. Then, click on **Bookmarks** and select the **Creating Manholes** bookmark.

3. In **Contents**, ensure the **Street_Centerlines** layer and **Forrest Park Subdivision** are visible. If desired, you can turn off the RW and Parcels layers to remove clutter. Remember, you will need to select **List by Draw Order** to do this. You can also turn off the **World Imagery Basemap**.

 Turning off unnecessary layers is always a good idea. This will help speed up map redraw and reduce overall clutter in the map. The result is increased efficiency and improved performance.

4. Click on the **List by Selection** button in the **Contents** pane. Make the **Street_Centerlines** layer the only selectable layer using the methods you have learned in previous recipes.

5. Click on the **List by Editing** button in the **Contents** pane. Ensure the **Street_Centerline** layer is enabled for editing.

6. Click on the **Edit** tab in the ribbon.

7. Close the **Create Features** pane if it is still open.

8. Activate the **Select** tool in the **Selection** group on the **Edit** tab.

9. Click on the centerline segment of Oak Place, as shown:

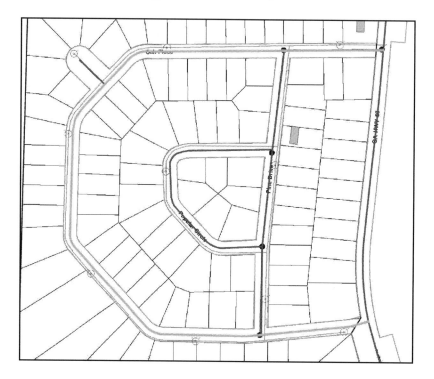

10. Click on the **Attribute** button located in the **Selection** group on the **Edit** tab in the ribbon. This will open the **Attribute** pane on the right-hand side of the interface by default.

    The **Attribute** pane is made up of two panels. The top panel displays a list of selected features. In your case, you should see only one. The bottom panel displays the list of fields and the associated value for each field:

11. Click in the cell located next to the **ST_NAME** field and type OAK PL. Press your *Enter* key when done.

12. Using that same process, fill out the remainder of the values as shown in the following screenshot:

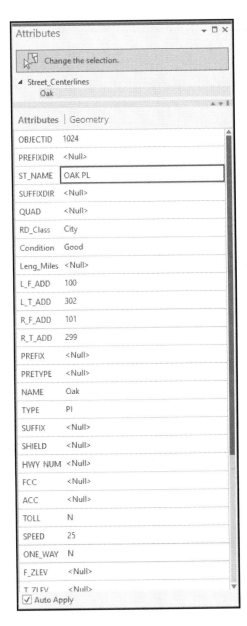

13. Save your attribute edits by clicking on the **Save** button in the **Manage Edits** group on the **Edit** tab in the ribbon.

14. Ensure the **Select** tool in the **Selection** group on the **Edit** tab is still active. Then, select the centerline for Pine Drive.

15. The **Attribute** pane should update to show the values for Pine Drive, most of which should be **<Null>**. Set the following values for Pine Drive:
    - **ST_NAME**: PINE DR
    - **RD_CLASS**: City
    - **Condition**: Good
    - **NAME**: Pine
    - **Type**: Dr
    - **TOLL**: N
    - **SPEED**: 25
    - **ONE_WAY**: N

16. Save your attribute edits by clicking on the **Save** button in the **Manage Edits** group on the **Edit** tab.

17. Select the centerline for Popular Circle and edit the attributes for it in the **Attributes** pane as you have done for the other two roads using the following values:
    - **ST_NAME**: POPULAR CIR
    - **RD_CLASS**: City
    - **Condition**: Good
    - **NAME**: Popular
    - **Type**: Cir
    - **TOLL**: N
    - **SPEED**: 25
    - **ONE_WAY**: N

18. Save your edits as you did with the previous two centerlines.

 Generally, it is best to update the attribute values for new features as you create them. That way, you do not forget to make the necessary updates to the attributes, which are just as important in a GIS as in the spatial data.

You have now edited attribute values for individual features in the Attributes pane. What if you have several features which all need to be assigned the same attribute value? You can do them individually just as you have been, but there is a more effective way. You will now learn how to do that by updating the pipe material for the sewer pipes you created in a previous recipe:

19. Click the **Clear** button in the **Selection** group in the **Edit** tab in the ribbon. This will deselect all currently selected features.

20. In the **Contents** pane, turn on the **Sewer Lines** layer and turn off the **Street_Centerlines** layer.

21. In the **Contents** pane, click on the **List by Editing** button. Then, set the **Sewer Lines** layer to be editable.

22. In the **Contents** pane, click on the **List by Selection** button. Then, set the **Sewer Lines**, to be the only selectable layer.

23. If required, click on the **Edit** tab in the ribbon and activate the **Select** tool in the **Selection** group.

24. Click at a location to the south-east of all the sewer lines in the new subdivision and then drag your mouse pointer to the north-west while holding down your mouse button. Release it once you have drawn a rectangle that encompasses all the sewer lines you drew in the previous recipe, as illustrated in the following diagram:

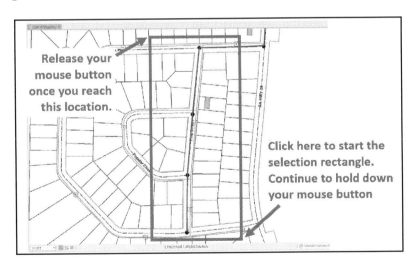

25. In the **Attributes** pane, you should see four features selected in the top panel. Click on **Sewer Line** located above the four selected features in the top panel of the **Attributes** pane.

26. Click on the cell located next to **PIPE SIZE** in the bottom panel of the **Attributes** pane and type 10. Press your *Enter* key when done to commit the change.

27. Then, click on the cell located next to **MATERIAL** and select **PVC** from the list.

28. Lastly, click on the cell located next the **Condition** field and select **Good** from the list that appears. Your **Attributes** pane should look like the following screenshot:

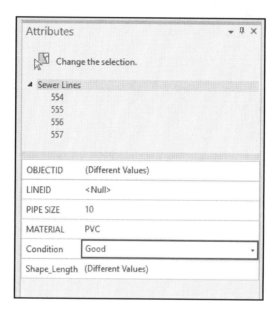

29. Save your edits if your **Attributes** pane matches the previous screenshot.

   By selecting the Layer name at the top of the upper panel, you were able to change the attributes for all selected features. This is a much more efficient and effective method for updating multiple features that share a common value.

30. If you are not continuing to the next recipe, save your project and close ArcGIS Pro. If you are continuing to the next recipe, you do not need to do anything more in this recipe.

Editing attributes in the Table view

In the last recipe, you learned how to update attribute values using the Attributes pane. You experienced editing attributes for individual features and multiple features. This is just one way you can edit attributes.

ArcGIS Pro also allows you to edit attributes directly in the table when you view the attribute table of the entire layer. Like the Attributes pane, you can edit individually or for multiple features at one time. When editing attributes for individual features, the workflow is very similar to editing in the Attributes pane. To edit the values for multiple features, you will need to use a new tool, Calculate Field.

The Calculate Field tool is very powerful. It allows you to create expressions or formulas that are used to calculate the values, which are then populated into the field. These expressions can be very simple or complex. Complex expressions must be written using Python. Python is the primary scripting language for ArcGIS.

In this recipe, you will update attributes for individual features in the Table view. You will then use the Calculate Field tool to calculate the length in miles for the new roads you drew in previous exercises.

Getting ready

Before starting this recipe, you will need to have completed all of the previous recipes in this chapter. This recipe can be completed with all licensing levels of ArcGIS Pro. You will also need to ensure you have internet access in order to make use of the Esri provided basemaps.

How to do it...

1. If you closed ArcGIS Pro before starting this recipe, you will need to start ArcGIS Pro and open the `Editing.aprx` project located in `C:\Student\ArcGISProCookbook\Chapter4\Editing` using the skills you learned in previous recipes.
2. Click on the **Map** tab in the ribbon. Then, click on **Bookmarks** and select the **Creating Manholes** bookmark.

3. In **Contents**, ensure the **Manhole** and **Street_Centerlines** layers are visible. If desired, you can turn off the **Forrest Park Subdivision**, **RW**, and **Parcels** layers to remove clutter. Remember, you will need to select **List by Draw Order** to do this. You can also turn off the **World Imagery Basemap**.

4. Click on the **List by Select** button in the **Contents** pane. Set the **Manhole** layer as the only selectable layer.

5. Click on the **List by Editing** button in the **Contents** pane. Ensure the **Manhole** layer is set to be editable.

6. If necessary, close the **Create Features** and **Attributes** panes.

7. Right-click on the **Manhole** layer in the **Contents** pane and select **Attribute Table**, as shown in the screenshot. This will open the table pane at the bottom of the interface:

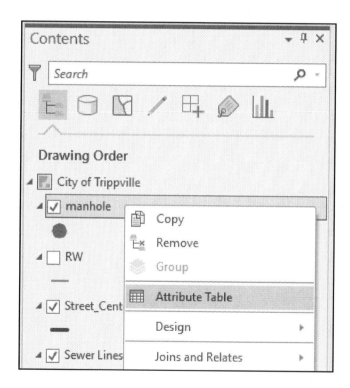

You can undock the Table view and move it to another location, including another monitor if you have one. Moving the Table View to another monitor is a common practice. It frees up more space for the map and allows you to enlarge the table to view it better. To undock the Table View, simply click on the tab containing the name of the open table and drag it to the new location.

8. Click on the **Edit** tab in the ribbon. Then, activate the **Select** tool located in the **Selection** group.

9. Click on the manhole located at the northern intersection of Oak Place and Pine Drive, as illustrated in the following screenshot:

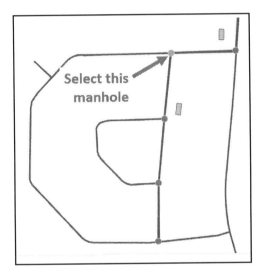

10. Look at the bottom of the Table view. You should see the number of selected features displayed. It should say **1 of 545**. Click on the **Show Selected Records** button located next to the text that indicates how many records are selected.

11. You should now only see the single record you have selected. Click in the cell located below the **Basin** field name. Type in Sweetwater, as shown in the following screenshot. This identifies which drainage basin the manhole is located in. You may need to press your *Enter* key to apply the new value:

Single selected record with updated value

12. Click on the cell located below **Depth** and type 4.0. You may need to press your *Enter* key to apply the new value.

13. Ensure the **Select** tool is still active and select the next manhole that is located due south of the one you were just editing. It is at the northern intersection of Pine Drive and Popular Circle.

14. Edit the following attribute values as indicated:
    - **Basin**: Sweetwater
    - **Depth**: 3.8

15. Select the manhole located due south at the southern intersection of Pine Drive and Popular Circle.

16. Edit the following attribute values as indicated:
    - **Basin**: Sweetwater
    - **Depth**: 3.0

17. Select the last manhole located at the intersection of Pine Drive and Oak Place.

18. Edit the following attribute values as indicated:
    - **Basin**: Sweetwater
    - **Depth**: 2.5

19. Save your edits by clicking on the **Save** button located in the **Manage Edits** group on the **Edit** tab on the ribbon.

You have just learned how to edit attribute values for individual features in the Table view. But what if you need to apply a common value to multiple features or calculate a value based on other information or a formula/expression? This is where the Calculate Field tool comes in.

Next, you will see how the Calculate Field tool works. You will start with a simple change. You will change the material of the sewer lines you added in a previous recipe. You will change their material from PVC to DI. Then, you will increase the complexity by creating an expression that will calculate the length of each road segment in miles.

20. Click the **Clear** button located in the **Selection** group on the **Edit** tab to deselect all selected features.

21. Using the skills you have learned, ensure the **Sewer Lines** layer is visible, selectable, and editable.

22. Click on the **Edit** tab in the ribbon and activate the **Select** tool located in the **Selection** group.

23. Click on one of the sewer lines you added in the *Splitting a line feature* recipe.

24. While holding down your *Shift* key, click on the remaining sewer lines you created in the *Splitting a line feature* recipe until they are all selected, as shown in the following diagram. You should have four sewer lines selected:

Multiple sewer lines selected and displayed in table and map

25. In the table view, right-click on the **Material** field name. Select **Calculate Field** from the menu that appears, as shown in the screenshot. This opens the **Calculate Field** tool in the **Geoprocessing** pane:

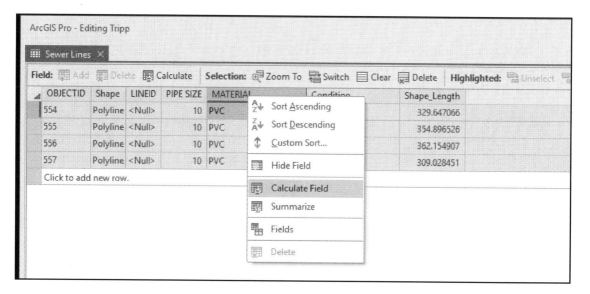

26. Ensure the **Input Table** is set to **Sewer Lines**. It should automatically be set because you evoked the tool from that table.

27. Ensure the **Field Name** is set to MATERIAL. Again, this should automatically be set.

28. Under **Expression**, below the **Fields** and **Helpers** panels, locate where it says **MATERIAL** = and the cell below that. Type the following into the cell: "DI". Your **Calculate Field** tool should look like the following screenshot:

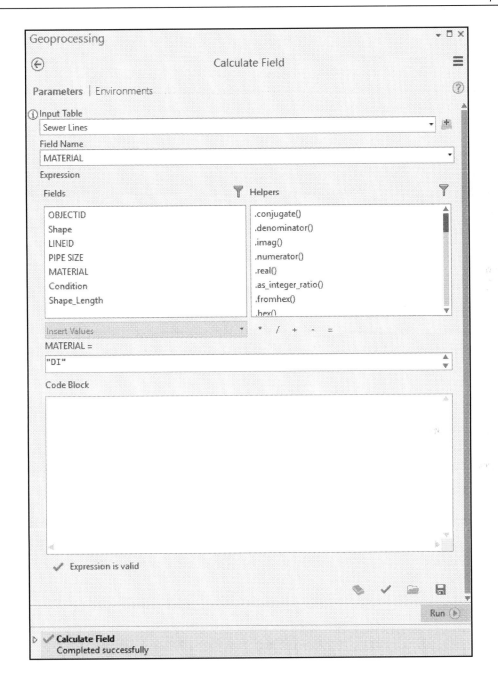

29. Click the **Validate** button located at the bottom of the **Geoprocessing** pane. It should look like a green check mark.

30. If the validation says **Expression is valid**, click on the **Run** button. If the validation gives you an error, review the error and fix it. The most common error is not including the double quotation marks around the DI value.

 If you run the Calculate Field tool without any features selected, it will populate new values for all records in the table based on the value or expression you inputted into the tool. In this recipe, you had four sewer lines selected, so only those four had their material values changed. If you had not selected those four and had run the Calculate Field tool, it would have changed the material value for all the sewer lines in the layer to DI.

31. You should see the material value for each selected sewer line change from **PVC** to **DI**. Save your edits if the values changed correctly.

32. Close the **Geoprocessing** pane.

Now that you know how to populate a simple value into multiple features, it is time to look at a way to create a simple expression. You will calculate the length of each road segment in miles using the shape length field as the base. This field shows the length of each segment in US feet.

33. Click on the **Clear** button in the **Selection** group on the **Edit** tab on the ribbon.

34. Right-click on the **Street_Centerlines** layer and select **Attribute** Table. The attribute table for the layer should open in the table view.

35. Right-click on the **Leng_Miles** field in the table view and select the **Calculate Field** tool from the menu that appears.

You will notice that the field already contains values. However, this is not a default field; you want to ensure the values are current and correct.

36. Ensure the **Input Table** is set to **Street_Centerline** and the **Field Name** is set to **Leng_Miles**. This should be automatically set because you right-clicked on the **Leng_Miles** field in the **Street_Centerlines** table.

37. Locate the cell below **Leng_Miles =**. It should be below the **Fields** and **Helpers** panel. Type in the following: `!Shape_Length!/5280`. This will divide the value in the **Shape_length** field for each feature by 5,280, which is the number of feet in a mile.

When creating expressions, syntax is extremely important. In this expression, the shape length field is identified as such using exclamation marks. To help reduce the risk of syntax errors, you could just locate the **Shape_Length** field in the **Fields** panel and double-click on it to add it to the expression with the proper syntax. For more information about how to use the Calculate Field tool, go to `http://pro.arcgis.com/en/pro-app/tool-reference/data-management/calculate-field.htm`.

Your **Calculate Field** tool should now look like this:

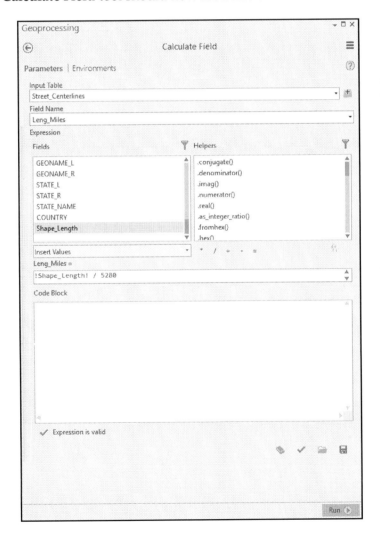

38. Validate your expression by clicking on the **Validate** button located near the bottom of the **Geoprocessing** pane.
39. If the validation is successful, click the **Run** button. If the validation returns an error, fix it and revalidate.
40. Activate the **Select** tool in the **Selection** group on the **Edit** tab on the ribbon.
41. Select the street center line for Oak Place.
42. In the table view, click on the **Show Selected Records** button located at the bottom.

You should now see only the record in the table for Oak Place. The value for the **Leng_Miles** field is now populated with a value of approximately half a mile. It was populated by the Calculate Field tool you just ran. The tool not only populated the value for the new roads you added in previous recipes, but it also updated the values for all the street centerlines in the layer:

43. Save your edits and your project.
44. Close ArcGIS Pro.

5

Validating and Editing Data with Topologies

In this chapter, we will cover the following recipes:

- Creating a new geodatabase topology
- Validating spatial data using a geodatabase topology
- Correcting spatial features with topology tools
- Editing data with a map topology

Introduction

GIS has the amazing capability to help us solve real-world problems. ArcGIS Pro includes a wealth of tools that allow users to perform all kinds of analysis to answer questions, find solutions, and determine patterns. However, like most computer systems, the results are only as good as the quality of the data the analysis is based on. The old adage *garbage in, garbage out* definitely applies.

So how do we ensure our GIS data is clean and accurate? One way is to make use of topology. Topology is a model of how features are related to one another spatially. Are they adjacent, connected, or coincident? This should not be confused with topography, which is how the ground changes in elevation. ArcGIS Pro allows you to use two types of topology, Geodatabase and Map.

A geodatabase topology is an item you create within a geodatabase, which allows you to apply rules to the data that is part of the topology. This might include rules such as: polygons must not overlap, lines must not intersect, or points must be inside a polygon. The rules are then used to validate the data to locate any features that violate the rules. ArcGIS Pro includes tools that allow you to fix the errors that are found. To make use of geodatabase topologies, you must store your data in a geodatabase, the feature classes must be in the same feature dataset, and you must have a standard or advanced license.

In addition to being able to validate data with geodatabase topology, ArcGIS Pro provides tools to help you edit data so as to not introduce new errors into your data. These topology edits allow you to edit multiple features so that whatever their existing spatial relationship happens to be, it is maintained after the edit. This can not only keep your data clean, but also greatly increases your editing efficiency because you can edit multiple features with a single edit operation.

Map topologies are not as complex as geodatabase topologies. They are temporary, only existing during a given ArcGIS Pro session when you have a map open. Map topologies do not allow you to validate your data to find errors. What they allow you to do is perform edits to existing data, using topology edit tools, so that the edited features maintain their current spatial relationships.

Map topologies are not limited to only data in a geodatabase or in a single-feature dataset. Geodatabase feature classes and shapefiles can all be included in a single Map topology. Another advantage of the Map topology is that it works at all licensing levels, so you can use them even with just a Basic license.

In this chapter, you will learn how to create a new Geodatabase topology. This will include adding rules and feature classes to it. Then you will validate the feature classes that take part in the topology to find the errors. Next you will use topology tools to fix the errors and validate again to ensure your edits have not introduced new errors. Lastly, you will explore a Map topology and how you can use it to edit multiple features at one time.

Creating a new geodatabase topology

A geodatabase topology is an item stored in a geodatabase, just like a feature class or table. They can only exist and function within a geodatabase. Other formats, such as shapefiles, do not support geodatabase topologies.

Like feature classes and tables, you must create the topology. This will include giving it a name, setting tolerances, adding rules, and adding participating feature classes. To create a new geodatabase topology, a couple of things must be true.

First, you can only create a geodatabase topology within a feature dataset. Second, only feature classes stored in the feature dataset containing the topology can participate in that topology. Third, participating feature classes must not be part of another topology or geometric network. A feature class can only participate in one topology or geometric network at a time. Lastly, you must have a Standard or Advanced license of ArcGIS Pro in order to create a new topology.

In this recipe, you will create a new geodatabase topology in the Trippville GIS database, which will ultimately be used to validate the parcel data for the City. For those that have done this in the older ArcMap application, you will find the ArcGIS Pro process much more complex, at least in version 2.0 and version 2.1. This will hopefully be more streamlined in future versions.

Getting ready

This recipe will require you to have a Standard or Advanced license for ArcGIS Pro. You will not be able to complete it with just a basic license. If you do not have a standard or advanced license, you can request a free trial license from Esri, at `http://www.esri.com/en/arcgis/products/arcgis-pro/trial`. Trial licenses are valid for 21 days.

You also need to ensure you have installed the sample data for the book. It is also recommended that you complete all the recipes in `Chapter 1`, *ArcGIS Pro Capabilities and Terminology*, before starting this recipe. This will ensure you have the foundational skills needed to complete this recipe.

How to do it...

1. To get started, you need to launch ArcGIS Pro as you have in previous recipes.
2. In the **ArcGIS Pro** start window, click on **Open another project**:

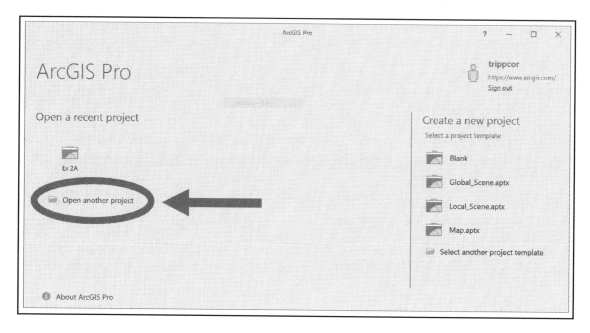

3. Select **Computer** from the **Open** window and then click **Browse** in the area on the right.
4. Navigate to `C:\Student\ArcGISProCookbook\Chapter5\Topologies` by clicking on `C:\` in the area on the left of the **Open Project** window. Then double-click on **Student, ArcGISProCookbook, Chapter5**, and **Topologies** folders.
5. Select the **Topologies.aprx** project file and click **OK**.

The project will open in the **Catalog** view. This project currently does not contain any maps. Before you create your new topology, you need to verify a couple of things first. You need to ensure that your geodatabase contains a feature dataset and that the parcels feature class, which you will validate later, is within a feature dataset:

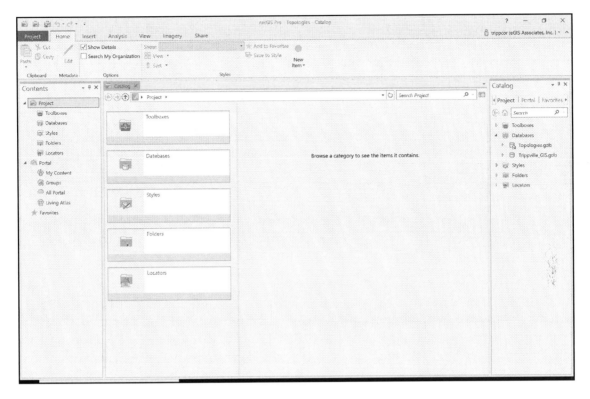

6. In the **Contents** pane, click on **Databases** so that the two geodatabases connected to the project are displayed in the **Catalog** view.

7. Double click on the **Trippville_GIS.gbd** geodatabase so you can see its contents. Then answer the question ahead:

Question: Does the geodatabase contain any feature databases, and if so, what are they?

Answer:

You should have seen that this geodatabase contains at least three feature datasets, Base, Sewer, and Water. So that means you can create a topology in this geodatabase. Now you need to locate the parcels feature class:

8. Double-click on the **Base** feature dataset to reveal its contents.

9. Scroll down to verify that it contains the **Parcels** feature class.

10. Scroll back through the feature dataset to see if it contains any topologies. Then answer the questions ahead:

   Question: Is the Parcels feature class within the feature dataset?

   Answer:

   Question: Does the feature dataset contain any other topologies?

   Answer:

Now that you have verified that the **Parcels** feature class is stored in the **Base** feature dataset, and there are no other topologies to contend with, you are now ready to begin building a new topology.

11. Click on the **Analysis** tab in the ribbon.

12. Click on the **Tools** button in the **Geoprocessing** group on the **Analysis** tab. This will open the **Geoprocessing** pane.

13. Click on the **Toolboxes** tab near the top of the **Geoprocessing** pane, just below the search cell, as shown in the following screenshot. This will open all the system toolboxes connected to the project:

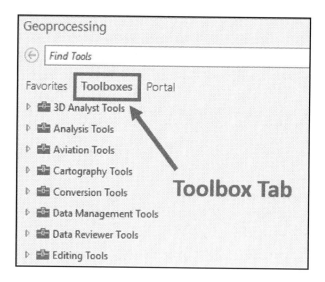

For those that have used the older ArcMap or ArcCatalog applications, this is the same as opening ArcToolbox. ArcGIS Pro does not include separate applications like the older ArcGIS Desktop did. In ArcGIS Pro, everything is all in one single application, at least up to version 2.1. There has been some discussion about creating an ArcCatalog-like app for performing general data management functions. However, it has not been determined if this will indeed happen.

14. Expand the **Data Management Tools** toolbox by clicking on the small arrowhead located to the left of the toolbox name.

15. Expand the **Topology** toolset located near the bottom of the **Data Management** toolbox.

16. Click on the **Create Topology** tool in the **Topology** toolset. This will open the tool in the **Geoprocessing** pane.

17. Click on the **Browse** button located at the end of the cell for the **Input Feature Dataset**.

18. Click on **Databases** in the panel on the left of the **Input Feature Dataset** window that opened. You may need to expand the **Project** folder to see it.

19. Double-click on the **Trippville_GIS.gdb** geodatabase in order to display its contents.

20. Select the **Base** feature dataset and click **OK**. *Do not double-click on the feature dataset*. Select it with a single click.

21. For the **Output Topology**, type Parcels. This is the name of the topology you are creating. Leave the **Cluster Tolerance** blank. ArcGIS Pro will calculate a default tolerance.

22. Verify that your **Create Topology** tool looks like the following, and then click
    Run:

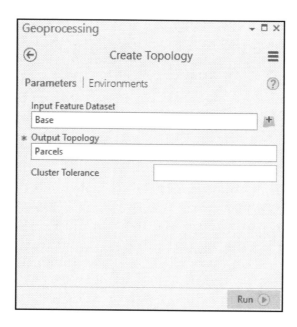

The Cluster Tolerance is the distance at which ArcGIS Pro believes
features should be considered to be in the same location. When you
validate the topology, ArcGIS Pro will automatically snap features
together that are within the cluster tolerance distance. This means that
when you validate, it will potentially move data. This is both good and
bad. It will often clean up data by connecting features that were
mistakenly not connected. It will remove small gaps and overlaps between
features. However, if your cluster tolerance is set to large, it could snap
features together that should not be. So, it is generally recommended to
keep the cluster tolerance small. Esri indicates that the best practice is to
use the default tolerance calculated by ArcGIS Pro, as it is typically small
enough to avoid any adverse effects to your data.

23. Close the Geoprocessing pane.

In the **Catalog** view you should now see the **Parcels** topology you just created.
The next step is to add the feature class or classes that will participate in the
topology. In this recipe it will be only one feature class, parcels. You will now add
that feature class to the topology:

24. In the **Catalog** view, scroll to the **Parcels** topology you just created. Right-click on it and select **Properties** from the menu that appears, as shown in the following screenshot:

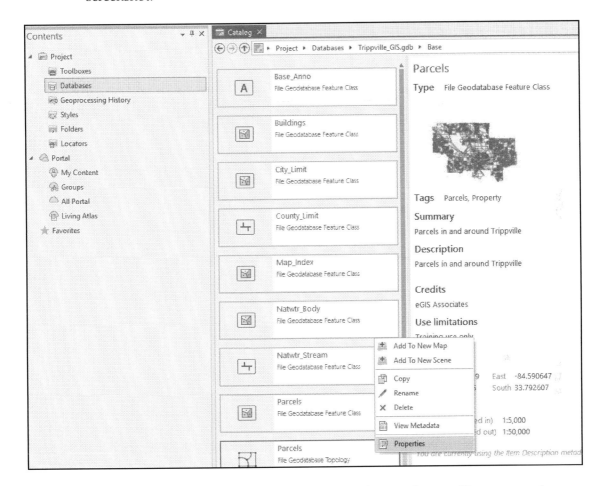

 Multiple topologies can exist in the same feature dataset. However, each feature class can only participate in one topology at a time.

25. The **Topology Properties** window should open. Click on the **General** option in the panel located on the left of the window. Review those settings. You can see that the cluster tolerance is set to a very small value. You will also see that the topology is not validated.

A topology cannot be validated until it includes both feature classes and rules. A topology can include one or more of both. Which feature classes and rules you include will depend on the purpose of the topology and your data.

26. Click on the **Feature** class option located in the panel on the left side of the **Topology Properties** window. Then click on the **Add Classes** button.
27. Scroll down the list of feature classes presented in the **Add Classes** window until you see the **Parcels** feature class. Click on the box to the left of the feature class name to select it. Then click **OK** to add it to the topology.

You can select multiple feature classes and add them all to the topology at the same time. You are not required to add them one at a time.

28. Verify that your **Topology Properties** window looks like the following screenshot and click **OK** to apply the changes you have made:

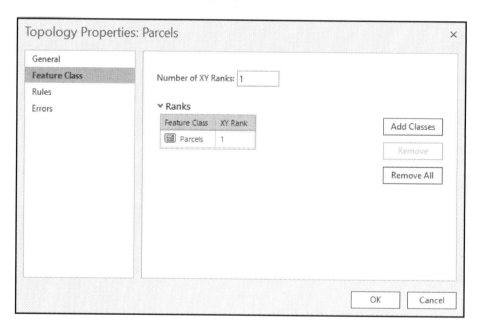

Topology Properties window

You have just added a participating feature class to the topology. Now you need to add rules, which you will use to validate your data against. We will keep it simple for this recipe. You will only add a single rule to validate against.

29. Right-click on the **Parcels** topology again and open the **Properties** as you did previously.
30. Click on the **Rules** option in the panel on the left of the **Topology Properties** window.
31. Click where it says **Click here to add a new rule.** in the panel on the right side of the window, as illustrated in the following screenshot:

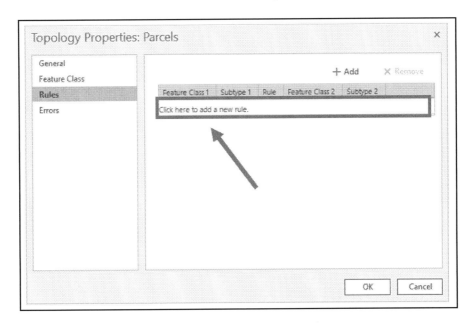

Topology Properties window - setting rules

32. Click on the cell located beneath the column titled **Feature Class 1**. Select **Parcels** from the list that appears. You may need to double-click to get the list to appear. Since you only have one participating feature class in this topology, it should be the only one in the list.
33. Click on the cell located beneath the column titled **Rule**. Select **Must Not Overlap (Area)** from the list of possible rules that appears.

34. Verify that your **Topologies Properties: Parcels** window looks like the following and then click **OK**.

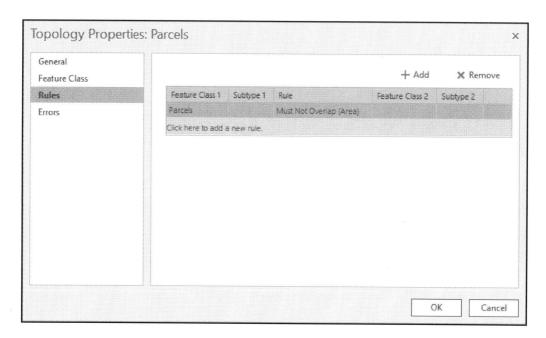

A topology can include many rules. The rules you can apply will depend on the type of feature classes that participate in the topology. For example, the rule you added in this recipe only applies to polygons in a single feature class. For more information about topologies in ArcGIS Pro, and the rules, go to `http://pro.arcgis.com/en/pro-app/help/data/topologies/topology-in-arcgis.htm`.

35. Save your project.
36. If you are not continuing to the next recipe you can close ArcGIS Pro. If you are, please leave the application open.

Validating spatial data using a geodatabase topology

You have just created a new topology in the previous recipe. This will allow you to find errors in the parcel feature class which violate the polygons must not overlap rule you included in the topology. To find any errors you must first validate the topology.

When you validate a topology, several things occur. First, all features participating within the topology are snapped together if they are within the cluster tolerance. This is done automatically for all features when you validate. Second, the participating feature classes are checked against the rules you have included in the topology. Any areas that include features that violate the rules are identified in the topology so you can easily locate the errors and fix them.

In this recipe, you will validate your topology to identify any errors in the Parcels feature class. To do this, you will create a new map and add the topology, along with the Parcels layer, to it.

Getting ready

You will need to have completed the previous recipe in order to complete this one. You will also need a Standard or Advanced license of ArcGIS Pro. You will not be able to perform this recipe with just a Basic license of ArcGIS Pro. If you only have a basic license, you can request a trial advanced ArcGIS Pro license from Esri, at `http://www.esri.com/en/arcgis/products/arcgis-pro/trial`.

How to do it...

1. To get started, you will need to launch ArcGIS Pro if it is not already open. If you closed ArcGIS Pro before starting this recipe, you will need to start ArcGIS Pro and open the `Topologies.aprx` project located in `C:\Student\ArcGISProCookbook\Chapter5\Topologies`, using the skills you have learned in past recipes.
2. Click on the **Insert** tab in the ribbon.

3. Click on the **New Map** button located in the **Project** group in the **Insert** tab. This will create a new blank 2D map in your project. The new map should automatically be opened.

4. In the **Contents** pane, right-click on the **Map** and select **Properties** from the menu that appears, as illustrated in the following screenshot:

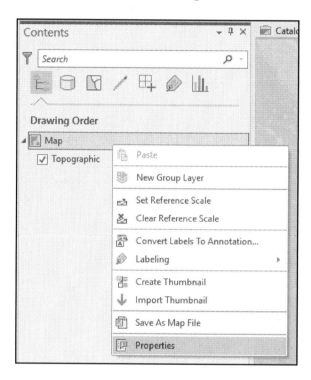

5. Ensure the **General** option is selected in the left panel in the **Map Properties** window that opened.

6. In the cell for **Name**, type `Parcel Topology` and click **OK**. Where it said **Map** prior, it should now read **Parcel Topology**.

7. Save your project.

8. In the **Catalog** pane, expand the **Databases** folder by clicking on the small arrowhead located to the left.

9. Expand the **Trippville_GIS.gdb** so you can see its contents.

10. Expand the **Base** feature dataset.

11. Right-click on the **Parcels Topology** and select **Add to Current Map** from the menu that appears, as shown in the following screenshot. This will add the topology and the participating feature classes as layers to the map:

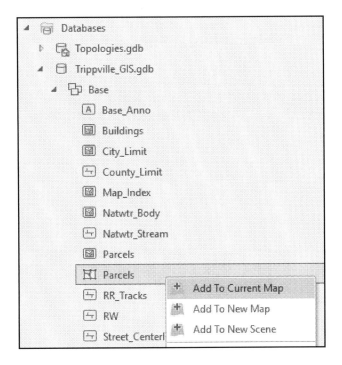

12. Right-click on the **Parcels** layer in the **Contents** pane. Select **Zoom to Layer** from the menu that appears. You should now be able to see the parcels for the city of Trippville.

13. In the **Contents** pane, examine the layers listed under the **Parcels Topology**. Then answer the following question:

Question: What layers are included in the topology?

Answer:

As you can see, a topology includes more than just the rules, participating feature classes, and cluster tolerance. It also includes the located errors and Dirty Areas:

14. Turn on the **Dirty Areas** layer in the **Parcels Topology**. You should see a big blue square appear around the parcels in the map, as shown in the following screenshot:

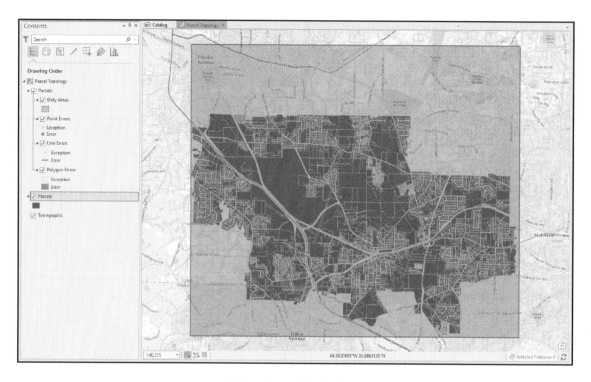

Topology dirty areas displayed in the map

 Dirty Areas are areas in your data that are participating in the topology which you have not validated. In this case, the entire area is considered a dirty area because you have not validated your topology. Just because a dirty area exists does not mean your data has errors or cannot be used. A Dirty Area is just an area within your data which you have not validated with the rules in your topology because you have either edited the data or just created the topology. Regardless of whether Dirty Areas exist, or if your data does have errors, you can always use your data.

15. Click on the **Edit** tab in the ribbon.

16. Click on the drop-down arrow located next to **No Topology** in the **Manage Edit** group on the **Edit** tab, and select **Parcels (Geodatabase)** from the list, as illustrated:

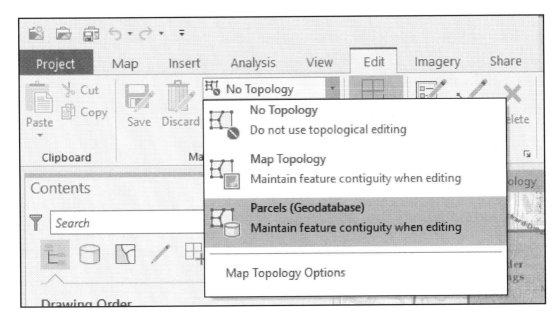

17. Now that you have selected the topology you will validate, you need to access the validate tool. Click on the **Modify** button in the **Features** group on the **Edit** tab. This will open the **Modify Features** pane.

18. Scroll down to the **Topographic** toolset. If necessary, expand it so you can see its contents.

19. Since this is the first time you have validated the topology since it was created, select the **Validate All** tool.

There are also geoprocessing tools you can use to validate your topology. These are located in the **Data Management** toolbox and the **Topology** toolset. The **Validate Topology** tool does the same thing as the **Validate All** tool.

When you validate the topology, it will look for any parcels that overlap other parcels. Any it finds, it will add those locations to the **Polygon Errors** layer. When the validation is complete, you should see some red polygons on the east side of the Parcels layer, which indicate the errors that were found.

20. Close the **Modify Features** pane and save your project.

21. Zoom in to the area indicated in the following diagram:

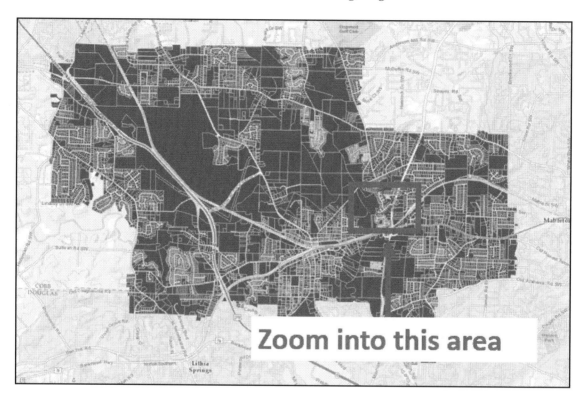

Zoom to the area indicated by the rectangle

Your map should now look similar to the following diagram. Remember your colors may be different as ArcGIS Pro assigns a random color to new layers when they are added:

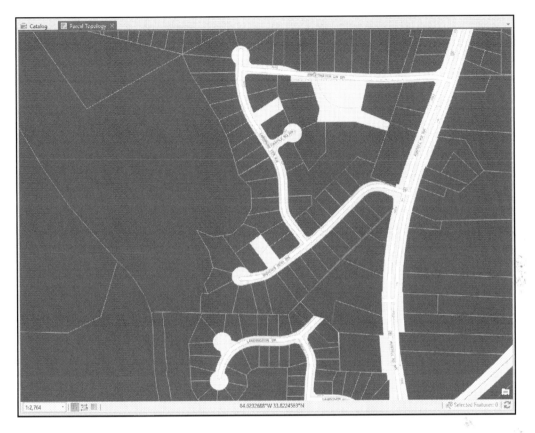

In this view, you can see the errors that were found in the parcel data once you verified it.

22. Let's create a bookmark so you can easily return to this area later. Click on the **Map** tab in the ribbon.

23. Click on the **Bookmarks** button in the **Navigate** group on the **Map** tab. Select **New Bookmark**. This will open the **Create Bookmark** window.

24. Name the new bookmark Parcels Overlap Area to Fix and click **OK**.

25. Save your project.

26. If you are not continuing to the next recipe, you may close ArcGIS Pro. Otherwise keep it open.

As you have seen in previous recipes, bookmarks allow you to quickly zoom in to a fixed spatial location. These are very handy for many purposes. Several things I use bookmarks for include printing a map at a specific location and scale, for meetings where I need to highlight specific areas or features, and to return to a specific location for a project or for editing. Each map has its own set of bookmarks. There is no limit to the number of bookmarks a project can contain.

Correcting spatial features with topology tools

Now that you know where the errors are in your data, you need to fix them. ArcGIS Pro includes specific tools for fixing topology errors. These are generally quick and easy to use for most situations. You may also use standard editing tools to correct errors as well. In either case, you should always validate your data after completing edits to ensure you have not introduced any new errors into your data.

In this recipe, you will fix several errors you uncovered when validating the topology. You will use the Error Inspector tool in ArcGIS Pro to correct the errors.

Getting ready

This recipe continues to build on the work done in the previous recipes in this chapter. You will need to have completed all the previous recipes included in this chapter before you can start on this one. As with those previous recipes, you will also need a Standard or Advanced license level to complete this recipe.

How to do it...

1. If you closed ArcGIS Pro before starting this recipe, you will need to start ArcGIS Pro and open the `Topologies.aprx` project located in `C:\Student\ArcGISProCookbook\Chapter5\Topologies` using the skills you have learned in past recipes.
2. In the **Contents** pane, click on the **List by Editing** button.
3. Ensure the **Parcels** layer is enabled for editing.
4. Click on **List by Selection** in the **Contents** pane.

5. Ensure the following layers at minimum are selectable: **Polygon Errors** and **Parcels**.

6. Click on the **Edit** tab in the ribbon.

7. Click on the **Error Inspector** button in the **Manage Edits** group on the **Edit** tab. This will open the **Error Inspector** pane at the bottom of the interface. Like all panes, this one may be undocked and moved to a different location if desired.

8. Select the first error presented in the pane by clicking on the gray square located to the far left of the first row, as illustrated here:

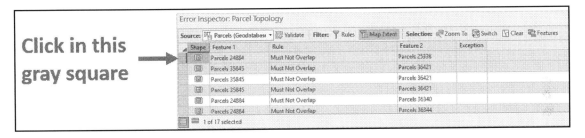

Select record in the table by clicking on gray square to the left

9. Click on the **Zoom To** option located at the top of the **Error Inspector** pane. This will zoom you in to the location of the selected error.

10. Right-click on the same square you clicked on to select the error to reveal a new context menu. Select **Merge**, as shown in the following screenshot:

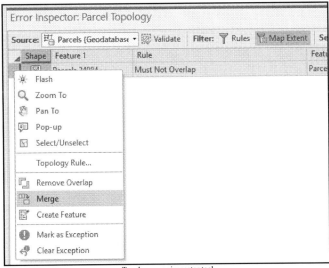

Topology error inspector tool

11. Select **Parcels 24884 (Largest)** and click the **Merge** button in the **Merge** window that appears. This will merge the overlap area with the selected parcel and subtract it from the smaller parcel you did not select, removing the overlap.

    For the sake of this recipe, we chose to merge the overlapping area with the larger parcel polygon for the sake of expediency. Normally you would want to do some research to see which parcel the area should belong to.

When you right-clicked on the row, in the table, a context menu appears. This menu contains many options. The top section of the context menu allows you to navigate to the location of the error. The second section allows you to review the rule the error has violated. The third section contains tools for correcting the error. The tools will vary based on the rule which has been violated and the type of data you are working with.

In this case you had three tools to choose from to fix the error: Remove Overlap, Merge, and Create Feature. You saw how the Merge tool worked, but what about the others? The Remove Overlay will remove the area where two or more polygons overlap one another. This creates a gap between the polygons. The Create Feature tool creates a new polygon from the overlapping area while subtracting that same area from the overlapping polygons.

12. A new dirty area should appear because you just edited the parcels layer but have not validated it. Click on the **Validate** button located at the top of the **Error Inspector** pane. This will remove the dirty area and allow you to see if any new errors have appeared due to your edit.

You should validate your data regularly when using topologies to ensure it remains clean. How often you validate is up to you, but here are some general guidelines: beginner users should probably validate after every edit or correction. More experienced users should validate before they save edits to ensure they are not saving erroneous data back to the geodatabase. Remember, you can always undo up until the last time you saved. Once you save, there is no going back.

13. Click the **Save** button in the **Manage Edits** group on the **Edit** tab.

14. In the **Error Inspector** pane, locate the three errors for **Feature 1** relating to **Parcels 35845**.

15. Click on each error, one at a time. Watch both the map and the **Preview** window at the right side of the **Error Inspector** pane. You should be able to see that each of these errors is related to the same two parcels.

> You can zoom in to get a closer look at each error in the **Preview** window on the **Error Inspector** pane. Simply use the scroll wheel on your mouse to zoom in or out within the **Preview**.

16. Click on the small square located next to the top record for the errors related to **Feature 1 Parcels 35845**. Holding your *Shift* key down, click on the last of the three records relating to **Parcels 35845**. All three errors should now be selected, as illustrated in the following screenshot:

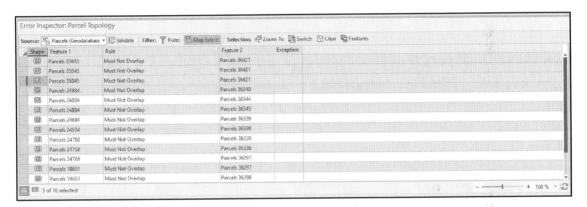

Selecting parcels 35845 in the table

17. In the panel on the right side of the **Error Inspector** pane, where you see the preview, click the **Fix** tab. It should show that you have three errors selected and display two active options: **Create Feature** and **Remove Overlap**. Your research has revealed that these overlapping areas are now easements which are tracked in another layer. So, you will select **Remover Overlap**.

> Merge was grayed out, because that tool requires you to select which feature you are merging the overlapping area into for each error. So, it can be used to perform mass corrections.

You just fixed three errors with a single edit operation. Using these tools to correct your data not only makes your data cleaner but it can be very efficient as well.

18. Validate your data using the **Validate** button at the top of the **Error Inspector** pane. If no new errors are found for the area you just fixed, save your edits.

19. Using the same processes, you have just fixed the remaining errors. Feel free to try different corrective tools in each case to see how they work. Make sure to validate after each corrective action, and to save your edits as you go.

20. If you are not continuing to the next recipe, save your project and close ArcGIS Pro. If you are continuing, leave ArcGIS Pro and the project open.

As you have now seen, the use of geodatabase topologies can greatly increase the overall accuracy of your GIS data and help you locate where errors may exist. The end result is improved data quality and better analysis results. One thing to remember when you want to use geodatabase topologies is you must have a Standard or Advanced ArcGIS Pro license.

Editing data with a map topology

You have now seen how powerful geodatabase topologies can be to help you find and correct errors in your data. However, to use geodatabase topologies, your data must be stored in a geodatabase and you must have a standard or advanced license. So, what do you do if you want to maintain data which is stored in a shapefile so that you do not introduce topological errors, or if you only have a basic license? This is where a Map topology should be used.

As said in the introduction, map topologies are temporary and do not allow you to validate data using rules. What they do allow you to do, though, is edit data using topology tools so that the existing spatial relationships are maintained. This keeps you from introducing any new errors into your data. Map topologies also have the advantage of allowing these topology editing tools to be used on shapefiles and geodatabase feature class-based layers at the same time. Being able to edit multiple layers with single edits, regardless of whether it is a shapefile or geodatabase, can greatly increase your efficiency. Map topologies also do not require all the geodatabase feature classes to be in the same feature dataset within the geodatabase. So, while map topologies do not allow you to validate your data like geodatabase topologies do, they do offer greater data flexibility.

In this recipe, you will use a map topology to edit data in multiple layers with a single edit. A road has been widened to include a turn lane. You need to adjust several layers including, the City Limits, Parcels, Rights of Way, and Voting Districts, to reflect the newly widened road. Several of these layers are in the Trippville GIS geodatabase you have been working with. However, the Voting Districts are stored in a shapefile because the voter registration system, which needs the layer, cannot read a geodatabase.

Getting ready

This recipe can be completed using all license levels of ArcGIS Pro. It is not required that you complete any previous recipes in order to complete this one, though it is recommended that you complete the recipes found in Chapter 1, *ArcGIS Pro Capabilities and Terminology* before starting this recipe to ensure you have the foundational skills required to complete this recipe. You also need to ensure you have installed the sample data for the book.

How to do it...

1. If you closed ArcGIS Pro before starting this recipe, you will need to start ArcGIS Pro. Then open the Topologies.aprx project located in C:\Student\ArcGISProCookbook\Chapter5\Topologies using the skills you have learned in past recipes.
2. If they are still open, close all panes with the exception of the **Contents** and **Catalog** panes.

3. Right-click on the **Parcels** topology group layer, which contains the **Dirty Areas**, **Point Errors**, **Line Errors**, and **Polygon Errors** layers, and select **Remove**, as illustrated in the following screenshot:

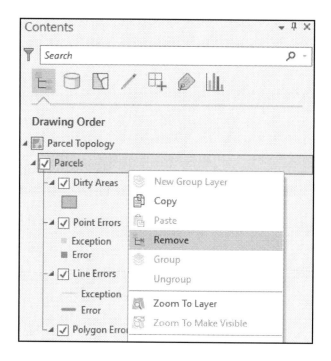

4. Save your project.
5. Click on the the **Add Data** button on the **Map** tab in the **Layer** group in the ribbon.
6. Click on the **Databases** folder located under **Project** in the left panel of the **Add Data** window.
7. Double-click on the **Trippville_GIS.gdb** geodatabase.
8. Double-click on the **Base** feature dataset.
9. Select the **City_Limit** feature class. Then, while holding down the *Ctrl* key, select the **RW** feature class. Then click **OK** to add these new layers to your map.
10. In the **Contents** pane, ensure you are viewing the **List by Drawing Order**. It is the first button on the top left of the pane.
11. Click on the **Symbol** patch, located below the **City_Limit** layer name in the **Contents** pane, to open the Symbology Pane.

12. Ensure you have **Gallery** selected at the top of the pane. Then scroll down and select the symbol named **Black Outline (2 Pts)** located in the **ArcGIS 2D Style**.

At the top of the **Symbology** pane, you should see a **Search** function. This allows you to find a symbol you are looking for using key words or tags. You could type `Black outline 2 pts` into the search to locate the symbol or related symbols.

13. Drag the **City_Limit** layer to the top of the layer list.
14. If desired, change the symbology for the **Parcels** and **RW** layers so you can easily see them.
15. Save your project.
16. In the **Catalog** pane, expand the **Folders** folder so you can see its contents.
17. Expand the **Topologies** folder so you can see its contents. You should see several files in this folder, including **Topologies.gdb**, **Topologies.tbx**, **Voting_Districts.lyrs**, and **Voting Districts.shp**, as shown in the screenshot:

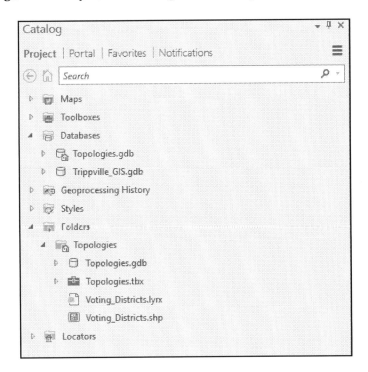

18. Right-click on the **Voting_Districts.lyrx** file and select **Add to Current Map**.

You just added a layer to a map using a layer file. Layer files store configuration settings for a layer so that, when added, they are automatically displayed based on those settings. Layer files can include settings for symbology, labeling, definition queries, scale-visibility ranges, and more. This allows you to standardize layer displays between multiple maps and projects within your organization.

Your map should now look like the following screenshot. Your symbology will most likely be different, depending on the colors ArcGIS Pro assigned when you added the layers and any adjustments you made to the symbology. Remember, ArcGIS Pro assigns a random color to newly added layers:

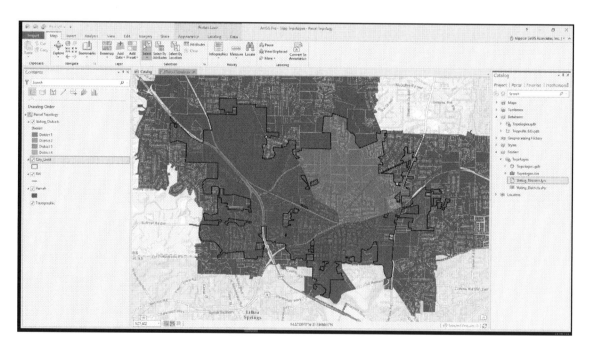

Map with voting districts added

19. Click on the **Map** tab and activate the **Explore** tool.

20. Hold down your *Shift* key so you can zoom in to a specific area. Zoom to the area indicated on the northern side of the City:

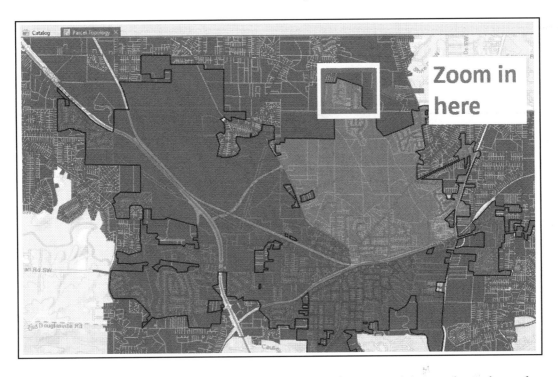

21. Now, save your project to ensure you do not lose any of the work you have done so far.
22. Click on the **List by Selection** button in the **Contents** pane. Make sure all layers are selectable.
23. Click on the **List by Snapping** button in the **Contents** pane and ensure all layers are snappable.
24. Click on the **List by Editing** button in the **Contents** pane and ensure all layers are editable.
25. Click on the **Edit** tab in the ribbon.

26. Click on the topology drop-down list, located in the **Manage Edits** group on the **Edit** tab in the ribbon, and select **Map Topology**, as illustrated:

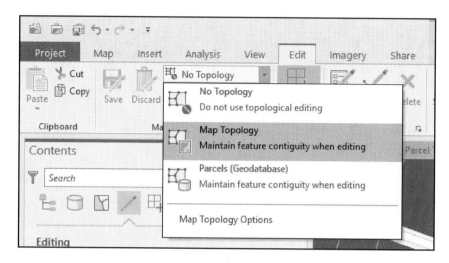

You are now ready to begin editing the layers to reflect the new turn lane that has been added to the entrance of Sweetwater Valley Road. This is a new right-turn lane, allowing cars to safely decelerate before turning, and cars continuing down Clay Road to pass turning cars.

27. Click on the **Select** tool in the **Selection** group on the **Edit** tab.

28. In the map, click and draw a selection rectangle, as illustrated in the following screenshot:

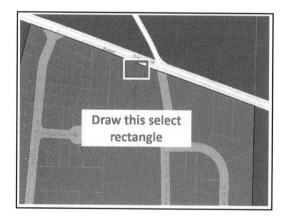

29. Click on the **List by Selection** button in the **Contents** pane. Verify that you have one feature in each layer selected, as shown in the following screenshot:

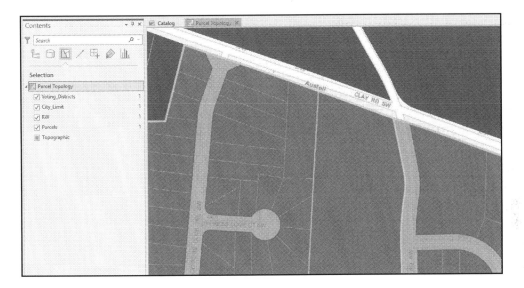

30. Click on the **Reshape** tool, located in the **Tools** group on the **Edit** tab in the ribbon, to open the **Modify Features** pane.

31. Click on the northwestern corner of the parcel, located to the west of Sweetwater Valley Road, as illustrated:

32. Then move your mouse pointer in a southerly direction, along the western boundary of the parcel, and right-click. Select **Direction/Distance** from the context menu that appears, as shown in the following screenshot:

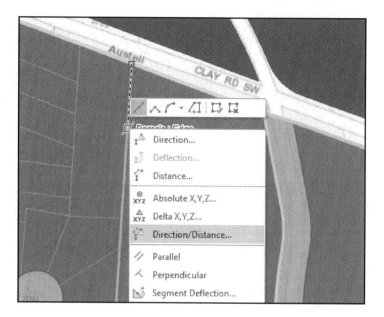

33. Set the **Direction** to be S3-42-19W QB and the Distance to 50.00 FtUS. You may need to press the *Enter* key after entering the distance to apply the values you entered.
34. Move your mouse pointer to the northern boundary of the parcel and right-click. Select **Parallel** from the context menu that appears, as illustrated in the following screenshot:

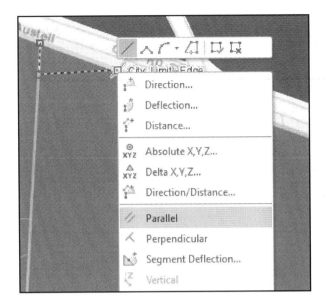

35. Your mouse pointer should now be locked in a direction parallel to the parcel boundary. Move your mouse pointer along that parallel course until it is snapping to the eastern right of way for Sweetwater Valley Road. Click at that location, as shown in the following diagram:

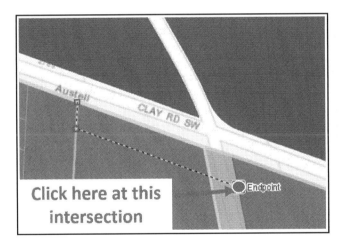

36. Move your mouse pointer until it snaps to the intersection of the eastern right of way for Sweetwater Valley Road and the southern right of way for Clay Rd, as shown in the next screenshot. Double-click when you get to the indicated location to finish your sketch:

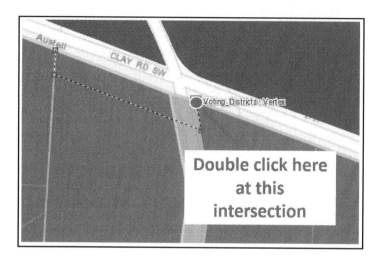

Your map should now show the new area for the new turn lane that was installed, as shown in the following diagram. This new turn lane required you to edit multiple layers. This included all the layers which were in your map. You could have edited each layer individually. However, by using the Map Topology, you were able to edit features in four different layers with a single edit. This included layers which were stored in different data formats as well.

To learn more about using topologies, go to http://pro.arcgis.com/en/pro-app/help/editing/introduction-to-editing-topology.htm.

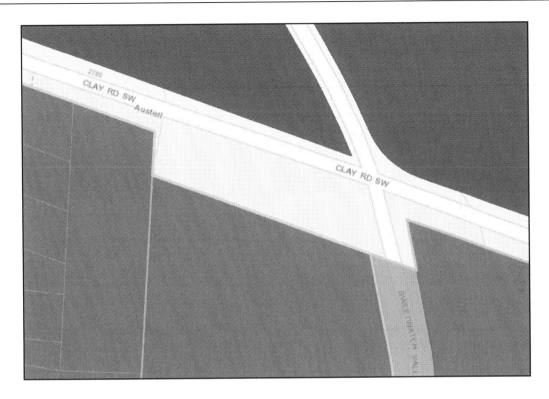

37. Once you verify that your edits were completed successfully, save your edits by clicking on the **Save** button in the **Manage Edits** group on the **Edit** tab.

Remember, saving data edits is different than saving a project. By default, these are two separate operations. Saving the project will save changes you have made to the contents of the project, such as adding a new map, changing the properties of a layer in a map, creating a new layout, and connecting to a new database. Saving the project is done using buttons or commands on the Quick Access Toolbar or the **Project** tab in the ribbon. The **Save** button on the **Edit** tab in the **Manage Edits** group saves changes to the spatial or attribute data referenced in a map or scene. It does not save edits to the project. In the options for ArcGIS Pro, you can enable the saving of edits when you save the project, if desired. Doing so is not a bad idea for new users who are not accustomed to having different saves within a single application.

38. Close the **Modify Features** pane to free up screen area and reduce the computer resources being used by ArcGIS Pro.

39. Save your project to ensure all your project changes are saved.

40. Close ArcGIS Pro.

You have now seen the power of Map topology. It allows you to edit multiple features at one time, regardless of which layer or layers they may be in, as long as they are coincident. This can greatly increase the efficiency of your editing. Unlike Geodatabase topologies, you can use Map topologies in any license level of ArcGIS Pro. The primary limitation of a Map topology is the inability to assign spatial rules and validate your data using the rules, as you can with a Geodatabase topology.

6
Projections and Coordinate System Basics

In this chapter, we will cover the following recipes:

- Determining the coordinate system for an existing map
- Setting the coordinate system for a new map
- Changing the coordinate system for a map
- Defining a coordinate system for data
- Projecting data to different coordinate systems

Introduction

One of the things that makes GIS such a powerful visualization and analytical tool is the ability to overlay multiple layers of information together in a map. Putting our GIS data in real-world coordinate systems and projections is how we are able to do this. By placing our data in a real-world system, we tie it to the Earth. This allows us to locate features anywhere on the Earth's surface and then bring them into a map so we can see how those features are related spatially.

There are two basic types of coordinate systems we can use in ArcGIS Pro, geographic and projected. A geographic coordinate system is based on a 3D model of the earth, called the ellipsoid or spheroid. The ellipsoid is then tied back to the physical Earth by the datum. Geographic coordinate systems use degrees as their primary unit of measurement.

Each degree can then be broken down into different sub-units, such as decimal degrees, minutes, decimal minutes, or minutes, and seconds. You will often hear geographic coordinate systems referred to as **Latitude** and **Longitude**:

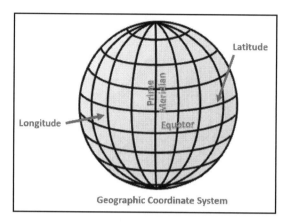

The primarily lines of reference used in a geographic coordinate system are the **Equator** and the **Prime Meridian**. These are the starting points for determining the latitude and longitude values required to locate a feature's position. Geographic coordinate systems can be used to identify the location of a feature on the Earth very accurately. However, as the diagram illustrates, the distance between the lines of latitude and longitude are not consistent. It varies depending where on the Earth you are located. This makes it difficult to measure distances and areas. This is where projected coordinate systems come in.

Projected coordinate systems locate and display data in a 2D plane, using a cartesian coordinate system. This allows us to apply standard units of linear measurement, such as feet and meters. The origin of the projected coordinate system is tied to a geographic coordinate system. This is what ties the projected coordinate system to the earth. From the origin, an x and y axis is defined, along with the units, as illustrated in the following diagram. Because projected coordinate systems use uniform units, we are able to easily measure distances and areas:

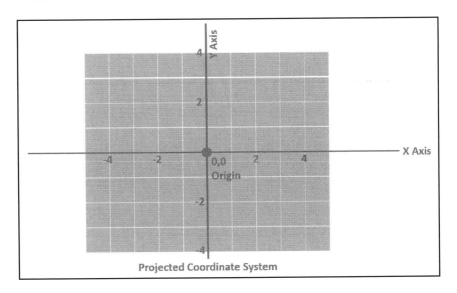

Projected Coordinate System

Of course, taking a 3D surface such as the Earth and flattening it does introduce distortions into our data. So, we have different methods of projecting the data from a 3D model to a 2D plane to reduce these distortions. There are three basic types of projections, planar, conic, and cylindrical. From there they can get more advanced.

As long as all your data is in a real-world coordinate system, regardless of what type, ArcGIS Pro can display it in a single map or scene, even if the layers are in different coordinate systems. It will project the data on the fly in that map or scene to a common coordinate system. So, it is important that all your spatial data is assigned the correct coordinate system. Otherwise your data may be displayed incorrectly and results of your analysis might be incorrect.

In this chapter, you will learn how to work with coordinate systems within ArcGIS Pro. You will start by learning how to determine the coordinate system for an existing map. Then you will learn how to set the coordinate system for a new map. Next, you will learn how to change the coordinate system for an existing map. Then you will learn how to define the coordinate system for data. Lastly you will learn how to project data from one coordinate system to another.

Determining the coordinate system for an existing map

Every map and scene you create in ArcGIS Pro makes use of a coordinate system in order to display data in a location. However, it not only can impact how and where features are displayed, but also what you can do with the map. The coordinate system used by a map can impact if you can share it as a web map via ArcGIS Online, how well layers overlay one another, and more. So, it is important to know what coordinate system your map is using.

The first layer you add to the map will define the coordinate system for that map. But what if you are working with an existing map, maybe one that was created by someone else? How do you determine the coordinate system for the existing map you are working with?

In this recipe, you will learn how to determine which coordinate system has been assigned to an existing map.

Getting ready

This recipe does require the sample data be installed on the computer. You are not required to have completed any previous recipes. However, it is recommended that you complete the recipes in Chapter 1, *ArcGIS Pro Capabilities and Terminology*, or have some experience using ArcGIS Pro before you start this recipe. You can complete this recipe with any ArcGIS Pro licensing level.

How to do it...

1. Please start by launching ArcGIS Pro using skills learned in Chapter 1, *ArcGIS Pro Capabilities and Terminology*, or based on your prior user experience.
2. In the **ArcGIS Pro** start window, click on **Open another project**:

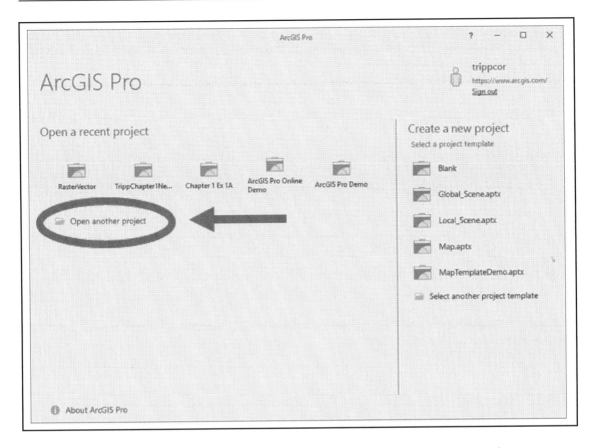

3. Select **Computer** from the **Open** window, and then click **Browse** in the area on the right.

4. Navigate to
   C:\Student\ArcGISProCookbook\Chapter6\CoordinateSystems by clicking on C:\ in the area on the left of the **Open Project** window. Then double-click on the **Student**, **ArcGISProCookbook**, **Chapter6**, and **CoordinateSystems** folders.

5. Select the **CoordinateSystems.aprx** project file and click **OK**.

The project will open with the Basic Map of Trippville visible. This is an existing map, which was obviously created by someone else:

6. Look down at the bottom of the **Map** view, and you should see a small status bar. This displays the current scale of the map, buttons to enable functionality, the coordinate display, and more:

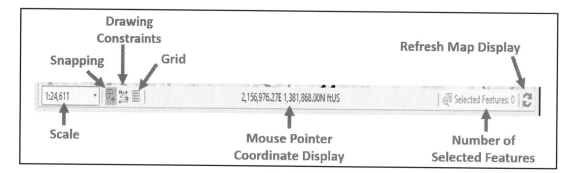

7. Move your mouse pointer around within the map while watching the Mouse Pointer Coordinate Display. Then answer the question ahead:

 Question: What units are being displayed in the map?

Answer:

As you moved your mouse within the map while watching the coordinate display, you should have seen the values change. The first value displayed is the X value for the location of your mouse pointer within the map. The second value is the Y value for the location of your pointer. The display is in US feet, as indicated by the **ftUS** located to the right of the coordinates.

 When working with projected coordinate systems, you may see the X value also referred to as the **Easting** and the Y as the **Northing**.

Looking at the values in the coordinate display can help you determine what type of coordinate system your map may be in, Geographic or Projected. X values greater than 180 and Y values greater than 90 might indicate that your map is using a projected coordinate system.

You can control the units used in the Mouse Pointer Coordinate Display within the **Map Properties** window. In the **General** option, you can set the display units to be any value you wish. This can differ from the primary Map Units, which are based on the coordinate system assigned to the map.

Now, it is time to determine exactly what coordinate system is being used in the Basic Map of Trippville.

8. In the **Contents** pane, right-click on the **Basic Map of Trippville**, and select **Properties** from the menu that appears, as illustrated:

9. In the **General** option in the **Map Properties** window, review the various settings and answer the following questions:

> **Question**: What are the Map Units?

> **Answer**:
>
> **Question**: What are the Display Units?
>
> **Answer**:

10. Click on the **Coordinate Systems** option in the left panel of the **Map Properties** window.

11. Look in the right panel of the **Map Properties** window, under **Current XY Coordinate System**. Answer the question that follows:

> **Question**: What is the Current XY Coordinate System for the map?
>
> **Answer**:

12. Click on **Details**, located just beside the **Current XY**, as shown in the following screenshot:

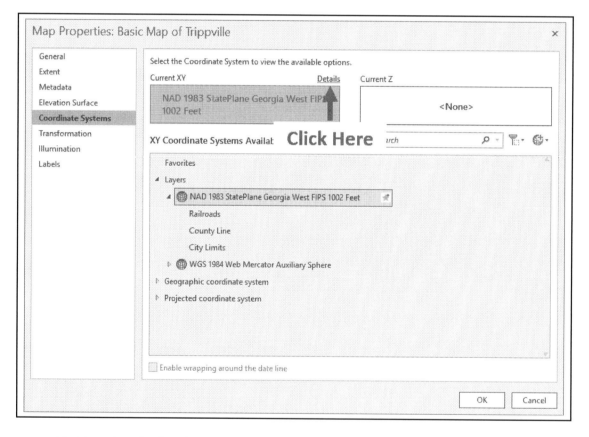

13. Examine the details associated with the coordinate system assigned to the map. Answer the following questions:

Question: What type of coordinate system is being used?

Answer:

Question: What datum is being used by the assigned coordinate system?

Answer:

Question: What spheroid or ellipsoid is referenced for the assigned coordinate system?

Answer:

As you can now see, the map is using the Georgia State Plane West Zone, which references the North American Datum of 1983 (NAD 83). This is a projected coordinate system that uses the GRS 80 spheroid.

14. Close the **Coordinate System Details** and **Map Properties** windows.
15. Save your project.
16. If you are not continuing to the next recipe you can close ArcGIS Pro. If you are continuing, keep ArcGIS Pro open.

You now know how to determine the coordinate system for an existing map. It is important to know what coordinate system you are working with because it forms the foundation for how layers interact with each other spatially. If a map is not assigned a coordinate system, then you will not be able to bring layers together into a single map and expect them to overlay one another properly.

Setting the coordinate system for a new map

You now know how to determine the coordinate system assigned to existing maps. But how do you assign one to a new map? That is pretty easy. As was mentioned earlier, the first layer you add to a new map will set the coordinate system for the map.

In this recipe, you will create a new map in the project you used in the previous recipe. You will then see what coordinate system has been assigned to the new map. Next, you will add a new layer to the map and see what that does to the coordinate system for your map. Lastly, you will add another layer to the map that is in a different coordinate system, and check to see if that changes the coordinate system for your map.

Getting ready

This recipe does require the sample data be installed on the computer. It is recommended that you complete the previous recipe in this chapter along with the recipes in `Chapter 1`, *ArcGIS Pro Capabilities and Terminology*, before you begin this recipe. This will ensure that you have the necessary skills and understanding required to complete this recipe successfully. You can complete this recipe with any ArcGIS Pro licensing level.

How to do it...

1. If you closed ArcGIS Pro before starting this recipe, you will need to start ArcGIS Pro. Then, open the `CoordinateSystems.aprx` project located in `C:\Student\ArcGISProCookbook\Chapter6\CoordinateSystems` using the skills you have learned in past recipes.
2. Click on the **Insert** tab in the ribbon.
3. Click on the **New Map** button located on the **Project** group in the **Insert** tab. As you have seen demonstrated in past recipes, this will create a new blank 2D map in your project. The new map should automatically be opened and named **Map**.
4. In the **Contents** pane, right-click on the **Map** and select **Properties** from the menu that appears, as illustrated in the following screenshot:

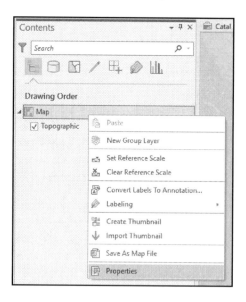

5. Click on **Coordinate** system in the panel located on the left of the **Map Properties** window. Then answer the following question:

Question: What coordinate system is currently assigned to the new map you just created?

Answer:

As you can see, the new map you added has been assigned a coordinate system even though you have not added a layer yet. The assigned coordinate system is based on the basemap which is automatically added by default. If the basemap is one of the Esri provided ones from ArcGIS Online, then the coordinate system assigned to your map will be the WGS 1984 Web Mercator (Auxiliary Sphere).

WGS 1984 Web Mercator (Auxiliary Sphere) is the standard coordinate system used by most commercial web mapping systems, including Google Maps, Bing Maps, and Esri ArcGIS Online content.

If you are using a custom basemap, the coordinate system will be whatever is assigned to the custom basemap. If you have configured ArcGIS Pro to not automatically use a basemap, the coordinate system will be undefined.

Now, let's see what happens when you add a layer to your new map.

6. Close the **Map Properties** window by clicking **Cancel**.
7. In the **Catalog** pane, expand the **Databases** folder so that you can see its contents.
8. Expand the **Trippville_GIS.gdb** geodatabase.
9. Right-click on the **Zoning** feature class and select **Add to Current Map**.
10. Save your project.

6. In the **Contents** pane, right-click on the **Zoning** layer that you just added, and select **Properties** from the menu that appears.

7. In the left panel, select the **Source** option, as illustrated on in the following screenshot:

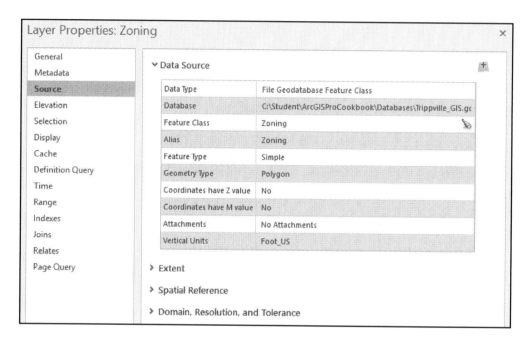

13. In the right panel, scroll down until you see the **Spatial Reference** option.

14. Expand the **Spatial Reference** by clicking on the small arrowhead located to the left so that you can see its contents.

15. Examine the **Spatial Reference** information for the layer and answer the following question:

Question: What is the Projected Coordinate System for the Zoning layer?

Answer:

Close the **Layer Properties** window by clicking **Cancel**.

16. Right-click on **Map** in the **Contents** pane, as illustrated in the following screenshot:

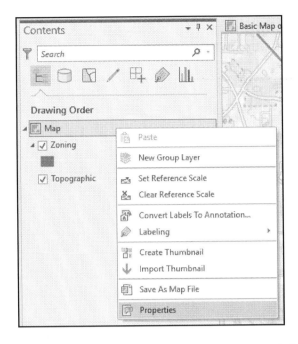

17. Select the **Coordinate System** option in the panel on the left of the **Map Properties** window.

18. Look at the area below **Current XY** in the right panel, then answer the following questions:

> **Question**: What is the coordinate system assigned to the map?
>
> **Answer**:

> **Question**: Has the coordinate system for the map changed since you added the new layer?
>
> **Answer**:

As you can see, the coordinate system for your map has changed. It is now using the NAD 1983 State Plane Georgia West FIPS 1002 Feet coordinate system. Now, let's see if it changes again if you add another layer to the map:

19. Close the **Map Properties** window by clicking **Cancel**.

20. In the **Catalog** pane, expand the **Folders** folder so that you can see its contents.
21. Expand the **Coordinate System** folder to see its contents.
22. Select the **Elevation Contours** shapefile, and drag and drop it into the map. This will add it as a new layer to your map.
23. Using the same method you used for the **Zoning** layer, examine the spatial reference for the **Elevation Contours** layer. Then answer the following question:

Question: What coordinate system is assigned to the Elevation Contours layer?

Answer:

24. Close the **Layer Properties** window.
25. Open the **Properties** for the **Map** again using the same method you used in *step 17* of this recipe. Verify the coordinate system used by the map, and answer the following question:

Question: Did the coordinate system for your map change again?

Answer:

Even though the Elevation Contours layer is in the GCS WGS 1984 Geographic Coordinate system, the coordinate system for your map has not changed. Only the first layer added to a map will change the coordinate system. All other layers are projected on the fly to match the coordinate system of the map:

26. Close the **Map Properties** window.
27. Save your project.
28. If you are not continuing to the next recipe, you may close ArcGIS Pro. Otherwise keep it open.

You can now set the coordinate system for any new map that you create. This is important for the same reason that you need to know the coordinate system of any existing map you may work with: GIS is reliant on the use of real world coordinate systems to properly display the location of data within our maps. As long as the data we use is in and properly assigned the correct coordinate system, ArcGIS Pro is able display the data in the common coordinate system we assign to a map.

Changing the coordinate system of a map

You now know how to determine the coordinate system for an existing map, and how to set one for a new map. But how do you change the coordinate system for a map or scene?

You might be wondering why you would want to change the coordinate system for a map. There are several reasons why you might want to change the coordinate system assigned to a map. As mentioned in the introduction, some coordinate systems are better suited for specific operations. If you need to measure areas or distances for analysis or editing, a projected coordinate system is best, especially for small areas such as a county, city, or district. If you are trying to show locations of features across large areas, such as a country or the world, then a geographic coordinate system is often best. If you are publishing as a web map then it might require the map be in the WGS 1984 Web Mercator (Auxiliary Sphere) coordinate system to conform with other datasets. So, if you need to do one of these and your map is in a different coordinate system, you might need to change it. Luckily it is not hard to change the coordinate system for a map, as you are about to see.

Changing the coordinate system for a map does not change the coordinate system for the underlying data referenced in the map. This means that if you have a shapefile in your map as a layer, and that shapefile is in NAD 83 UTM Zone 16N Meters, then if you change the Map Coordinate system to the WGS 1984 Web Mercator (Auxiliary Sphere), this will not change the coordinate system the shapefile is stored in. In other words, changing the coordinate system of the map does not project the data it references to a new coordinate system. You will learn how to project data to a different coordinate system later in this chapter.

In this recipe, you will learn how you can change the coordinate system used within a map.

Getting ready

It is recommended that you complete all previous recipes in this chapter before starting this one. That will ensure that you have the basic knowledge and understanding required to successfully complete this recipe. This recipe can be completed with all license levels of ArcGIS Pro. You do need to have the sample data installed as well.

How to do it...

1. If you closed ArcGIS Pro before starting this recipe, you will need to start ArcGIS Pro and open the `CoordinateSystems.aprx` project located in `C:\Student\ArcGISProCookbook\Chapter6\CoordinateSystems` using the skills you have learned in past recipes. If you are continuing from the previous recipe, the project should already be open and you can continue to the next step.

2. Make sure the Basic Map of Trippville is the active map in the map view. If the map is still open, click on the tab for the **Basic Map of Trippville** at the top of the map view area, as illustrated in the following screenshot. If you closed the map during a past recipe, you will need to reopen it. To reopen the map, expand the **Maps** folder in the **Catalog** pane. Then right-click on the **Basic Map of Trippville** in the **Maps** folder and select Open from the menu that appears, as illustrated:

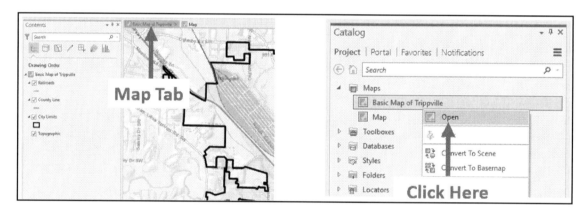

Activating the map or opening it if needed

3. Move your mouse pointer to the approximate center of the map and answer the question. Try to remember the location you use. You will need to know it for a later task in this recipe.

Question: What is the x and y coordinate for the location of your mouse pointer? (Remember, you can get this value from the status bar at the bottom of the map view.)

Answer:

As you can see, the x coordinate will be somewhere around a value of 2,150,000, and the y coordinate somewhere around a value of 1,390,000. Of course, your values will be different, but should be in the general ballpark:

4. Right-click on the **Basic Map of Trippville** in the **Contents** pane, as shown in the following screenshot, and select **Properties**:

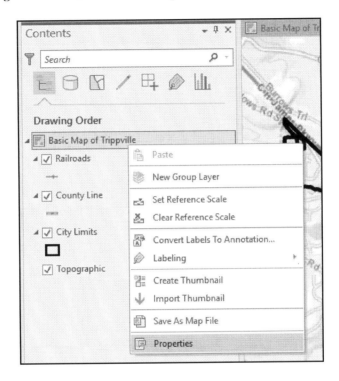

 You can also just double-click on the map name in the **Contents** pane to open the map properties. This also works with layers.

5. Click on the **Coordinate Systems** option in the left panel of the **Map Properties** pane. It should look like the following:

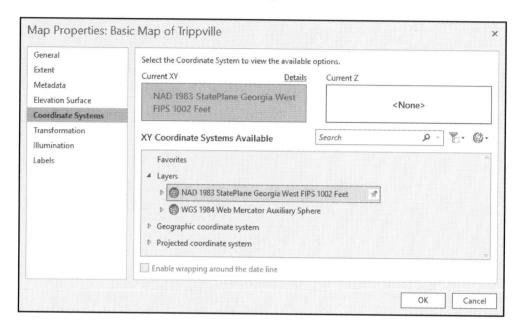

You are going to change the map's coordinate system from the NAD 1983 State Plane Georgia West FIPS 1002 Feet to the WGS 1984 Web Mercator (Auxiliary Sphere) so it will be ready to publish as a web map later:

6. Expand the **Projected coordinate system** option by clicking on the small arrowhead located to the left of it.

7. Scroll down to **World** and expand it as well.

8. Scroll down until you see WGS 1984 Web Mercator (auxiliary sphere). It will be located near the bottom of the list.

9. Select the WGS 1984 Web Mercator (auxiliary sphere) from the list. Your **Current XY** value should change to reflect the coordinate system you selected, as shown in the following screenshot:

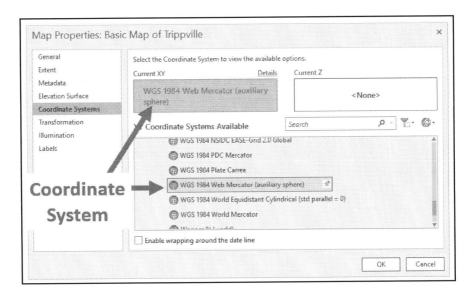

10. Once you have verified that you have selected the correct coordinate system, click **OK** to apply the change.

11. Save your project.

12. Now move your mouse pointer to approximately the same location that you used in *step 3* as the estimated center of the map.

13. Compare the results to those you got in *step 3*, and answer the following question:

Question: Are the coordinates for the approximate center of the map different now that you have changed the coordinate system?

Answer:

As you can see, the coordinates for the approximate center of the map have indeed changed. They are very different. But has this also changed the coordinate system for the layers and their source data? It was said earlier that they should not have changed, but let's verify just to make sure:

14. In the **Contents** pane, open the **Properties** for the **City Limits** layer using skills you have learned in past recipes.

You access the properties for a layer the same way you access the properties for a map.

15. Click on the **Source** option located in the left panel of the **Layer Properties** window.

16. Scroll down in the right panel until you see **Spatial Reference**. Then expand **Spatial Reference** by clicking on the small arrowhead.

17. Look at the **Project Coordinate System** assigned to the **City Limits** layer. Then answer the following question:

> **Question**: Is the coordinate system assigned to the layer the same or different from the map?
>
> **Answer**:

18. Close the **Layer Properties** window by clicking **Cancel**.

19. If you are not continuing to the next recipe, save your project and close ArcGIS Pro. If you are continuing, leave ArcGIS Pro and the project open.

As you have just verified, the coordinate system for the layer source has not changed. It is still being stored in the same coordinate system it has always been in. So just changing the coordinate system for the map does not change the source data's coordinate system. It only changes how it is displayed in that specific map. ArcGIS Pro projects the data on the fly from the coordinate system it is stored in to that the map is displaying. This is very useful when working with data from multiple organizations which may not use the same coordinate system as yours. One thing to remember though is that projecting on the fly does use more computer resources and will slow down the rendering of the data every time you pan or zoom in the map.

Defining a coordinate system for data

You now know how to assign and change the coordinate system used in a map. Maps are not the only thing that are assigned a coordinate system. Our data is also assigned a coordinate system, or at least it should be. If your data is not assigned a coordinate system then ArcGIS Pro may not be able to display the correct location with all your other data. This is also true if your data is assigned the wrong coordinate system.

Where is the coordinate system information stored within your data? Well, that depends on what type of data you are working with. If it is a feature class stored in a geodatabase, then the coordinate system information is stored within the geodatabase itself. If you are working with shapefiles, then the assigned coordinate system is stored in a file with a .prj file extension.

If you are working with CAD data, meaning .dwg, .dxf, or .dgn files, then you will also need a .prj file in order for ArcGIS Pro to know what coordinate system it is in. While some CAD files can be assigned a coordinate system within the drawing itself, ArcGIS Pro cannot access that part of the file, so you must have an external .prj file.

As you saw in Chapter 2, *Creating and Storing Data*, in the *Creating a new Geodatabase* recipe, when you create a new feature class in a geodatabase, you are asked to assign the coordinate system as part of the Create Feature Class tool. So, in most cases, when you create new feature classes or shapefiles, you will assign the coordinate system for that data as you create it. However, you will find that many existing or legacy datasets do not have a coordinate system defined. This is true mostly for shapefiles and CAD files.

Just because a dataset does not have an assigned coordinate system does not mean it was not created in a real-world coordinate system. The majority of all shapefiles are created in a real-world coordinate system. They are just missing the .prj file required by ArcGIS Pro and other Esri products to know what the coordinate system is. The same is true of many CAD files as well, though you will encounter a larger number of CAD files that are not in a real-world coordinate system. You will learn more about that in a later chapter. If the data that is missing from the coordinate system was created in the same coordinate system as the rest of your data, you can still use it for maps, to perform analysis, and more, without defining the coordinate system for the data. It is when you try to mix data in different coordinate systems that you will start to encounter problems if you try to publish the data to a web service or convert it to another format. So, it is generally considered best practice to always define a coordinate system for all your data.

In this recipe, you will learn how to define a coordinate system for data that does not have one. In this case, it will be a CAD file that was created in a real-world coordinate system, which is different from all your other data.

Getting ready

It is recommended that you complete all the recipes in Chapter 2, *Creating and Storing Data*, of this cookbook before you begin this recipe. Chapter 2, *Creating and Storing Data*, will provide you with a better understanding of data and how it is created in ArcGIS Pro. That lays part of the foundational understanding needed to work and understand this recipe.

This recipe can be completed with all license levels of ArcGIS Pro. You will need to ensure the sample data is also installed before starting.

How to do it...

1. If you closed ArcGIS Pro before starting this recipe, you will need to start ArcGIS Pro. Once ArcGIS Pro has started, open the `CoordinateSystems.aprx` project located in `C:\Student\ArcGISProCookbook\Chapter6\CoordinateSystems` using the skills you have learned in past recipes. If you are continuing from the previous recipe, the project should already be open and you can continue.

2. Make sure the **Basic Map of Trippville** is the active map in the map view. If you are not sure how to do this, refer back to *step 2* in the previous recipe.

3. In the **Catalog** pane, expand the **Folders** folder so you can see its contents.

4. Expand the **CoordinateSystems** folder.

5. Expand the **Northern Subdivision.DWG** file. This is an AutoCAD drawing file that contains information about a new subdivision being built near the City of Trippville.

6. Right-click on the **Polyline** feature class within the **Northern Subdivision.DWG** file and select **Add to Current Map**.

The new layer should appear in the **Contents** pane, however, you will not see it drawn in your map. You will now begin to investigate why:

7. Right-click on the **Northern Subdivision–Polyline** layer and select **Zoom to Layer**, as illustrated:

8. Move your mouse pointer to the map view and watch the map display the coordinate readout in the Status Bar at the bottom of the map view.

As you can see, the layer was drawn in the map. It is just not appearing in the right location. Let's continue to investigate a little more to see why it is not drawing the layer in the correct location in relation to all your other data:

9. Double-click on the **Northern Subdivision-Polyline** layer to open the **Layer Properties** window.
10. Select the **Source** option from the panel on the left side of the window.
11. Scroll down in the panel on the right until you see **Spatial Reference**.
12. Expand the **Spatial Reference** and answer the following question:

Question: What is the coordinate system assigned to the Northern Subdivision–Polyline layer?

Answer:

As you can see, ArcGIS Pro indicates that this new layer has an Unknown Coordinate System. This means that as far as ArcGIS Pro is concerned, the data is not in a real-world coordinate system. However, after talking with the person that created the drawing file, you have found out it is in the UTM 16N coordinate system. ArcGIS Pro just does not know this because there is no projection file to tell it that the data is in that coordinate system. You need to create the projection file for the drawing file:

13. Click on the **Analysis** tab in the ribbon.
14. Click on the **Tools** button located in the **Geoprocessing** group in the **Analysis** tab. This will open the **Geoprocessing** pane.

15. In the **Geoprocessing** pane, click on the **Toolboxes** tab near the top. This will display all the system toolboxes included in ArcGIS Pro.

16. Expand the **Data Management** toolbox.

17. Select the **Define Projection** tool, as indicated:

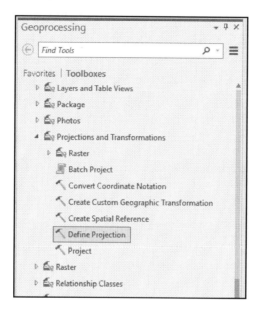

18. Scroll down until you see the **Projections and Transformations** toolset.

19. For the **Input Dataset or Feature Class**, click on the drop-down arrow and select the **Northern Subdivision–Polygon** layer from the list.

20. For the **Coordinate System**, click on the Select Coordinate System icon, which looks like a small wireframe globe. This will open the **Coordinate System** window.

21. In the area available under **XY Coordinate Systems Available**, expand the projected coordinate systems, as illustrated in the following screenshot:

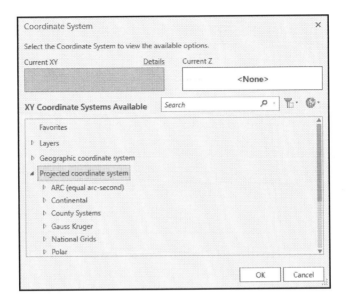

22. Scroll down the list and expand **UTM**.

23. Scroll down and expand **NAD 1983**.

24. Scroll down and select **NAD 1983 UTM Zone 16N**, as shown in the following screenshot, then click **OK**:

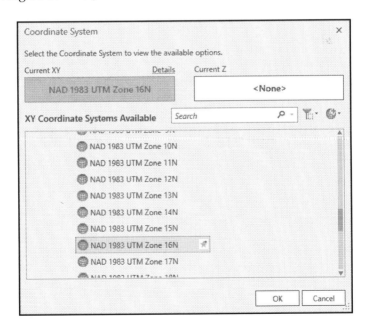

25. Verify that your **Define Projection** tool looks like the screenshot, and click on **Run**:

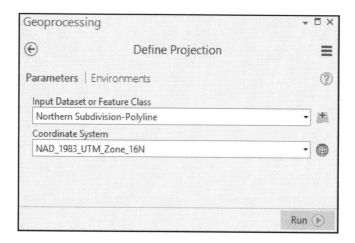

When the Define Projection tools completes, the Northern Subdivision–Polyline layer should disappear from view in the map:

26. Right-click on the **Northern Subdivision–Polyline** layer in the **Contents** pane and select **Zoom to Layer**. If necessary, zoom out using the scroll wheel on your mouse so that you can see the layer in relation to the other layers.

Your map view should look similar to the following screenshot. The new subdivision is located due north of the City of Trippville. This is the correct location. Remember that your colors and scale might be different:

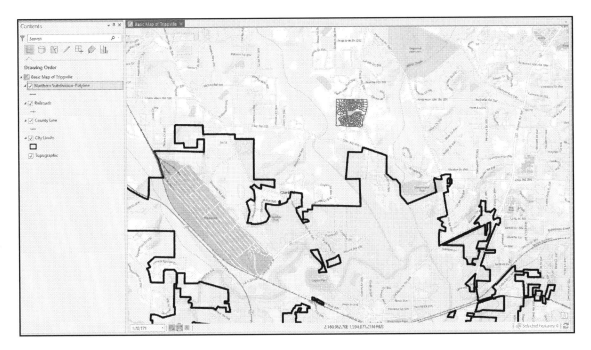

New subdivision shown in the correct location in relation to the City of Trippville

The layer is now showing up in the correct location because you defined the coordinate system, creating the .prj file for the drawing file referenced by the layer. This allowed ArcGIS Pro to project the layer from NAD 1983 UTM 16N coordinate system, which the data was created in, to NAD 1983 State Plane GA West, which is used by the map. ArcGIS Pro does project the data on the fly once the coordinate system is defined:

27. Close the **Geoprocessing** pane to free up screen space.

The Define Projection tool will also assign a coordinate system and generate a .prj file for shapefiles, DXF, and DGN files. You do need to ensure that the data is in a real-world coordinate system and what that coordinate system is before you use the tool. The Define Projection tool will not georeference data that was not created in a real-world coordinate system, nor will it project data from one coordinate system to another.

28. Save your project to ensure you do not lose any of your work.

29. If you are not continuing to the next recipe, close ArcGIS Pro. If you are continuing, keep ArcGIS Pro open.

This recipe illustrates the importance of having a coordinate system assigned to your GIS data. As you saw, without it, the data will not display in the correct location. This makes it impossible to use as part of a map or to perform analysis. It is also not unusual to get data which has been assigned the wrong coordinate system. The behavior and process described in this recipe can also be used to assign the correct coordinate system to data that has been wrongly assigned.

Projecting data to different coordinate systems

You now know how to change the coordinate system for a map, and how to assign one to data that is missing a coordinate system. But how do you change the coordinate system for data? That process is called projecting data.

When you need to move or project data from one coordinate system to another, it requires a lot more than just redefining the assigned coordinate system like you did in the previous recipe. It requires ArcGIS Pro to recalculate all the coordinate values for the features within that dataset. This means all those features will have new coordinates that represent values in the coordinate system it has moved to. To calculate the new coordinate values, ArcGIS Pro must perform many calculations for each feature to account for possible changes in datums, units, reference locations, earth models, and more. So, it can take a long time for larger datasets.

The tool you use to move data from one coordinate system to another is the Project tool. This tool is located in the Data Management Tools toolbox and the Projections and Transformations toolset. In this recipe, you will use the Project tool to move data from one coordinate system to another. You will project the Trippville City Limits from its current coordinate system to the WGS 1984 Web Mercator (Auxiliary Sphere) coordinate system for publishing to ArcGIS Online.

Getting ready

As with the previous recipe, it is recommended that you complete all the recipes in Chapter 2, *Creating and Storing Data*, of this cookbook before you work with this recipe. Chapter 2, *Creating and Storing Data*, will provide you with a better understanding of data and how it is created in ArcGIS Pro. That lays part of the foundational understanding needed to work through and understand this recipe.

This recipe can be completed with all license levels of ArcGIS Pro. To complete the last part of this recipe you will also need a connection to ArcGIS Online. Your user account will need to be tier two and have publisher rights.

How to do it...

1. If you closed ArcGIS Pro before starting this recipe, you will need to start ArcGIS Pro. Then open the `CoordinateSystems.aprx` project located in `C:\Student\ArcGISProCookbook\Chapter6\CoordinateSystems` using the skills you have learned in past recipes. If you did not close ArcGIS Pro when you completed the previous recipe, the project should already be open and you can continue.

2. Make sure the **Basic Map of Trippville** is the active map in the map view. If you are not sure how to do this, refer back to *step 2* in the *Changing the coordinate system of a map* recipe located in this chapter.

3. In the **Contents** pane, double-click on the **City Limits** layer to open the **Layer Properties**.

4. Click on the **Source** option in the left panel of the window.

5. In the right panel of the **Layer Properties** window, scroll through the options until you get to **Spatial Reference**.

6. Expand the **Spatial Reference** option and answer the following question:

> **Question**: What is the Projected Coordinate system for the City Limits layer?
>
> **Answer**:

You can see that the City Limits layer is being stored in the NAD 1983 State Plane Georgia West coordinate system. You want to project this layer so that it is in the WGS 1984 Web Mercator (Auxiliary Sphere) coordinate system, so it will be easier to integrate with other online content. The WGS 1984 Web Mercator (Auxiliary Sphere) coordinate system is the one used by most public mapping websites, such as Google Earth, Bing Maps, and Esri ArcGIS Online:

7. Close the **Layer Properties** window by clicking **Cancel**.

8. Click on the **Analysis** tab in the ribbon.

9. Click on the **Tools** button, in the **Geoprocessing** group on the **Analysis** tab, to open the **Geoprocessing** pane.

10. Click on the **Toolboxes** tab at the top of the **Geoprocessing** pane, as shown in the following screenshot:

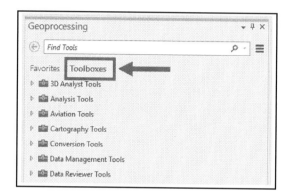

11. Expand the **Data Management Tools** toolbox by clicking on the small arrowhead located next to it.
12. Scroll down and expand the **Projections and Transformations** Toolset by clicking on the small arrowhead next to it.
13. Click on the **Project** tool to open it.

The Batch Project tool does the same thing as the Project tool, but allows you to input multiple feature classes or datasets.

14. Click on the drop-down arrow for the **Input Dataset or Feature Class** and select **City Limits** from the list.
15. Click on the **Browse** button located to the right of the **Output Dataset or Feature Class** cell, as indicated:

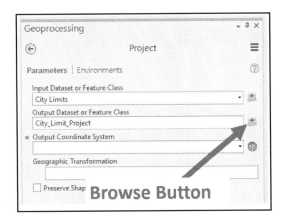

16. In the **Output Dataset or Feature Class** window, select **Databases** from the panel on the left. You may need to expand the **Project** option first.

17. Double-click on the **Trippville_GIS.gdb** geodatabase in the right panel.

18. In the **Name** cell located at the bottom, type City_Limits_Web.

19. Verify, your **Output Dataset or Feature Class** window looks like the following screenshot, and click **Save**:

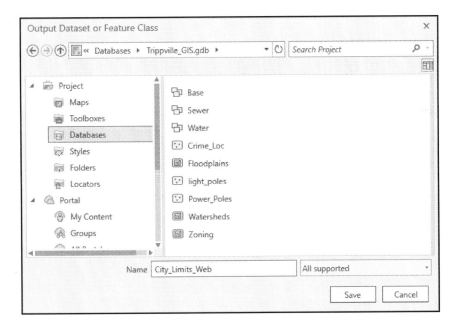

20. Click on the small wireframe globe, located to the right of the **Output Coordinate System**, to open the **Coordinate System** window.
21. In the bottom panel, expand the **Projected coordinate systems**.
22. Scroll through the list of the different types of projected coordinate systems until you see **World**. Expand the **World** option so you can see its contents.
23. Scroll down until you see **WGS 1984 Web Mercator (auxiliary sphere)** and select it.
24. Verify that your **Coordinate System** window looks like the screenshot and click **OK**:

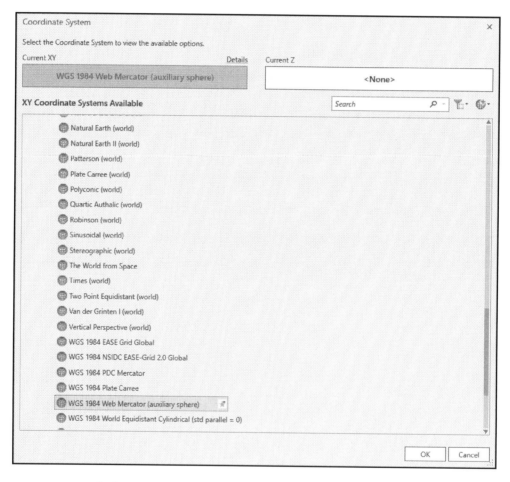

Coordinate system window, selecting the WGS 84 Web Mercator (auxiliary sphere) coordinate system

25. Verify that your **Project** tool looks like the following screenshot, then click on the **Run** button at the bottom. The new City_Limits_Web layer will be added to your map when it is complete:

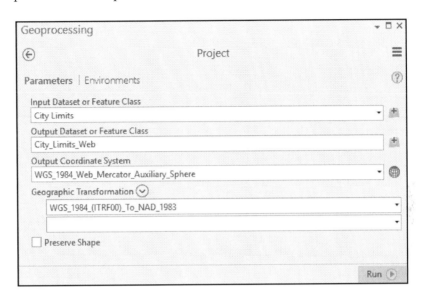

Notice that a Geographic Transformation is automatically applied. Transformations apply mathematical adjustments when projecting data, to account for differences in datums. The original coordinate system for the City Limits layer referenced the North American Datum of 1983 (NAD 1983). The WGS 1984 Web Mercator (auxiliary sphere) coordinate system references the WGS 84 datum. While these are both Earth-centered datums, they are slightly different. That difference must be accounted for when the data is projected. That is what the transformation does.

Also, note that the Project tool creates a new feature class, leaving the original one intact. This provides a safety net in case you were to select the wrong output coordinate system:

26. Close the **Geoprocessing** pane when the **Project** tool is complete and save your project.

27. Right-click on the **City_Limits_Web** layer in the **Contents** pane and select **Copy**, as illustrated in the following screenshot:

28. Click on the **Insert** tab in the ribbon.
29. Select the **New map** button in the **Project** group on the **Insert** tab to add a new map to your project.
30. Right-click on the **Map** in the **Content** pane and select **Paste**, as shown in the following screenshot:

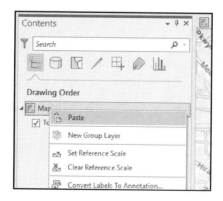

If the Paste option is grayed out, you may need to go back to the Basic Map of Trippville and copy the layer again.

31. Click on the **Share** tab in the ribbon.
32. Click on the **Web Layer** button located in the **Share As** group on the **Share** tab. This will open the **Share as Web Layer** tool pane.

If this button is grayed out or not accessible, it may be because you are not logged in to ArcGIS Online. Look in the upper-right corner of the ArcGIS Pro interface. If it says **Sign in**, you are not connected to ArcGIS Online and need to do so. Click on **Sign in** to **log in** to your ArcGIS Online account.

33. In the **Name** cell, type `City_of_Trippville_Limits`.

Spaces and special characters are not allowed in the name of a web layer, with the exception of an underscore.

34. Ensure **Layer Type** is set to **Feature**.
35. Type the following for the **Description**: `This layer represents the current boundary for the City of Trippville`.
36. Type the following for **Tags**, and make sure to press the *Enter* key between each one: `Trippville, City, Boundary, Limits`.
37. Set your **Sharing Options** as desired. If you are using your organization's primary ArcGIS Online account, it is probably best to leave it set to **My Content** only, otherwise other users in your organization may see and have access to the layer you are about to share.

38. Verify that your **Share As a Web** layer tool looks like the following screenshot, then click the **Configuration** tab located near the top of the pane:

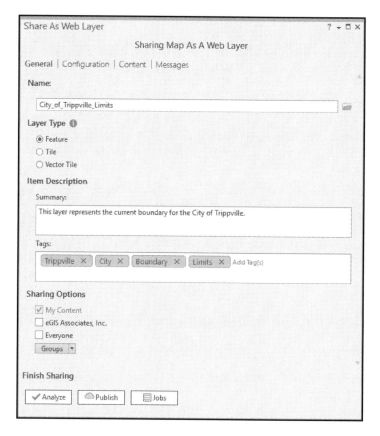

Share Map As Web Layer window

39. Review the options under **Configuration**; you are not going to change these. When you are done reviewing the options, click on the **Content** tab near the top of the pane.

40. Verify that your **Web Layer** will include the **City_of_Trippville_Limits** with the **City_Limits_Web**.

41. Click the **Analyze** button at the bottom of the pane to see if there are any issues that might prevent the web layer from being published successfully.

You should get two warnings, as illustrated in the screenshot. Warnings are signified by exclamation points in a yellow triangle. Warnings indicate something that violates recommended settings or practices, but which will not stop the web layer from publishing. Errors, on the other hand, will cause the publishing of the web layer to fail:

The first warning, as shown, indicates that a layer is missing a feature template. Since you are not allowing editing of this layer when it is published to the web, this is not going to be a problem and can be ignored. The second warning, indicating that the layer's data source is not supported, is referring to the Basemap. We are not concerned with the basemap since one can be added in ArcGIS Online if you use the City_Limits_Web layer in a web map. You will learn more about creating web maps in Chapter 12, *Introducing ArcGIS Online* and Chapter 13, *Publishing Your Own Content to ArcGIS Online*. These warnings should not adversely impact the publishing of the layer to the web.

42. Click the **Publish** button at the bottom of the **Share As Web Layer** pane. This will publish this layer to ArcGIS Online. Depending on your web connection, this operation might take some time to complete.

43. Once the tool has successfully published the web layer, click on **Manage the web layer**, located at the bottom of the tool, as illustrated in the following screenshot. This will launch your web browser and take you to your ArcGIS Online login screen:

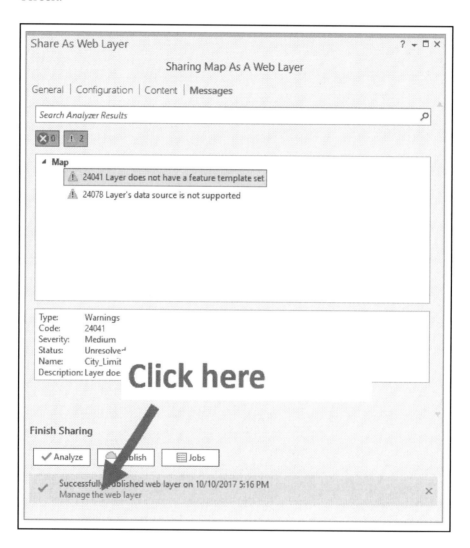

44. Log in into your ArcGIS Online account, as shown in the following screenshot:

ArcGIS Online Login page

You should now see the properties associated with the web layer that you just published. The web layer is a copy of your data now stored in ArcGIS Online and served out as a web feature service. Now, let's look at the web layer you just published in the ArcGIS Online Map Viewer:

45. Click on the **Open in Map Viewer** button located on the right side of the web page in your web browser. This will open the web layer you created in a web map:

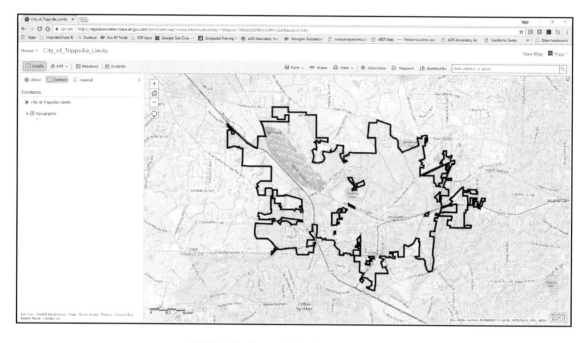

ArcGIS Online Map Viewer application with your web layer displayed

46. Explore the web layer you created in the web viewer. Once done, close your browser.
47. Return to ArcGIS Pro.
48. Close the **Share As Web Layer** pane.
49. Save your project.
50. Close ArcGIS Pro.

You have just projected a layer to a new coordinate system using the Project tool. You projected the City Limits layer to the coordinate system used by most web mapping applications, so it could be more easily integrated with other web-based GIS data in the future, then you published that layer to ArcGIS Online. Next, you viewed the new layer that you published in a web map via the ArcGIS Online Map Viewer. In Chapter 12, *Introducing ArcGIS Online*, you will learn more about ArcGIS Online and how you can use it to share and access data with those both in and outside your organization.

7
Converting Data

In this chapter, we will cover the following recipes:

- Converting shapefiles to a Geodatabase feature class
- Merging multiple shapefiles into a single geodatabase feature class
- Exporting tabular data to an Excel spreadsheet
- Importing an Excel spreadsheet into ArcGIS Pro
- Importing selected features into an existing layer

Introduction

As you may have noticed by now, GIS data comes in many formats. There are geodatabases, shapefiles, CAD files, DBF files, rasters, spreadsheets, and more. ArcGIS Pro allows you to use all of these. However, there are limits to what ArcGIS Pro allows you to do with some of these formats. Some of these are read only, such as CAD files or spreadsheets. Others you can read and edit, such as shapefiles and geodatabases. Also, if you have data spread across multiple locations, formats, and files, it can make it difficult to use.

If you are going to be editing and analyzing data, it is recommended that you consolidate all the required data into a single format. For ArcGIS Pro, the primary storage format is the geodatabase. Shapefiles are generally considered a secondary option. In order to consolidate your data sources, you may need to convert and combine data from one or more sources into a single source. ArcGIS Pro provides several methods and tools to accomplish this. Which one works best will depend on several factors, including:

- The existing data format
- The target data format

- How much data needs to be converted and the number of files?
- Are you performing a wholesale conversion or do you need to select specific features?
- Are you trying to combine multiple files into one?
- Are you importing into the GIS or exporting out to use in another application?

All of these considerations will help to determine which conversion method and tools will work best for your situation.

In this chapter, you will learn several different methods and tools that will allow you to convert and combine data within ArcGIS Pro. You will start by learning how to convert a simple shapefile into a new geodatabase feature class. Then you will expand those skills to learn how to merge multiple shapefiles into a single geodatabase feature class.

Next, you will learn how to export tabular data in your GIS to a spreadsheet, so you can easily include it in a report or perform additional calculations. Then you will reverse that workflow and import a spreadsheet into your GIS.

From there, you will learn how you can convert specific features from one source into another. The method you will learn provides you with a high level of control and accuracy when converting data.

Lastly, you will learn how to georeference CAD and raster files so that they are located in the proper location according to a specific coordinate system. This will make converting that data much easier.

Converting shapefiles to a geodatabase feature class

Shapefiles are one of the most common GIS data formats you will encounter during your career in GIS. Just about every GIS-enabled application can read, import, export, and edit a shapefile. This includes applications such as QGIS, AutoCAD Map 3D, Civil 3D, Geomedia, and many others. This has resulted in shapefiles becoming a common format for sharing GIS data with multiple platforms. It is not uncommon to receive data from engineering, planning, and surveying firms in a shapefile format.

In this recipe, you will receive a shapefile containing the location of several stormwater drainage structures, which were collected by a local surveying firm. You will integrate this shapefile into the geodatabase for the City of Trippville.

Getting ready

This recipe does require the sample data be installed on the computer. While it is not required to have completed any previous recipes, it is recommended that you at least review `Chapter 1`, *ArcGIS Pro Capabilities and Terminology*, to ensure you have the proper skills required to successfully complete this recipe. You can complete this recipe with any ArcGIS Pro licensing level.

How to do it...

1. You will need to launch ArcGIS Pro to begin this recipe.
2. In the **ArcGIS Pro** start window, click on **Open another project**:

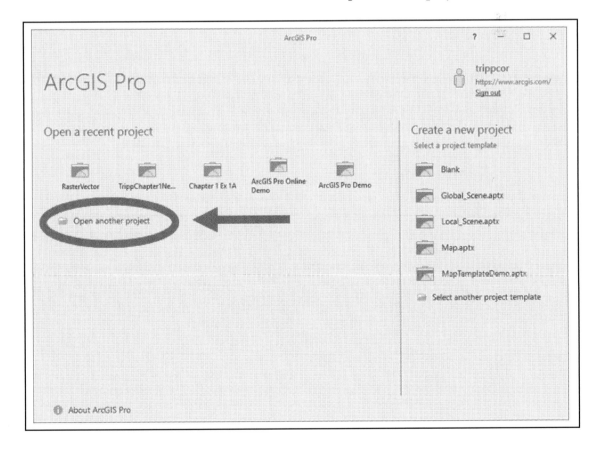

3. Select **Computer** from the **Open** window and then click **Browse** in the area on the right.

4. Navigate to C:\Student\ArcGISProCookbook\Chapter7\Convert Single Shapefile by clicking on **C:** in the area on the left of the **Open Project** window. Then double-click on the **Student**, **ArcGISProCookbook**, **Chapter7**, and **Convert Single Shapefile** folders.

5. Select the **Convert Single Shapefile.aprx** project file and click **OK**.

The project will open with the Trippville Stormwater Map visible. This is an existing map that was obviously created by someone else. You will notice, if you look at the **Contents** pane, that the map does not contain any stormwater layers. You will add the shapefile you have received from the local surveying firm:

6. In the **Catalog** pane, click on the small arrowhead located next to the **Folders** folder so you can see its contents. Then expand the **Convert Single Shapefile** folder so you can see its contents.

7. You should see the **Stormwater_Structures.shp** file in the folder you just expanded. Before you use this file you should examine its metadata to ensure it is the one you are looking for.

8. Right-click on the **Stormwater_structures.shp** file and select **View Metadata** from the menu that appears, as shown in the following screenshot:

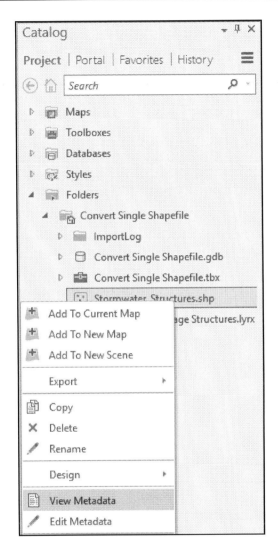

 ArcGIS Pro uses different colored icons to identify data formats. Shapefiles are shown with a green icon, CAD files with a blue icon, and geodatabases with a gray icon.

The **Catalog** view should open, displaying the metadata for the shapefile you selected. This will provide you with basic information concerning the shapefile.

Metadata is data about your data. It provides information about how the data was created, when it was created, how often it is updated, what its intended purpose is, and more. It is considered best practice to create and maintain metadata for all GIS datasets. However, it is not uncommon to find data without metadata. This is especially true of shapefiles, since they must be manually created and maintained. ArcGIS will automatically create at least some metadata for geodatabase feature classes and tables.

9. Take a moment to read over the metadata for the shapefile. When done, close the **Catalog** view by clicking on the **x** in the tab entitled **Catalog** at the top of the view area. This should return you to the map.

10. Now it is time to add the shapefile to the map. Right-click on the **Stormwater_Structures.shp** file and select **Add to Current Map** from the menu that appears, as illustrated here:

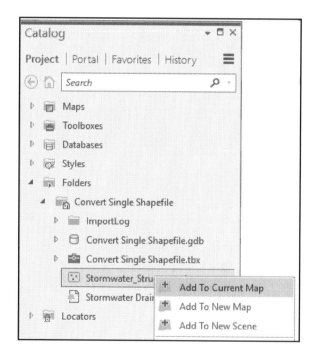

Add new layer to current map from Catalog pane

The **Stormwater Structures** layer should now appear in your **Contents** pane. Next you will review the attribute data associated with the layer you just added.

11. Right-click on the **Stormwater_Structures** layer in the **Contents** pane. Select the **Attribute Table**, as shown in the following screenshot. This will open the attribute table for the shapefile below the map view unless you have moved the table window to another location:

Question: What fields are located in the attribute table for the shapefile?

Answer:

Question: How many structures/features are stored in the shapefile?

Answer:

The table window is dockable and undockable, so, you can move it wherever you wish, including to another monitor. Unlike ArcMap, ArcGIS Pro allows you to open each table in its own window, providing greater viewing flexibility.

You should see only four fields in the attribute table, FID, Shape, Id, and Typ. The FID and Shape are default fields for a shapefile. The Id and Typ are user-defined fields. Default fields are created and maintained by the software that created the data. User-defined fields are those created and maintained by users. The default and user-defined fields will vary from application to application and format to format.

The Typ field identifies the type of structure, CB is a catch basin, AD is an area drain, DI is a drop inlet. These are all common stormwater drainage structures.

After viewing the metadata and the attribute fields, you now have a better understanding of the data you will be converting. It is always good to make sure you know the data you are working with before you start using it to perform analysis or create maps.

12. Close the **Table** window by clicking on the **x** in the tab labeled **Stormwater_Structures**. Now the map should fill the entire view area once more.
13. In the **Catalog** pane, expand the **Databases** folder so you can see its contents.
14. Expand the **Trippville_GIS.gdb** geodatabase by clicking on the small arrowhead located to the left of the database name.
15. Look at the contents of the geodatabase. You should notice that there are three feature datasets included: **Base**, **Sewer**, and **Water**.

Feature datasets serve several purposes within a geodatabase. First, they help you better organize related data. Second, they ensure all data stored within them shares a common spatial reference, which means they are all in the same coordinate system. This allows the data to take part in topologies and geometric networks which are used to ensure data quality and provide additional functionality.

Early versions of ArcGIS Pro do not support Geometric networks, but version 2.1 and later will. Geometric Networks will be renamed to Utility Network. The Utility Network will allow you to trace your utility network and perform various types of analysis. To learn more about the Utility Network, go to http://www.esri.com/esri-news/arcnews/spring17articles/introducing-utility-network-for-arcgis.

Before you convert the **Stormwater_Structures** shapefile into a geodatabase feature class, you will create a new feature dataset for the stormwater system. This will allow you to easily find the data in the geodatabase later and allow you to create a utility network in the future if you need to.

16. In the **Catalog** pane, right-click on the **Trippville_GIS.gdb** geodatabase. In the menu that appears, go to **New** and select **Feature Dataset**, as illustrated in the following screenshot. This will open the **Create Feature Dataset** tool in the **Geoprocessing** pane:

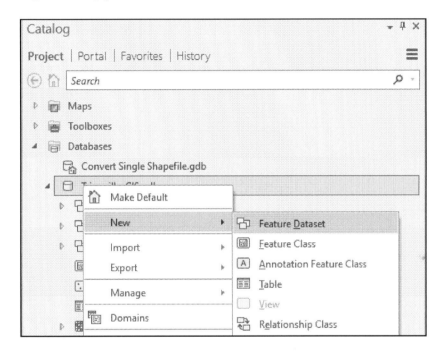

17. The **Output Geodatabase** should automatically be set to **Trippville_GIS.gdb** because it was the one you selected and right-clicked on. For the **Feature Dataset Name**, type Stormwater.

18. Under the **Coordinate System** option, click on the small drop-down arrow located on the far-right side of the cell. Select **Street Rights of Way** from the list, as shown here:

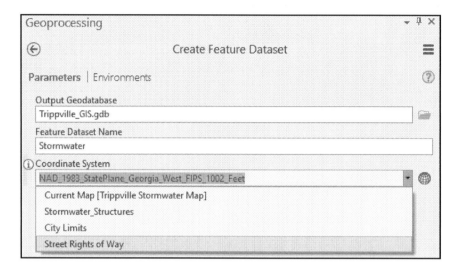

The **Coordinate System** should now be set to
NAD_1983_StatePlane_Georgia_West_FIPS_1002_Feet.

19. Verify that the **Create Feature Dataset** tool looks like the screenshot that follows. If it does, click the **Run** button located at the bottom of the pane:

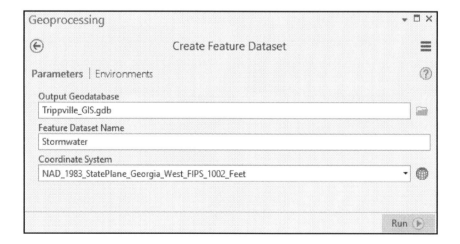

When the tool finishes, you should see the new feature dataset that you just created appear in the **Trippville_GIS.gdb** geodatabase. You will convert the shapefile containing the stormwater structures to a new feature class which will be stored in the feature dataset you just created.

20. In the **Contents** pane, right-click on the **Stormwater_Structures** layer. In the menu that appears, go to **Data** and select the **Export Features** option as illustrated in the following screenshot. This will open the **Copy Features** tool in the **Geoprocessing** pane. This normally appears on the right side of the interface:

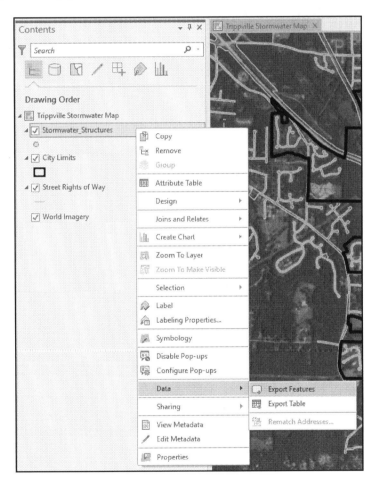

Exporting features from the Contents pane

21. The **Input Features** should automatically be set because you right-clicked on a specific layer to access the tool. Click the **Browse** button located on the far-right side of the **Output Feature Class**.

22. In the **Output Feature Class** window that opens, select the **Databases** folder located under **Project** in the left panel of the window. Two databases should appear in the right panel: **Convert Single Shapefile.gdb** and **Trippville_GIS.gdb**.

23. Double-click on the **Trippville_GIS** geodatabase.

24. Double-click on the **Stormwater** feature dataset that you created earlier.

25. In the **Name** cell located near the bottom of the **Output Feature Class** window, type Stormwater_Structures and click **Save**.

26. Verify that the **Copy Features** tool looks like the screenshot, and click the **Run** button:

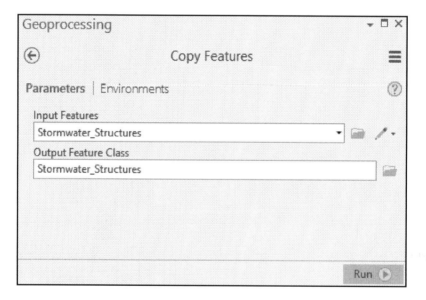

If the tool ran successfully, a new layer should appear in your map. Now you will verify that ArcGIS Pro converted the shapefile successfully.

27. Close the **Geoprocessing** pane by clicking on the small **x** located in the upper-right corner of the pane.

28. In the **Contents** pane, click on the **List by Source** button. It should be the second one from the left and looks like a cylinder.

29. Notice that you have two **Stormwater_Structures** layers. However, they are in two different locations.

Question: Where are the two stormwater_structures stored?

Answer:

As you can see, one of the stormwater_structures layers is stored in the **Trippville GIS** geodatabase. The other is stored in the **Convert Single Shapefile** folder. The one in the geodatabase is the one you just converted. The other is the original shapefile. The Copy Features tool created a new feature class in the geodatabase and left the source shapefile alone. Now that you have verified that it did create the feature class in the geodatabase, you need to verify that it converted all the features.

30. Right-click on the **Stormwater_Structures** layer, which is stored in the **Trippville_GIS.gdb**, and select **Attribute Table** from the menu that appears.

31. Look at the bottom of the table window to see the total number of records/features contained in the layer.

Question: Does it match the number of features that were in the Shapefile? (Look back to earlier in this recipe when you opened the attribute table for the shapefile and answered the question of how many features were stored in it if you don't remember.)

Answer:

Both the shapefile and geodatabase feature class should contain the same number of records/features if the Copy Features tool worked correctly.

32. Right-click on the **Stormwater_Structures** shapefile layer in the **Contents** pane, and select **Remove** from the menu that appears. You no longer need the shapefile layer in your map.

33. Click on the **Save Project** button located in the Quick Access menu at the top left of the ArcGIS Pro interface.

There's more...

As with most things you can do in ArcGIS Pro, there is more than one way to accomplish a task. Converting a Shapefile to a geodatabase feature class is no exception. For example, you could have accessed the **Copy Features** tool directly from the **Data Management Tools** toolbox and the **Features** toolset in the **Geoprocessing** pane.

There is also a third way that you can convert shapefiles to a geodatabase feature class. You can use the Feature Class to Feature Class geoprocessing tool as well. Let's take a look at how that works.

You have received a shapefile containing stormwater drainage pipes from the same local surveying firm. You want to convert those into the feature dataset that you created earlier in this recipe:

1. In the **Catalog** pane, expand the contents of the **Trippville_GIS.gdb** if needed. It may still be expanded from your previous work.
2. Right-click on the **Stormwater feature dataset**. Select **Import** and **Feature Class...**. This will open the **Feature Class to Feature Class** conversion tool in the **Geoprocessing** pane:

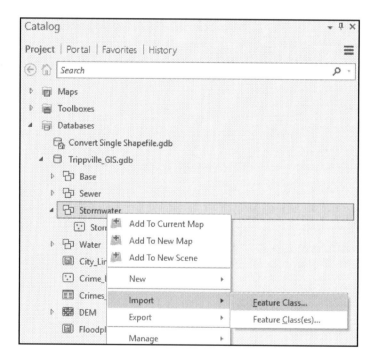

3. The **Output Location** should already be set. Click on the **Browse** button at the far-right end of the **Input Features**.

4. In the **Input features** window, select the **Folders** folder in the left panel under **Project**. The **Convert Single Shapefile** folder should appear in the right panel of the window.

5. Double-click on the **Convert Single Shapefile** folder.

6. Click on **Stormwater_Pipes.shp** and click **OK**.

7. Set the **Output Feature Class** to `Pipes`. You will not need to change any other tool settings.

8. Verify that your **Feature Class to Feature Class** tool looks like the following, and click **Run**:

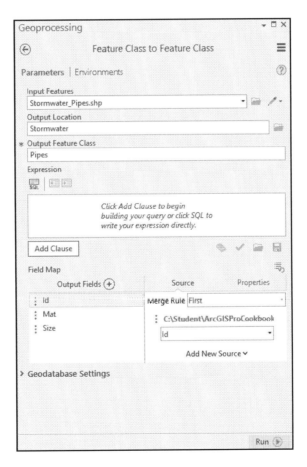

Feature class to feature class conversion tool

9. If the tool is successful, a new **Pipes** layer should appear in your map. This new layer points to a new feature class, you just created in the **Trippville_GIS** geodatabase.

10. Let's verify that the tool did create a new feature class. In the **Catalog** pane, expand the **Databases** folder, then expand the **Trippville_GIS.gdb** geodatabase and the Stormwater feature dataset.

11. Verify that you see the **Pipes** feature class.

12. If you do, close the **Geoprocessing** pane and save your project.

If any geoprocessing tool, such as the Feature Class to Feature Class tool, fails, you can always click on the **History** tab in the **Catalog** pane to review what happened. You can click on any geoprocessing operation you have performed during your ArcGIS Pro session and see if it was successful or not. If it was not, you can see the errors which were generated so you can troubleshoot why it did not work.

13. If you are not continuing to the next recipe you can close ArcGIS Pro. If you are continuing, keep ArcGIS Pro open.

So, you have now seen two different tools you can use to convert shapefiles into geodatabase feature classes. These tools are not just limited to converting shapefiles. They can also convert other spatial data formats, including coverages, DWGs, DGNs, DXFs, and more as well.

Merging multiple shapefiles into a single geodatabase feature class

You now know how to convert a single shapefile into an individual geodatabase feature class. What if you have several shapefiles that you need to merge into a single common geodatabase feature class? Can you do that in ArcGIS Pro?

Of course you can. This is not an uncommon workflow. You often need to combine multiple shapefiles or geodatabase feature classes into a single feature class. Combining multiple sources into a single one makes working with the data easier. For example, you are working on a regional transportation study and you receive road data from three counties. If you wish to analyze traffic flow or calculate the total length of roads by type for the region, it would be much easier to do if all the data was in a single feature class. Maybe you are responsible for maintaining data for a 911 center that services both the city and county. The city and county assign addresses for new construction and update the address point file for their respective jurisdiction. You would need to combine these two files for use in the 911 software. These are just two possible examples of situations where you would want to combine multiple shapefiles or geodatabase feature classes together into one.

In this recipe, you will merge three different shapefiles into a single common geodatabase feature class. You have had three field crews out collecting the location of street signs as part of a sign inventory the roads superintendent asked you to create. Each crew has collected the sign location data into a shapefile. So, you now have three separate shapefiles which need to be merged into a single geodatabase feature class. This will make the data much easier to manage and work with in the future.

Getting ready

This recipe does require the sample data be installed on the computer. You do not need to complete any previous recipes. Though it is recommended that you review Chapter 1, *ArcGIS Pro Capabilities and Terminology*, plus the previous recipe in this chapter, to ensure that you have a basic understanding of the skills required to complete this recipe. This recipe can be completed with any ArcGIS Pro licensing level.

How to do it...

1. If you closed ArcGIS Pro before starting this recipe, you will need to start ArcGIS Pro.
2. Open the `Convert Multiple Shapefiles.aprx` project located in `C:\Student\ArcGISProCookbook\Chapter7` using the skills you have learned in past recipes.

The project should open with the Street Sign Inventory map. If you look in the **Contents** pane you will see three **Street_Signs** layers. These are the three shapefiles collected by your field crews. You will take a moment to investigate these three layers so you know what you have to work with.

3. Right-click on the **Street_Signs_Day1** layer in the **Contents** pane and select **Attribute Table** from the menu that appears. Take a moment to investigate the Attribute Table and then answer the following questions:

    Question: What type of shapefile is this layer?

    Answer:

    Question: What attribute fields does it contain?

    Answer:

4. Repeat this process for the other two **Street_Signs** layers. Compare the answers to the previous two questions with each of these layers. Note any similarities or differences.

    As you have just found out, all three layers are point features and have a common attribute table structure or schema. While a common schema is not always required when merging multiple fields together, it does often help. One thing that must match in order to merge multiple layers together is the feature type. You can only merge points with points, lines with lines, and polygons with polygons.

    Now that you have verified that the feature types match and the attribute fields are the same, you are ready to merge the three layers together to create a single one:

5. Close the **Attribute Tables** for the three **Street_Signs** layers. This will free up some screen space.
6. Click on the **Analysis** tab in the ribbon.
7. Click on the **Tools** button in the **Geoprocessing** group in the **Analysis** tab. This will open the **Geoprocessing** pane.

8. Click on the **Toolboxes** tab in the **Geoprocessing** pane, as illustrated:

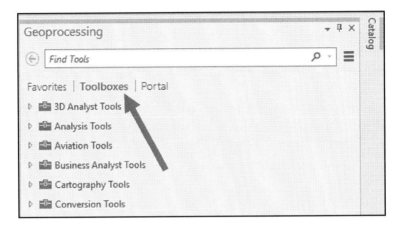

9. In the Search box at the top of the **Geoprocessing** page, type `Merge` and press your *Enter* key to locate the **Merge** tool.

10. Select **Merge (Data Management Tools)** from the list that is presented. It should be near the top, as shown in the following screenshot:

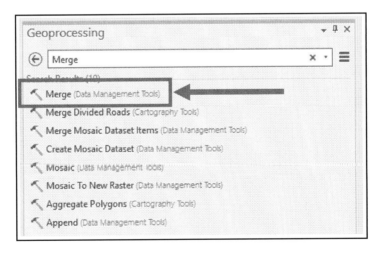

Selecting the Merge tool in the Geoprocessing pane.

The **Merge geoprocessing** tool should now be open in the **Geoprocessing** pane. This is the tool you will use to combine the three individual shapefiles.

11. Under **Input Datasets**, click on the small drop-down arrow and select **Street_Signs_Day1**. When you do that, another input box should appear below it, allowing you to add another input.

12. Click on the small drop-down arrow at the end of the second input box that appeared and select **Street_Signs_Day2**.

13. Repeat that process to add **Street_Signs_Day3** as the last input for the **Merge** tool.

14. Click the **Browse** button at the right side of the **Output Dataset** box.

15. In the **Output Dataset** window that appears, select **Databases** from the panel on the left side of the window.

16. Double-click on the **Trippville_GIS** geodatabase in the panel on the right side of the window.

17. In the **Name** cell, type StreetSigns and click **Save**.

18. Verify that your **Merge** tool looks like the following screenshot. If it does, click **Run**:

The Merge geoprocessing tool

When the tool runs successfully, you should see a new **StreetSigns** layer added to your map. This new layer should cover all the points in the original three layers, but notice they still exist. The Merge tool, like most geoprocessing tools, creates new data and does not alter the original input data. But let's verify that just to be sure.

19. Click on the List by Source tab located in the **Contents** pane. It is the button that looks like a gray cylinder.

20. Locate all **Street Signs** layers that are visible in the map. Note where their source is stored and answer the following questions:

> **Question**: Where is the StreetSigns layer you that just created being stored?
>
> **Answer**:

> **Question**: Where are the three Street_Signs shapefiles being stored?
>
> **Answer**:
>
> **Question**: Are these the same?
>
> **Answer**:

As you can now see, the **StreetSigns** layer is referencing a geodatabase feature class that is being stored in the **Trippville_GIS** geodatabase, whereas the shapefiles for the **Street_Signs** shapefiles are stored in the **Convert Single Shapefile** folder. These are two very different locations. Because we don't see a red exclamation point located beside any of the layer names, we know the data sources still exist and none have been deleted.

Any time that you see a red exclamation point located just before the layer name in the **Contents** pane, you know that layer has lost the connection to its source data.

21. Right-click on each of the **Street_Signs** layers and select **Remove** from the menu that appears. This removes them from the map to reduce clutter and confusion. Removing a layer from the map does not delete the source data.

22. Right-click on the **StreetSigns** layer and select **Attribute Table** from the menu that appears.

23. Review the **Attribute Table** and compare it with what you saw when looking at the attribute tables for the shapefiles.

   Question: How does the attribute table for the StreetSigns layer compare to the ones for the three shapefiles?

   Answer:

24. Save your project.

As you can see, the Attribute Table for the new StreetSigns layer contains the same exact fields as the original three shapefiles. Also, the number of records equals the sum of the total records from the three shapefiles. The Merge geoprocessing tool combined the content, both spatial and attributes, of the three shapefiles into a single geodatabase feature class.

There's more...

The Merge geoprocessing tool works great if you want to combine multiple files or feature classes into a new single feature class. What if you want to add new data from a shapefile or geodatabase feature class to an existing layer of information? For example, your field crews go out and locate additional street signs. You would not want to create another layer. Instead you would want to add the new signs to the existing layer. How would you do that?

This is where the Append geoprocessing tool comes in to play. The Append tool will add new records from an input table, file, or feature class to an existing one. Let's see it in action so you can gain a better understanding of how it works. You will append a new shapefile that contains additional sign locations to the StreetSigns layer you just created:

1. Click on the **Map** tab in the ribbon.
2. Click on the **Add Data** button in the **Layer** group on the **Map** tab.
3. Click on the **Folders** folder located under **Project** in the panel on the left side of the **Add Data** window.
4. Double-click on the **Convert Single Shapefile** folder in the right-side panel.
5. Select the **Street_Signs_Day4.shp** file and click **OK** to add the shapefile as a layer to the map.

6. Right-click on the **Street_Signs_Day4** layer you just added to your map, and select **Zoom to Layer** from the menu that is presented. This will allow you to more easily see the layer you just added. As you can see, this layer contains data for more signs located on the west side of the city.

7. Open the **Attribute Table** for the **Street_Signs_Day4** layer using the same process you used earlier in this recipe.

8. Review the Attribute Table contents and note the number of features/records in the table. Use that information to answer the following question:

Question: How many records/features does the Street_Signs_Day4 shapefile contain?

Answer:

9. Open the attribute table for the StreetSigns layer and note the number of records/features it contains. Use that information to answer the following question.

Question: How many records/features does the StreetSigns layer contain?

Answer:

10. Click on the **Analysis** tab in the ribbon.

11. Click on the **Tools** button located in the **Geoprocessing** group on the **Analysis** tab.

12. In the **Geoprocessing** pane that appears, click on the **Toolboxes** tab.

13. Locate and expand the **Data Management Tools** toolbox.

14. Expand the **General** toolset and locate the **Append** tool, as illustrated in the following screenshot:

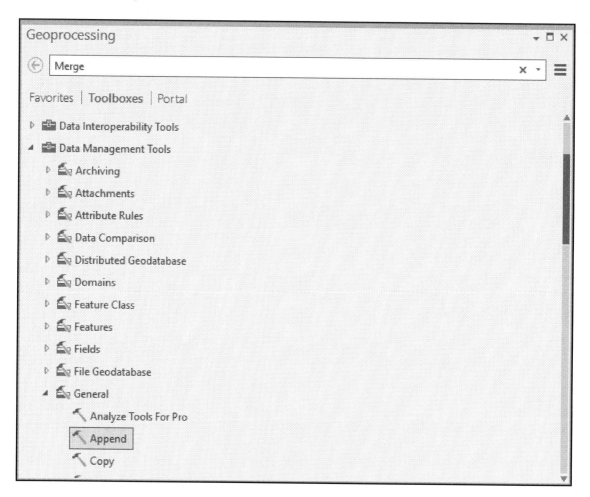

15. Click on the **Append** tool to open it in the **Geoprocessing** pane.
16. Click on the small drop-down arrow located to the right of the **Input Datasets** cell and select **Street_Signs_Day4**.
17. Click on the small drop-down arrow located to the right of the **Target Dataset** and select **StreetSigns** from the list presented.

18. Verify that your **Append** tool looks like the following and click **Run**:

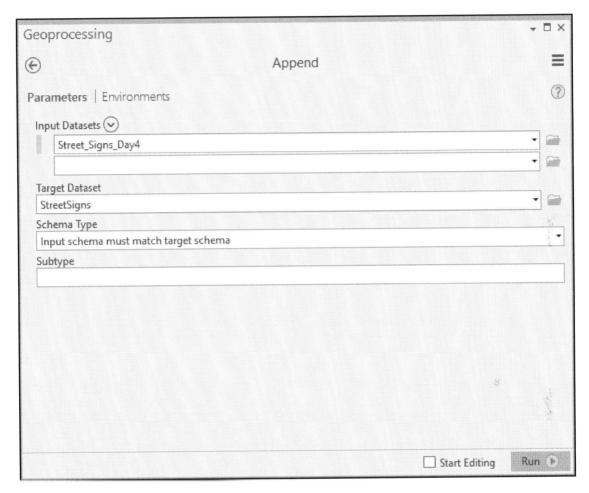

The Append tool in the Geoprocessing pane.

Notice that no new layers were added to your map, unlike when you used the **Merge** tool. This is because no new layers were created. The features from the **Street_Signs_Day4** shapefile have been added to the existing **StreetSigns** shapefile. Let's verify that is what happened.

19. In the **Contents** pane, select the **List by Draw Order** button. It is the first one on the left-hand side.

20. Turn off the **Street_Signs_Day4** layer by clicking on the box to the left of the layer name so it no longer contains a check mark.

    You should now see a copy of the features that were in the shapefile displayed in the StreetSigns layer. This shows that the features from the shapefile were copied to the geodatabase feature class. Now check the attributes to ensure they were copied.

21. In the **Contents** pane, select the **List by Selection** button.
22. Ensure the **StreetSigns** layer is set as selectable.
23. Right-click on the **Street_Signs_Day4** layer and select **Zoom to Layer**. This ensures that you are zoomed in to the area covered by this layer.
24. Click on the **Map** tab in the ribbon.
25. Click on the **Select** button in the **Selection** group on the **Map** tab.
26. On your map, click on the lower-right side, as indicated in the following diagram. Continue to hold your mouse button down and drag your mouse pointer to the north-west until you reach the approximate location shown, creating a rectangle which will allow you to select all the features copied from the shapefile:

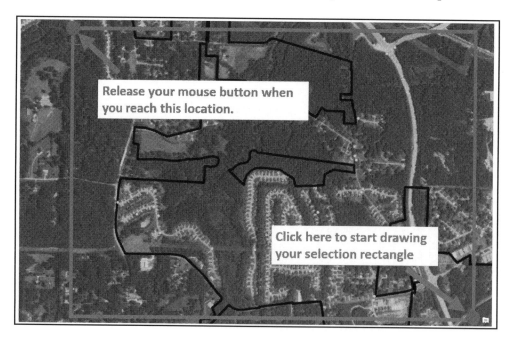

Selection rectangle for street signs

27. Right-click on the **StreetSigns** layer and select **Attribute Table**.

28. Click the **Show Selected Records** button located at the bottom of the **Attribute Table**. This filters the table so that only the selected features are visible.

29. Note the total number of records. Compare that to the number of records in the table before you used the Append tool. Use that information to answer the following questions:

> **Question**: Do the selected records all include attribute values?
>
> **Answer**:
>
> **Question**: How does the total number of records in the table compare to the number before you ran the Append tool?
>
> **Answer**:

As you can see, the attribute values were also copied from the shapefile to the new geodatabase feature class. The new total number of records in the StreetSigns layer should equal the sum of the number of records in the shapefile plus the pre-append tool record count for the StreetSigns layer. The Append tool simply added the records/features from the shapefile to the StreetSigns layer.

30. Close the **Attribute Table** and **Geoprocessing** pane if it is still open.

31. Save your project and close ArcGIS Pro.

As you have now experienced, the Merge and Append geoprocessing tools are great for combining multiple datasets into one. This can reduce the total number of datasets you must manage and make performing analysis much easier.

Exporting tabular data to an Excel spreadsheet

Many times, the people we work with are not GIS professionals or do not have access to GIS software. They may request data in another format. One of the most commonly requested formats is a spreadsheet. Spreadsheets are something just about everyone with a computer can work with. They can run calculations, summarize data, create graphs, and more.

While you cannot export the spatial data to a spreadsheet, ArcGIS Pro will allow you to export tabular data to a spreadsheet-compatible format. This includes Microsoft Excel XLS, XLSX, and CSV files. You are able to export attribute and stand-alone database tables to spreadsheets with ArcGIS Pro. As with most other operations, there is more than one way to do it.

In this recipe, you will learn two different methods for converting tables to spreadsheet compatible formats. The roads superintendent has asked you to provide him with a copy of the street sign inventory you have been working on so he can get a general count of all signs by type, and so he can compare it to his list of signs he has been keeping in a notebook. He also wants you to get him a spreadsheet with all the roads located within the city. You will use a different method for each of these tasks.

Getting ready

This recipe requires that you have completed the previous recipe. It also requires you to have spreadsheet software installed, such as Microsoft Excel or Open Office. This recipe can also be completed with all license levels of ArcGIS Pro.

How to do it...

1. You will first need to start ArcGIS Pro and open the `Convert Multiple Shapefiles.aprx` project located in `C:\Student\ArcGISProCookbook\Chapter7\` using the skills you have learned in past recipes.
2. Locate the **StreetSigns** layer in the **Contents** pane.
3. Right-click on the **StreetSigns** layer and go down to **Data**. Then select **Export Table**, as illustrated in the following screenshot. This will open the **Copy Rows** tool in the **Geoprocessing** pane:

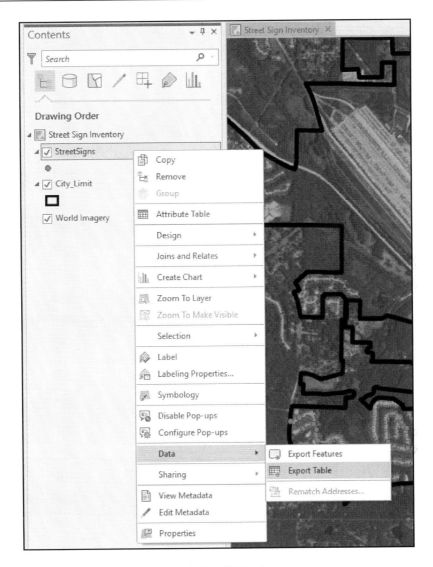

Accessing Export Table function

4. The **Input Rows** should already be set to the **StreetSigns** layer since you right-clicked on it to access the tool. Now click on the **Browse** button located to the right of the **Output Table**.

5. Click on the **Folders** folder located under **Project** in the left panel of the **Output Table** window.

6. Double-click on the **Convert Single Shapefile** folder in the right panel.
7. In the **Name** cell, type `StreetSignsInventory.csv` and click the **Save** button at the bottom of the window.
8. Verify that your **Copy Rows** tool looks like the following and click **Run**:

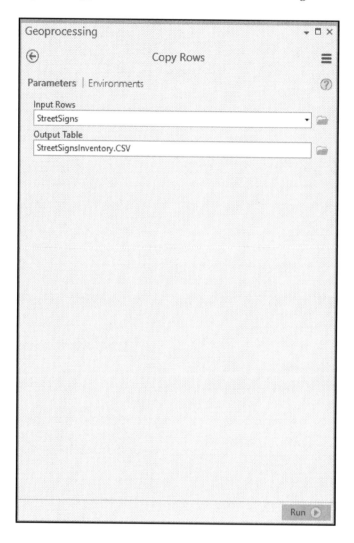

The Copy Rows tool can be used to convert multiple types of tabular data to other formats. Input for this tool can include Geodatabases, shapefiles, dBase tables, Microsoft Excel spreadsheets, CSV files, and TXT files. Output can be geodatabase standalone tables, dBase tables, and CSV and TXT files. To learn more about the Copy Rows tool, go to `http://pro.arcgis.com/en/pro-app/tool-reference/data-management/copy-rows.htm`.

Remember, if you have features or records selected in a layer or table, the **Copy Rows** tool will only export the selected items to the new output table.

When the **Copy Rows** tool is complete, you should see a new table appear in the **Contents** pane. This is the CSV file you just created. Let's see if it will open in Microsoft Excel or the spreadsheet application you have installed.

9. Open your **Windows Explorer** or **File Explorer** depending on what version of Windows you are using. There is typically an icon on the Taskbar located at the bottom of your monitor which will open **Windows Explorer** or **File Explore**. The icon looks like a file folder sitting in a stand.

File/Windows Explorer is not the same as Internet Explorer. Internet Explorer is a web browser. File/Windows Explorer allows you to browse the contents of your computer, network, and connected drives.

10. In the directory tree located in the panel on the left of the **File Explorer** window, locate **Desktop** and expand it so you can see its contents.

11. Locate **This PC** or **My Computer** within the **Directory Tree** and expand it so you can see its contents.

12. Click on the **C:** drive. It is normally named either **Local Drive** or **OS**.

13. In the right panel, locate the **Student** folder and double-click on it.

14. Double-click on the **ArcGISProCookbook** folder to open it.

15. Double-click on the **Chapter7** and the **Convert Single Shapefile** folders to open them.

16. Scroll down until you find the **StreetSignsInventory.CSV** file and double-click to open it.

17. Take a moment to look over the contents of the file. You should see three columns. The first row should contain the field names from the **Attribute Table**. The remaining rows contain the data from the attribute table. It should look similar to the following:

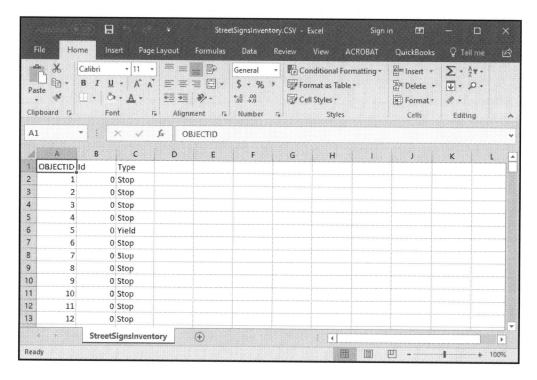

18. Once you are done reviewing the CSV file, close it. If asked to save it, do not.

You have just converted the Attribute Table for the StreetSigns layer to a CSV file which you opened as a spreadsheet. So, you have completed the first task. Now you need to export the street centerline attributes. This will actually require you to prepare the data before you export it, because, as you will see, your street centerline data actually extends beyond the City Limits.

19. Return to ArcGIS Pro. If you accidentally closed ArcGIS Pro, please refer back to the first step in this recipe to reopen the correct project.

20. In the **Catalog** pane, expand the **Databases** folder so you can see its contents.

21. Next, expand the **Trippville_GIS.gdb** geodatabase and the **Base** feature dataset.

22. Drag and drop the **Street_Centerlines** feature class into the map view.

As you can see, the data extends outside the City Limits of Trippville. The roads superintendent only wants data for the portions of the roads inside the City Limits, so you will need to clip the data.

23. Click on the **Analysis** tab in the ribbon.
24. Click on the **Clip** tool located in the **Tools** group on the ribbon. This will open the **Clip** tool in the **Geoprocessing** pane.
25. Click on the drop-down arrow for the **Input Features** located at the far right side of the cell. Select **Street_Centerlines** from the list.
26. Repeat this process for the **Clip Features**, selecting the **City_Limit** layer.
27. Accept the default name for the **Output Feature Class**. Verify that your **Clip** tool looks like the following, and click **Run**:

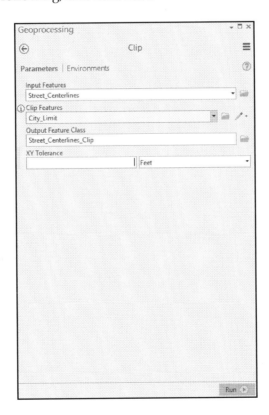

Clip tool in the Geoprocessing pane

When the **Clip** tool completes, a new layer will appear in your map which contains only the portion of the roads within the City Limits of Trippville:

28. Close the **Geoprocessing** pane and save your project.

29. Click on the **Analysis** tab in the ribbon to ensure it is active. Next click on the **Tools** button located in the **Geoprocessing** group.

30. Click on the **Toolboxes** tab at the top of the **Geoprocessing** pane, as illustrated in the following screenshot:

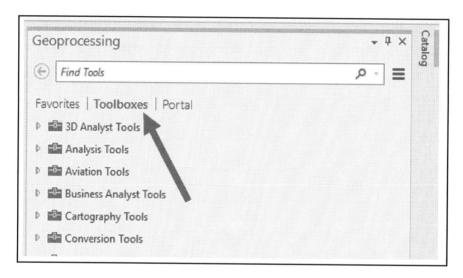

Click on Toolboxes tab in center

31. Locate and expand the **Conversion Tools** toolbox in the **Geoprocessing** pane.

32. Expand the **Excel** toolset to reveal the **Excel to Table** and the **Table to Excel Python** script tools.

You may wonder how you can tell these are Python script tools. It is because of the icon located next to the tool. Scrolls, as displayed next to these two tools, indicate Python script tools. Hammers indicate system tools such as the Clip tool, you used earlier in this recipe. A group of connected multi-colored diamonds indicates a model tool created with ModelBuilder.

33. Select the **Table to Excel** tool. This will open the tool in the **Geoprocessing** pane.

34. Click the drop-down arrow for the **Input Table** and select **Street_Centerline_Clip** from the list.

35. For the **Output Excel File**, click the **Browse** button located on the far-right side.

36. In the left panel of the **Save As** window that just opened, locate **This PC** or **My Computer** and click on it.

37. In the right panel, locate the **C:** drive and double-click on it. The C:\ drive is often named **Local Drive** or **OS**.

38. Locate the **Student** folder in the right-hand side panel and double-click on it.

39. Locate the **ArcGISProCookbook** folder and double-click on it.

40. Locate the **My Projects** folder and double-click on it.

41. In the **File Name** box located near the bottom of the **Save As** window, type `Street_Centerlines_Trippville` and click **Save**.

42. Verify that your **Table to Excel** tool looks like the following, and click **Run**:

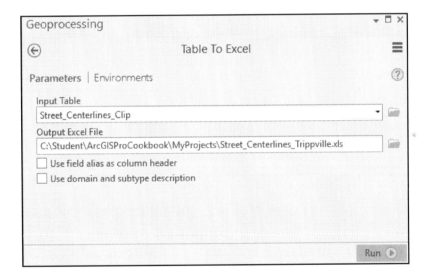

If the tool runs successfully it should create a new spreadsheet in the folder you designated. Now you will verify the results.

43. Open **Windows Explorer** or **File Explorer** like you did earlier in this recipe.

44. Using the same method you did in *steps 10-14* of this recipe, navigate to `C:\Student\ArcGISProCookbook\MyProjects`.

45. Locate the **Street_Centerlines_Trippville.xls** file that you just created and double-click on it to open the file.

46. Take a moment to examine the spreadsheet you created. It should look similar to the screenshot that follows. If you desire, open the **Attribute Table** for the **Street_Centerlines** layer in ArcGIS Pro and compare the two:

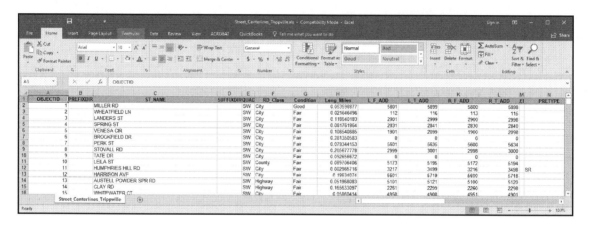

Exported spreadsheet

47. When you are done examining the contents of the spreadsheet, close it and your **File Explorer** window.

48. Return to ArcGIS Pro and save your project.

49. If you are not continuing on to the next recipe, close ArcGIS Pro. If you are, you may leave ArcGIS Pro open.

You have now used two methods to export data from GIS to a format that can be opened by applications such as Microsoft Excel. This capability further expands the usefulness and flexibility of your GIS. It opens up the ability to integrate with other non-spatial applications.

Importing an Excel spreadsheet into ArcGIS Pro

You have learned how to export data from GIS formats to a spreadsheet within ArcGIS Pro. But what if you need to go the other way? People use spreadsheets to store all kinds of information. This is because they are quick and easy to create and are very versatile. So, what does it take to bring one into your GIS using ArcGIS Pro?

When working with spreadsheets in ArcGIS Pro, remember, simpler is always better. ArcGIS Pro allows you to view XLS and XLSX files. It displays the spreadsheet as a database table. You can view, query, and link a spreadsheet. The linking is limited to using a join or a relate, which you learned about in Chapter 3, *Linking Data together*.

There are some limitations when trying to use a spreadsheet in ArcGIS Pro. ArcGIS Pro treats a spreadsheet like a database table. So, it applies database limitations to the spreadsheet. This includes the following:

- The values in the first non-empty row in the spreadsheet become the field names.
- Each column must have a unique name.
- Each column cannot contain special characters. Underscores (_) are allowed.
- The field names (values in the first row) are limited to 64 characters.
- No value in a cell can exceed 255 characters.
- Each field must start with an Alpha character. It cannot start with a number.

If the spreadsheet fails to meet any of these limitations, ArcGIS Pro will not allow you to view the spreadsheet. This means that you may need to customize or simplify the spreadsheet for it to work in ArcGIS Pro. Also, ArcGIS Pro will not allow you to edit a spreadsheet.

If you need to edit the data in a spreadsheet or make it a permanent part of your GIS data, you will need to convert it. ArcGIS Pro has a tool that converts the spreadsheet into a database table. This can be a dBase or standalone geodatabase table.

In this recipe, you will view a spreadsheet containing inspection information in ArcGIS Pro. This will start with you reviewing the contents of the spreadsheet in Excel or other spreadsheet application to ensure that it does not violate some of the limitations. Then you will open it in ArcGIS Pro.

Getting ready

It is recommended that you complete all the recipes in Chapter 3, *Linking Data together*, of this cookbook before you work this recipe. Chapter 3, *Linking Data together*, will provide you with a better understanding of how to work with database tables in ArcGIS Pro. You will also need to have Microsoft Excel or a similar spreadsheet application installed. This recipe can be completed with all license levels of ArcGIS Pro.

How to do it...

1. Open Windows/File Explorer. It should be an icon that looks like a file folder on your Taskbar.
2. In the panel on the left, expand the contents of **This PC** or **My Computer**, depending on your operating system.
3. Locate and expand the **C:** drive, which is typically labeled as **OS** or **Local Drive**.
4. Click on the **Student** folder so that its contents appear in the right-hand side panel.
5. Double-click on the **ArcGISProCookbook** folder
6. Double-click on the **Chapter7** folder.

7. Double-click on the **Inspections2016to2017.xls** file to open it. The spreadsheet
    should open in your spreadsheet application such as Microsoft Excel. It should
    look like the screenshot that follows:

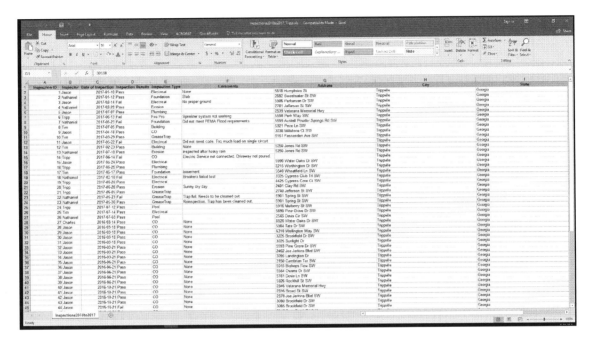

Inspection spreadsheet

8. Review the spreadsheet, comparing it to the limitations listed in the opening of
    the recipe. Then answer the following questions:

Question: What are the values in the first row, which will become the column names when you open the spreadsheet in ArcGIS Pro?

Answer:

Question: Is each value in the first row unique?

Answer:

Question: Do the values in the first row contain any special characters?

Answer:

Question: Do any of the values in the first row exceed 64 characters?

Answer:

Question: Do any of the values in any cell exceed 255 characters?

Answer:

As you can see, this is a simple spreadsheet. It does not contain a lot of title information or complicated equations which can cause issues in ArcGIS Pro. As a matter of fact, it meets most of the restrictions required by ArcGIS Pro. However, several of the values in the first row do violate the restrictions because they contain special characters (spaces). You will need to adjust these before you can bring the spreadsheet into ArcGIS Pro.

9. You need to change the value in cell **A1**. Replace `Inspection ID` with `Insp_ID`.
10. Replace `Date of Inspection` in cell **C1** with `Date_Insp`.
11. Replace `Inspection Results` in cell **D1** with `Insp_results`.
12. Replace `Inspection Type` in cell **E1** with `Insp_Typ`.
13. Verify that you have properly replaced the values in row 1, and then save the spreadsheet and close it:

	A	B	C	D	E	F
1	Insp_ID	Inspector	Date_Insp	Insp_results	Insp_Typ	Comments
2	1	Jason	2017-01-10	Pass	Electrical	None
3	2	Nathaniel	2017-01-12	Pass	Foundation	Slab
4	3	Jason	2017-02-14	Fail	Electrical	No proper ground
5	4	Nathaniel	2017-02-20	Pass	Erosion	
6	5	Jason	2017-07-07	Pass	Plumbing	
7	6	Tripp	2017-06-13	Fail	Fire Pro	Sprinkler system not working
8	7	Nathaniel	2017-05-23	Fail	Foundation	Did not meet FEMA Flood requirements.
9	8	Tim	2017-07-05	Pass	Building	
10	9	Jason	2017-04-18	Pass	CO	
11	10	Tim	2017-03-29	Pass	GreaseTrap	
12	11	Jason	2017-05-22	Fail	Electrical	Did not meet code. Too much load on single circuit.
13	12	Tim	2017-02-23	Pass	Building	None
14	13	Nathaniel	2017-07-10	Pass	Erosion	Inspected after heavy rain.
15	14	Tripp	2017-06-14	Fail	CO	Electric Service not connected. Driveway not poured.
16	15	Jason	2017-05-24	Pass	Electrical	
17	16	Tripp	2017-05-25	Pass	Plumbing	

14. Start ArcGIS Pro and open the `Import Spreadsheet.aprx` project located in `C:\Student\ArcGISProCookbook\Chapter7` using the skills you have learned in past recipes. The project should open with the City of Trippville map.

15. You will now add the spreadsheet you just edited to ArcGIS Pro. Click on the **Add Data** button in the **Layer** group on the **Map** tab in the ribbon.

16. In the panel on the left side, expand the **Computer** option so you can see its contents.

17. Click on the **C:** drive so its contents appear in the right panel.

18. Scroll down in the right panel until you see the **Student** folder. Double-click on the **Student** folder.

19. Double-click on the **ArcGISProCookbook** folder.

20. Double-click on the **Chapter7** folder.

21. Double-click on the **Inspections2016to2017.xls** file. Select the **Inspections2016to2017$** worksheet and click **OK**. The worksheet should appear as a standalone table in the **Contents** pane.

22. Right-click on the **Inspoections2016to2017$** standalone table and select **Open** from the menu that appears. The worksheet opens as a table and should look very familiar. Notice the fields of information this workshop contains:

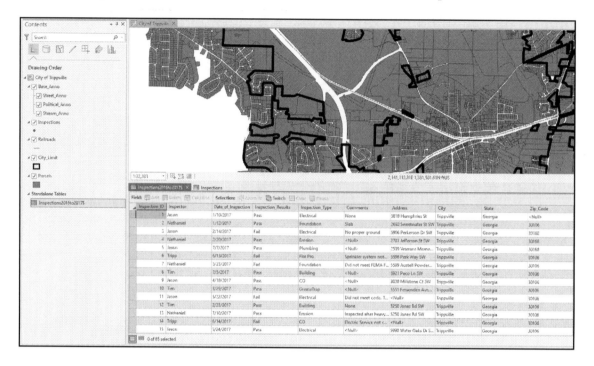

If you look at the list of layers in the map, you will see an **Inspections** layer. This layer shows the locations of the inspections referenced in the worksheet you just brought into ArcGIS Pro. Now you will examine that layer:

23. In the **Contents** pane, right-click on the **Inspections** layer and select **Attribute Table** from the menu that appears.

As you can see, this table is very simple. It only contains three fields, ObjectID, Shape, and InspID, so the layer only stores the location of each inspection. If you were to join it with the worksheet you added, then you would know a lot more about each inspection. This would in turn increase your ability to use the data in ArcGIS Pro. Now you will join the worksheet to the **Inspections** layer.

24. In the **Contents** pane, right-click on the **Inspections** layer, select **Joins and Relates**, and then **Add Join**, as illustrated in the following screenshot. This will open the **Add Join** tool in the **Geoprocessing** pane:

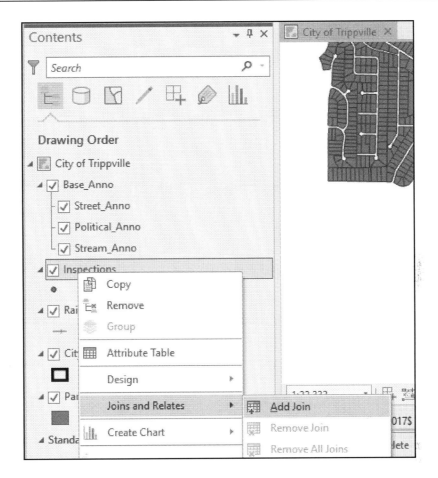

25. The **Layer Name or Table View** should already be assigned. Click the drop-down arrow for the **Input Join Field** and select **InspID** from the list presented.

26. The **Join Table** should also be automatically assigned as the **Inspections2016to2017$** worksheet because it is the only standalone table in your map. Click on the drop-down arrow for the **Output Join Field** and select **Inspection_ID**.

27. Verify your **Add Join Table** tool looks like the following screenshot and click **Run**:

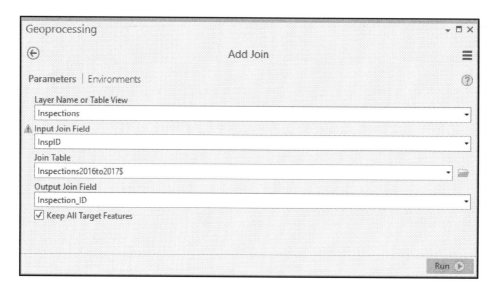

28. Look back at the **Inspections Attribute Table**, which originally contained only two fields. Now you should see that the information from the worksheet has been added to that table.

29. Close the **Geoprocessing** pane.

30. Save your Project.

Now that you have joined the worksheet data to the **Inspections** layer, you can use that additional information to label, symbolize, and query, just as if the additional information was part of the layer to start with. The one thing you cannot do is edit the information that comes from the worksheet in ArcGIS Pro. That requires you to convert it.

The method you use to convert it will depend on how you intend to use the data from the spreadsheet. If you want to keep the spreadsheet data in a separate table, you can use the Excel to Table tool. If you wish to permanently join the data to the layer, you can export the joined layer to a new feature class. You will do both now.

31. Right-click on the **Inspections** layer and go to **Data** in the menu that appears. Then select the **Export Features** option, as illustrated in the following screenshot. This will open the **Copy Features** tool in the **Geoprocessing** pane.

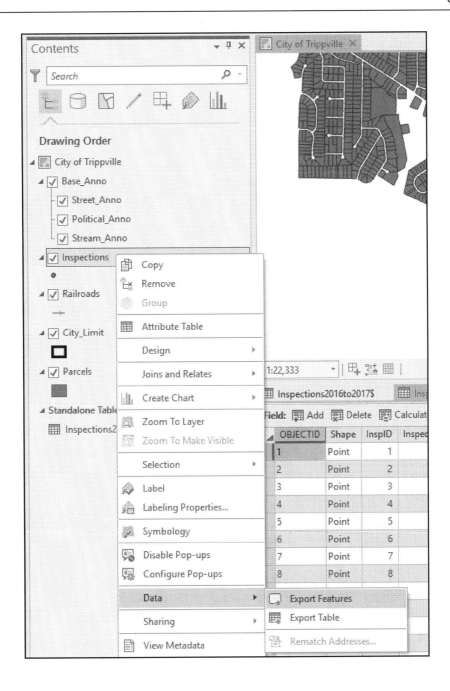

32. The **Input Features** value should be automatically populated. Click the **Browse** button at the end of the **Output Features Class** cell.

33. Select the **Databases** folder under **Project** in the left panel of the **Output Feature Class** window.

34. Double-click on the **Trippville_GIS.gdb** geodatabase in the right panel of the window. Then, in the **Name** cell near the bottom of the window, type `Inspections_more_data` and click the **Save** button.

35. Verify that your **Copy Features** tool looks like the following screenshot and click **Run**:

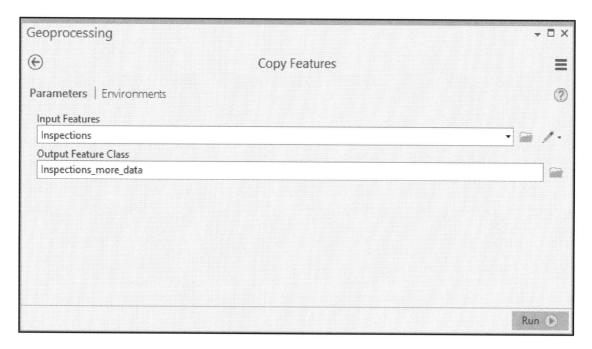

Copy Features tool in the Geoprocessing pane

36. Close the **Geoprocessing** pane.

37. The new **Inspections_more_data** layer should appear in the **Contents** pane. Open the **Attribute Table** for this new layer and answer the following question:

Question: What attribute fields does the layer you created contain?

Answer:

As you can see, the new layer contains all the information that was in the Attribute Table for the **Inspections** layer and the **Inspections2016to2017$** worksheet standalone table. Now that all that information is part of a single layer, you can edit all the data.

38. Save your project using the **Save** button on the Quick Access toolbar.

The ability to import and use data from outside sources greatly increases the flexibility of your GIS. It can provide you with access to a plethora of new information to include in your analysis.

There's more...

You just joined a spreadsheet to the Inspections layer, and then exported that to a new feature class which contains the combined information from both the joined sources. But what if you wanted the Inspections layer and the data from the spreadsheet to remain separate but still be editable from ArcGIS? How would you do that?

In that case, you would want to convert the spreadsheet to a true standalone database table. This would allow the two to remain separate, but they could still be joined as needed or maybe even a relationship class could be set up between them. Keeping them separate would have other advantages as well. First, you could easily replace the standalone table with a new copy of the spreadsheet as needed if your organization wanted to continue to input data through the spreadsheet. Being a standalone table, you could share just the table with others for editing and updating via web forms or mobile applications. These are just a few of the advantages.

Let's look at how you would export the spreadsheet to a standalone table in your GIS database:

1. Click on the **Analysis** tab in the ribbon.
2. Click on the **Tools** button in the **Geoprocessing** group on the **Analysis** tab. This will open the **Geoprocessing** pane once again.
3. If required, click on the **Toolboxes** tab located near the top of the **Geoprocessing** pane.

4. Locate and expand the **Conversion Tools** toolbox.

5. Locate and expand the **Excel** toolset in the **Conversion Tools** toolbox.

6. You should see two tools, **Excel to Table** and **Table to Excel**. You used the **Table to Excel Python** tool in the previous recipe. Now you will use the **Excel to Table** tool. Click on the **Excel to Table** tool. This will open the tool in the **Geoprocessing** pane.

7. Click on the **Browse** button for the **Input Excel File**. This will open a new window that allows you to navigate to the Excel file you will convert.

8. In the panel on the left, locate and expand **This PC** or **My Computer**.

9. Select **C:**, which is typically labeled **OS** or **Local Drive**. The contents of the **C:** drive should appear in the panel on the right.

10. Scroll down until you see the **Student** folder, then double-click on the **Student** folder.

11. Double-click on the **ArcGISProCookbook** folder.

12. Double-click on the **Chapter7** folder.

13. Select the **Inspections2016to2017.xls** file and click the **Open** button.

Do not double-click on the **Inspections2016to2017.xls** file. That will open its contents and not select it, as desired. This will cause the tool to ultimately fail.

14. Click the **Browse** button for the **Output Table**.

15. Click on the **Databases** folder in the left panel of the **Output Table** window, located under **Project**.

16. Double-click on the **Trippville_GIS.gdb** geodatabase.

17. In the **Name** cell, near the bottom of the **Output Table** window, type `Inspections_2016_2017`. Then click the **Save** button.

18. Verify that your **Excel to Table** tool looks like the following, and click **Run**:

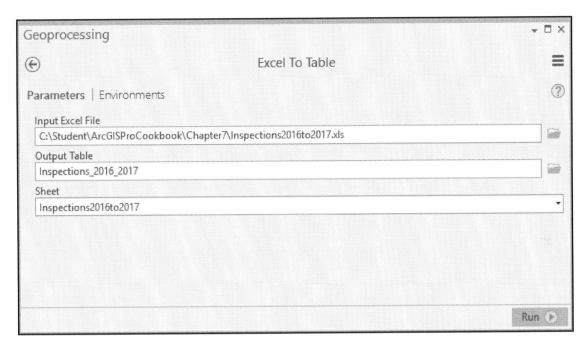

Excel to Table tool in the Geoprocessing pane to import the spreadsheet into a geodatabase

When the tool is complete, a new standalone table will appear in the **Contents** pane. This is the new table that you just created. Now you will remove the join between the **Inspections** layer and the spreadsheet, and replace it with a join to the new table:

19. Right-click on the **Inspections** layer and go to **Joins and Relates** in the menu that appears. Select **Remove Join**, as illustrated in the following screenshot. This will open the **Remove Join** tool in the **Geoprocessing** pane:

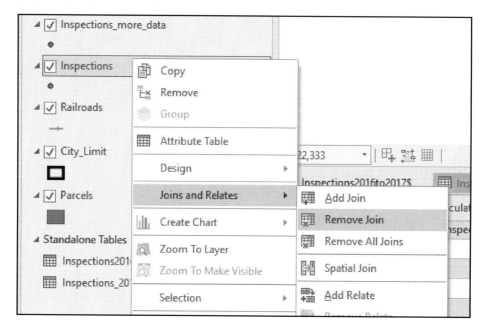

Removing the data table joins

20. All the required parameters should be automatically populated, since there is only one join in place associated with the **Inspections** layer. So verify that your **Remove Join** tool looks like the following screenshot and click **Run**:

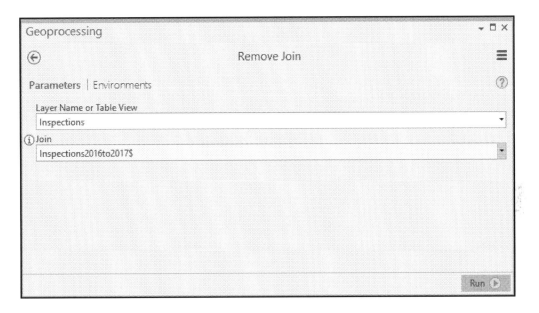

You can join or relate multiple tables to a single layer or table if needed within ArcGIS Pro. However, be careful how many you join or relate as it can have a negative impact on performance and become difficult to manage.

21. Using the skills you learned in Chapter 3, *Linking Data together*, and earlier in this recipe, join the Inspections_2016_2017 standalone table to the Inspections layer.

22. Right-click on the **Inspections2016to2017$** standalone table and select **Remove**. This will remove the table from the map, but does not delete the file.

23. Open the **Attribute Table** for the **Inspections** layer and verify the data from the **Inspections_2016_2017** is joined.

24. Close the **Geoprocessing** pane and any open tables that you are viewing.

25. Save your project and close ArcGIS Pro.

Importing selected features into an existing layer

Throughout this chapter, you have learned various methods for importing entire datasets into your geodatabase or exporting from your geodatabase to other formats. What if you only want to import a few selected features or records?

By default, the geoprocessing tools you have already used, such as Copy Features, Merge, Append, and Excel to table, will automatically be limited to selected features or records if you have them selected. However, most of these tools create new feature classes or tables. They do not just add data to an existing dataset. ArcGIS Pro will allow you to copy data from one layer and paste it into another existing layer. This allows you to choose exactly which features you want to convert or import.

In this recipe you will copy records from a shapefile and paste them into an existing layer which points to a geodatabase feature class. You will do this by first performing a query to select the features in the shapefile you wish to import into the existing geodatabase layer. Then you will copy and paste those features from the shapefile into the geodatabase layer. The shapefile you are working with represents a new subdivision being constructed in the City of Trippville.

Getting ready

You are not required to have completed previous recipes in order to complete this one. This recipe can be completed with all license levels of ArcGIS Pro. You will need to ensure the sample data for the book has been installed. It is assumed that by this point you have completed some recipes from the book or at least have worked with ArcGIS Pro in the past and know how to open an existing project.

How to do it...

1. Start ArcGIS Pro and open the `Convert Selected Data.aprx` project located in `C:\Student\ArcGISProCookbook\Chapter7` using the skills you have learned in past recipes.
2. Notice the large parcel in the center of the map view. This is the parcel that is going to become the new subdivision. In the **Contents** pane select the **List by Draw Order** button. It is the first button on the left side.

3. Turn on the **New Subdivision Shapefile** layer. Once it is visible you will be able to see the new subdivision.

4. The new project should open with the City of Trippville map zoomed to the area for the new subdivision. Click on the List by Editing button in the **Contents** pane. The buttons icon looks like a pencil.

5. Right-click on the **Street Rights of Way** layer and select **Make this the only editable layer** from the menu that appears, as illustrated here:

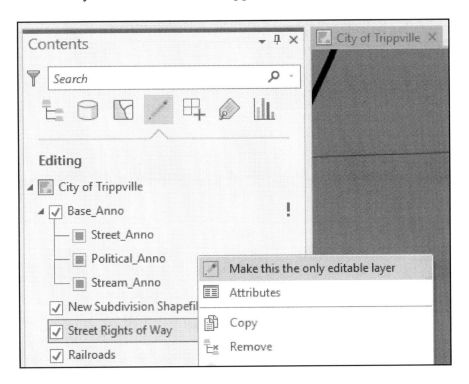

6. Click on the **List by Selection** button in the **Contents** pane. It is located to the left of the **List by Editing** button.

7. Click on the **Map** tab in the ribbon. Select the **Select by Attribute** tool in the **Selection** group. This will open the **Select Layer by Attribute** tool in the **Geoprocessing** pane.

8. Click on the drop-down arrow for the **Layer Name and Table View**. Select the **New Subdivision Shapefile** from the list presented.

9. Ensure the **Selection Type** is set to **New Selection**.

10. Click on the **Add Clause** button.

6. Build your expression as shown in the following screenshot, and click the **Add** button:

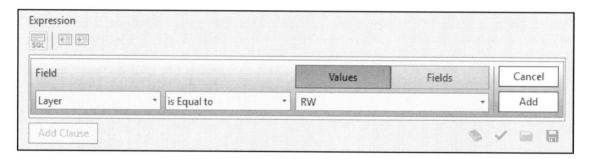

12. Click the **Verify** button, which looks like a green check mark, below the selection expression you just created. If it says **The SQL expression is valid**, click the **Run** button. This will select all the lines in the **New Subdivision Shapefile** that are attributed as being RW, which stands for **Rights of Way**.

You should have 258 features selected, which you can verify by looking in the **Contents** pane. You should see the number of selected features next to the **New Subdivision Shapefile** layer. The selected features will be highlighted in the map, as shown the following screenshot:

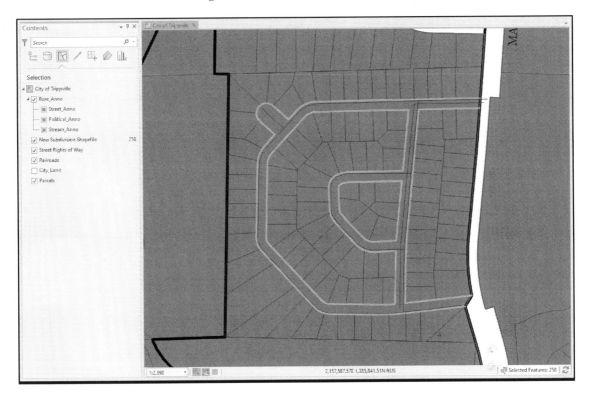

Selected street rights of way lines

Now, you will copy the features you have selected and paste them to the **Street Rights of Way** layer.

13. Click on the **Edit** tab in the ribbon.
14. Click on the **Select** tool in the **Selection** group on the **Edit** tab.
15. Click on the **Copy** button located in the **Clipboard** group on the **Edit** tab.

16. Click on the drop-down arrow located below the **Paste** tool in the **Clipboard** group on the **Edit** tab, and select **Paste Special**, as illustrated in the following screenshot:

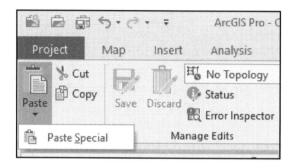

17. Ensure the **Paste into Template** is set to **Street Rights of Way**, as shown in the following screenshot, and click **OK**:

18. Look in the **Contents** pane. Notice that there are now no features selected in the **New Subdivision Shapefile** layer. Instead, there are now 258 features selected in the **Street Rights of Way** layer. You just copied the features from one layer and pasted them into another existing layer.

19. Click on the **Clear** button, located in the **Selection** group on the **Edit** tab in the ribbon, to clear your selected features.

20. In the **Contents** pane, click on the **List by Draw Order** button and turn off the **New Subdivision Shapefile** layer to verify that you did successfully copy the features to the **Street Rights of Way** layer.

21. Click the **Save** button in the **Manage Edits** group on the **Edit** tab in the ribbon to save the new features you just copied into the **Street Rights of Way** layer. When asked to save all edits, click **Yes**.

22. Save your project and close ArcGIS Pro.

This method will allow you to copy features from layers that reference CAD files (DWG, DGN, or DXF), shapefiles, and geodatabase feature classes to another layer as long as the layer references a shapefile or geodatabase feature class.

8
Proximity Analysis

In this chapter, we will cover the following recipes:

- Selecting features within a specific distance
- Creating Buffers
- Determining the nearest feature using the Near tool
- Calculating how far features are using the Generate Near Table tool

Introduction

If you have been working through the previous chapters in this book, you have learned how to access, visualize, convert, and maintain data using ArcGIS Pro. While these capabilities alone would make ArcGIS Pro a very powerful tool, those are by no means the limits of what you can accomplish with ArcGIS Pro.

ArcGIS Pro is capable of performing some amazing analysis. These capabilities are generally broken down into four categories: overlay, proximity, network, and statistical. These can be further specialized as well. As was pointed out in `Chapter 1`, *ArcGIS Pro Capabilities and Terminology*, there are two things that determine what tools are available to you, license level and extensions. The license level will determine what core tools are available to you. The extensions will determine what specialized tools you will be able to access. So, it is always important to know what license level you are using and what extensions you have access to. Review `Chapter 1`, *ArcGIS Pro Capabilities and Terminology*, for more information about license levels.

Let's now focus on proximity analysis in ArcGIS Pro. Proximity analysis is simply determining how far or close features are from one another. This could be as simple as selecting features that are within a specified distance from other features, or as complex as calculating the distances between features in one or more layers. Examples of proximity analysis include creating a buffer around selected features to show the area around those features at a set distance. It might be calculating how far features in one layer are from features in another layer and writing those values to a data table. It might be determining which feature in one layer is the closest to a feature in another layer.

In this chapter, you will get some first-hand experience of performing various types of proximity analysis. This will include creating buffers, selecting features based on distance, determining the nearest feature, and calculating how far features are from other features. Some of these recipes will require you to have an Advanced license for ArcGIS Pro.

Selecting features within a specific distance

For this recipe, the roads superintendent has told you he will be starting a new project along Sloan St. and needs to notify those living and working near the street. He has asked you to generate a list of all the parcels located within 500 feet of Sloan Street, so he can notify them of the upcoming work.

In this recipe, you will use the Select by Location tool to select all the parcels within 500 feet of Sloan Street, and then export the selected parcels to an Excel spreadsheet to give to the superintendent. Before you can use the Select by Location tool, you will need to select all the road centerline segments that make up Sloan Street. You will use the Select by Attribute tool to do that.

Getting ready

This recipe does require the sample data be installed on the computer. It is recommended that you complete the recipes in Chapter 1, *ArcGIS Pro Capabilities and Terminology*, or have some experience working with ArcGIS Pro before you start this recipe in order to ensure you have the required foundational skills and knowledge needed to successfully complete this recipe. You can complete this recipe with any ArcGIS Pro licensing level.

How to do it...

1. The first step is to launch ArcGIS Pro. You can do this, several ways depending on how your computer is set up. You can go through the Start menu and **All Programs**. Then to **ArcGIS** and **ArcGIS Pro**.

2. In the **ArcGIS Pro** start window, click on **Open another project**:

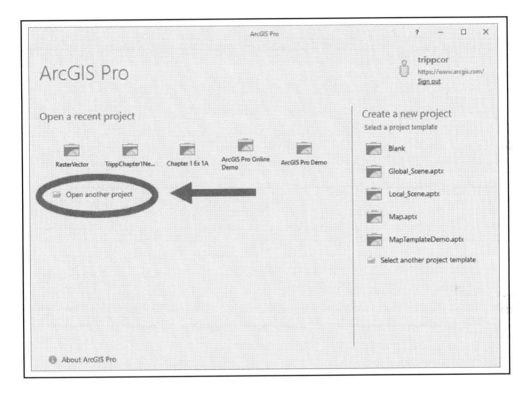

3. Select **Computer** from the **Open** window and then click **Browse** in the area on the right.

4. Navigate to `C:\Student\ArcGISProCookbook\Chapter8\Proximity Analysis` by clicking on `C:\` in the area on the left of the **Open Project** window. Then double-click on **Student**, **ArcGISProCookbook**, **Chapter8**, and **Proximity Analysis** folders.

5. Select the **Proximity Analysis.aprx** project file and click **OK**.

The project will open with the **Select in a distance** map. This is an existing map that already contains the layers you will need to work with in this recipe.

6. Click on the **Bookmarks** button in the **Navigate** group in the **Map** tab on the ribbon.

7. Select the **Sloan St** bookmark, as illustrated in the following. This will zoom you to the work area for this recipe:

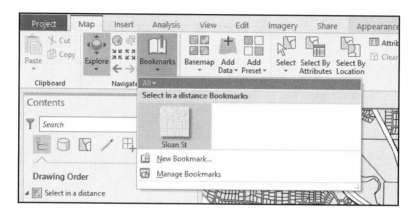

8. Now you need to select all the segments which form Sloan St. You will use the **Select by Attribute** tool to do this. Click on the **Select by Attributes** tool located in the **Selection** group on the **Map** toolbar. This will open the **Select Layers by Attributes** tool in the **Geoprocessing** pane.

9. Click on the drop-down menu for the **Layer Name or Table view**. Select **Street Centerlines** from the list that appears.

10. Ensure the **Selection** type is set to **New selection**.

11. Click on the **Add Clause** button to start building your query.

12. Set the **Field** to **ST_NAME** using the drop-down arrow.

13. Ensure the operator is set to **is Equal to**.

14. Type SLOAN ST into the values cell. It should start to auto-populate as you begin typing.

15. Verify that your query looks like the following, and click the **Add** button:

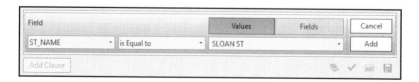

16. Verify your **Select Layer by Attribute** tool looks like the following image and click **Run**:

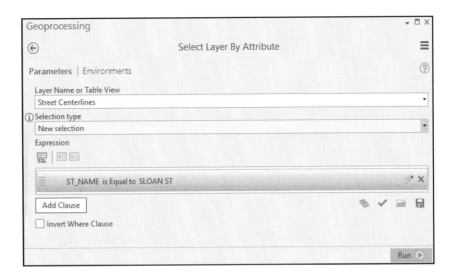

17. If you look at the lower-right corner of the ArcGIS Pro interface, you should see that three features are selected. Close the **Geoprocessing** pane once you have verified that you have three features selected.

Since Sloan St. is such a short road, you could have simply selected them from the map using the **Select** tool.

You have just selected the road segments that make up Sloan Street within your GIS data. Now, you need to select the parcels that are within 500 feet, so you can create the notification list to give to the superintendent.

18. With the **Sloan Street** segments selected, click on the **Select by Location** tool in the **Selection** group on the **Map** tab in the ribbon. This will open the **Select Layers by Location** tool in the **Geoprocessing** pane.

19. Set the **Input Feature Layer** to **Parcels** by clicking on the drop-down arrow and selecting the layer from the list.

20. Set the **Relationship** to **Within a distance** using the drop-down arrow and selecting the option from the list.

21. Set the **Selecting Features** to **Street Centerlines** from the list presented to you when you click on the drop-down arrow.
22. Type 500 in the **Search Distance** cell and ensure the units are set to feet.
23. Verify that the **Selection type** is set to **New selection**.
24. Review whether your **Select Layer by Location** tool looks like the following screenshot, and click **Run**:

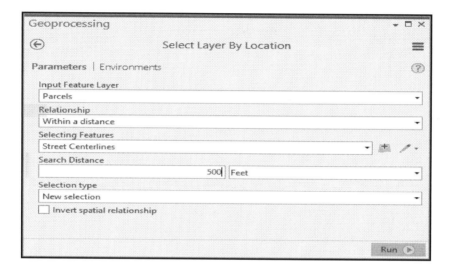

The Select Layer by Location tool automatically uses only selected features in the Selecting Features layer because it is a geoprocessing tool. Geoprocessing tools automatically run using selected features for any input layers or tables. So, unlike the Select by Location tool in ArcMap, you are not required to tell ArcGIS Pro to use selected features.

The Select Layer by Location tool is not limited to only selecting features within a specified distance. It can be used to select features based on several types of spatial relationships, including intersect, are contained by, share a boundary, and more. This makes it a very powerful tool when you need to select features based on their spatial relationship.

When the tool finishes, you should end up with 107 total selected features. That includes three selected Street Centerline segments and 104 parcels. Now, all that is left is to export the selected parcels to an Excel spreadsheet.

25. In the **Geoprocessing** pane, click on the **Back** button located in the upper-left corner of the pane, as indicated in the following image. This will take you back to the general **Geoprocessing** pane:

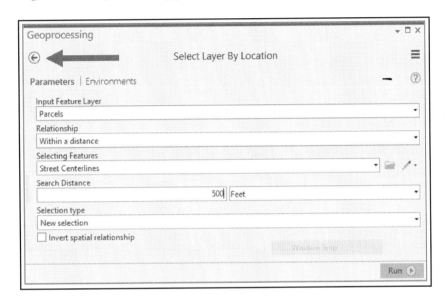

26. Click on the **Toolboxes** tab at the top of the **Geoprocessing** pane.
27. Expand the **Conversion Tools** toolbox and the **Excel** toolset.
28. Click on the **Table to Excel** tool. This will open the tool in the **Geoprocessing** pane.
29. Set the **Input table** to **Parcels** using the drop-down arrow and selecting the layer from the list that appears.
30. Click the **Browse** button for the **Output Excel File**.
31. In the **Save As** window that appears, click on **This PC** or **My Computer** in the panel on the left.
32. In the panel on the right, double-click on the **C:** drive located under **Devices and drives**. It should be labeled **OS or Local Drive**.
33. Scroll down in the right panel and double-click on the **Student** folder.
34. Continue this same process until you have navigated to `C:\Student\ArcGISProCookbook\MyProjects`.
35. Type `Parcels_near_SloanDr` in the **File Name** cell, then click **Save**.

36. Verify that your **Table to Excel** tool looks like the following, and click **Run**:

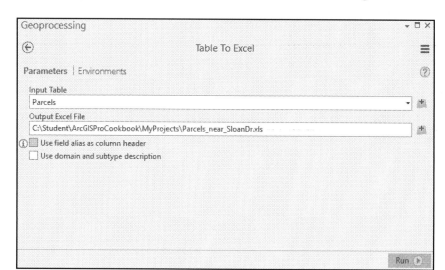

When the tool is complete it will have exported a copy of all the attribute information linked to the selected parcels to a Microsoft Excel spreadsheet.

37. In the **Selection** group on the **Map** tab in the ribbon, click on the **Clear** button to deselect all selected features.

38. Save your project.

39. If you are not continuing to the next recipe you can close ArcGIS Pro. If you are continuing, keep ArcGIS Pro open.

So, in this recipe, you needed to create a list that the roads superintendent could use to notify all those that live or work near Sloan Street of an upcoming project. To do this you first had to select all the segments that made up Sloan Street in the GIS database. You performed an attribute query using the Select by Attributes tool. You then used this selection in the Select by Location tool to select all parcels within 500 feet of the selected segments of Sloan Street. Lastly, you exported the selected parcels that were near Sloan Street to a spreadsheet. The roads superintendent will then be able to use it to notify all those near the upcoming road project.

This recipe has not only shown you how to select features that are within a specified distance of other features, it has also illustrated that analysis is often a multiple step process. It requires you to use a range of tools and skills to arrive at an answer.

Creating buffers

Buffers allow you to see what features are within a specific distance of other features. It generates polygons around the buffered features that provide the visual reference of the specified distance. These polygons can then be used to perform additional analysis or select features that are within, or intersect, the buffers.

In this recipe, you will create a buffer around the creeks and streams in the City of Trippville that will represent a protective zone where special permits are required to perform work. This is due to a recent ordinance passed by the city council to protect water quality in and around the city.

Getting ready

This recipe does require the sample data be installed on the computer. It is recommended that you complete the recipes in Chapter 1, *ArcGIS Pro Capabilities and Terminology*, as well as the other recipes in this chapter before you start this recipe. This will ensure that you have the skills required to successfully complete the steps in this recipe. You can complete this recipe with any ArcGIS Pro licensing level.

How to do it...

1. If you closed ArcGIS Pro before starting this recipe, you will need to start ArcGIS Pro and open the Proximity Analysis.aprx project located in C:\Student\ArcGISProCookbook\Chapter8\Proximity Analysis, using the skills you have learned in past recipes.
2. In the **Catalog** pane, expand the **Maps** folder. Then right-click on the **Buffer** map and select **Open** from the menu that appears. This will open a map that contains the layers you need to perform the work you will be doing in the remainder of the recipe.
3. Click on the **Analysis** tab in the ribbon.
4. Click on the **Buffer** tool in the **Tool** group. This will open the **Buffer** tool in the **Geoprocessing** pane.
5. Set the **Input Features** to **Creeks and Streams** by clicking on the drop-down arrow and selecting the layer from the list.
6. Accept the default **Output Feature Class**.

While the input for the Buffer tool can be any feature type (point, line, or polygon), the output will always be a polygon.

7. Type 60 into the **Distance** value and select **Feet** from the units drop-down list.
8. You will also accept the defaults for the **Side Type** and **End Type**. The **Side Type** should be **Full** and the **End Type** should be **Round**.

 You are only able to access and change these options if you have an Advanced license.

9. Because the protective zone is consistent for all creeks and streams, you will set the **Buffer** tool to **Dissolve all output features into a single feature** class by clicking on the drop-down arrow for the **Dissolve Type**. This will create a single buffer that takes less space and is easier to manage.
10. Verify that your **Buffer** tool looks like the following, and click the **Run** button:

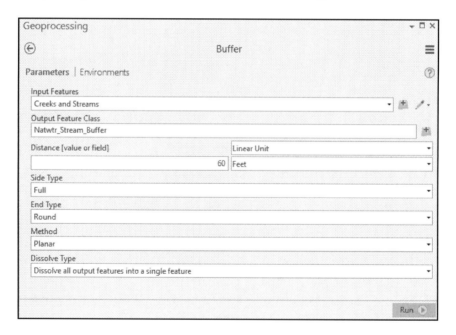

11. When the **Buffer** tool completes, a new layer will appear in your **Contents** pane. This is the buffer feature class you just created. Close the **Geoprocessing** pane to free up screen space.

12. Save your project.

You have just created a new feature class in the project geodatabase, that represents the protective area around the creeks and streams. You can easily see the areas that are impacted by this new protective zone. You could also use this layer to perform various analyses. For example, you could use the Select by Location tool to select all parcels that intersect the protective buffer. This will allow you to know exactly which parcels would need a permit for any work they do near one of the creeks or streams. You could use the Union geoprocessing tool to calculate how much of each parcel is within the protective zone and how much is outside.

Challenge:
Using the skills you learned in this recipe and in the Selecting Features within a distance recipe, select all the parcels that are intersected by the new protective zone buffer you just created, then export the selected parcels to an Excel spreadsheet.

There's more...

You have just learned how to create a single buffer around features using the Buffer tool. But what if you need to create several buffers at various distances around a set of features or a single layer? You could just use the buffer tool multiple times. However, there is an easier way.

The fire chief for the city of Trippville is working on a fire protection study and needs your help to determine the level of protection provided by the fire hydrants within the city. He needs to know how much of each parcel is 100, 200, and 300 feet from each hydrant. You will use the Multiple Ring Buffer tool to accomplish this:

1. First we will clean up the **Buffer** map you have been using. Right-click on the **Natwtr_Stream_Buffer** layer and select **Remove** from the menu that appears.

2. Repeat this process for the Creeks, Streams, Lakes and Rivers layers.

3. In the **Catalog** pane, expand the **Databases** folder so you can see its contents.

4. Expand the **Trippville_GIS.gdb** geodatabase.

5. Expand the **Water** feature dataset and right-click on the **fire_hyd** feature class. Select **Add to Current Map** from the menu that appears.

6. Save your project.

7. Click on the **Analysis** tab in the ribbon.

8. Click on the **Tools** button in the **Geoprocessing** group to open the **Geoprocessing** pane.

9. Click on the **Toolboxes** tab near the top of the **Geoprocessing** pane.

10. Expand the **Analysis** toolbox and the Proximity toolset.

11. Click on the **Multiple Ring Buffer** tool to open it in the **Geoprocessing** pane. Notice that it has a different icon from all the other tools. That is because this tool is actually a Python script.

 Python is the primary scripting language for ArcGIS. It allows you to create custom tools that help automate tasks. These can then be scheduled to run automatically, at specified times, or run manually. To learn more about creating Python scripts for ArcGIS, you may want to check out Programming ArcGIS with Python by Eric Pimpler, at `https://www.packtpub.com/application-development/programming-arcgis-python-cookbook-second-edition`.

12. Set the **Input Features** to the **fire_hyd** layer you just added by clicking on the drop-down arrow and selecting it from the list.

13. Accept the default value for the **Output Feature Class**.

14. Type 100 in the cell under **Distances** and press the *Enter* key. Another cell should appear.

15. Type 200 in the new cell that appears and press the *Enter* key. Again, another cell should appear.

16. Type 300 in the new cell that appears and press the *Enter* key.

17. Set the **Buffer Units** to **Feet** using the drop-down arrow.

18. Accept the provided default for the **Field Name**.

19. Set the **Dissolve Option** to **Non-overlapping (Rings) or All depending on your ArcGIS Pro version**. This will allow the fire chief to know how much coverage he has at each distance.

 The Dissolve Option determines whether you create rings/donuts or disks. The Non-overlapping or All options will generate rings that resemble donuts. The overlapping area from the other specified distances is cut out. So in this example, you will get a single ring that extends out to 100 feet. The next ring will cover from 100 to 200 feet. The last ring will cover from 200 to 300 feet.

The Overlapping (disks) or None option creates solid disks that overlap.

Using this recipe as an example, you will have one disk that extends out to 100 feet. You will have a second disk that extends out to 200 feet and overlaps the first disk. The last disk will extend out to 300 feet and overlap the other two disks.

You are not required to set your buffer distances to equal intervals. They can be any distance you wish. To learn more about the Multiple Ring Buffer tool, go to `http://pro.arcgis.com/en/pro-app/tool-reference/analysis/multiple-ring-buffer.htm`.

20. Verify that your **Multiple Ring Buffer** tool looks like the following, and click **Run**:

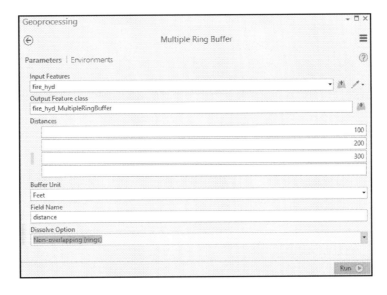

The new layer should appear in the **Content** pane, which shows the results of the **Multiple Ring Buffer** tool. Now let's verify the results.

21. Select the **fire_hyd_MultipleRingBuffer** layer in the **Contents** pane.
22. Click on the **Appearance** tab in the **Feature Layer** contextual menu in the ribbon.
23. Click on the **Import** button in the **Drawing** group.
24. Verify that the **Input Layer** is set to **fire_hyd_MultipleRingBuffer**.
25. Click on the **Browse** button for the **Symbology** Layer. Then select the **Folders** folder under **Project** in the left panel of the **Symbology Layer** window.

26. Double-click on the **Proximity Analysis** folder in the right panel.
27. Select the **Distance_from_Hydrant.lyrx** and click **Ok**.
28. Verify that your **Apply Symbology from Layer** looks like the following, and click **Run**:

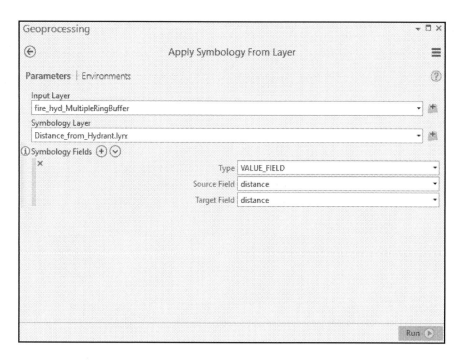

The symbology should change for the multiple ring buffer layer you created. Now you can see each ring.

29. Close the Geoprocessing pane.
30. Save your project.
31. Click on the **Map** tab and the **Bookmarks** button. Select the **Hydrant** bookmark to zoom in closer to the **Hydrants**.
32. Ensure that the layer is still selected in the **Contents** pane, and click on the drop-down arrow below the **Symbology** button in the **Drawing** group on the **Appearance** tab in the ribbon. Select **Unique Values** from the menu that appears, as illustrated in the following screenshot:

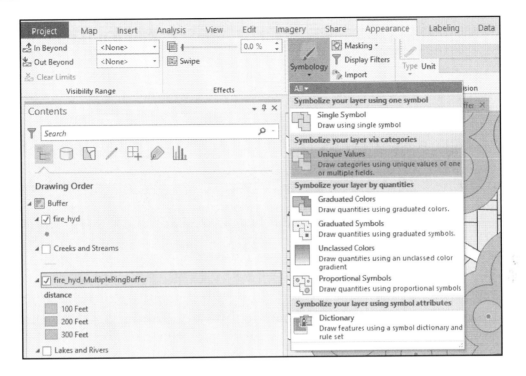

The **Symbology** pane should open.

33. In the grid that displays the three distances, right-click on the row for **200 Feet** and select **Remove**. This will remove the area from 100 to 200 feet from the map so you can see how the rings work.

Removing values from the symbology grid does not remove them from the actual data source. It just removes those features from the display. You can always add the removed value back.

34. Click on the **Undo** button in the **Quick Access** toolbar located in the upper-left corner of the ArcGIS Pro interface. This will return the 200 value symbology.

35. Save your project and close ArcGIS Pro.

So, you have just created a new layer that represents distances around the fire hydrants in the city. This will allow the fire chief to easily determine how much protection the fire hydrants provide the citizens and businesses. Using this data, he can determine if any new fire hydrants should be installed to improve the fire protection in the city.

Determining the nearest feature using the Near tool

You have seen how we can use buffers to show areas that are within a specified distance from features. This allows us to see if other features are within that area. We can also use those areas to perform additional analysis. However, these are all general measurements. They do not tell us which feature is the closest to another feature. How do we determine which feature is closest to another feature?

If you have an advanced license for ArcGIS Pro, this is pretty easy. The Near tool will determine the closest feature for you. Not only will it determine which feature is closest, but it also has options to calculate the distance, direction, coordinates, and more of the closest features. The Near tool works with points, lines, and polygons. You can also specify that it only searches for the closest feature within a specified distance. So lets put this tool into action.

In this recipe, you will continue to assist the Fire Chief. He is still working on his fire protection study. He wants to know which fire hydrant is closest to each parcel, so the department will know exactly which hydrant they should connect to when responding to a given location. You will use the Near tool to calculate which hydrant is closest to each parcel.

Getting ready

You will need to make sure you have an Advanced license for ArcGIS Pro to complete this recipe. You will not be able to do it with a Basic or Standard license. If you are not sure what license level you have or how to determine it, refer to Chapter 1, *ArcGIS Pro Capabilities and Terminology*, and the recipe entitled *Determining your ArcGIS Pro license level*. That recipe outlines the steps required to determine your license level, if you do not remember.

If you are limited to a Basic or Standard license, then please read through this recipe and then proceed with the *There's more...* section, which can be completed with a lower license level.

It is also recommended, you complete the other recipes in this chapter before starting this one. This will ensure that you have a good basic understanding of proximity analysis within ArcGIS Pro.

You will also need to ensure the sample data is installed before you continue.

How to do it...

1. To begin, launch ArcGIS Pro using the same method you have in previous recipes, and then launch the `Nearest Feature.aprx` project located in `C:\Student\ArcGISProCookbook\Chapter8\Proximity Analysis` using the skills you have learned in past recipes.

2. It should open with the **Trippville Fire Protection Map**. Verify that this map contains the **Fire Hydrant** and **Parcels** layers at a minimum. It should look like the following. Your scale may be different depending on the size of your monitor and what panes you have open:

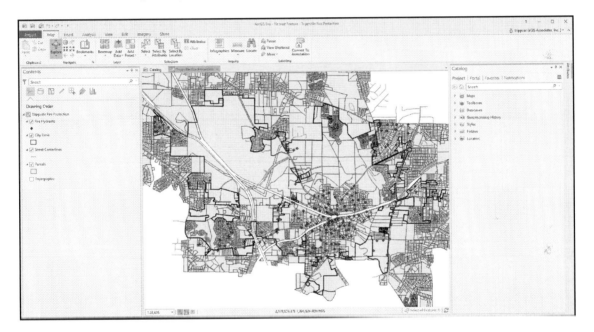

3. Right-click on the **Parcels** layer in the **Contents** pane and select **Attribute Table** from the menu that appears.

4. Review the available fields and answer the following question:

   Question: What fields are associated with the parcels in the attribute table?

   Answer:

As you can see, there are only a few fields associated with the parcels. The attribute table is currently storing the ObjectID, Shape, LOTNUM, STNUMBER, STNAME, STSUFFIX, Shape_Length, Shape_Area, and Acres. There is nothing here that tells you which fire hydrant is closest to each parcel. You are about to change that.

5. Close the **Parcels attribute** table by clicking the small **X** next to the table name in the tab at the top of the table view. This will free up more screen real estate.

If you have multiple monitors, or a really large one, you could also undock and drag the table pane to a different monitor or location as well. This would free up space for viewing the map, but also allow you to continue to view the table. Also, ArcGIS Pro lets you display each table in its own window if you desire, unlike ArcMap, which forces all tables into a single window.

6. Click on the **Analysis** tab in the ribbon, then click on the **Tools** button in the **Geoprocessing** group. This opens the **Geoprocessing** pane.
7. Click on the **Toolboxes** tab at the top of the **Geoprocessing** pane.
8. Expand the **Analysis Tools** toolbox and the **Proximity** toolset.
9. Click on the **Near** tool in the **Proximity** toolset.
10. Set the **Input Features** to **Parcels** by clicking on the drop-down arrow and selecting the layer from the list presented.
11. Set the **Near Features** to **Fire Hydrants** using the drop-down arrow and selecting it from the list.

You can set more than one layer or feature class as the Near Features. Also, Input Features and Near Features can be the same if you are looking for the nearest feature in the same layer.

12. Set the **Search Radius** to 300 feet by typing in 300 and ensuring the units are feet. The Fire Chief has indicated that any parcel over 300 feet from a hydrant is considered to not be adequately protected.
13. Go ahead and click on the **Location and Angle** boxes. This will provide additional information for the closest Hydrant.

The Location option will add the *x* and *y* coordinates for the nearest hydrant to the Parcel attribute table. The Angle option will add the angle to the nearest hydrant based on grid north.

 It should be noted that the Near tool is one of the few geoprocessing tools that actually edits existing data. In the case of the Near tool, it will add new fields to the Parcels attribute table since the Parcels layer is set as the Input Features. For more information on the Near tool, go to http://pro. arcgis.com/en/pro-app/tool-reference/analysis/near.htm.

14. Ensure the **Method** is set to **Planar**.
15. Verify that your **Near** tool looks like the following, and then click **Run**:

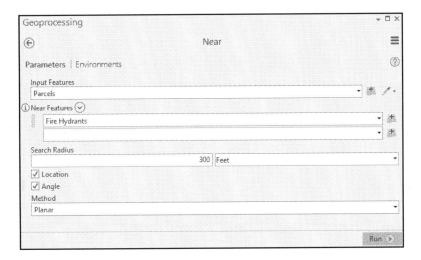

Notice, this time no new layers were added to your map unlike the Buffer and Multiple Ring Buffer. That is because the Near tool does not create a new feature class or table. Instead, it adds new fields to the Input Features attribute table. Lets see what fields were added by the Near tool to the Parcels layer.

 You must also have edit permissions to the Input Features layer in order to use this tool.

16. Close the Geoprocessing pane to free up screen space.

17. Open the **Attribute** table for the **Parcel** using the same method you did earlier in this recipe. Then answer the following question:

Question: What fields have been added to the Parcels Attribute table by the Near tool?

Answer:

As you can see, several new fields now appear in the **Parcels** attribute table. This includes the **Near_FID**, **Near_Dist**, **Near_X**, **Near_Y**, and **Near_Angle**, as shown in the following screenshot:

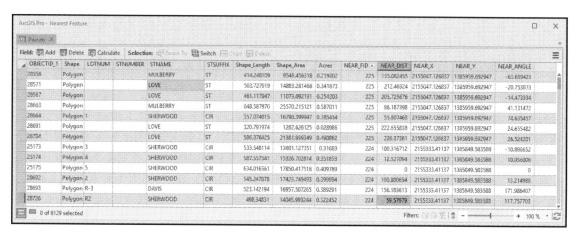

Those parcels with a -1 value in the fields are not within the 300 foot search radius you specified when your ran the Near tool. So those are easily identified as not having adequate fire protection. Those parcels that were within 300 feet of a hydrant now have the hydrants' feature ID (Near_FID), distance to the hydrant (Near_Dist), angle to the hydrant (Near_Angle), and X,Y coordinates (Near_X and Near_Y) assigned to each parcel. This allows you to learn which hydrant is closest to each parcel.

The Near_FID is the ObjectID for the nearest fire hydrant. You could use those two fields to join, relate, or create a relationship class between the two layers. This would allow you to access even more information.

18. Close the **Parcels** attribute table when you are done reviewing it.
19. Save your project.

Challenge:

Try linking the Parcels layer to the Fire Hydrants layer using a Join or Relate. Refer to `Chapter 3`, *Linking Data together*, using a Join or Relate. Determine which you should use, a Join or a Relate. (Hint: The cardinality between the tables is a many to one.) Then, link them using the best method. Verify your choice by opening the Parcels attribute table and seeing if you can see or access the linked information from the nearest Fire Hydrant. Remember, those with a -1 will not have linked information.

There's more...

The Near tool requires you to have an advanced license to determine which feature is the closest. What happens if you only have a basic or standard license? Is it possible to determine the closest feature without an advanced license?

Yes, you can, although it is not as straightforward and does produce a new feature class. You can use the Spatial Join tool. Let's see how it works. This will assume that you have not been able to complete the recipe up to this point because you did not have an advanced license.

1. Click on the **Analysis** tab in the ribbon.
2. Click on the **Spatial Join** tool in the **Tools** group on the **Analysis** tab. This will open the **Spatial Join** tool in the **Geoprocessing** pane.

You can also find this tool in the Overlay analysis toolset in the Analysis Tools toolbox. The Spatial Join allows you to join layers or feature classes together based on many spatial relationships.

3. Set the **Target Features** to the **Parcels** layer using the drop-down arrow and selecting it from the list.
4. Set the **Join Features** to **Fire Hydrants**, also using the drop-down arrow.
5. Accept the default **Output Feature Class**, which should be something similar to **Parcels_SpatialJoin**.

Unlike the Near tool, the Spatial Join tool creates a completely new feature class. It does not simply add new fields to an existing layer. This means that your original Parcels layer is left unchanged.

6. Set the **Join Operation** to **Join one to one** using the drop-down arrow. You are using the one to one option because only one hydrant should be the closest to each parcel.

7. Ensure the **Keep All Target Features** checkbox is checked. This will ensure the resulting output feature class will contain all the parcels, even if they do not have a fire hydrant nearby.

8. Scroll down to the **Match Option** and select **Closest** using the drop-down arrow. This is the spatial relationship that ArcGIS Pro will use to join the data. Closest is near the bottom of the list. Take the time to see what other options are available.

9. Set the **Search Radius** to 300 feet, as we did when using the **Near** tool. This limits the search for the closest fire hydrant to 300 feet.

10. Verify that your **Spatial Join** tool looks like the following, then click **Run**:

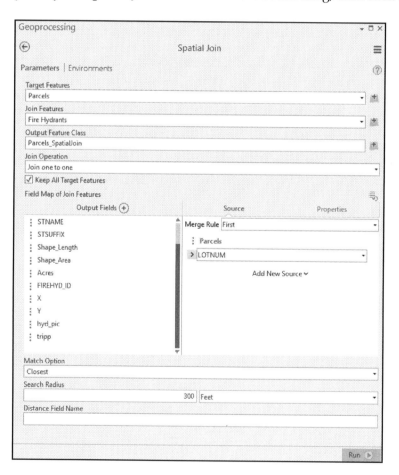

Depending on your computer, this tool may take a few minutes to run. So don't be worried if it takes some time. This analysis requires a lot of processing to complete.

11. A new layer should appear in your **Contents** pane. This new layer is the result of the **Spatial Join** tool. Close the **Geoprocessing** pane.

12. Right-click on the new layer that was just added. Select **Attribute table** from the menu that appears.

13. The attribute table contains information from both the **Parcels** and **Fire Hydrants** layer. Take a moment to review the results.

   The Join_Count field tells you how many fire hydrants were joined to the parcels. Because you chose the Join one to one option, this number should either be a 1 or a 0. The Target_FID is the ObjectID for the closest fire hydrant to the parcel. The FireHyd_ID, X, Y, Picture, and Picture 2 fields all come from the closest fire hydrant to the parcel. The remaining fields all came from the parcels layer.

14. Close the attribute table when you are done.

15. Save your project and close ArcGIS Pro.

So, you now have two ways to calculate the nearest feature in ArcGIS Pro. If you have an advanced license you can use either method. If you only have a basic or standard, then you must use the Spatial Join. If you can use either, which is best? That depends on what you need to do with the resulting data. The Spatial Join is best when you are creating data that is intermediate to a large process and will not be needed later. Otherwise, it creates yet another layer you must maintain. The Near tool does not create more data for you to manage. It only adds to an existing layer of information that you are already maintaining.

Calculating how far features are using the Generate Near Table tool

You now know a couple of different ways to find the closest feature. What if you want to calculate the distance from one group of features to another group? Not just looking for the closest. The Generate Near Table tool can do this.

The Generate Near Table tool will create a new database table that lists how far the features in the input are from those in the near feature layer.

Like the Near tool, you have the option to include additional fields for location and angle as well. This tool also requires an advanced license.

The city of Trippville has several water quality monitoring stations that monitor the quality of the water in the creeks, streams, and rivers in the city. Recently, several of them have been reporting poor or bad water quality.

It is believed that this might be due to run off from an industrial site in the city.

In this recipe, you will use the Generate Near Table tool to identify all industrial parcels located near the stations reporting bad water quality. These will be the ones you need to inspect first to see if they are the cause of the bad water quality.

Getting ready

You will need to make sure you have an advanced license for ArcGIS Pro to complete this recipe. You will not be able to do it with a basic or standard license. If you are not sure what license level you have or how to determine it, refer to Chapter 1, *ArcGIS Pro Capabilities and Terminology*, and the recipe entitled *Determining your ArcGIS Pro license level*. That recipe will tell you how to determine your license level.

If you are limited to a basic or standard license, then please read through this recipe and then proceed with the *There's more...* section, which can be completed with a lower license level.

It is also recommended that you complete the other recipes in this chapter before starting this one. This will ensure that you have a good basic understanding of proximity analysis within ArcGIS Pro.

You will also need to ensure the sample data is installed before you continue.

How to do it...

1. You will start by launching ArcGIS Pro. Then open the Near Table.aprx project located in C:\Student\ArcGISProCookbook\Chapter8\Proximity Analysis using the skills you have learned in past recipes. The project should open with the **Trippville** map. You will start by selecting the industrial-zoned parcels.

2. Activate the **Map** tab in the ribbon and select the **Select by Attributes** tool in the **Selection** group. The **Select Layer by Attributes** tool will open in the **Geoprocessing** pane.

3. Set the **Layer Name or Table View** to **Zoning** using the drop-down arrow and selecting it from the list.

4. Ensure the **Selection Type** is set to **New selection**.

5. Click on the **Add Clause** button to begin building your query.

6. Set the **Field** to **ZONING** using the drop-down arrow.

7. Make sure the operator is set to **is Equal to**.

8. The value should be set to **HI** using the drop-down arrow.

9. Verify that your query looks like the following, and click the **Add** button:

10. Click the **Add Clause** button again. The clause you just added will only select those parcels that are in the **Heavy Industrial** (**HI**) zone. You also need to select those that are **Light Industrial** (**LI**).

11. Where it says **And**, click the drop-down arrow and select **Or**.

And and Or are clause connectors. They determine how clauses in a query work together. If you had left the query with And, then the selection would have to meet both clauses. Since a parcel cannot be zoned both heavy and light industrial, that means nothing would be selected. Or means it only has to meet the requirements of one of the two clauses. So in this case, the query will select all features that are zoned either light or heavy industrial.

12. Set the **Field** to **ZONING**, the operator to **is Equal to**, and the value to **LI**. Then, click **Add** once you verify it looks like the following screenshot:

13. Your **Select Layer by Attributes** tool should now contain two SQL Where clauses. This will select all the parcels that are zoned either light or heavy industrial. Verify that your tool looks like the following, and click **Run**:

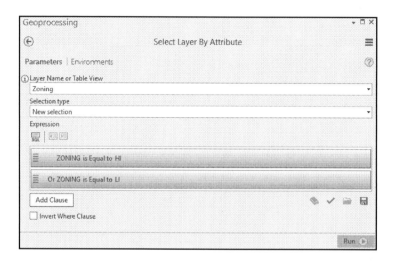

When you run the query, approximately 152 parcels should be selected within the map. All of them should be zoned either light or heavy industrial. Next, you need to select the **Water Quality Stations** that are reporting bad water quality. You will do this with another Select by Attribute query.

14. If you closed the **Geoprocessing** pane with the **Select Layer by Attribute** tool, click on the **Select by Attributes** button in the **Selection** group on the **Map** tab. If it is still open, go to the next step.

15. In the **Geoprocessing** pane, ensure the **Select Layer by Attribute** tool is still active.

16. Set the **Layer Name or Table View** to **Water Quality Station** using the dropdown arrow. If your old query is still present in the expression, an error may appear when you make this change. You can ignore it for now as you will be creating a new query soon.

17. Ensure the **Selection type** is still set to **New selection**.

18. Click on the Clear Expression button located below the query expression. It looks like a small eraser, as illustrated in the following screenshot:

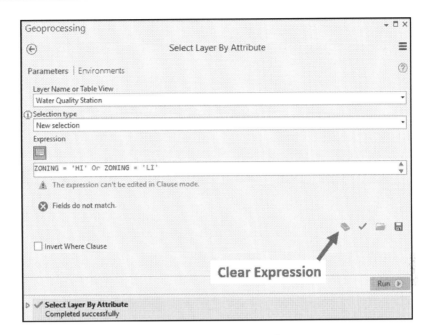

19. If you do not see the **Add Clause** button, click on the Switch to Edit Clause Mode button near the top of the expression area and below the word Expression, as illustrated in the following:

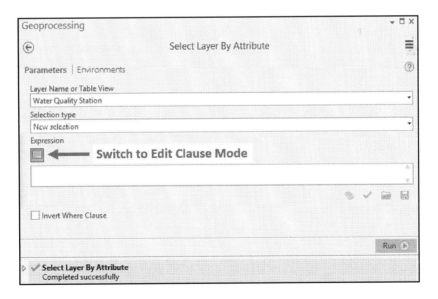

20. Click on the **Add Clause** button.
21. Set the **Field** to **Current Status**, the operator to **is Equal to**, and the value to **Bad**, all using the drop-down arrows.
22. Verify that your expression looks like the following, then click the **Add** button:

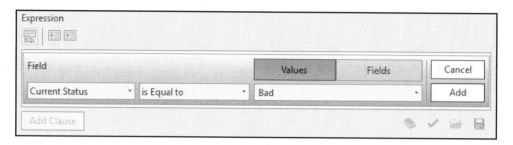

23. Verify that your **Select Layer by Attribute** tool looks like the following, and then click **Run**:

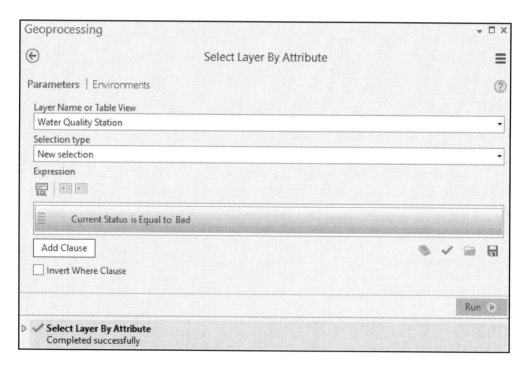

24. In the **Contents** pane, click on the **List by Selection** button. It is the third one from the left. You should now have approximately two Water Quality Stations and 151 Zoning polygons selected.

   Now that you have selected the appropriately zoned parcels and water quality stations, you need to create the table that lists which of the selected parcels is near the selected water quality stations. You will limit your search to a 1,500 feet radius around the water quality stations.

25. Click on the **Analysis** tab in the ribbon.

26. Click on the **Generate Near Table** tool in the **Tools** group. If you don't see the tool, click on the arrows located on the right side of the group to navigate up and down in the list of tools in the group.

27. The **Generate Near Table** tool will appear in the **Geoprocessing** pane. Set the **Input Features** to **Water Quality Station** using the drop-down arrow.

28. Set the **Near Features** to **Zoning** using the drop-down arrow on the far-right side.

29. Accept the default value ArcGIS Pro generates for the **Output Table**.

 This tool is creating a new table. By default, the table is being stored in the Project Geodatabase. This happens to be the Proximity Analysis geodatabase.

30. Set the **Search Radius** to 1,500 feet by typing 1500 and verifying the units.

31. Uncheck the **Find only closest feature** if it is checked. You want to find all industrial zoned-parcels within 1500 feet of the water quality monitoring stations that are reporting bad quality, not just the closest one. Leave the maximum number of closest matches to 0. This will ensure all matches within 1500 feet are returned.

32. The **Method** should be set to **Planar**.

33. Verify that your **Generate Near Table** tool looks like the following, and click **Run**:

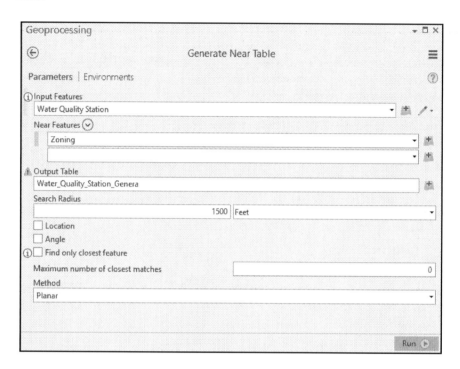

When the tool finishes, a new standalone table should appear in your **Contents** pane. This table is the results of the tool you just ran. Let's take a look at the results.

34. Close the Geoprocessing pane.

35. Right-click on the new table you just created, which was added to the **Contents** pane. Select **Open** from the menu that appears.

As we have mentioned before, geoprocessing tools, such as the Create Near Table tool, only use selected features automatically. Since you selected specific features in the Water Quality Stations and Zoning layers, this tool only used those selected features to run its analysis.

36. Review the newly created table.

In the new table, you should see several fields. The **IN_FID** field contains the object id for the Water Quality Station. You should see a value of 3 or 4 which matches the object id for those stations in the attribute table for the Water Quality Stations that have a current status of **Bad**. The **Near_FID** field contains the object id of the nearby industrial-zoned parcel. Each water quality station should be paired with multiple parcels. The **Near_Rank** field identifies which is closest to each water quality station. This helps you prioritize which parcels you should begin with.

37. Close the table and save your project.

There's more...

So, can you do this without an advanced license of ArcGIS Pro? The answer is yes. You can use the Spatial Join tool to accomplish something very similar. However, the result is not a table. It is a new feature class that will contain many overlapping features. If you just want a table, you can then export the records from the results of the Spatial Join tool to a new table. Here is how all that works:

1. If you still have the features selected from the Water Quality Station and Zoning layers, proceed to the next step. If you do not, repeat *steps 2-24* from the recipe. You should have two Water Quality Stations and 151 Zoning polygons selected.

2. Click on the **Analysis** tab in the ribbon. Then select the **Spatial Join** tool in the **Tools** group. This will open the tool in the **Geoprocessing** window.

3. Set the **Target Features** to **Water Quality Station** using the drop-down arrow.

4. Set the **Join Features** to **Zoning** using the drop-down arrow.

5. Click the **Browse** button to set the **Output Feature Class**.

6. Select databases from the panel on the left. Then double-click on the **Proximity Analysis.gdb** geodatabase in the panel on the right.

7. Type WaterQual_IndustZoned_SpatialJoin into the **Name** and click **Save**.

8. Set the **Join Operation** to **Join one to many**. This will ensure the result has all the industrial-zoned parcels within 1,500 feet of the water quality stations reporting bad quality.

9. Set the **Match Option** to **Within a distance** using the drop-down arrow.

10. Set the **Search Radius** to 1,500 feet.

11. Verify that your **Spatial Join** tool looks like the following, and click **Run**:

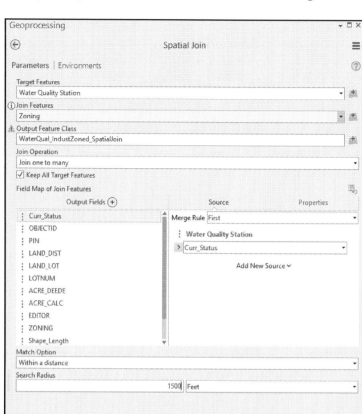

12. A new layer will appear in your **Contents** pane. This is the results of the **Spatial Join** tool. Close the **Geoprocessing** pane.
13. Select the **List by Draw Order** in the **Contents** pane. It is the first button at the top-left of the pane.
14. Click on the **Map** tab in the ribbon. Then click on the **Clear** button in the **Selection** group. You should now be able to see what looks like two new features that overlap the two Water Quality Stations that had bad water quality. Time to verify how many features are actually in those locations.
15. Right-click on the new layer and select **Zoom to Layer**.
16. Select the new layer in the **Contents** pane.

17. Click on the drop-down arrow located below the **Explore** tool and select **Selected in Contents**. Now click on one of the two new features. The information popup should appear when you click on one of the features.

18. Look at the lower-left corner of the information popup to see how many features are actually in the location you selected. If you clicked on the northernmost location, you should have about 30 features. If you clicked on the southernmost location, you should have about 14 features. This is illustrated in the following:

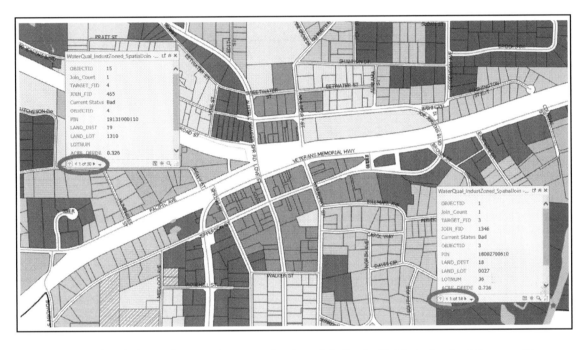

19. Right-click on the new layer and select **Attribute Table** to look at the resulting attributes. Review the table and see if you can identify what the fields mean and where they came from.

20. Close the attribute table and save your project.

21. Close ArcGIS Pro.

As you can see, you have created another new feature class. If you wanted to export this as a standalone table, you could right-click on the layer and go to **Data**. Then select **Export Table**. If you wanted to export it to an Excel spreadsheet you could use the Table to Excel tool you have used in past recipes.

Spatial Statistics and Hot Spots

9

In this chapter, we will cover the following recipes:

- Identifying hot spots
- Finding the mean center of geographic distribution
- Identifying the central feature of geographic distribution
- Calculating the geographic dispersion of data

Introduction

If you have completed the previous chapter, you have begun to get an idea of the analytical power ArcGIS Pro brings to the table. You have seen how it can be used to find features that are near one another and calculate those distances in addition to other attributes. But what if you are not looking to find just the closest feature or calculate how far features are from one another? What if you want to determine whether there are any spatial clusters in your data, to see whether there is some pattern or possible point of origin?

This type of analysis is often called Cluster or Hot Spot analysis. It uses various methods to determine the spatial distribution of data and associated values, so you can see clusters, determine center points, directional distribution, and more. This is done by calculating spatial statistics that can be weighted by other attributes, such as size, total amounts, or counts.

ArcGIS Pro contains over 25 different tools for calculating spatial statistics. These are all stored in the Spatial Statistics toolbox and divided between five different toolsets, including Analyzing Patterns, Mapping Clusters, Measuring Geographic Distributions, Modeling Spatial Relationships, and Utilities. All but a couple of the tools in this toolbox work with the core ArcGIS Pro product at all license levels. This means that even with a Basic license, you can perform some pretty amazing analysis.

In this chapter, you will get an opportunity to work with a few of the spatial statistics and hot spot analysis tools that are in ArcGIS Pro. You will perform a hot spot analysis to determine which areas in a city have experienced the most damage or loss due to crime. This will help the city determine where it might want to focus law enforcement activities.

Next, you will calculate the mean center of the members of a professional organization, so you can determine where to look to hold a conference so that it is located at the average center of mass for all the members.

Then, you are going to determine the central building for a company to use, to determine where to relocate its Corporate Headquarters, so it is at the center of all its other offices. This will make it easier for everyone to travel to Headquarters for meetings and reduce overall travel budgets.

Lastly, you will look at a series of crimes to determine whether they are concentrated or clustered in not only a general area but also along a focused direction. This will help determine whether a specific road or other mode of travel may be a contributing factor.

Identifying hot spots

The Police Chief has come to you for help. He is working on a grant to help fund more police officers through a neighborhood policing program. He needs to determine whether there are areas where crime has been occurring that have experienced more damage or loss than others. If such areas exist, he could include that as justification in his grant proposal.

He has provided you with crime data for the city that covers the years 2013 and 2014. This data has been geocoded, so you have a point layer that shows the location of the crimes and is attributed with the Crime Type, Date it occurred, Officer Responding, Damage or Loss in dollars, and number of victims involved. The grant requires all numbers to be summarized to the Census Block level. You will have to use the Spatial Join tool to aggregate the crime data by Census Block.

In this recipe, you will use the Hot Spot Analysis tool to see whether there are any geographic clusters of crimes that have resulted in higher-than-normal damage or loss to the victims. In order to perform this analysis, you will first need to aggregate the point data to the census blocks using a spatial join to summarize the crime data.

Getting ready

This recipe requires the sample data to be installed on your computer. It is recommended that you complete the recipes in the previous chapter before working on these. It is also recommended that you have completed the Joining Features Spatially recipe found in Chapter 3, *Linking Data together*. This will ensure, you have a better foundational understanding of how to access analysis tools and general workflows. You can complete this recipe with any ArcGIS Pro licensing level.

How to do it...

1. Using the skills you have acquired from performing the previous recipes, start ArcGIS Pro and open the `Spatial Stats Hotspots.aprx` project located in `C:\Student\ArcGISProCookbook\Chapter9\Spatial Stats Hotspots`.

2. The project should open with the **Union City Crime** map. This map contains the Crime Locations provided by the Police Chief, streets, City Limits, Parcels, Census Blocks, and Police Beat Zones. Before we begin with the analysis, we will need to get a better idea of the data we have to work with. Right-click the **Crime Locations** layer in the **Contents** pane and select the **Attribute Table**. Take a moment to explore the table and answer the following questions:

   Question: What fields are in the attribute table for the Crime Locations layer?

   Answer:

   Question: What type of crimes are identified in the attribute table?

   Answer:

   Question: What is the largest amount of loss or damage you can find in the table?

   Answer:

You can sort fields in ascending or descending order by right-clicking the field name in the table and selecting the desired sorting, much like you can do in a spreadsheet.

3. Open the attribute table for the **Census Blocks** layer using the same process. Review its contents and answer the following question:

Question: What fields are in the attribute table for the Crime Locations layer?

Answer:

You now have a better understanding of the data you will be working with. Since the hot spot analysis is looking for spatial clusters within an area, you will generally get better results using polygon inputs that points. So, it is recommended that you aggregate or summarize your point data to get the best results. That means you will need to aggregate the **Crime Locations** data into the **Census Blocks** layer, so you can see how many crimes occurred in each block and the total amount of damage in each block. You will use the **Spatial Join** tool to do this.

4. Close the open **Attribute tables** for the **Crime Locations** and **Census Blocks** layers.
5. Click the **Analysis** tab in the ribbon. Then click the **Spatial Join** tool in the **Tools** group. This will open the tool in the geoprocessing ribbon.
6. Set the **Target Features** to **Census Blocks** using the drop-down arrow.
7. Set the **Join Features** to **Crime Locations** using the drop-down arrow.
8. Accept the default value for the **Output Feature** class.
9. Set the **Join Operation** to **Join one-to-one** using the drop-down arrow and ensure **Keep All Target Features** is checked.

If you remember from `Chapter 3`, Linking Data together, you have two options for the Join Operation: Join one-to-one or Join one-to-many. The Join one-to-one option will aggregate data or sum values if more than one match is found. This is what we want. If the Join one-to-many option is selected, the tool will create multiple records for each match it finds between the Target and Join features. To learn more about the Spatial Join tool, go to `http://pro.arcgis.com/en/pro-app/tool-reference/analysis/spatial-join.htm`.

10. In the **Output Fields** panel, scroll down until you see **DL_Dollars** and select it. This is the **Damage and Loss** field from the **Crime Locations** layer. As illustrated in the following image, set the **Merge Rule** to **Sum** in the right panel so it adds the total damage from all the crimes that happen within the associated **Census Block**:

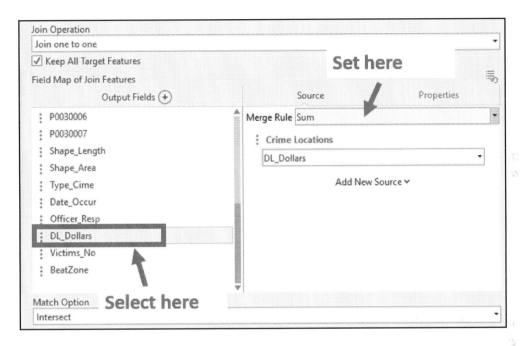

11. Select **Victims_No** located below **DL_Dollars** and set the **Merge Rule** for it to **Sum** too.
12. Set **Match Option** to **Contains**. This will aggregate all the crime locations contained in a specific census block.
13. Do not set a search radius since we only want to aggregate the crimes contained within the census blocks.

14. Verify that your **Spatial Join** tool looks like the following and click **Run**:

15. Close the **Geoprocessing** pane.

A new layer should have appeared in the **Contents** pane. This is the result of the Spatial Join tool. It should have the aggregated the crime data by census block. Let's examine the result to verify.

16. Right-click the **Census_Blocks_SpatialJoin** layer and select the **Attribute** table from the menu that appears.

17. Take a moment to scroll through the fields to see which ones are present. Then answer the following questions:

> **Question**: What fields does this new layer contain which the original Census Blocks layer did not?
>
> **Answer**:

> **Question**: What Census Block contains the largest amount of damage or loss from crime?
>
> **Answer**:

As you can see, the fields from the **Crime Locations** table have been added to those of the **Census Blocks** in the new layer you created. The **Damage or Loss in Dollars** and **Number of Victims** now represent the totals for all crimes that occurred within the given Census block. You should have also seen a new field, **Join_Count**. This provides you with a count of the number of crimes that were contained in each Census Block.

Now, it is time to perform the hot spot analysis to determine areas where the greatest amount of damage or loss has occurred due to crime. But before we do that, we need to update those census blocks that have a null damage value with a 0 to avoid issues with performing our analysis.

18. Click the **Map** tab in the ribbon. Then click the **Select by Attributes** tool in the **Selection** group.

19. Ensure the **Layer Name** or **Table View** is set to the new layer you just created.

20. The **Selection Type** should also be set to **New Selection**.

21. Click the **Add Clause** button.

22. Set the field to **Damage or Loss in Dollars** and the operator to **Null** using the drop-down arrows. Verify that your clause looks like the following, then click **Add**:

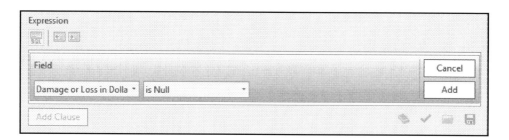

23. Verify that your **Select Layer by Attribute** tool looks like the following and click **Run** to select all blocks that have no value for the **Damage or Loss in Dollars** field:

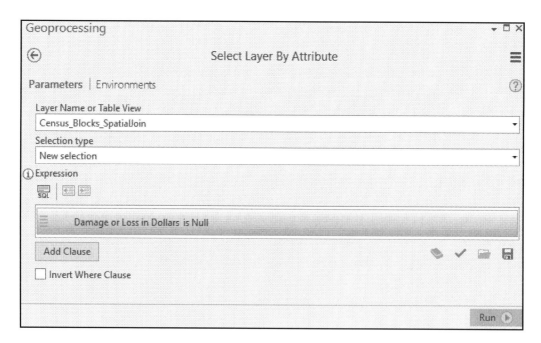

24. In the **Census_Blocks_SpatialJoin Attribute** table, right-click the **Damage or Loss in Dollars** field and select **Calculate Field** from the menu that appears.

25. This will open the **Calculate Field** tool in the **Geoprocessing** pane. In the expression cell located just beneath where it says **DL_Dollars**, and just above the **Code Block** area, type 0. Then click **Run**.

You have just used the Calculate Field tool to populate the Census blocks that did not have any matching crime data with a damage or loss value of 0. The Hot Spot analysis tool you will soon use does not work well when the field it will be analyzing has missing or Null values. Now it is time to begin the hot spot analysis.

26. Close the **Attribute** table for the **Census_Blocks_SpatialJoin** layer.

27. Ensure the **Map** tab is active in the ribbon. Then click the **Clear** button in the **Selection** group to deselect all selected records.

Remember, all geoprocessing tools will automatically only make use of selected features when you run them. To ensure we analyze every census block, we have to ensure none were selected. If we had run the tool with the census blocks still selected, it would not have found any hot spots or clusters because they all had a damage or loss value of 0.

28. Click the **Analysis** tab in the ribbon. Then click the **Tools** button in the **Geoprocessing** group to open the **Geoprocessing** pane.

29. Click the **Toolboxes** tab at the top of the pane. Scroll down to the **Spatial Statistics Tools** toolbox. It is near the bottom of the list.

30. Expand the **Spatial Statistics Tools** toolbox. Then expand the **Mapping Clusters** toolset.

31. Click the **Hot Spot Analysis (Getis-Ord GI*)** tool to open it in the **Geoprocessing** pane.

32. Set your **Input Feature Class** to **Census_Blocks_SpatialJoin** using the drop-down arrow.

33. Set the **Input Field** to **Damage or Loss in Dollars** using the drop-down arrow. This is the field you will be analyzing.

The **Input field** must be a numeric field type. This means it must be a long or short integer, or a float or double field type. It cannot be a text, date, or other field type.

34. Set the **Output Feature** class to be **Crime_Hotspots_DamageLoss** by typing that into the cell.

35. Leave the **Conceptualization of the Spatial Relationships** set to the **Fixed distance band**. This setting determines how features are analyzed in spatial relation to one another.

36. Leave **Distance Band** or **Threshold Distance** and **Self Potential Field** undefined as these are optional parameters.

37. Verify that your **Hot Spot Analysis (Getis-Ord Gi*)** tool looks like the following and click **Run**:

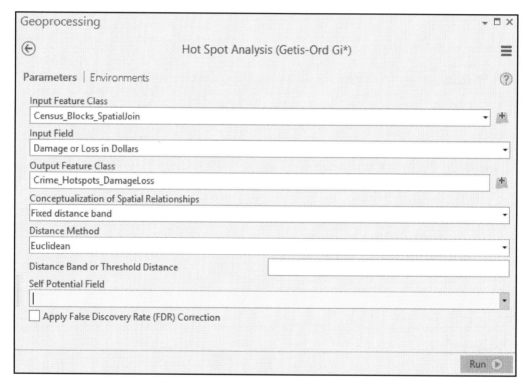

When the Hot Spot Analysis tool completes, a new layer will be added to your map. This layer will automatically be symbolized based on the statistical significance or confidence of the data. The higher the confidence, the more hot or cold it is. In this case, the hot spots are those areas that have the highest level of **Damage or Loss in Dollars**. The cold spots would be those where there was significantly less **Damage or Loss in Dollars**.

The results of your analysis have identified two hot spots or clusters where the amount of damage or loss in dollars is significant when compared to the surrounding areas:

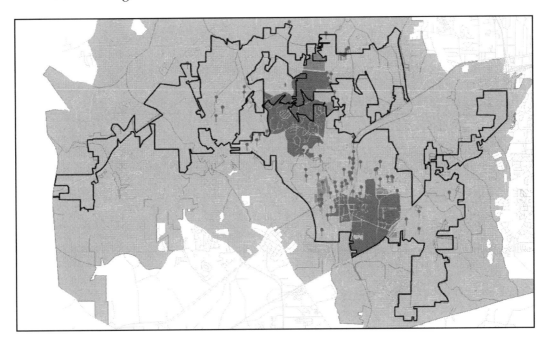

As you can also see, there are no Cold Spots. This means that there are now areas that are significantly below the average damage when compared to their surrounding neighbors.

38. Save your project.
39. If you are not continuing to the next recipe, you can close ArcGIS Pro. If you are continuing, keep ArcGIS Pro open.

Finding the mean center of geographic distribution

When we are looking for clusters of data or trying to determine the overall geographic distribution of our data, one of the first things many of these tools do is determine a center of mass for the data. From there, it can compare nearby features looking for clusters, determine area concentrations of data, look at directional distribution, and more.

However, finding the center of the geographic distribution of our data can be a powerful analytical tool. This can allow us to strategically locate new facilities, pick a central meeting place, plan a reaction to events, and more. There are three types of centers we can calculate: mean, feature, and median.

The Mean Center is the easiest to calculate. It is simply the average of all the x and y coordinates for all features in the layer you are analyzing. The result is the mean center. This can be useful in tracking movement or shifts over time, such as population shifts from urban to suburban areas. You might also use this to locate a good place to hold a meeting that would be centrally-located for all attendees.

The Median Center is sometimes referred to as the Minimum Distance center. Simply put, it is the coordinate pair that represents the location closest to all features in a given layer. Areas will automatically be weighted by the number of features present. Those with a large number of features will pull the median center toward them more than those with fewer features. This can be useful in locating new facilities that may rely on other structures for support.

The Center Feature locates an existing feature that is closest to all other features. This might be helpful if you are looking for a location that would be centrally-located to other facilities. For example, you are planning training for firefighters. You want to hold it at an existing fire station because they have the equipment you need for the training. The Center Feature would allow you to locate the fire station that would be closest to the other stations.

In this recipe, you have been asked to find a central location to hold a conference for a professional organization. You have been provided with a layer showing the locations of all the members. You will use the Mean Center tool to determine the geographic mean center of all the members. This will then identify the area you should look to for holding the conference.

Getting ready

This recipe requires the sample data to be installed on the computer. You do not need to complete any previous recipes, though it is recommended that you work through the first three chapters of the book, or have similar experience with ArcGIS Pro, to ensure that you have the proper foundational understanding to complete this recipe. You can complete this recipe with any ArcGIS Pro licensing level.

How to do it...

1. If you closed ArcGIS Pro before starting this recipe, you will need to start ArcGIS Pro and open the Spatial Stats Hotspots project located in `C:\Student\ArcGISProCookbook\Chapter9\Spatial Stats Hotspots`, using the skills you have learned in past recipes.

2. In the **Catalog** pane, expand the **Maps** folder. Then right-click the **Member Center** map and select **Open** from the menu that appears. This will open a map that contains the layers you need to perform the work for the remainder of the recipe.

    As you can see, this organization has members located across the US. So, it is important to pick a central location for the conference to reduce travel time and costs for all members.

3. Click the **Analysis** tab in the ribbon.

4. Click the **Tools** button in the **Geoprocessing** group to open the **Geoprocessing** pane.

5. Click the **Toolboxes** tab at the top of the pane.

6. Scroll down to the **Spatial Statistics Tools** toolbox and expand it so you can see its contents.

7. Expand the **Measuring Geographic Distribution** toolset. Notice the various tools included in this toolset. You should see tools for calculating the various centers that were discussed earlier, along with others.

8. Click the **Mean Center** tool to open it.

9. Set the **Input Features Class** to **Members** using the drop-down arrow.

10. Accept the default value for the **Output Feature Class**.

11. Leave the **Weight Field**, **Case Field**, and **Dimension Field** blank for this analysis. You will use those in a future analysis.

12. Verify that your **Mean Center** tool looks like the following and click **Run**:

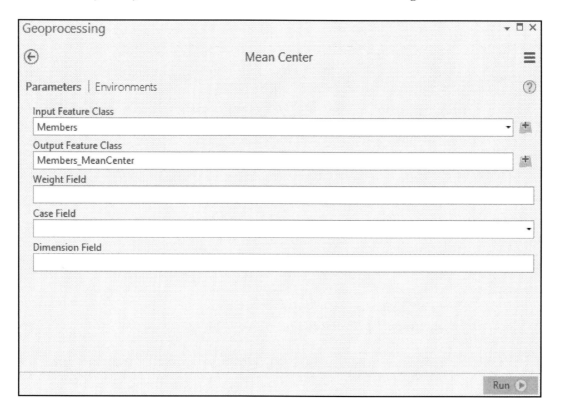

The results should produce a point that is located just north of Lebanon, Missouri, and west of Richland, Missouri, as shown in the following screenshot. This represents the mean geographic center of all the members in the organization:

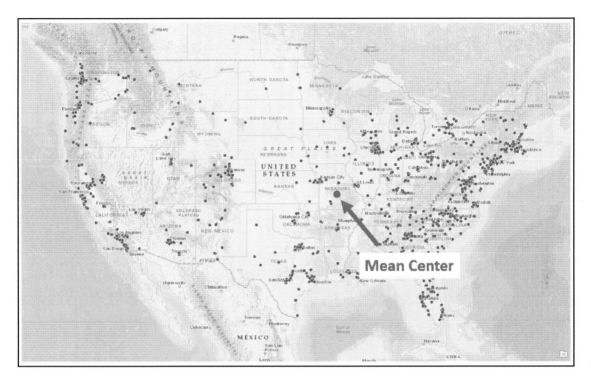

Results of mean center analysis

13. Close the Geoprocessing pane.
14. Save your project.

You have just calculated the mean center for the members of a professional organization to help them pick a location for their next conference. You used the Mean Center tool located in the Spatial Statistics Tools toolbox and the Measuring Geographic Distributions toolset to do this.

There's more...

You just calculated the mean center for the members of a professional organization using the Mean Center tool. However, when you ran the tool, you left several parameters blank, including **Weight Field** and **Case Field**. Both of these parameters can change the results of the tool and greatly increase its flexibility.

Often when we are analyzing data, not all the inputs are equal, even in a single layer. Some may need to be given more influence over others. This is certainly true when we are trying to calculate centers. We can reflect this unequal influence by using a weighted field.

When we calculate centers without using a weighted field, as you did with the members, all features are treated the same. No single feature or location carries more weight or influence on the final result than another. However, if you use a **Weight Field**, some locations receive greater consideration than others when calculating the mean center. This will cause the center to be pulled toward those weighted locations, as illustrated in the following screenshot:

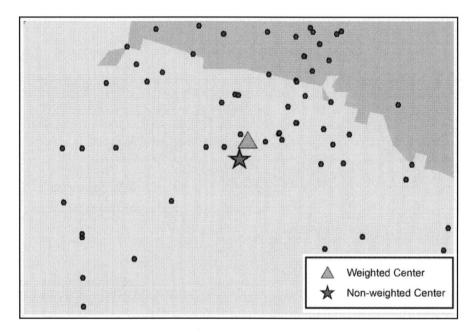

The weight each feature carries when running the analysis is based on a field in the attribute table of the **Input Feature Class**. This attribute field must be a numeric type field. Text fields cannot be used as a weighted field. Those with a higher number will have more pull when calculating the center than those with a lower number. This will cause the calculated center to be pulled closer to those with a higher weight.

The **Case Field** groups features for analysis based on values found in that field. This means that your results will have more than one center point returned. You will get a center location calculated for each grouping of features.

So, let's see how these two fields work. The Police Chief needs more help with his grant application. He is trying to determine the possible location of new precincts within each of the Police Beat Zones. These Zones represent patrol and response areas for the precincts. He needs to know the mean center of the crimes that occur in each Zone. He wants those crimes with the greatest number of victims to be considered more than those with the least. You will use the same Mean Center tool to perform this analysis for the Police Chief. However, this time you will provide values for the **Weight Field** and **Case Field** parameters:

1. Ensure the Spatial Stats Hotspots project is still open.
2. Click the **Union City Crime** map tab at the top of the map view. The map you used to perform the hot spot analysis in the previous recipe should now be displayed.
3. Right-click the **Crime_Hotspots_DamageLoss** layer and select **Remove** from the menu that appears. Repeat this process for the **Spatial Join** and **Census Blocks** layers as well. This just cleans up the map, so it is easier to read and work with.
4. In the **Contents** pane, make sure you are on **List by Draw Order**. It is the first button on the left at the top of the pane.
5. Turn on the **Police Beat Zones** layer so it is visible. Now you can see the Zones the Police Chief was referring to.
6. Using the skills you have learned, open the **Mean Center** tool in the **Geoprocessing** pane.

   If you don't remember how you did that, refer to *steps 3-7* when you calculated the Mean Center of the members earlier in this recipe.

7. Set **Input Feature Class** to **Crime Locations** using the drop-down arrow.
8. Accept the default value provided for the **Output Feature Class**.
9. Set the **Weight Field** to the **Number of Victims** using the drop-down arrow.
10. Set the **Case Field** to the **Police Beat Zone**.

11. Verify that your **Mean Center** tool looks like the following then click **Run**:

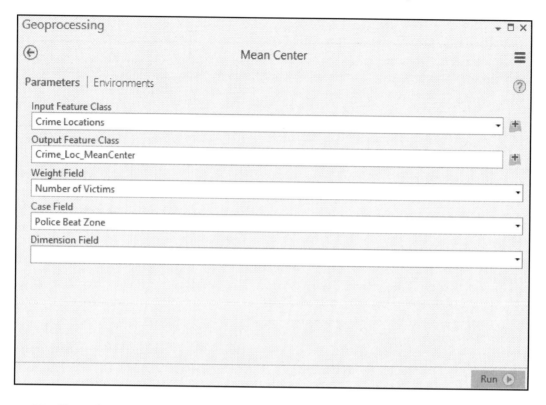

12. Close the Geoprocessing pane.

You should now see that a center point has been located for each of the Police Beat Zones. This is the geographic mean center of all the crimes that occurred in each zone, weighted by the number of victims:

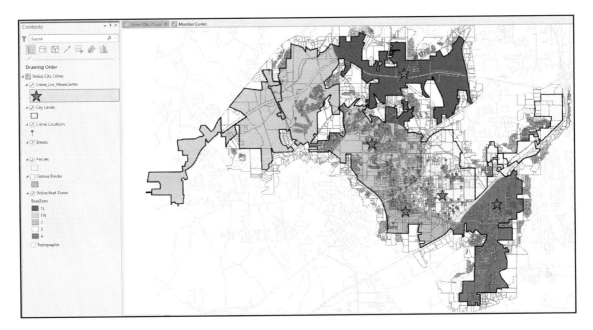

Results of the mean center using a case field

This means the centers were pulled toward those crimes with the greatest number of victims. If you wanted to see the impact the weight field had on the results, you could re-run the Mean Center tool without the Weight Field being applied. Depending on the number of victims, the difference between the weighted and non-weighted center will vary.

13. Save your project.
14. Close ArcGIS Pro.

Identifying the central feature of geographic distribution

You now know how to calculate the geographic center for a group of features. As you have seen, this can be very useful to help locate new structures, event sites, and so on. It can also be used to compare two sets of data to see whether there is a shift or movement over time. But what if you need to know what feature within a group is the most central? Can you do that?

You can do this using the Center Feature tool. This tool is in the Spatial Statistics Tools toolbox and the Measuring Geographic Distributions toolset. The Central Feature tool identifies the most central feature in a point, line, or polygon in the input feature class. It does this by calculating the distances from the centroid of each feature to every other feature's centroid. Once that has been calculated, the tool selects the feature that has the shortest distance to all other features and copies it to a new output feature class. The shortest distance calculation will honor Z (elevation) coordinates as well, if they exist. Like the Mean and Median Center tools, you can also use a Weight and Case field if desired. This tool works best with a projected coordinate system. Use of a geographic coordinate system can skew the results due to the inconsistency of the units. To learn more about the specifics of how this tool calculates the center feature, go to `http://pro.arcgis.com/en/pro-app/tool-reference/spatial-statistics/h-how-central-feature-spatial-statistics-works.htm`.

In this recipe, you are working for the ACME GIS company that recently merged with another company. This resulted in many new locations being added. The CEO thinks it might be best to move to the Corporate Headquarters, currently located in the Chicago area, to a more centrally-located office. This will help reduce travel time for meetings and other events. So, he has asked you to determine the most central office within the organization. He does want you to take into account the number of employees at each location as well. The offices with more employees should be given greater consideration in your analysis.

Getting ready

It is recommended that you complete the other recipes in this chapter before starting this one. This will ensure that you have a good foundational understanding of where to access the required tools and basic concepts required to complete this recipe.

You will also need to ensure the sample data is installed before you continue.

How to do it...

1. Start ArcGIS Pro and open the `Spatial Stats Hotspots.aprx` project, located in `C:\Student\ArcGISProCookbook\Chapter9\Spatial Stats Hotspots`, using the skills you have learned in past recipes. If you completed the previous recipes recently, this project should be included in your list of recently opened projects.

2. In the **Catalog** pane, expand the **Maps** folder. Then right-click the **ACME GIS Office Locations** map and select **Open**. This will open a map, as illustrated in the following screenshot, that shows the locations of all the offices for the ACME GIS company:

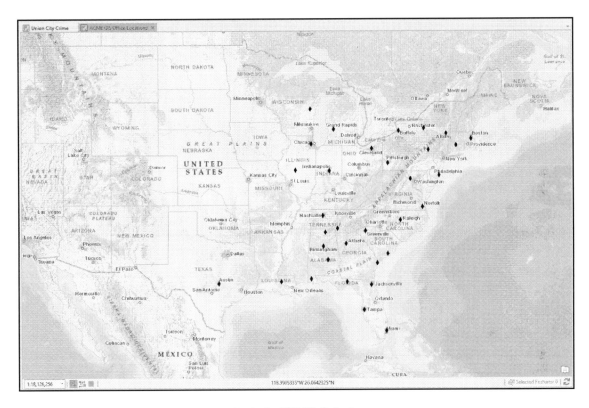

Map showing ACME GIS office locations

3. As always, you should get to know your data before you use it. So, right-click the **Office Locations** layer in the **Contents** pane and select **Attribute Table** from the menu that appears.

4. Review the fields that are available and answer the following questions:

Question: What fields are associated with the Office Locations in the attribute table?

Answer:

Question: How many offices does ACME GIS have?

Answer:

Question: Which office has the most staff?

Answer:

As you can see, this table has many attributes for each office. It has fields containing the address information for each location as well as the number of staff currently employed at the location.

5. Close the **Office Locations** attribute table by clicking the small **X** next to the table name in the tab at the top of the table view.

6. Take a moment to look at the spatial distribution of the offices. See if you can estimate which office is the central feature.

As you can see, many are located along the east coast of the United States. There is a gap along the Appalachian Mountains and Kentucky. This is because ACME GIS mostly had offices in the northeastern part of the Unite States before it merged with another company. The other company had offices mostly in the southeast of the United States.

7. Click the **Analysis** tab in the ribbon. Then click the **Tools** button in the **Geoprocessing** group. This opens the **Geoprocessing** pane.

8. Click the **Toolboxes** tab at the top of the **Geoprocessing** pane.

9. Expand the **Spatial Statistics Tools** toolbox and the **Measuring Geographic Distribution** toolset.

10. Click the **Central Feature** tool to open it.

11. Set the **Input Feature Class** to **Office Locations** by clicking the drop-down arrow and selecting the layer from the list presented.
12. Type `Central_Office` for the **Output Feature Class**, replacing the default value completely.
13. Accept **Euclidean for Distance Method**.
14. For this attempt to locate the central feature, you will not use a weight field as requested by the CEO. So, leave it blank. You will re-run this tool later using the **Staff Number** field to weight the results. That will allow you to see the difference that the **Weight Field** can make to the results.
15. Leave **Self Potential Weight Field** and **Case Fields** blank as well.
16. Verify that your **Central Feature** tool looks like the following and click **Run**:

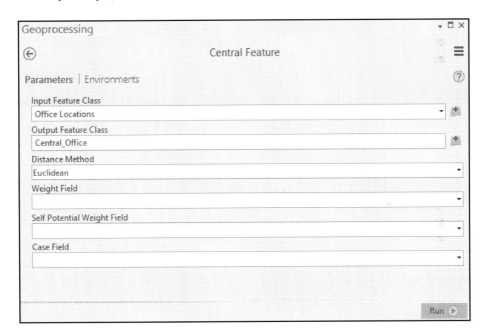

Central Feature tool in the Geoprocessing pane

A new layer will appear in your **Contents** pane, which is the result of the Central Feature tool. As you can see, and is illustrated ahead, the office located in Greenville, South Carolina is the most central office if you do not use a Weight field:

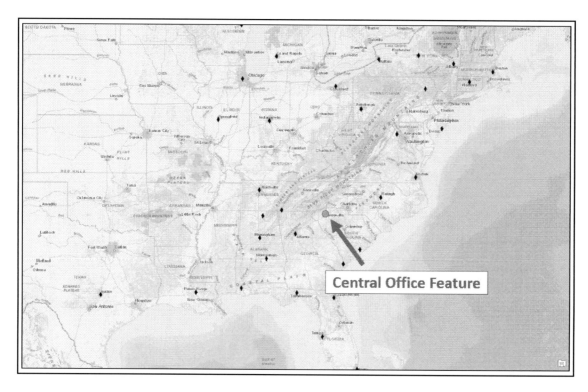

Now let's see what happens when you apply the number of staff in each office to the analysis as the Weight Field.

17. The **Geoprocessing** pane should still be open, with the **Central Feature** tool open. The **Input Feature Class** should still be set to **Office Locations**.

18. Change the **Output Feature Class** to `Central_Office_Weighted`.
19. Again, accept **Euclidean** for the **Distance Method**.
20. Set the **Weight Field** to **Number of Staff**.
21. Leave the other parameters blank. Verify that your **Central Feature** tool looks like the following, and then click **Run**:

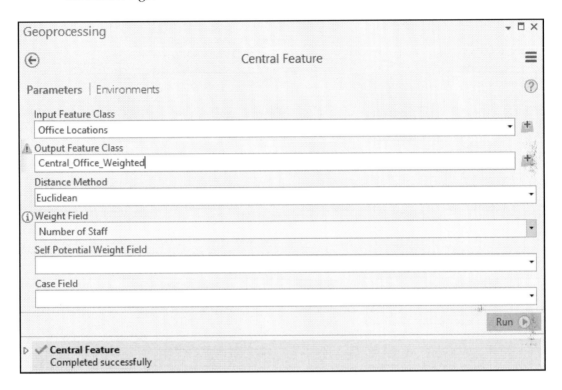

When you apply the weight of the total staff in each office to the analysis, the results shift. The central office is now the Indianapolis office. That is a big shift toward the north west:

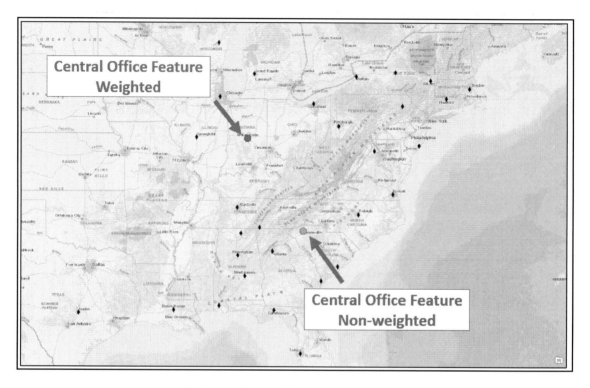

Map showing the different results between weighted and non-weighted

This shows that the northern offices have more staff than those to the south. The difference is great enough to pull the central feature to a completely new location.

22. Save your project.
23. If you are not continuing to the next recipe, you can close ArcGIS Pro. If you are continuing, leave the project open.

You now know how to locate the central feature within a layer. This can be very useful for a number of purposes, such as locating a new operation in an existing facility, trying to find the starting point for a spreading fire by comparing sightings, or to locate a new facility based on where the most people are.

Calculating the geographic dispersion of data

You can now determine the geographic center and central feature for a grouping of data. As you have seen, this can be a very powerful type of analysis. It can help you sight new locations, determine the focal point of a series of incidents, find the center of mass for a group of features, and more. But what if you need to know where the area of greatest concentration of features is, or how compact or spread out the data is around its geographic center? Such analysis can help you to locate clusters of data or see shifts in behavior.

ArcGIS Pro's Standard Distance tool, located in the Spatial Statistics Tools toolbox, and the Measuring Geographic Distributions toolset allows you to do this. It measures the compactness of a distribution around the mean center of a group of features. The smaller the distance calculated, the less the data is dispersed. It is more compact. The larger the distance calculated, the more the data is dispersed, meaning it is less compact. The output from this tool will either be a new polygon feature class for 2D analysis or a Multipatch 3D Sphere. So, this tool works with 3D data analysis as well. To learn more about how this tool calculates the dispersion of data, go to `http://pro.arcgis.com/en/pro-app/tool-reference/spatial-statistics/h-how-standard-distance-spatial-statistic-works.htm`.

Because of your help with his Neighborhood Policing Grant, the Police Chief was impressed and is back for more help. He believes that there is a shift in crime patterns as the year progresses and the holiday season draws closer. He wants to shift patrols from the residential areas to the area around the mall, commercial district, and interstates as the holiday season approaches. However, the City Council believes that this might make the citizens unhappy, so they oppose the shift in police resources.

The Chief has asked for your help to determine whether there is indeed a change in the crime patterns as he believes, and to provide him with something he can take to City Council to make his case. He also wants analysis for each Police Beat Zone. In this recipe, you will use the Standard Distance tool to determine the concentration of crimes for the first half of the year and the last half by Beat Zone. This will allow you to see whether there is truly a change in the crime patterns as the year progresses, by demonstrating whether there is a shift in the central location as well as the area of concentrations.

Getting ready

It is recommended that you complete the other recipes in this chapter before starting this one. This will ensure that you have a good foundational understanding of where to access the required tools and basic concepts required to complete this recipe.

You will also need to ensure the sample data is installed before you continue.

How to do it...

1. If you closed ArcGIS Pro after the last recipe, reopen the `Spatial Stats Hostspots.aprx` project using the skills you have learned in previous exercises. If ArcGIS Pro is still open from the last recipe, continue to the next step.
2. If needed, turn off all layers in the map with the exception of City Limits, Crime Locations, Streets, Parcels, and Police Beat Zones. You map should look like the following:

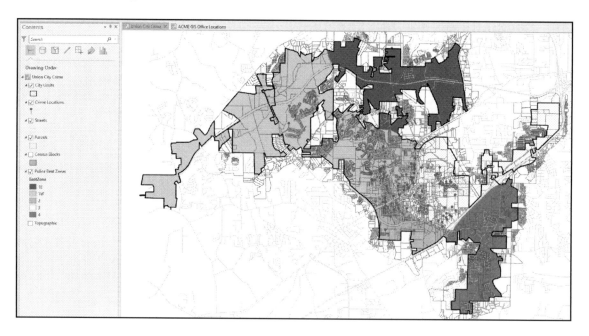

3. Add the new crime data to your map. In the **Catalog** pane, expand the **Databases** folder.

4. Expand the **Spatial Stats Hotspots.gdb** geodatabase.

5. Expand the **UnionCity** feature dataset and right-click the **Crimes_Loc_2017** feature class and select **Add to Current Map**. This will add a new layer to your map.

6. Ensure the new layer is selected in the **Contents** pane, then click the **Appearance** tab in the ribbon.

7. Click the **Import** button located in the **Drawing** group. This will open the **Apply Symbology From Layer** tool in the **Geoprocessing** pane.

8. Ensure the **Input Layer** is set to **Crim_Loc_2017**.

9. Set the **Symbology Layer** to **Crime Locations** using the drop-down arrow.

10. All other parameters should remain empty. Click **Run** to apply the symbology from the **Crime Locations** layer to the **Crime_Loc_2017** layer.

11. Close the **Geoprocessing** pane when the tool finishes.

12. Right-click the **Crime Locations** layer and select **Remove**.

You have prepared the map for the analysis you need to conduct for the Police Chief. Now to begin analyzing the distribution of the crimes for the first half of the year. We will start by selecting all the crimes that occurred on or before June 30, 2017.

13. Select the **Map** tab in the ribbon and then click the **Select by Attributes** button in the **Selection** group. This will open the **Select Layer by Attributes** tool in the **Geoprocessing** pane.

14. Ensure the **Layer Name or Table View** is set to **Crime_Loc_2017** using the drop-down arrow if needed.

15. Ensure the **Selection Type** is set to **New selection**.

16. Click the **Add Clause** button to begin building your query.

17. Set the **Field** to **Date_Occur** using the drop-down arrow.

18. Make sure the operator is set to **is On or Before** using the drop-down arrow.

19. The value should be set to **06/30/2017**. You can either type that in or use the calendar button located to the right of the value.

20. Verify that your query looks like the following, and click the **Add** button:

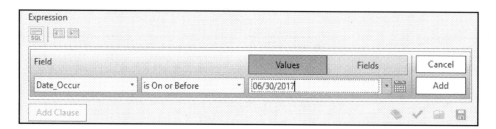

21. Your **Select Layer by Attributes** should look like the following. Verify it does and click **Run**:

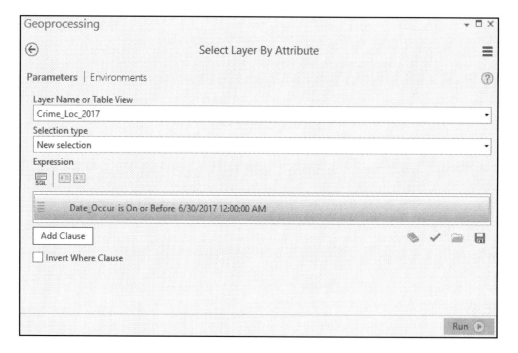

When you run the query, approximately 70 crimes should be selected within the map. This should be all the crimes that occurred during the first half of the year. You can verify that by opening the attribute table for the **Crime_Loc_2017** layer and setting the table to only display selected records. Then sort on the **Date_Occur** field.

Now that you have selected the crimes that occurred during the first half of the year, it is now time to analyze their geographic distribution.

22. In the **Geoprocessing** pane, click the **Back** button that is located in the upper-left corner of the pane. It is a small arrow inside a circle. Then click the **Toolboxes** tab at the top of the pane.

23. Scroll down through the list of toolboxes until you see the **Spatial Statistics Tools** toolbox and expand it.

24. Expand the **Measuring Geographic Distributions** toolset.

25. Click the **Standard Distance** tool to open it in the **Geoprocessing** pane.

26. Set the **Input Feature Class** to **Crime_Loc_2017** using the drop-down arrow.

27. Set the **Output Standard Distance Feature Class** to **Crime_Distribution_First_Half** by typing that value into the cell.

28. Leave the **Circle Size** set to **1 standard deviation**.

29. Leave the **Weight Field** blank. You do not need to apply a weight to the features for this analysis because the Chief has not told you to apply any greater weight to some crimes over others. They are to all be treated the same.

30. You will apply a **Case Field**, so that you can break the analysis down by Police Beat Zone. Set the **Case Field** to **Police Beat Zone**.

31. Verify that your **Standard Distance** tool resembles the following, and click **Run**:

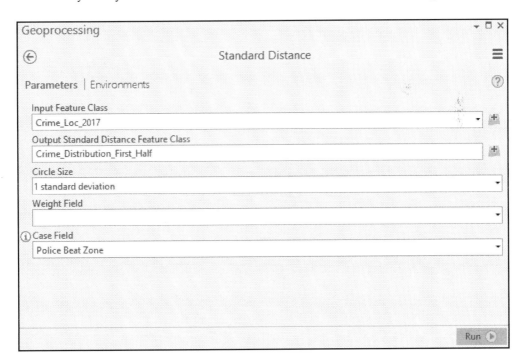

A new layer will appear in your map once the tool is complete. This represents the geographic distribution for the crimes that occurred during the first half of 2017 in the city. The map should look something like this:

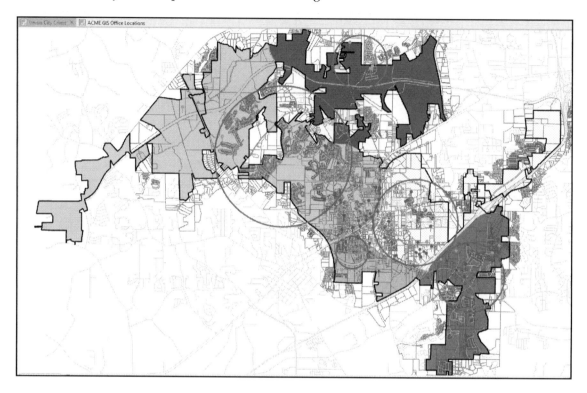

The circles represent the concentration of the crimes around the mean center for each group by Police Beat Zone. So, you should have five circles. Notice that not all the crimes that occurred in each Zone are inside the circle. That is because the circle represents the overall distribution or concentrations of the crimes.

Now that you know the distribution for the first half of the year, it is time to analyze the last half of the year.

32. Select the **Map** tab in the ribbon. Then click the **Clear** button located in the **Selection** group to deselect all selected features.
33. Click the **Select by Attributes** button in the **Selection** group so that you can build a query to select all crimes that occurred during the last half of 2017.
34. Set the **Layer Name or Table View** to **Crimes_Loc_2017** using the drop-down arrow.

35. Ensure the **Selection Type** is set to **New selection**.
36. Click the **Add Clause** button to begin building your query.
37. Set the **Field** to **Date_Occur** using the drop-down arrow.
38. Make sure the operator is set to **is After** using the drop-down arrow.
39. The value should be set to **06/30/2017**. You can either type that in or use the calendar button located to the right of the value.
40. Verify that your query looks like the following and click the **Add** button:

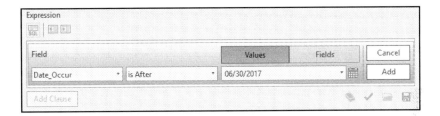

41. Your **Select Layer by Attributes** should look like the following. Verify that it does and click **Run**:

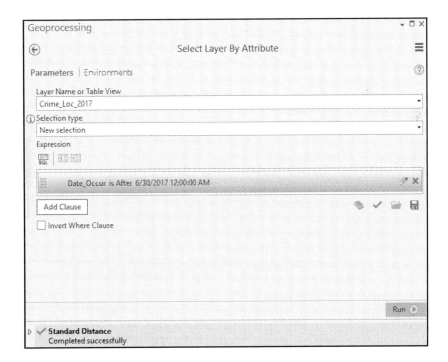

Now you should have all the crimes selected that occurred during the last half of the year. That means you should have 82 crimes selected. You can verify this using the same method you used to verify the previous selection.

42. In the **Geoprocessing** pane, click the **Back** button that is in the upper-left corner of the pane. It is a small arrow inside a circle. Then click the **Toolboxes** tab at the top of the pane.

43. Scroll down through the list of toolboxes until you see the **Spatial Statistics Tools** toolbox and expand it.

44. Expand the **Measuring Geographic Distributions** toolset.

45. Click the **Standard Distance** tool to open it in the **Geoprocessing** pane.

46. Set the **Input Feature Class** to **Crime_Loc_2017** using the drop-down arrow.

47. Set the **Output Standard Distance Feature Class** to **Crime_Distribution_Last_Half** by typing that value into the cell.

48. Leave the **Circle Size** set to **1 standard deviation**.

49. Leave the **Weight Field** blank. You do not need to apply a weight to the features for this analysis because the Chief has not told you to apply any greater weight to some crimes over others. They are to all be treated the same.

50. You will apply a **Case Field**, so you can break the analysis down by Police Beat Zone. Set the **Case Field** to **Police Beat Zone**.

51. Verify that your **Standard Distance** tool resembles the following, and click **Run**:

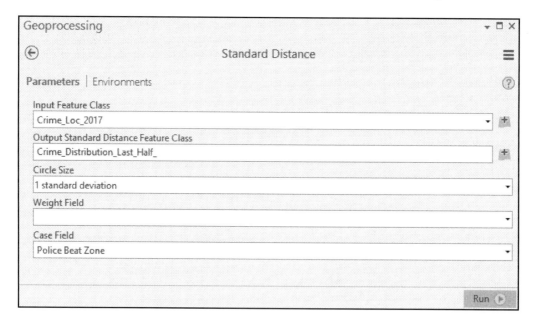

52. Close the Geoprocessing pane when the tool completes.
53. Click the **Clear** button located in the **Selection** group on the **Map** tab to deselect all features.

You can now see the distribution of crimes for the last half of the year and visually compare it to the first half:

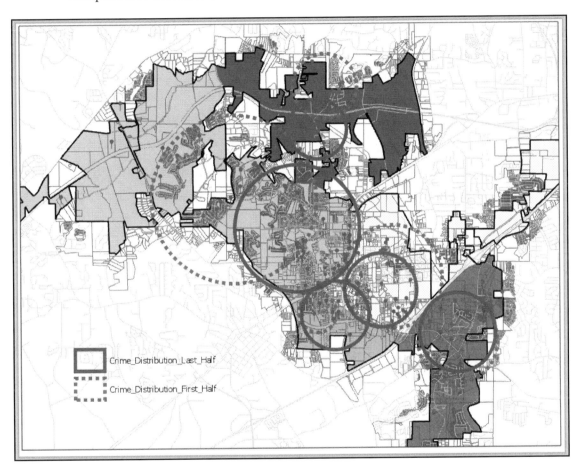

It would appear that the Police Chief is correct. The data does show that the concentration of crimes does shift toward the commercial district, mall, and interstate area. You can see that the distribution for Zone 1W contracts and shifts southeast toward the commercial district located along Roosevelt Highway that runs through the middle of the City. The same is true for Zone 3 that contracts along Shannon Parkway, another major commercial thoroughfare. Zone 2 actually expands toward both Shannon Parkway and Roosevelt Highway during the last half of the year. The concentration for Zone 1E stays about the same size but certainly shifts south toward the intersection of US Highway 29, Scarborough Road, and Stonewall Tell Road. This is another major artery with a lot of commercial development.

54. Save your project and close ArcGIS Pro.

So, as you saw, your analysis supported the Police Chief's theory. He seems to be correct. You can now provide him with the data he needs to take to the City Council, so they can make an informed decision about the distribution of police resources.

10
3D Maps and 3D Analyst

In this chapter, we will cover the following recipes:

- Creating a 3D scene
- Enabling your data to store Z (elevations)
- Creating Multipatch features from 2D
- Creating 3D features
- Calculating the volume of a polygon

Introduction

Since its beginnings over 50 years ago, GIS has relied on 2D maps. They were what we created and where we performed all our analyses. Recently, this is changing. More and more, we are having to take the third dimension, Z, into account. This is because the world is becoming more crowded. Our infrastructure is stacking up upon itself, both above ground and below. So, the need to track and view data in 3D is increasing. Supporting technologies, such as **Light Detection and Ranging** (**LiDAR**), **Unmanned Aerial Vehicles** (**Drones/UAS/UAV**), and increasing computer power are also adding to this push.

As you have seen if you have completed previous recipes in this book, ArcGIS Pro is a very powerful tool for visualizing and analyzing data. However, up to this point, we have been working in a 2D environment. While we can do a lot in 2D, it does have limitations because we live in a 3D world. ArcGIS Pro brings new 3D capabilities to the table that we have not had in previous desktop GIS applications. It natively supports the 3D viewing, querying, and limited analysis of data. When you add the 3D Analyst extension, then you open up a whole new world of possibilities.

Working in 3D provides much better ways to view and manage our infrastructure. We can begin to see the true spatial relationships between the features we are maintaining, viewing, and analyzing. ArcGIS Pro allows you to create 3D Maps, called **Scenes**, using the core application, as illustrated here:

The preceding scene was created using ArcGIS Pro. You can see the buildings, power poles, light poles, and fire hydrants, all depicted in 3D. This allows you to see things such as whether a building will be in the way of a power line or whether a building will cast a shadow over an area that might prevent certain species of plants from growing. If you add the 3D Analyst extension, then you can begin to calculate the slope of road or pipe, determine whether one building might block the view from another, and more.

Don't limit your 3D thinking or displays to infrastructure. Any data can be displayed in 3D. This opens up a whole new way to look at your data, as illustrated in the following maps:

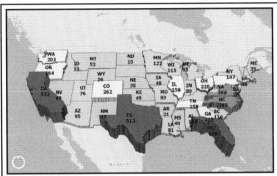

Number of GIS Certified Professionals (GISP) per state

Total Population by Census Block of Union City, GA

As you can see, these two maps have nothing to do with infrastructure. Instead they are highlighting areas with higher and lower values. The use of 3D makes those areas with higher and lower values stand out visually even more so than using traditional symbology. These maps also illustrate that you can combine traditional categorical and quantitative symbology with 3D to produce even more impactful maps. This capability is included in the core functionality of ArcGIS Pro.

What if I need to do more than visualize data in 3D? What if I need to analyze the data so that I can make use of elevational or height information? Well, we have already hinted at that. Esri has an extension for ArcGIS Pro called **3D Analyst**. This extension greatly enhances ArcGIS Pro's ability to work within 3D. The 3D Analyst extension adds a new toolbox to your arsenal that contains 11 toolsets and over 100 tools for creating, converting, and analyzing 3D data. The 3D Analyst extension is not part of the core ArcGIS Pro product. It must be purchased as an additional license. However, it will work with all license levels of ArcGIS Pro. To learn more about the 3D Analyst extension, go to `https://www.esri.com/software/arcgis/extensions/3danalyst`.

In this chapter, you will get an opportunity to explore some of the 3D capabilities of ArcGIS Pro. You will start by creating a 3D scene. Then you will learn how you can enable your features classes to store Z coordinates like it does *x* and *y*. Then you will move on to more advanced concepts and begin to make use of the 3D Analyst extension.

Creating a 3D scene

As we said, ArcGIS Pro allows you to create 3D maps as part of its core functionality regardless of license level. So that is what you are about to do. In this scenario, you are working for an engineering firm that is working on a project to possibly turn a quarry into a water reservoir. The lead engineer on the project has asked you to create a 3D map of the area that he will use during a presentation to the client. This will help the client and engineer visualize the area as he creates his plan.

In ArcGIS Pro, a 3D map is called a **scene**. When creating a new 3D scene, one of the first things you need to determine is what data will serve as the ground surface. The ground surface becomes the canvas that all 2D layers are draped across. Yes, a 3D scene will include both 2D and 3D layers. Typical 2D layers might include an aerial photo, parcels, political boundaries, and natural water features. These often help put your 3D layers into context. The ground surface can also serve as the starting point for displaying the 3D layers. It may provide the starting elevation for those features. They are then extruded above or below that surface. Esri provides a terrain model that is the default ground surface for any new 3D scene. This model is a web service published through ArcGIS Online. You can also use your own elevation or terrain data. This can include a Digital Elevation Model (**DEM**), **Triangulated Irregular Network** (**TIN**), or other web services.

In this recipe, you will create a simple 3D scene of the project area. This scene will include both 2D and 3D layers. You set the elevation source for the map that will serve as the ground surface. You will start all this by creating a new project that contains a local scene.

Getting ready

This recipe requires the sample data to be installed on the computer. It is recommended that you complete the recipes from Chapter 1, *ArcGIS Pro Capabilities and Terminology* before starting this recipe. This will ensure you have a better foundational understanding of how to add layers, set symbology, and navigate within a map. You can complete this recipe with any ArcGIS Pro licensing level.

It is also recommended that you verify your computer hardware is sufficient for working with 3D data. This requires more power than working with traditional 2D Maps. It is recommended that you have at least an i5 or better processor with 8 GB or more RAM (16 GB if you don't have a dedicated video card), dedicated video card with **Graphics Processing Unit** (**GPU**), and both 4 GB video RAM and 12 GB of free hard drive space. If you computer does not meet or exceed these specifications, you may have issues completing this and other recipes in this chapter.

How to do it...

1. You will start by launching ArcGIS Pro as you have done in previous recipes. In the **Create a new project** panel located on the right side, select `Local_Scene.aptx`, as shown here:

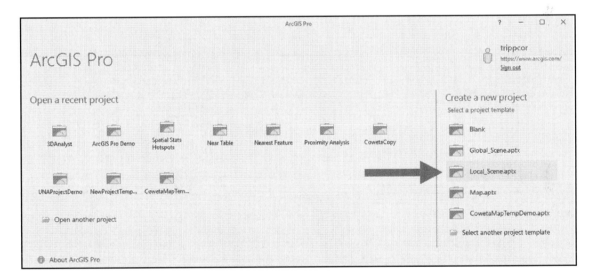

2. In the **Create a New Project** window that appears, name your new project `3DAnalyst`.
3. Click the **Browse** button at the end of the **Location** cell. Then in the left panel of the **Select a folder to store the project** window, click **Computer**.
4. In the panel on the right, double-click the `C:` drive. It is sometimes labeled as OS or local drive.
5. Scroll down and double-click the `Student` folder. Then repeat for the `ArcGISProCookbook` folder.

6. Scroll down and select the `Chapter 10` folder. Do not double-click it. Once selected so that `Chapter10` appears as the **Name**, click **OK**.

Remember, for this part of creating a new project, you are selecting the location where the new project will be stored, not what the project is being named. So you must select an existing folder on a local drive or network share. If you double-click instead of single-clicking to select, you will need to back up one folder. You can do that simply by clicking the **Back** button located in the left corner. It looks like an arrow inside a circle.

7. Verify your **Create a New Project** window looks like the following and click **OK**:

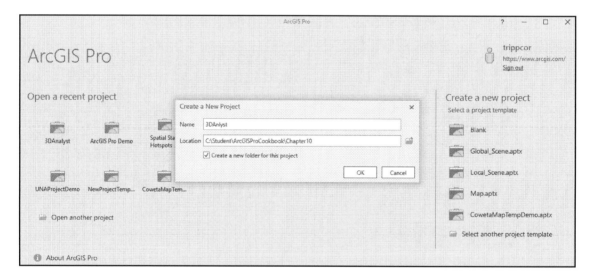

You have just created a new project. This new project contains a single local scene. Now you will need to add data and folder connections to the project that you will need in order to add layers and access data.

8. In the **Catalog** pane, right-click the **Folders** folder and select **Add Folder Connection**.
9. In the panel on the left of the **Add Folder Connection** window, select **Computer**. Then double-click the **C:** drive.
10. Scroll down and double-click the **Student** folder.
11. Select the **ArcGISProCookbook** folder with a single click and click **OK**.

12. Expand the **Folders** folder in the **Catalog** pane and answer the following question.

Question: What folders do you see connected to your project?

Answer:

You should see that two folders are now connected. The first is your project folder. This has the same name as the project you just created. The second folder is the connection you just added. If you were to expand the **ArcGISProCookbook** folder connection, you will see all the other folders inside. Adding the connection to that folder allows you to access and use data contained in any of those folders inside this project. Now you will connect to a couple of databases that you will need in this and future recipes.

13. Right-click the **Databases** folder in the **Catalog** pane and select **Add Database**.
14. Click **Folders** located under **Project** in the left panel of the **Select Existing Geodatabase** window. You may need to expand the **Project** folder to see it.
15. Double-click the **ArcGISProCookbook** folder.
16. Scroll down and double-click the **Databases** folder.
17. Select the **AthensQuarry.gdb** and click **OK**.

You have just added the connection to the primary database you will be using in this recipe. But since you will be using this project for other recipes in this chapter, you will go ahead and connect to the **Trippville_GIS.gdb** geodatabase that you will need later.

18. Repeat that same process to add the **Trippville_GIS.gdb** geodatabase to the project. The one difference being that you need to select the **Trippville_GIS.gdb** at the end before you click **OK**.
19. Right-click the **Local_Scene.gdb** database and click **Remove**. You will not be using that database, so removing it cleans up the project.
20. Save your project.

So, you have added the databases and folder connections that you need to the project. Now you are ready to begin configuring your 3D scene. You will need to first configure some properties for the scene.

21. In the **Contents** pane, right-click **Scene** and select **Properties** from the menu that appears.

22. On the **General** tab, rename the scene to Quarry Project.
23. Set the **Display units** to **US Feet** using the drop-down arrow. This project is located in Georgia, which is in the southeastern United States.
24. Set the **Elevation Units** to the same value.
25. Click **Elevation Surface** in the left panel of the window.
26. Expand the **Elevation sources** option located near the bottom of the window. You should see the **WorldElevation3D/Terrain3D** web service listed. This is the default surface used for new scenes.
27. Add your own local **Elevation source** that is more accurate than the one provided by Esri. Click the **Add Elevation Source** button.
28. Click the **Databases** folder under **Project** in the left panel of the **Add Elevation Source** window.
29. Double-click the **AthensQuarry.gdb** geodatabase in the right panel.
30. Select **quarry_dem** and click **OK**. This is a digital elevation model that was created by a surveyor in the firm you are working at for this project. It is based on actual field survey data for the project site.

    You should now have two **Elevation sources** listed for this project. You may also see a warning telling you a datum transformation was applied. This is normal because your DEM and the Esri web service make use of two different coordinate systems and datums. You can click the **Transformation** page in the properties if you want to learn more.

    It is not unusual for a scene to have more than one **Elevation source**. It depends on the area covered by both the project and local elevation sources. ArcGIS Pro treats overlapping elevation sources much like layers in the **Contents** pane. It will use the top one that covers the area in question if two or more of the sources overlap. In this case, it will use the local DEM you just added until you reach the spatial edge where the DEM ends. Then it will make use of the Esri Terrain Model as the source.

31. Click **Coordinate System** in the left panel. The engineer wants everything in the local state plane coordinate system since that is what the survey data was collected in.

32. Click the **Add Coordinate System** button and select **Import Coordinate System** as illustrated in the following screenshot:

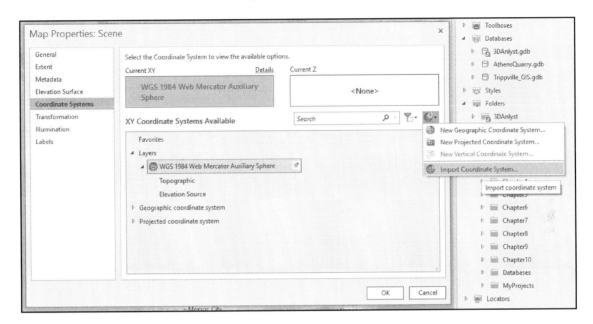

33. In the **Import Coordinate System**, select **quarry_DEM** from the right panel. If you do not see it, you will need to navigate to the **AthensQuarry.gdb** geodatabase located in the **Databases** project folder. Click **OK** once you select **quarry_DEM**.

34. You may get a warning about the imported coordinate system. If you do, ignore it. You should now have both a **Current XY** and **Current Z** coordinate system assigned, as illustrated in the following graphic. Click **OK** if you do to apply these changes to the scene's properties:

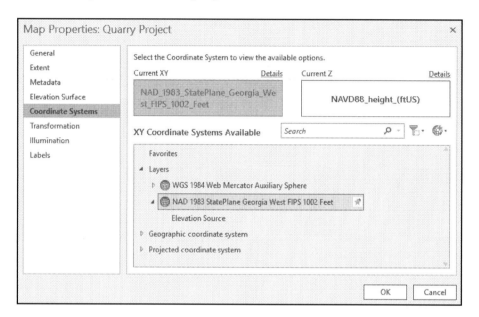

Your scene will change in such a way that the earth will appear to be oblong in shape. This is because you have assigned a local coordinate system to your map that is designed to preserve the data as much as possible in the project area. Now you will add layers to the scene.

35. Save your project.
36. Click the **Add Data** button on the **Map** tab in the **Layer group**.
37. Double-click the **Databases** folder and then the **AthensQuarry.gdb**.

38. Select the **Bldg, HydroLine, HydroPoly,** and **Parcels** feature classes. Click **OK** once you have the feature classes selected.

Holding down your *Ctrl* key while selecting will allow you to select multiple feature classes.

The new layers you added should appear in your map as 2D Layers. You will need to adjust the draw order for the layers and the symbology.

39. In the **Contents** pane, select and drag the **Lakes** layer so it is above the **Parcels**.
40. Select and drag the **Bldg** layer so it is above the **Parcels** layer as well. It can be either above or below the **Lakes** layer.

All layers should now be visible in your map. No layer should be hiding behind another one. Now, let's work on the symbology.

41. Click the symbol patch located below the **Streams** layer name. This should open the Symbology pane.
42. Ensure you are viewing the **Gallery** by clicking the **Gallery** tab next the top of the pane. Select the **Water** (line) predefined symbol.
43. Click the symbol patch located below the **Lakes** layer name. Then select the **Water** (area) predefined symbol on the **Symbology** pane.
44. Click the symbol patch below the **Bldg** layer name. Then select the **Building Footprint** predefined symbol. If you see more than one, select any one you want to use.
45. Click the symbol patch located below the **Parcels** layer name. Select the **Black Outline** predefined symbol.

46. Close the **Symbology** pane.

Your scene should now look like the following graphic. So far, you have created a new project that contains a 3D scene. You then configured the source elevation, which is the ground surface for the scene, using a local digital elevation model. Lastly, you added several layers to the scene. These layers are all being displayed as 2D layers, which means they are just being draped across the DEM you specified as the elevation source:

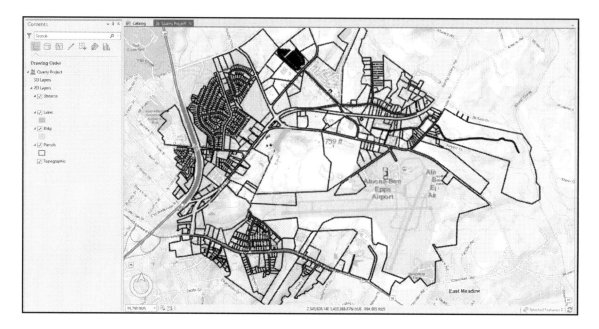

Now it's time to make one of the 2D layers a 3D layer. This is fairly easy to do.

47. Select the **Bldg** layer in the **Contents** pane.

48. Drag and drop it on the 3D Layers in the list. The 3D Layers will highlight in blue when your mouse pointer is on top of it. This is the indication to release your mouse button. The **Bldg** layer should now appear under **3D Layers** indicating it is now a 3D layer. This means you will be able to display the buildings as 3D objects in the scene.

49. In the **Extrusion** group, click the drop-down arrow located below **Type**. Select **Min Height**, as shown in the following screenshot:

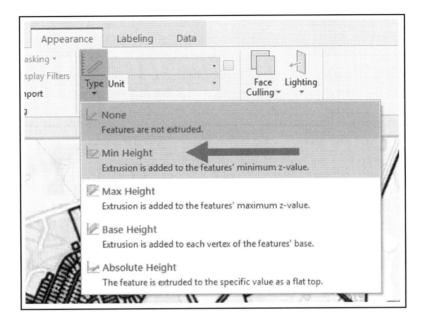

50. In the cell located next to the **Type** option, click the drop-down arrow and select **[Est_HGT]** from the list, as illustrated in the following graphic. This is a field from the attribute table for the **Bldg** layer:

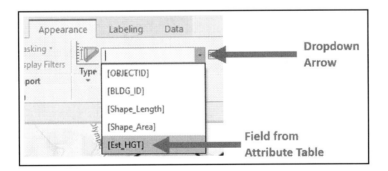

You have just extruded the building in the **Bldg** layer based on a field in the attribute table that has each building's estimated height. Let's look at the results of your work so you can see the buildings are indeed 3D.

51. Place your mouse pointer on the southern side of the scene; anywhere on the southern side will work.

52. Press the scroll wheel located in the center of your mouse. While holding it down, push the mouse away from you. This should rotate the scene around the *z* axis. Rotate it until you can begin to see the building heights above the ground and 2D layers. Then release your scroll wheel.

53. Roll your scroll wheel so that you zoom in closer, so you can see the buildings and verify they are being shown above the ground and 2D layers.

Your scene should look similar to the following screenshot. Yours might be a little different depending on how far you rotated the scene along the Z axis and how much you zoomed in:

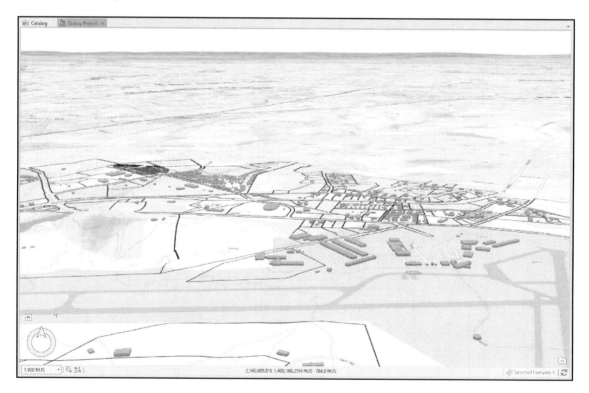

54. Click the **Map** tab in the ribbon. Then click the drop-down arrow located in the **Layer group**. Select the Imagery basemap from the list provided. This provides a more realistic 3D view of the quarry project area.

 If you do not see the Imagery basemap, it may be that you are not connected to ArcGIS Online or are connected to your organization's portal for ArcGIS. If possible, connect to ArcGIS Online using your login details. If you are not able to, skip to *Step 57*.

55. Save your project.

56. Continue to navigate through the scene. Try zooming in and out, panning, and rotating along all axes. Make sure to examine the area around the quarry. You should be able to see all the piles of rock and the quarry pit itself in detail, as shown here:

 If you use a trackball or touch pad on a laptop, you can also use the compass located in the lower-left corner to navigate in the scene. Simply clicking the ring with your pointer will pan the view. If you click the arrow located in the upper-left corner of the compass, you can access more controls.

57. When you are done exploring the scene, right-click the **Bldg** layer in the **Contents** pane and select **Zoom** to layer.

58. Save your project and close **ArcGIS Pro**.

You have just created a very basic 3D Scene using the core functionality found in ArcGIS Pro. What you just did can be accomplished at all license levels of ArcGIS Pro and does not require any extensions. If you want to learn more about creating 3D Scenes in ArcGIS Pro, you may want to examine *Chapter 5, Creating 3D Maps*, in *Learning ArcGIS Pro* by Tripp Corbin, GISP from Packt Publishing and watch the author's YouTube video on creating 3D maps with ArcGIS Pro: `https://www.youtube.com/watch?v=CRWE-CXO58st=58s.`

Enabling your data to store Z coordinates (elevation)

In chapter 2, *Creating and storing data*, we learned that vector data, points, lines, and polygons store data using the X and Y coordinates for the features. This determines their location, which is then displayed in a map. We expanded on that in chapter 6, *Projections and Coordinate System Basics*, where we learned those X and Y coordinates were referencing locations in a specific, real-world coordinate system that ties our data to the Earth. This allowed us to bring data from all over into our maps, so we could see their spatial relationships. ArcGIS Pro will project data that is in different coordinate systems on the fly, so they are displayed together. However, that only represents two dimensions.

Can you enable data in **ArcGIS Pro** to store Z, the third dimension? Of course you can. You typically do this when you first create the feature class or shapefile. Some formats, such as an AutoCAD DWG and DXF file, are always Z-enabled. The 3D Analyst extension for ArcGIS Pro also has tools that allow you to convert existing 2D data to 3D Z-enabled data.

In this recipe, you will continue to work with the data for the quarry project you used in the last recipe. The engineer is now concerned about the nearby airport. He needs to see the runways in relation to the quarry and may need to make calculations concerning runoff from the quarry to those runways. He has acquired a shapefile that contains the location of runways, taxi ranks, and parking areas at the airport. However, they are not Z-enabled. You will create a new feature class in the `Athens_Quarry` geodatabase that is Z-enabled. Then, you will import the data from the shapefile into it. Lastly, you will calculate the elevation of the features based on the **Digital Elevation Model** you selected as the ground elevation in the previous recipe.

Getting ready

This recipe requires the sample data to be installed on the computer. You will need to have completed the previous recipe before starting this one. You will also need to have the 3D Analyst extension to complete this recipe.

To determine whether you have access to the 3D Analyst extension, open ArcGIS Pro. Then, open any project you have previously opened. Click the **Project** tab in the ribbon. Click the **Licensing** option in the left panel of the **Project** pane. This will tell you what license level and extensions you currently have access to, as illustrated in the following screenshot:

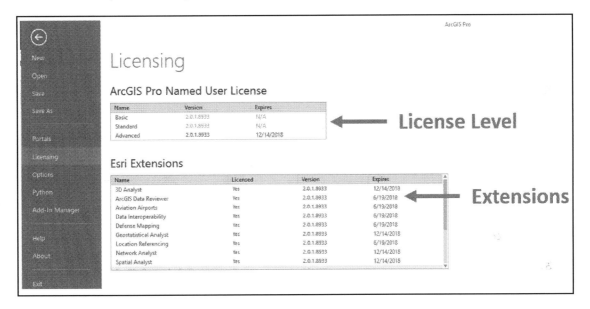

If you do not have access to the 3D Analyst extension, first contact your administrator to see whether they can provide one for you. If you do not have a license for this extension, you can request a trial license from Esri at `https://www.esri.com/arcgis/trial`.

This recipe can be completed with any license level of ArcGIS Pro, as long as you have the 3D Analyst extension.

How to do it...

1. Start ArcGIS Pro and open the `3D Analyst` project you created in the previous recipe. It should be in your list of recently opened projects.

2. Ensure the **QuarryProject** scene you created in the previous recipe is open. If not, open it from the **Catalog** pane by right-clicking it and selecting **Open Local View**.

3. In the **Catalog** pane, expand the **Database** folder. Right-click the **AthensQuarry.gdb** geodatabase. Then, go to **New and Feature Class**, as shown in the following screenshot. This will open the **Create New Feature Class** geoprocessing tool in the **Geoprocessing** pane:

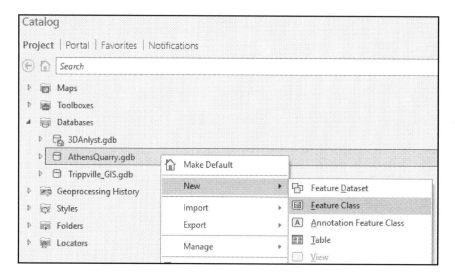

4. **Feature Class Location** should automatically be set because you right-clicked the geodatabase where you are creating the new feature class. Type `Airport_Runways` into the feature class name.

5. Verify the **Geometry** type is set to **Polygon**. If is it not, select it using the drop-down arrow.

6. For **Template Feature Class**, click the **Browse** button located to the far right of the cell. It looks like a yellow folder with a black plus sign on it.

7. Click the **Folder** folder located under **Project** in the left panel of the **Template Feature Class** window.

8. Double-click the **3DAnalyst** folder that appears in the right panel of the window.

9. You should now see at least two geodatabases and two shapefiles in this folder. Select **Airport.shp** and click **OK**.

10. Set **Has M** to **No** using the drop-down arrow.

11. Ensure **Has Z** is set to **Yes**. If not, use the drop-down arrow to set it.

12. Click the **Wireframe** globe located to the right of the **Coordinate System**. This will open the **Coordinate System** window so you can set both the horizontal (XY) and vertical (Z) coordinate systems the new feature class will use.

13. Click the wireframe globe with a green plus sign located to the right of the **XY Coordinate Systems Available** and select **Import Coordinate System**, as illustrated here:

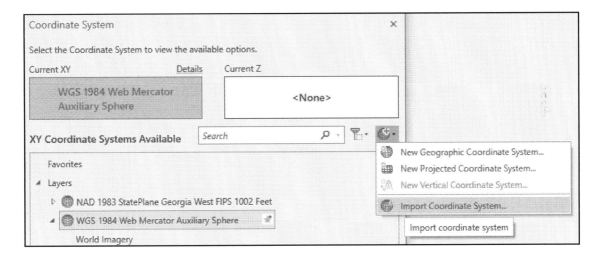

14. Select the **Databases** folder under **Project** in the left panel of the **Import Coordinate System** window.

15. Double-click the **AthensQuarry.gdb** geodatabase in the right panel of the window.

16. Select **quarry_DEM** and click **OK**. You may get a warning about the **Imported Coordinate System**. If you do, ignore it.

17. Your **Current XY** should now be set to the **NAD_1983_StatePlane_Georgia_West_FIPS_1002_Feet** horizontal coordinate system and the **Current Z** set to the **NAVD88_height_(ftUS)** vertical coordinate system. If it is, click **OK**.

18. Verify your **Create Feature Class** tool looks like the following and click **Run**:

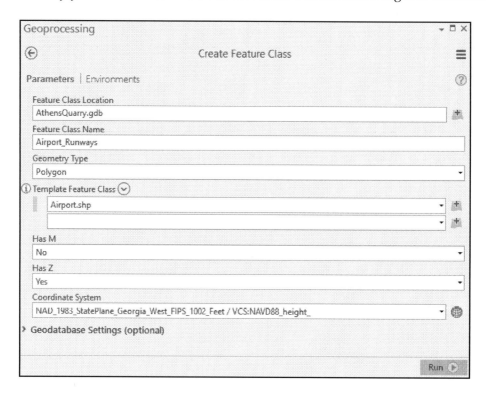

When the tool completes, a new layer should appear in the **QuarryProject Scene**. This new layer references the new feature class you just created. This new feature class will not only store the X and Y coordinates for all the features it contains but it will allow you to store the Z coordinates as well. Since this is a brand-new feature class, it is currently empty. You will next import the features that are in the shapefile you used as the **Template Feature Class** when you created the new feature class. You will use the **Append** tool to do this.

19. In the **Geoprocessing** pane, click the **Back** button located in the upper-left corner. This will take you back to either your favorites, Toolboxes, or Portal.

 If you closed the Geoprocessing pane when the **Create New Feature Class** tool completed, you can easily reopen it by going to the **Analysis** tab in the ribbon and clicking the **Tools** button in the **Geoprocessing** group.

20. Click the **Toolboxes** tab at the top of the **Geoprocessing** pane.

21. Scroll down the list of toolboxes to the **Data Management Tools** toolbox and expand it so you can see its contents.

22. Expand the **General** toolset. Notice the various tools included in this toolset.

23. Click the **Append** tool to open it.

24. For the **Input Dataset**, click the **Browse** button located to the right.

25. Select the **Folders** folder under **Project** in the left panel of the **Input Datasets** window.

26. Double-click the **3DAnalyst** folder.

27. Select the **Airport.shp** shapefile and click **OK**. This will set the dataset you want to add or import into the target dataset.

28. Set the **Target Dataset** to **Airport_Runways** using the drop-down arrow.

> You had to use the **Browse** button to set the **Input Dataset** because the **Airport.shp** shapefile was not already a layer in your map. The drop-down arrows only list existing layers or tables included in the active map or scene.

29. Since you used the shapefile as the template for the new **Airport_Runways** feature class, you should be able to leave the **Schema Type** set to `Input Schema must match target schema`. The schemas for the input and target should be the same.

30. Since the **Airport_Runways** feature class does not include subtypes, you can leave that parameter blank. Verify your **Append** tool looks like the following and click **Run**:

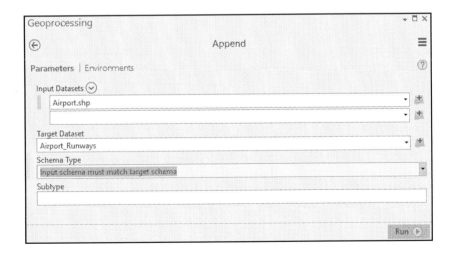

For those that might have used ArcMap in the past, you may have used the **Simple Data Loader** or **Load Object** tools to accomplish this task. ArcGIS Pro 2.1 and earlier versions do not include that functionality. The author is not sure if or when Esri will add those tools to ArcGIS Pro.

When the **Append** tool completes, it will have copied the features from the shapefile to the **Airport_Runways** feature class. You will not be able to see them because their Z coordinate is still currently set to 0 because the shapefile was a 2D shapefile. Next, you will need to calculate a Z coordinate for each vertex associated with the features in the new feature class.

You will use a tool from the 3D Analyst extension that will calculate the z for the vertices based on where it lies in relation to the DEM you set as the ground surface.

31. Click the **Back** button in the Geoprocessing pane that has the **Append** tool open.
32. Click the **Toolboxes** tab at the top of the pane.
33. Expand the **3D Analyst** toolbox so you can see its contents.
34. Expand the **3D Features** toolset.
35. Scroll down the list of tools until you come to the **Update Feature Z** tool. Click this tool to open it. This tool will calculate the Z coordinates of features based on an input surface.
36. Set the **Input Features** to **Airport_Runways** using the drop-down arrow.
37. Click the **Browse** button for the **Input Surface**.
38. In the **Input Surface** window, click **Databases** in the panel on the left located under **Project**.
39. Double-click the **AthensQuarry.gdb** geodatabase in the right panel.
40. Select **quarry_DEM** in the same panel and click **OK**.
41. ArcGIS Pro will automatically determine which **Interpolation Method** it believes is best. Accept the one determined by ArcGIS Pro.
42. The **Status Field** will be left blank. You can use this field to track which features are not updated with new Z coordinate values. This is typically because the features do not overlap the surface. In this case, all the features in the **Input Features** layers overlap the **Input Surface** for the project area so there is no need to be concerned. There are parts of some of the runway features that are outside the project area, but those are not a concern.

43. Verify your **Update Feature Z** tool looks like the following and click **Run**:

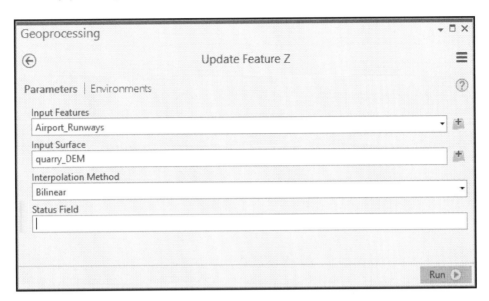

Once the tool completes, you should start to see parts of the **Airport_Runways** layers. It maybe partially hidden by the **World Imagery** basemap. This is because both are at the same elevation. Not being able to see the entirety of the features on the layer is not a big concern. The fact that you can see some of them where before you could not see any is proof you successfully added the Z coordinates to the features in the layer.

However, we will further verify the success of the tool by using another tool that will add and calculate several attribute fields that are based on the 3D characteristics of the feature. This is the **Add Z Information** tool that is also included in the 3D Analyst extension.

44. Save your project.
45. In the **Geoprocessing** pane that contains the **Update Feature Z** tool you just used, click the **Back** button.
46. If needed, click the **Toolboxes** tab in the **Geoprocessing** pane.

47. Expand the **3D Analyst Tools** toolbox to see its contents.

48. Expand the **3D Features Toolset**. Then click the **Add Z Information Tool** to open it.

49. Set the **Input Features** to **Airport_Runways** using the drop-down arrow.

50. Under the **Output Property** options, select the following:

- **Lowest Z**
- **Highest Z**
- **Average Z**
- **Average Slope**

51. Verify your **Add Z Information** tool looks like the following and click **Run**:

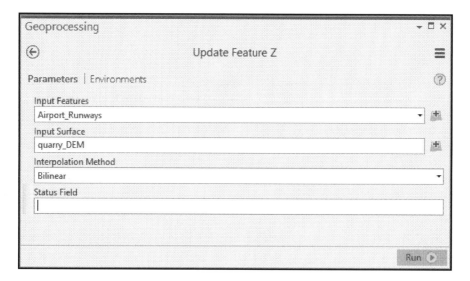

Fields for the properties you checked in the **Add Z Information** tool should now be added to the attribute table for **Airport_Runways** along with the appropriate values. Now, to verify that the tools worked.

52. Close the **Geoprocessing** pane.

53. Right-click the **Airport_Runways** layer and select **Attribute Table** from the menu that appears. Then answer the following questions.

> **Question**: What fields did the Add Z Information tool add to the attribute table?
>
> **Answer**:
>
> **Question**: Did the Update Feature Z tool work?
>
> **Answer**:
>
> **Question**: How can you tell whether it did or did not work?
>
> **Answer**:

> Hopefully you were able to pick out the four fields that were added to the attribute table for the **Airport_Runways** layer. These correspond to the options you selected in the tool. The values stored in these newly added fields allow you to see that the **Update Feature Z** tool was successful except for the two features that extended beyond the project area.

54. Save your project and close ArcGIS Pro.

You have just created a new Z-enabled feature class and imported data from a 2D shapefile into it. You then used the **Update Feature Z** to calculate the Z coordinates for all the vertices for the features in the new feature class you created. You then used the **Add Z Information** tool to verify that the Z coordinates had been successfully added.

Creating multipatch features from 2D

In working through the recipes in this chapter, you have learned how to display 2D data in 3D and how to create basic Z-enabled layers. All of these methods for working in 3D open the door to a wealth of capabilities within ArcGIS Pro from display to analysis. However, they all still have limitations. Extruding 2D data to display in 3D does allow us to see those features and their relationships in three dimensions compared to other features, but we are not able to easily calculate volumes or locate a position vertically within the extruded feature. Adding Z coordinates to a point, line, or polygon allows us to place it in the correct space but again they still only form a single plane. What do we need to create a solid shape (meaning something that has volume)? There is a more advanced 3D data format that is supported in ArcGIS Pro that allows for this. It is called **Multipatch**.

Multipatch is a true 3D object. It is constructed using a series of planes or polygons that are drawn in a 3D environment. They are connected together to form a 3D feature. The planes or polygons that form the feature are also called **patches**. Thus, the term multipatch. ArcGIS Pro is not the only application that allows for the display and creation of Multipatch features. Most **computer-aided drafting and design (CADD)** software also can be used to create multipatch features. Because of the complexity of a multipatch feature, you are often able to show more detail than what you can accomplish with simple extrusion. Multipatch feature classes also increase the number of analysis tools you can use from the 3D Analyst extension for calculating line of sight and more.

The City Planner for the City of Trippville wants to incorporate line of sight requirements into the development regulations for the City. He will want to see whether new buildings will adversely impact the views of existing buildings to key elements, such as parks and rivers, in the City. Many of these types of calculations require the use of multipatch features. In this recipe, you will convert the building footprints from extruded buildings to a new multipatch feature class.

Getting ready

To complete this recipe, you will need access to the 3D Analyst extension for ArcGIS Pro. You will need to have completed the other recipes in this chapter and ensure the sample data is installed before you continue. This recipe can be completed with all license levels of ArcGIS Pro.

How to do it...

1. Start ArcGIS Pro and open the 3DAnalyst.aprx project you used in the previous recipes in this chapter. This project should be included in your list of recently opened projects.
2. In the **Catalog** pane, right-click the **Maps** folder and select **New Scene**.
3. A new scene should open in the view area. Unless you have changed the default options, the new scene will display in the **Global** view. Since you are working with a single small city, you need to change it to a local view. Click the **View** tab in the ribbon.

4. Click the **Local** button located in the **View** group. This will change your scene to be a local view, as illustrated in the following screenshot:

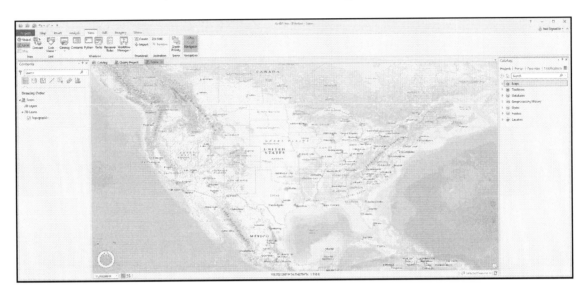

Scenes will either be global or local. Global scenes are used for large area 3D maps where the curvature of the earth can impact the display and analysis of the data. Local scenes are for smaller areas such as a City, Township, or County. In these cases, the curvature of the earth has less impact due to the scale of the 3D map. Local scenes most often make use of a projected coordinate system, whereas Global uses a geographic. For more information about global and local scenes, go to `http://pro.` `arcgis.com/en/pro-app/help/mapping/map-authoring/scenes.htm`.

5. Set the elevation source, which will be the surface for this new scene. Right-click the **Scene** in the **Contents** pane and select **Properties** from the menu that appears.

6. Click **Elevation Surface** in the left panel of the **Map Properties** window.

7. Expand the **Elevation sources** option in the middle of the right panel of the window.

8. Click the **Add Elevation Source** button.

9. Click the **Databases** folder on the left panel of the **Add Elevation Source** window.

10. Double-click the **Trippville_GIS.gdb** geodatabase in the right panel.

11. Select DEM and click **OK** to assign this as an elevation source. You may receive a warning that a datum transformation was applied. This is because the DEM and the Esri default terrain surface use different horizontal and vertical datums.

12. You will now remove the Esri Terrain as an **Elevation source** because it is not needed. Click the small red **X** located to the right of the Esri **WorldElevation3D** service, as indicated here:

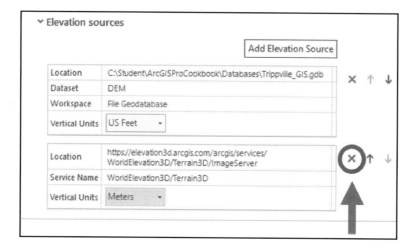

13. Set the **Surface color** to **No Color** using the drop-down arrow. This will allow you to see layers below the surface.

14. Set the coordinate system for the scene. Click the **Coordinate System** option in the left panel of the **Map Properties** window.

15. Click the **Add Coordinate System** button that looks like a small wireframe globe with a green plus symbol on it, located on the right side of the window.

16. Select **Import Coordinate System** from the menu that appears.

17. Select DEM in the right panel of the window and click **OK**. If you do not see the DEM listed, use the skills you have learned to navigate to the **Trippville_GIS** geodatabase in the project. You may again see the warning about the imported coordinate system. If you do, ignore it.

18. Click the **General** option in the left panel of the window.

19. Name the **Scene Trippville Buildings**.

20. Set the **Elevation Units** to **US Feet** using the drop-down arrow and click **OK**.

Your map view may now appear empty after you click **OK**. Do not worry if it does. This is normal. When you add layers, you will see the basemap and newly added layers displayed in the view.

The new scene is ready to begin adding layers. You will add a few layers to the new scene now.

21. Save your project.

Just a reminder, you should save your projects often because ArcGIS Pro does not have an autosave option for projects. Working with 3D scenes requires a lot more resources than 2D Maps. This makes them more prone to crashing and failure. To allow you to quickly recover if this happens, save your project any time you have made major changes to it, such as adding and configuring a new scene.

22. Click the **Add Data** button in the **Layer** group on the **Map** tab in the ribbon.
23. Click the **Databases** folder on the left panel of the **Add Data** window under **Project**.
24. Double-click the **Trippville_GIS** geodatabase in the right panel.
25. Double-click the **Base feature** dataset.
26. Select the **Buildings and Parcels feature** classes. Hold your *Ctrl* key down to select both. Click **OK** once both are selected.

The two layers are added as 2D layers to your scene. If your map view was blank, it should now display the two layers you just added along with your basemap. Now we will work on adjusting the symbology for both layers.

27. Click the small symbol patch located below the **Parcels** layer name in the **Contents** pane.
28. In the **Symbology** pane that appears, ensure you are looking at the **Gallery**. The **Gallery** contains preconfigured symbols. Scroll down until you find the **Black Outline** (1pt) symbol and select it.
29. Click the small symbol patch located below the **Buildings** layer in the **Contents** pane.
30. Scroll down through the list of symbols until you come to the dark gray **Building Footprint** symbol that is in **Category 3**. Select that symbol for your buildings layer.

If you hover your mouse pointer over a symbol in the **Symbology** pane, you will see information about the symbol including its name, the style in which it is stored, and its category. Also at the top of the **Symbology** pane is a **Search** function that you can use to locate predefined symbols based on a keyword. For example, you could have searched **Building** and it would have returned all symbols that are associated with buildings, including the one you were looking for.

31. Close the **Symbology** pane.
32. Right-click the **Buildings** layer in the **Contents** pane and select **Zoom** to **Layer**. You scene should now look very similar to the following screenshot. The scale may be different, depending on the size of your monitor and your resolution:

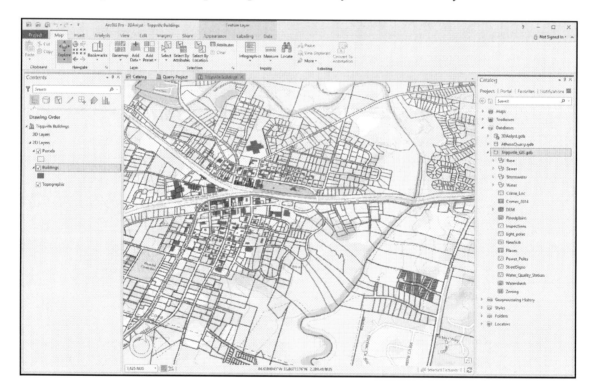

33. Drag and drop the **Buildings** layer from the 2D Layers to the 3D Layers.
34. Save your project.
35. Click the **Appearance** tab in the ribbon.

36. Click the drop-down arrow below **Type** in the **Extrusion group**. Select **Max Height** from the list presented.

37. Ensure the **Unit** is set to **US Feet**.

38. In the **Extrusion Expression** cell located to the right of the **Type** button, click the drop-down arrow and select the **[Est_HGT]** field from the list. This will extrude the buildings based on their estimated height stored in the attribute table for the layer.

39. Using the skills you learned in the first recipe of this chapter, *Creating a 3D map*, zoom in on the downtown area and rotate your scene so it looks similar to the following screenshot:

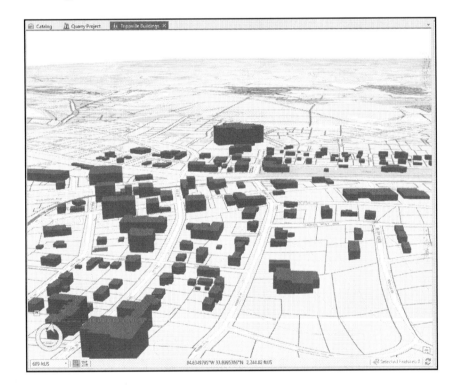

You can now see the buildings extruded to their estimated height. While they look 3D, they are still just 2D features that are being artificially expanded along the *z* axis to appear 3D. Now you will convert them to 3D Multipatch features.

40. Click the **Analysis** tab in the ribbon.
41. Click the **Tools** button on the **Geoprocessing** group to open the **Geoprocessing** pane.
42. Click the **Toolboxes** tab in the **Geoprocessing** pane.
43. Expand the **3D Analyst Tools** toolbox.
44. Expand the **Conversion** toolset and select the **Layer 3D** to **Feature Class** tool.
45. Set the **Input Feature Layer** to **Buildings** using the drop-down arrow.
46. Click the **Browse** button for the **Output Feature Class**.
47. Click the **Databases** folder under **Project** in the left panel of the **Output Feature Class** window. Double-click the **Trippville_GIS** geodatabase.
48. Type **Buildings_MP** for the **Name**. Click **Save**.
49. Verify your **Layer 3D** to **Feature Class** tool looks like the following and click **Run**:

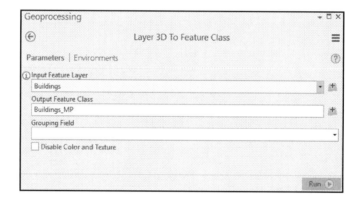

50. Turn off the **Buildings** layer to confirm your conversion was successful. You should still see 3D buildings on the map. These are the multipatch features you just created.
51. Right-click the **Buildings_MP** layer and select **Attribute Table**. Then answer the following question.

Question: What is the shape for the layer you just created?

Answer:

As you can see, the new layer is a Multipatch shape. It is no longer a polygon. Now let's see an example of the increased capability a multipatch allows you to have. We will use a tool you are already familiar with, **Add Z Information**.

52. Close the attribute table for the **Buildings_MP** layer.
53. Open the **Add Z Information** tool in the **3D Analyst Tools** and **3D Features Toolset**, using the skills you have learned.
54. Set the **Input Features** to the **Buildings_MP** layer. Then look at the **Output Property** options that are available.
55. Now set the **Input Features** to the **Buildings** layer and notice the **Output Property** options available for this layer.
56. Answer the following question:

Question: What is the difference between the two layers when they are set as the Input Features?
Answer:

When you set the **Buildings_MP** as the **Input Features** for the **Add Z Information** tool, you are presented with many output options. You can have the tool calculate the volume of each building, the total surface area, and more. When you set the **Buildings** layer as the input, you are presented with no options. That is because that layer, though being displayed in 3D, is not a true 3D layer. So the tool will not work with it.

57. If you want, you can run the **Add Z Information** tool using the **Buildings_MP** layer as the input and whatever options for the **Output Property** you want just so you can see the results. If you do, close the **Geoprocessing** pane when it is complete. If you do not want to try this step, simply close the **Geoprocessing** pane.
58. Save your project and close ArcGIS Pro.

Creating 3D features

So far you have learned how to create 3D features from existing 2D features. The first method you learned was creating a new Z-enabled feature class and importing existing 2D features into it. Then, updating the Z coordinates based on a elevation surface. Next, you learned how to convert extruded features into a new multipatch feature class. So how do you create new 3D features from scratch?

Like most things in ArcGIS Pro, there are several methods you can use. You can create new 3D features in either a 2D map or a 3D scene. You can then specify a specific Z coordinate or have them automatically inherit the ground surface elevation.

In this recipe, you will create a few new 3D features. These are based on requests from the Director of Planning for the City of Trippville. For the first, he wants to flesh out the 3D view of the City, so it includes fences. So, you will begin digitizing fences. You will start in a 2D map and then move to the 3D Scene. Next, the Director is concerned about the construction of a new proposed building. He believes it will block the view to one of the main parks in the City from an existing building. So, he needs you to establish a few observation points that you will use in a later recipe to establish sight lines and determine visibility.

Getting ready

You must have completed the other recipes in this chapter before starting this one. This will ensure you have the required project, maps, scenes, and data to complete this project. It will also confirm you have a good foundational understanding of where to access the required tools and basic concepts required to complete this recipe.

You will also need to ensure the sample data is installed before you continue.

How to do it...

1. Start ArcGIS Pro and open the `3DAnalyst.aprx` project you used in the previous recipes in this chapter. This project should be included in your list of recently opened projects.
2. Add an existing 2D map that contains the layers you need. Right-click the **Maps** folder in the **Project** pane and select **Import** for the menu.
3. In the **Import** window, expand the **Computer** folder in the left panel.
4. Select the `C:` drive that may be labeled as OS or local drive.
5. Scroll to the **Student** folder in the right panel and double-click it.
6. Double-click the **ArcGISProCookbook** folder in the right panel.
7. Scroll down and double-click the **Chapter10** folder.
8. Select the **Trippville_2Dd_Map.mapx** file and click **OK**. This is a map file. Importing this file will create a new 2D map in your project.

A new 2D map should be added to your project. You should now see this new map in your map view area of the ArcGIS Pro interface, as shown in the following screenshot:

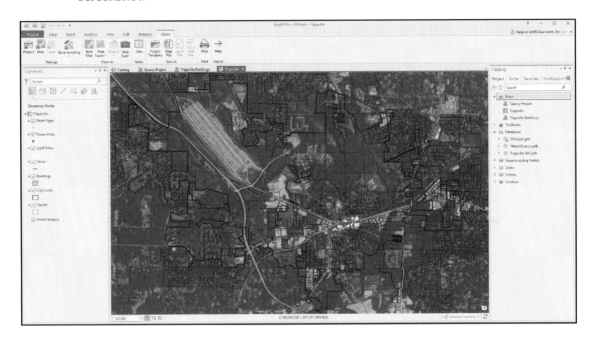

Before you can edit 3D data in a 2D map, you need to ensure it has an elevation surface assigned. Next, you will make sure the new 2D map is using the DEM for the City of Trippville.

9. Save your project.
10. Right-click the Trippville map at the top of the **Contents** pane.
11. Select **Properties** from the menu that appears.
12. Select the **Elevation Surface** option from the left panel of the **Map Properties** window.
13. Expand the **Elevation sources** option.
14. Click the **Add Elevation Source** button.
15. Click the **Databases** folder in the left panel of the **Add Elevation Source** window.
16. Double-click the **Trippville_GIS** geodatabase in the right panel of the window.
17. Select the DEM and click **OK**.

18. Verify your **Map Properties** window looks like the following screenshot and click **OK**:

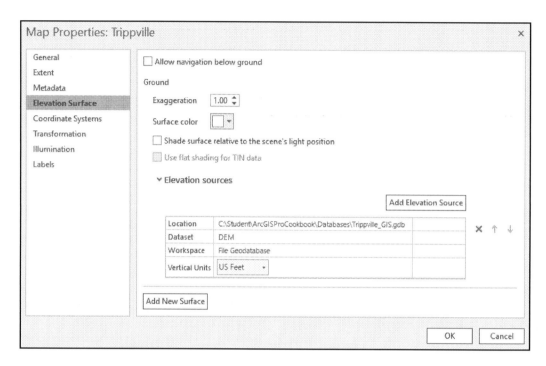

19. Save your project.

You have prepared your 2D Map, so it allows you to edit 3D data by ensuring it has an **Elevation Surface** assigned to it. Sometimes it is easier to edit 3D data in a 2D map because you are more comfortable with those tools. Now, to digitize a fence.

20. Click the **Map** tab to activate it in the ribbon.
21. Click the **Bookmark** button in the **Layer** group and select the **Fence 1** bookmark. This will zoom you to the area that has two fences you will digitize.

22. Zoom in to the parcel indicated in the following screenshot. Zoom in as close as you need to see the fence surrounding the backyard:

23. Click the **List by Editing** button at the top of the **Contents** pane. It is the one that resembles a pencil.

24. Ensure the **Fence** layer is enabled for editing.

25. Click the **Edit** tab in the ribbon.

26. Since the **Fence** layer is Z-enabled, you need to tell ArcGIS Pro where the Z coordinate will come from when you draw a new fence. You will need to configure the Z mode to do this. Click the small arrow located below the **Z Mode** button.

27. Select **Surface** from the small menu that appears. This should make **Ground** appear in the cell located to the lower right of the button. This means the Z value for each vertex will be determined based on the ground surface elevation where you click.

Selecting **Constant** allows you to manually enter a constant Z value that will be applied to all new Z-enabled features you create.

28. Click the **Create** button in the **Feature** group on the **Edit** tab. This will open the **Create Features** pane.

29. Select the **Fence** feature template in the **Create Features** pane.
30. Digitize the fence in by clicking at the locations shown in the following screenshot:

Click where the points are located to create the fence

31. Click the **Attributes** button located in the **Selection** group on the **Edit** tab. This will open the **Attribute** pane. You need to set the height of the fence.
32. In the **Height** cell, type 6 and press the *Enter* key to show it is a 6 foot tall fence.
33. Click the **Geometry** tab in the **Attribute** pane and look at the values. Now answer the following question.

Question: How did the Z values get populated when all you did was click a 2D location in the map?

Answer:

As you can see, even though you were creating the Z-enabled fence features in a 2D map, ArcGIS Pro was still able to determine a value for the Z coordinate as well as the X and Y. It did this by comparing the location you clicked to the ground surface and interpolating the Z value for that location.

34. Close the **Attributes** pane.
35. Click the **Save** button in the **Manage Edits** group on the **Edit** tab to save your edits. When asked to **Save** all edits, click **Yes**.
36. Click the **Clear** button in the **Selection** group to deselect the new fence you just created.

37. Click the **Trippville Buildings** scene you have worked with in previous recipes. It should be at the top of the view area.

 If you closed the **Trippville Buildings** scene, you can reopen it from the **Project** pane. Simply locate the scene in the **Maps** folder in the **Project** pane. Then right-click and select **Open Local View**.

38. Activate the **Map** tab in the ribbon. Then click the **Basemap** button in the **Layer** group and select the **Imagery** basemap.
39. Click the **Add Data** button in the **Layer** group on the **Map** tab.
40. Click the C: drive located under Computer. Then navigate to the C:\Student\ArcGISProCookbook\Chapter10 folder.
41. Select the Fence_3D layer file and click **OK**. The fence layer should appear in your scene with the symbology already configured.
42. Click the **Bookmarks** button and select the **Fences 1** bookmark. This will zoom you to the same area you were just working with in your 2D map.
43. Click the **Explore** tool and zoom out until you see the house with the pool located to the northwest of the parcel with the fence you just drew.
44. Zoom in on the house with the pool until your view looks similar to the following screenshot:

45. Click the **Edit** tab in the ribbon.
46. Click the drop-down arrow below the **Z Mode** button and review your options. Answer the following question.

Question: What options are available for the Z mode in the scene you are working with?

Answer:

As you can see, the surface options are grayed out. This is because in a 3D scene, the ground surface is automatically used to determine the Z coordinates for any new features. You do not need to set this when creating new Z-enabled features in a scene like you do in a 2D map.

47. The **Create** features plane should still be open from when you created the first fence in the 2D map. If not, click the **Create** button to open it.

48. Select the **Fence** feature template and digitize in the new fence, as illustrated in the following screenshot:

Click where the points are located to create the fence

The fence may not be visible after you complete it. This is because it has no height. It is running along the ground with all the other non-extruded layers. You will fix that now.

49. Click the **Attribute** button in the **Selection** group on the **Edit** tab. This will open the **Attributes** pane.

50. In the **Height** cell type 8 to make the height of the new fence display at eight feet. You should now see the fence in the scene.

51. Close the **Attributes** and **Create Features** panes to free up screen space.

52. Click the **Clear** button in the **Selection** group in the ribbon.
53. Click the **Save** button in the **Manage Edits** group to save the new fence you just created. Again, when asked if you want to save all edits, click **Yes**.
54. Activate the **Explore** tool in the **Map** tab in the ribbon.
55. Using the skills you have learned in previous recipes, rotate the view so you can see the new 3D fence you just created. It should look similar to the following graphic:

You can see that the fence you created is being displayed in 3D using the Z coordinates for the starting elevation and extrusion to show the height. You are off to a good start with the request from the **Planning Director** to create and populate a new fence layer. However, he really wants to know whether that proposed new building will create a problem for the existing buildings by blocking their view of the park.

So, you will move on to conducting a line-of-sight analysis, the first part of which is establishing observation points from the existing buildings. These must be 3D points. You will start by creating a new Z-enabled point feature class. Then you will digitize new observation points from the existing buildings the **Planning Director** is concerned about. In the next recipe, you will complete the analysis.

56. In the **Project** pane, expand the **Databases** folder so you can see its contents.

57. Right-click the **Trippville_GIS** geodatabase and go to **New**. Then select **Feature Class**, as illustrated in the following screenshot:

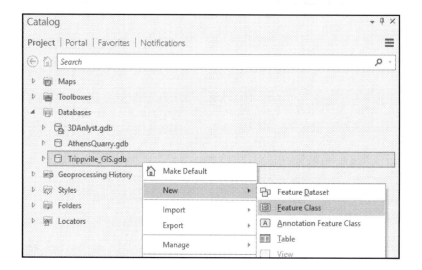

58. Name the new **Feature Class** as Observ_PT.

59. Set the **Geometry Type** to **Point** using the drop-down arrow.

60. Since this is a completely new feature class, not based on any existing ones, you will not specify a **Template Feature Class**. So, leave it blank.

61. Set **Has M** to **No** using the drop-down arrow.

62. Set **Has Z** to **Yes** if needed using the drop-down arrow.

63. Click the wireframe globe next to the **Coordinate System** to set the coordinate system for the new feature class so that it matches the rest of the Trippville data.

64. Click the **Add Coordinate System** button that looks like a wireframe globe with a green plus sign on it, as shown here. Select **Import Coordinate System**:

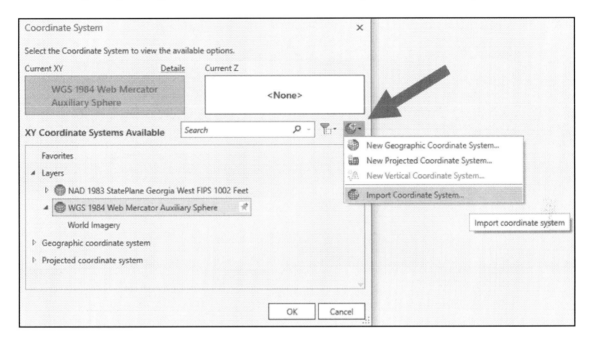

65. Double-click the **Trippville_GIS** geodatabase in the right panel of the window.
66. Select the DEM and click **OK** to import the coordinate system settings from it to the new feature class you are creating.

67. Both a **Current XY** and **Current Z** coordinate system should now be set, as illustrated in the following screenshot. If yours matches, click **OK**:

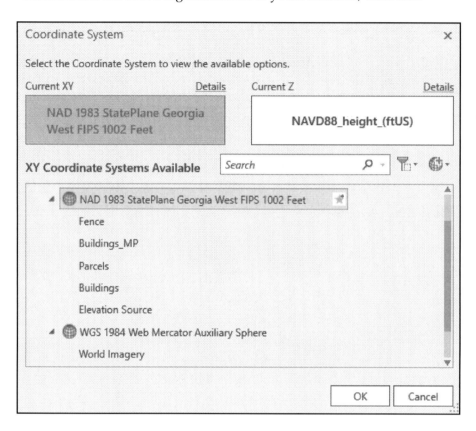

68. Verify your **Create Feature Class** tool looks like the following and click **Run**:

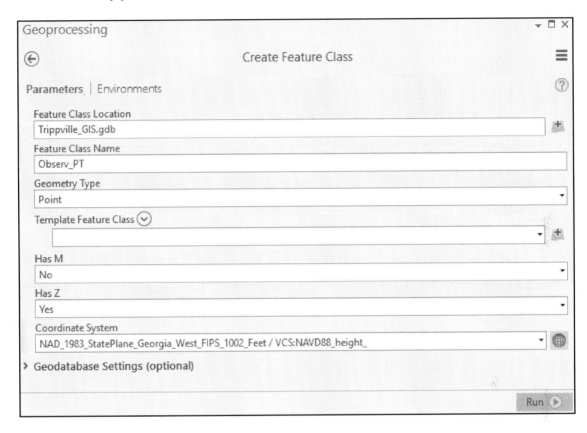

When the **Create Feature Class** tool completes, you should see a new layer appear in your **Contents** pane. This new layer references the new feature class you just created. Now you need to digitize some points into the new layer that represent the observation locations the **Planning Director** is concerned about.

69. Close the **Geoprocessing** pane that contains the **Create Feature Class** tool.

70. Save your project.

71. Now you need to zoom to the proposed building location. You will do this by selecting the proposed building and then zooming to it. In the **Map** tab, click the **Select By Attributes** button.

72. Set the **Layer Name** or **Table View** to **Buildings** using the drop-down arrow and ensure the **Selection Type** is set to **New Selection**.

73. Click the **Add Clause** button to build your SQL query.

74. Using skills you have learned in the previous recipes, set the **Field** to **Building Status**, operator to is Equal too, and **Values** to **Pr-Proposed**. Depending on your version of ArcGIS Pro, you may only see **Proposed** as the displayed value. Then click **Add**.

75. Verify your **Select Layer** by **Attribute** tool looks like the following and click **Run**:

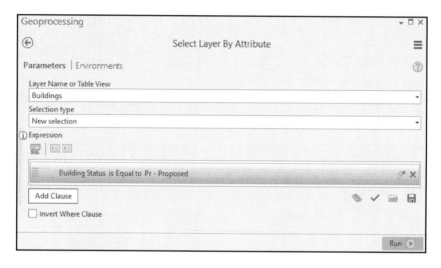

76. Close the **Geoprocessing** pane that contains the **Select Layer** by **Attributes** tool.

77. Right-click the **Buildings** layer in the **Contents** pane. Then go to **Selection** and select **Zoom** to **Selection**, as illustrated in the following graphic:

The scene will zoom to the location of the proposed building that is causing all the concern. Your scene should now look similar to the following screenshot. Depending on the size of your monitor and the size of your ArcGIS Pro application, yours may look slightly different:

 You can still query and zoom to features in a layer that have been turned off so they is not visible.

78. Using skills you have learned previously, add the **Parks** feature class located in the **Trippville_GIS** geodatabase to the scene. This will allow you to see the location of Washington Park, which is located to the northeast of this building. Ensure the **Selection Type** is set to **New selection**.

79. Zoom and rotate the **Trippville Buildings** scene you are working in so that you can see the area surrounding the proposed building. Something similar to the following screenshot should work well. You may need to drag the Parks layer to the 2D Layers group in order to see it:

The proposed building is the lighter gray one near the center of the scene. Washington Park is the light green area to the northeast of the proposed building. Now you need to digitize observation points for the buildings directly south and west of the proposed building.

80. In the **Contents** pane, click the **List by Snapping** button. Ensure the **Buildings_MP** layer is set as snappable.

81. Click the **List by Editing** button in the Contents pane. Right-click the **Observ_PT** layer and select **Make this the only editable layer**.

82. Click the **Edit** tab in the ribbon.

83. Click the **Create** button to open the **Create Features** pane.

84. Ensure snapping is turned on and it is set to **Edge**, **Vertex**, **End Point**, and **Intersection**.
85. Select the **Observ_PT** feature template in the **Create Features** pane.
86. Click the locations shown in the following screenshot. You may need to zoom in to get the exact locations:

87. Click the **Map** tab in the ribbon and activate the Explore tool.
88. Rotate your scene so you can see the location of the new points you just digitized. They should be snapped to the tops of their associated buildings.
89. If they are, click the **Edit** tab in the ribbon. Then click the **Save** button to save the new points you just created.
90. Close the **Create Features** pane.
91. Save your project and close ArcGIS Pro.

In this recipe, you created several new 3D features. You created two new fence features. The new fences inherited the Z coordinate from the location you clicked using the ground surface as a reference. You then specified a height for each fence that was then used to extrude them, so they displayed at their true height above the ground. Then, you created a completely new Z-enabled feature class to store observation points that you will use in the following recipe to analyze the ability to see Washington Park from those locations. The Z coordinates for those new points were determined by the corner of the buildings you snapped to.

Calculating lines of sight

You've learned several ways to create new 3D features. Now it is time to investigate some analyses you can perform with these features that you cannot do with 2D. A common analysis is to determine lines of sight. This has many uses. It can be used by property appraisers to determine whether a property has a good line of sight to a key feature, such as a river or ocean, which might increase its value. It is used by police to establish security perimeters for special events. It might be used to help plan a parade route. So, as you can see, there are many uses for such an analysis.

In this recipe, you will use the observation points you created in the previous recipe to determine whether there are lines of sight to Washington Park or whether the proposed building will block the view of the park entirely. This will be one of the determining factors the Planning Director will use to for deciding whether or not to approve the new building. This will require the use of several geoprocessing tools from the 3D Analyst extension for ArcGIS Pro.

Getting ready

You must have completed the other recipes in this chapter before starting this one. This will ensure you have the required project, maps, scenes, and data to complete this project. It will also confirm you have a good foundational understanding of where to access the required tools and basic concepts required to complete this recipe.

You will also need to ensure the sample data is installed before you continue and access to the 3D Analyst extension for ArcGIS Pro.

How to do it...

1. Start ArcGIS Pro and open the `3DAnalyst.aprx` project you used in the previous recipes in this chapter. This project should be included in your list of recently opened projects.
2. Click the **Analysis** tab in the ribbon. Then click the **Tools** button in the **Geoprocessing** group.
3. Click the **Toolboxes** tab in the **Geoprocessing** pane. Then expand the **3D Analyst Tools** toolbox.
4. Scroll down to the **Visibility** toolset and expand it so you can see its contents.
5. Select the **Construct Sight Lines** tool to open it.

6. Set the **Observation Points** to the **Observ_PT** layer using the drop-down arrow.

7. Set the **Target Features** to the **Parks** layer using the drop-down arrow.

8. For the **Output**, click the **Browse** button and navigate to the **Trippville_GIS** geodatabase using the skills you have learned from previous recipes. Name the new output feature class **Park_Sight_Lines** and click **Save**.

9. Ensure both the **Observer Height Field** and **Target Height Field** are set to **Shape.Z**.

10. Set the **Sampling Distance** to 200.

11. Verify your **Construct Sight Lines** tool looks like the following and click **Run**:

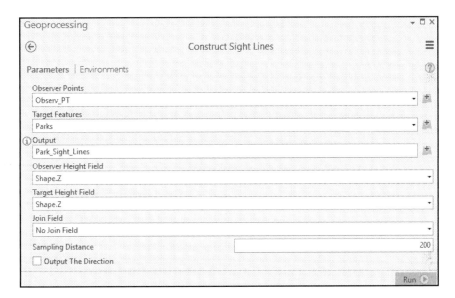

A new layer appears in your scene that represents every possible sight line from the observation point to the park using the interval you specified in the **Sampling Distance**. This tool ignores any possible obstructions. Next, you will use another tool that will investigate each of the sight lines you created to see whether they are blocked by the ground surface or other obstructions, such as buildings.

12. In the **Contents** pane, turn off the **Park_Sight_Lines** layer you just created. You do not need to see the layer to use it for further analysis.

Turning off layers that you do not need to see for the final results of any analysis process you are pursuing can improve overall performance and reduce map clutter.

13. Click the **Back** button in the **Geoprocessing** pane that contains the **Construct Sight Lines** tool. This will take you back to the toolboxes view.

14. Select the **Line of Sight** tool in the **Visibility** toolset in the **3D Analyst Tools** toolbox.

15. Click the **Browse** button for the **Input Surface**. Navigate to the **Trippville_GIS** geodatabase and select the **DEM**. Click **OK** once the **DEM** is selected.

16. Set the **Input Line Features** to **Park_Sight_Lines** using the drop-down arrow.

17. Set the **Input features** to **Buildings_MP** using the drop-down arrow.

 The **Input Features** is a layer that contains additional features you want to the tool to consider that might block the line of sight along the sight lines. This must be a multipatch feature class-based layer.

18. Name your **Output Feature Class** `Buildings_to_Park_LOS`.

19. You can leave the **Output Obstruction Point Feature Class** blank. This would create a new point feature class that shows exactly where the views are obstructed. For this analysis, we are not interested in those exact positions.

20. Verify your **Line of Sight** tool looks like the following and click **Run**:

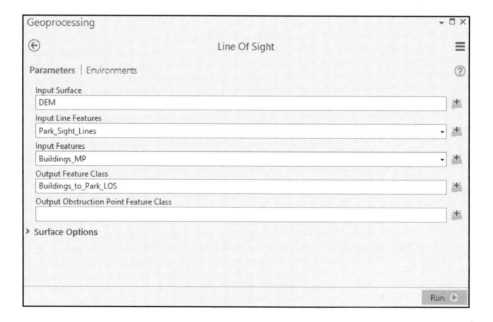

When the tool completes, you will see a new layer added that has identified which sight lines are visible and which are not, as shown in the following screenshot. Remember, this tool takes the ground as well as the buildings into account when determining what is visible and what is not:

You can now easily see which sight lines are being blocked by the proposed building and which are not. This is the information the Planning Director needed.

21. Close your **Geoprocessing** pane.
22. Save your project and close ArcGIS Pro.

Now you have performed your first 3D analysis to determine lines of sight from specified points to an existing feature. This required you to have the 3D Analyst extension for ArcGIS Pro. In addition, you had to create several 3D layers before you were able to perform this analysis. This included creating a multipatch layer representing the buildings in Trippville and observation points.

You could have performed this same analysis in a 2D Map. ArcGIS Pro can still perform 3D analysis in a 2D map. However, the results will not be as impactful or informative when displayed in a 2D map.

Calculating the volume of a polygon

Another common 3D analysis task is to calculate the volume of the area covered by a polygon feature. This is done by overlaying the polygon feature across a surface and then calculating the volume that exists between the plane created by the polygon features and the surface they overlay.

In this recipe, you will return to the quarry project you worked on earlier. The project engineer has determined the optimum full pool elevation and created a polygon layer for you. He wants you to determine what the total volume of water will be needed to fill the quarry to this level in gallons.

You will use the **Polygon Volume** tool that is part of the 3D Analyst extension to accomplish part of this analysis. You will then use the **Calculate Field** tool to calculate the total gallons required to fill the quarry.

Getting ready

You must have completed the other recipes in this chapter before starting this one. This will ensure you have the project, maps, scenes, and data required to complete this project. It will also confirm you have a good foundational understanding of where to access required tools and basic concepts required to complete this recipe.

You will also need to ensure the sample data is installed before you continue and access to the 3D Analyst extension for ArcGIS Pro.

How to do it...

1. Start ArcGIS Pro and open the **3DAnalyst.aprx** project you used in the previous recipes in this chapter. This project should be included in your list of recently opened projects.
2. Close all the Trippville maps and scenes. If needed, reopen the **Quarry Project** scene.

Remember, you can right-click a map or scene in the **Catalog** pane to open it.

3. Now you need to add the **Full Pool Layer** created by the project engineer. Click the **Add Data** button located on the **Map** tab in the ribbon.

4. Navigate to the `C:\Student\ArcGISProCookbook\Chapter10` folder and select the `Full_Pool_Level.lyrx` layer file. Click **OK**. A new layer should have been added to your scene that shows the water level of the quarry when it is filled, as shown in the following screenshot:

5. Click the **Analysis** tab in the ribbon.

6. Click the **Tools** button and the **Toolboxes** tab in the **Geoprocessing** pane.

7. Expand the **3D Analysis Tools** toolbox. Then expand the **Triangulated Surface** toolset.

8. Click the **Polygon Volume** tool to open it.

9. Click the **Browse** button for the **Input Surface**.

10. Expand the **Computer** folder in the left panel of the **Input Surfaces** window.

11. Select the **C:** drive. Then navigate to the **Student\ArcGISProCookbook\Databases** folder.

12. Select **quarry_tin** and click **OK**.

For this tool, the input surface must be a TIN, LAS, or terrain dataset. It will not accept a DEM surface as the input.

13. Set the **Input Features** to **Full Pool Level** using the drop-down arrow.
14. Set the **Height Field** to **Z_Mean** using the drop-down arrow.
15. Ensure the **Reference Plane** is set to **Calculate below the plane**. The plane it is referring to is the one created by the **Input Features**.
16. Accept the default values for the **Volume** and **Surface Area Field**.
17. Verify your **Polygon Volume** tool looks like the following and click **Run**:

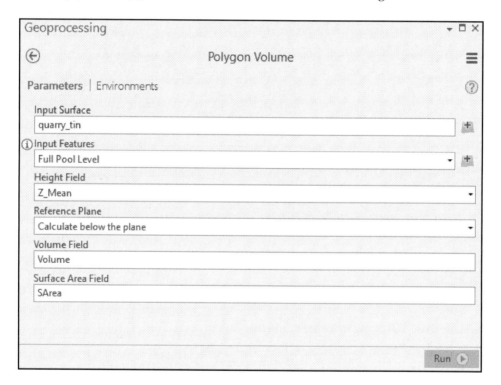

18. Close the **Geoprocessing** pane when the tool completes successfully.
    This particular tool does not create a new feature class or layer like so many of the other tools you have used. It instead adds two new fields to the attribute table for the input features. You will now examine the results.

19. Right-click the **Full Pool Level** and select **Attribute Table**. You should see two fields that were added: **Volume** and **SArea**.
    The volume is in cubic feet because your horizontal and vertical units for the layer are set to **US Feet**. The engineer needs to know the volume in US gallons. You will now create a new field to contain the volume in gallons and use the **Calculate Field** tool to populate it.

20. In the **Table** pane, click the **Add Field** button. It is located on the top left of the pane.

21. Name the new field **Gallons** then press your *Tab* key to move over to the **Data Type**.

22. Set the **Data Type** to **Float** using the drop-down arrow. This will allow it to store decimal values.

23. Verify your table design looks like the following and click the **Save** button in the **Changes** group on the **Fields** tab in the ribbon:

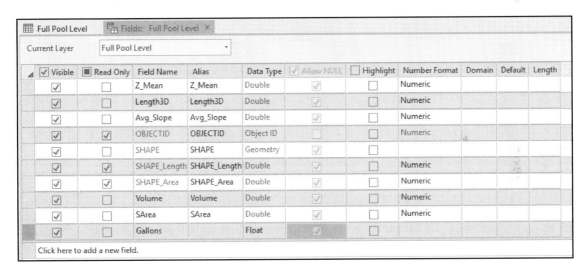

24. Close the **Design View** for the table.

    You have just added a new field to the attribute table for the **Full Pool Level** layer. This new field will be used to store the number of gallons that will be required to fill the quarry.

25. Right-click the **Gallons** field you just added in the table view and select **Calculate Field**. The **Calculate Field** tool will open in the **Geoprocessing** pane.

26. Scroll down so you can see the blank cell just above the words **Code Block**. You will need to enter the conversion expression here.

27. Type the following value into that cell: `!Volume! * 7.48052`. The number `7.48052` is the conversion factor for gallons per cubic foot.

28. Verify your **Calculate Field** tool looks like the following and click **Run**:

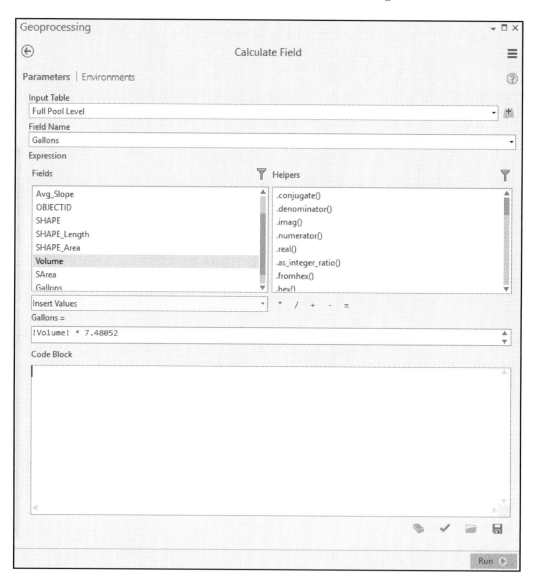

29. When the tool completes successfully, close the **Geoprocessing** pane.
30. Review the number that has now been populated into the **Gallons** field.
31. Close the **Full Pool Level** attribute table.
32. Save your project and close ArcGIS Pro.

You have just calculated the volume for an area covered by a polygon. This required you to have two datasets. You needed an elevation surface. The **Polygon Volume** tool you used required the surface to be in TIN, Terrain or LAS formats. The other dataset you needed was a polygon that formed the plane that was used to overlay the surface.

11
Introducing Arcade

In this chapter, we will cover the following recipes:

- Applying prebuilt Arcade expressions
- Creating an Arcade labeling expression
- Creating an Arcade symbology expression

Introduction

Over the years, Esri products have supported many different expression and scripting languages. These have included AML, Avenue, JScript, VB Script, SQL, and Python. Some of these languages were developed by Esri, such as AML and Avenue, while others were common IT industry languages, such as JScript, VB Script, Python, and SQL. Each of these were suited to specific uses on the desktop, servers, or online. However, now we find ourselves regularly having to work in all these environments at the same time. We create a map in ArcGIS Pro on our desktop, then publish to ArcGIS Enterprise, and later access it through the web on a mobile device.

This has begun to cause a problem as we work through these environments. Sometimes things we create that work great on the desktop do not translate to server or internet environments. This is often true for labels and symbology. So, to help bridge that gap, Esri has developed what they are calling a new expression language, Arcade.

Arcade is a lightweight and portable language that can be used across the ArcGIS platform. This means expressions you create in ArcGIS Pro will also work in ArcGIS Server, Portal, and ArcGIS Online. It can be used to control and display labels, perform mathematical calculations, manipulate symbology, and more. What makes Arcade unique is its inclusion of geometry types.

It was created from the beginning with that in mind, unlike other languages such as Python, which had to be customized to work with geometry.

What is the difference between an expression language and other programming or scripting languages? The primary difference is that an expression language cannot be used to create standalone apps or add-ins. It must be used inside of another application such as ArcGIS Pro. So Arcade is not as flexible as a scripting language like Python. Having said that, the expressions you can create with Arcade can be very complex, including multiple lines of code. For this reason, you may see Arcade expressions also referred to as scripts.

The syntax for Arcade is similar to other scripting languages such as Python or VB Script. For example, to indicate a text string, you simply enclose the desired string in single quotes. So, if you were creating an Arcade labeling expression and were to include Lot Number in the expression, those words would display as part of the label, as illustrated in the following screenshot:

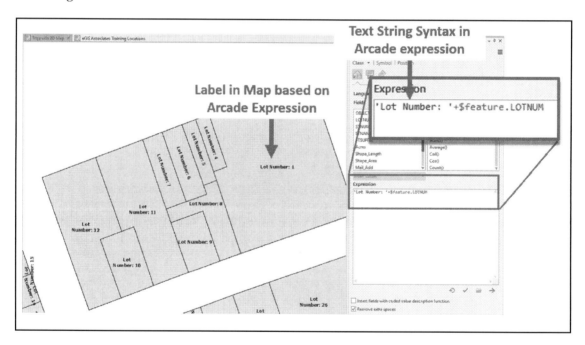

Sample of an Arcade expression for labeling a parcel with lot number

If you have ever created any labeling expressions in ArcGIS Pro or even in ArcMap, then the syntax shown in the graphic should look somewhat familiar. It is not that much different from Python or VB Script expressions. So, if you are already familiar with those, you should be able to pick up Arcade fairly quickly.

A few things you should know about Arcade syntax: first, it is not case sensitive, unlike Python. So a variable named Parcel is the same as parcel. To comment within your code, you can use either // for single-line comments or /* */ for multiple-line comments.

The following is an example of a single-line comment:

```
//Labels parcels with lot number
'Lot Number: '+$feature.LOTNUM
```

The following is an example of multiple-line comments:

```
/*
This expression was built using Arcade.
It is intended for use with ArcGIS Pro 2.1 and ArcGIS Enterprise 10.5 or
later versions.
*/
Proper($feature.NAME, 'firstword')
```

Lastly, variables may be declared within Arcade expressions and reassigned with new values, as illustrated in the following code block:

```
var x = 1;
return x;
//This will return a value of 1 for the variable x
x = 5;
return x;
//This will return a value of 5 for the variable x.
```

Arcade is still very new. It first came out with the release of ArcGIS 10.5 and ArcGIS Pro 1.4. With each new release of ArcGIS and ArcGIS Pro, Esri increases the capabilities of Arcade. This means you can expect to do more and more with this new expression language as time goes on. If you would like to take a deeper dive into Arcade, you may want to go to https://developers.arcgis.com/arcade/. This is Esri's primary resource for information about Arcade.

In this chapter, you will be introduced to Arcade and how it works in ArcGIS Pro. You will start by exploring existing expressions and learn how you can apply them in your projects. Then you will begin creating your own Arcade expressions. You will start by creating a labeling expression. Then you will learn how to create symbology expressions.

Applying prebuilt Arcade expressions

One of the nice things about creating Arcade expressions is that you can save them so that they can be used in other maps or scenes, or even with other layers in the same map. These expression files have a .lxp file extension. This also allows you to easily share expressions with others, so you do not have to reinvent the wheel every time you need to make use of an Arcade expression.

In this recipe, you will examine and apply a couple of existing Arcade expressions to layers within a map. You will start with a labeling expression that labels parcels with their **parcel identification number** (**PIN**) and the mapped acreage. Then you will examine another one that controls the visibility of a layer.

Getting ready

This recipe will require you to access an ArcGIS Pro license and have the sample data installed. This recipe is able to be completed at all ArcGIS Pro license levels. You will also need a web browser that supports HTML 5 and JavaScript. This includes current versions of Chrome, Edge, Firefox, and Safari. Internet Explorer 11 or newer is also acceptable. Other browsers may also work but have not been tested by Esri.

How to do it...

1. You will start by launching ArcGIS Pro and opening the Arcade project located in C:\Student\ArcGISProCookbook\Chapter11\Arcade using skills you have learned in previous recipes. The project should open with a map of the City of Thomaston, zoomed in to an area near the city center, as illustrated in the following screenshot:

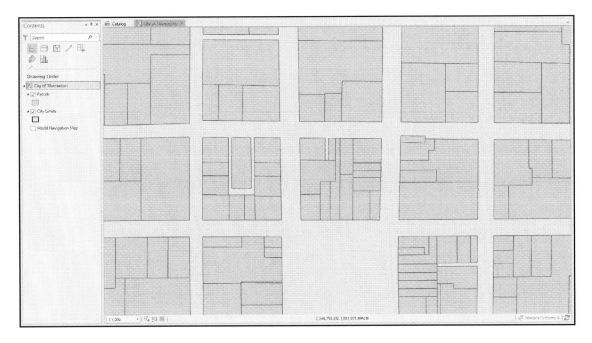

City of Thomasville map

2. In the **Contents** pane, select the **Parcels** layer so the **Feature Layer** contextual menu appears in the ribbon.

3. You will notice that none of the parcels in the map are labeled, so you need to turn on labeling for the layer. Click on the **Labeling** tab in the ribbon.

3. Click on the **Label** button located in the **Layer** group on the **Labeling** tab. This will turn on the labels for the parcels, as shown in the following screenshot:

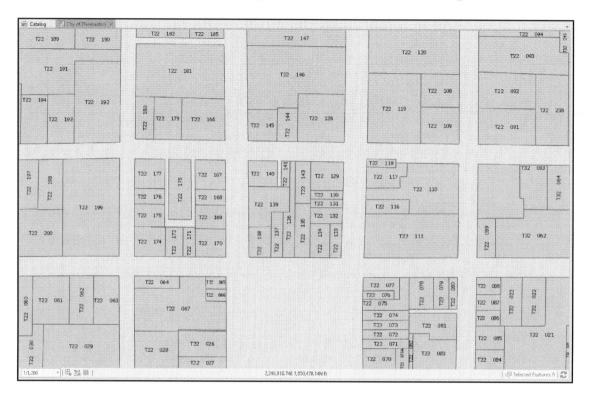

Now you can see that each parcel contains a label that identifies one attribute associated with each parcel. If you look at the setting for the **Field** in the **Label Class** group in the **Label** tab, you will see it is displaying the values found in the **PIN** field. This is the tax parcel identification number. What you want to do is label each parcel with not only its PIN but also with its mapped acreage. Luckily, someone has already created an expression file that will do just that.

You can also right-click on a layer in the **Contents** pane and select **Label** from the menu to turn labeling on and off for a specific layer.

5. In the **Labeling** tab, click on the **Expression** button located to the right of the **Field** option in the **Label Class** group, as illustrated in the following screenshot. This will open the **Label Class** pane where you create labeling expressions:

6. In the **Label Class** pane, set the **Language** to **Arcade** using the drop-down arrow.
7. Look at the labeling expression now. It should read **$feature.PIN**.

$feature is one of two global variables used by Arcade. It allows you to access or call information associated with the features in the target layer. In this example, it is letting you access the PIN field in the attribute table. You can also use it to access geometry information such as area, length, and coordinates.

8. Below the **Expression** area, click on the **Import** button, which resembles a file folder. This will open the **Import** window.

9. In the **Import** window, navigate to
   `C:\Student\ArcGISProCookbook\Chapter11` and select **Label Parcels** with
   PIN and **Acres.lxp**. Then click **OK**. This will import the expression into the
   Expression area in the **Label Class** pane. Now your **Label Class** pane should
   look similar to the following screenshot:

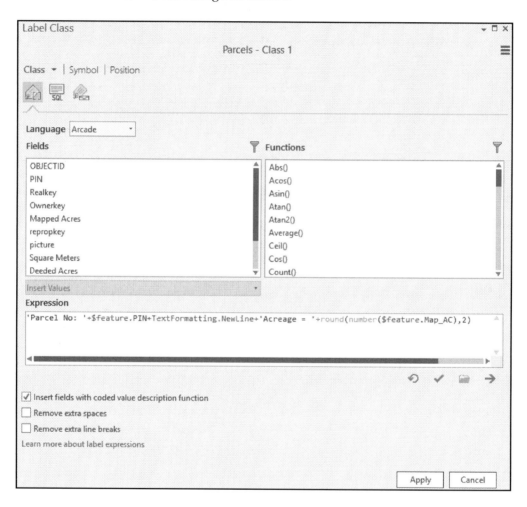

Now that you have imported the expression into the **Label Class** pane, let's take a look at it. This expression is set up to do a lot, as shown in the following:

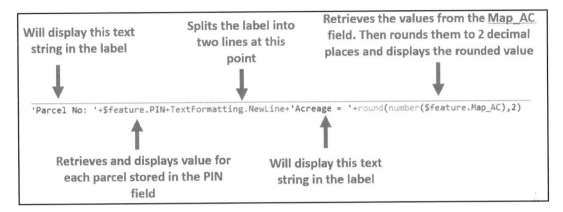

The expression starts with a text string, which will be displayed in the label. This is identified by the use of the single quotes enclosing the text string. That is followed by a **+**, which acts as a connector to the next part of the expression. The expression then retrieves the value for each parcel found in the **PIN** field of the layers attribute table. That value is then displayed after the **Parcel No:** text string from the first part of the expression. This is then followed by the **TextFormatting** variable, which creates a new line so that the following parts of the expression are displayed in another line. After that, the expression displays another text string, Acreage. Lastly, the expression retrieves the values for each parcel found in the **Map_AC** field of the attribute table. However, it does not just display the exact value. This expression takes it a step forward and rounds the values to two decimal places. It does this by invoking the round mathematical function and limiting it to two decimal places. The two decimal place limit is applied using the value after the field name.

Now that you know how this expression is supposed to work, let's apply it and then compare the results we see in this map to the explanation just provided.

10. Click on the **Apply** button at the bottom of the **Label Class** pane to apply the expression you just imported.

11. Notice how the labels in the map change and answer the question ahead:

Question: Did the labels change so that they now match the description of how the expression is supposed to work?

Answer:

If your map looks like the following screenshot, then yes, the expression performed exactly as described:

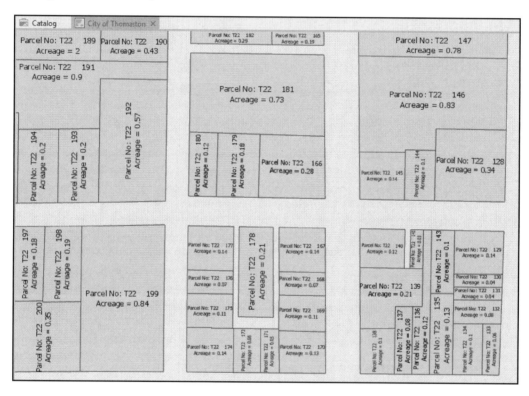

Results of labeling expression being applied

To a new user, this expression may seem complicated. However, it is a fairly simple one. These expressions can be much more complex, as you will find out next.

12. Close the **Label Class** pane and save your project.

13. Select the **Streets** layer in the **Contents** pane. Turn on the labels for this layer using skills you have learned earlier in this recipe. If you cannot remember, refer to *step 4*. The street names should appear in the map.

    Since you are working for the **City**, you want to make it possible to easily identify streets belonging to the **City**. To do this, your **City** streets need to be labeled in red and appear in a bold font. One of your co-workers has created an Arcade expression that will do that.

14. Click on the **Expression** button in the **Label Class** group on the **Labeling** tab, as you did previously in this recipe. This will open the **Label Class** pane.

15. In the **Label Class** pane, ensure the **Language** is set to **Arcade**. Then click on the **Import** button located near the bottom of the pane. You may remember that its icon resembles a file folder.

16. In the **Import** window that opens, navigate to `C:\Student\ArcGISProCookbook\Chapter11` using the skills you have learned and select the **City Streets Labels Red.lxp** file. Then click **OK**. You should now see the following expression appear in the **Label Class** pane:

    ```
    var type=($feature.FEATURE_TY)
    if (type == "City Street"){
    return "<BOL><CLR red='255'>"+$feature.ROAD_NAME+"</CLR></BOL>"
    } else {
    return $feature.ROAD_NAME
    }
    ```

17. Click the **Apply** button to apply the expression logic to the labels. Look at how the labels change. Some of the street names now appear in a bold red font. Those are the streets that belong to the **City**.

    Let's take a moment to examine how the expression accomplishes this. As you read this explanation, refer to the following diagram to help you better understand what is happening. It starts by defining a variable on the first line, which reads the road type from the **Feature_TY** field in the layer attribute table:

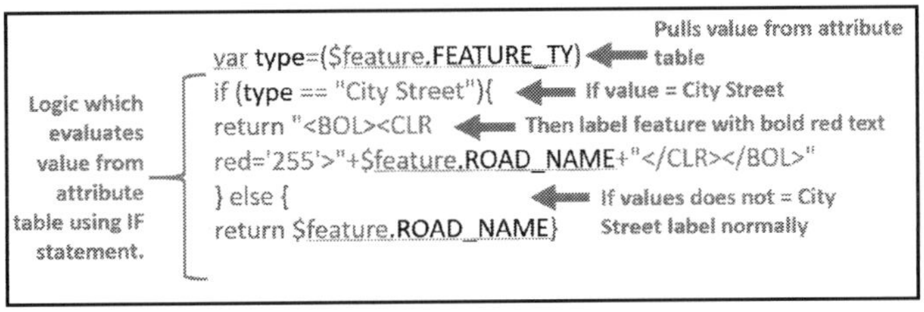

Once the variable is defined, the expression moves into a logic block that evaluates the value from the variable. It does this using an `if` statement. If the variable value for the feature is equal to **City Street**, then it returns a label for the feature from the **Road_Name** field in the attribute table, in bold red text. Otherwise, it just labels it with the value in the **Road_Name** field normally. The end result is a map with labels that look like those in the following screenshot:

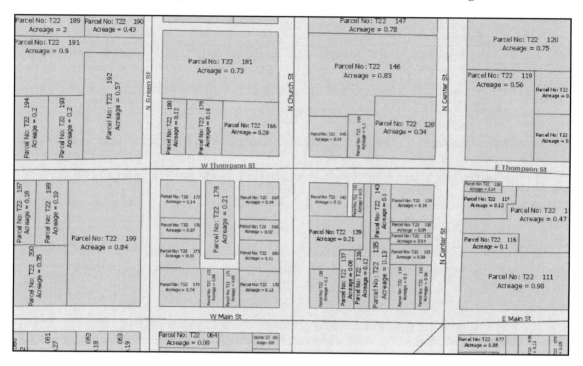

Results of labeling expression using if statements

As you can see, some road names appear in red and bold while others are black and normal. Those that are red and bold belong to the **City**.

18. Close the **Label Class** pane and save your project.
19. Close ArcGIS Pro.

You have now explored two Arcade expressions, so hopefully you are beginning to get some idea of how it works and what you can do with it. The first expression you used was fairly simple but still powerful. It labeled the parcels in the City of Thomaston with a PIN and the acreage on two different lines. The second expression you used included logic that controlled how features would be labeled. This is a much more complex expression. This is just the tip of the iceberg.

As you will learn later in this chapter, Arcade not only works with labels but can also be used to control symbology. This further increases the value of Arcade.

Creating an Arcade labeling expression

You have now had the opportunity to explore a couple of Arcade expressions. This has given you a chance to begin learning Arcade's syntax as well as some of the things you can do with these expressions. Now it is time for you to start building your own.

In this recipe, you will create an Arcade expression that will label the streets in Trippville with their name. This will require you to concatenate two separate fields that make up the full street name.

Getting ready

To complete this recipe, you need to have completed the previous recipe in this chapter as well as all those in Chapter 1, *ArcGIS Pro Capabilities and Terminology*. This will ensure you have the knowledge and skills needed to complete this recipe.

This recipe can be completed with any ArcGIS Pro license level and no extensions are required. You will need to ensure you have installed the sample data before you begin.

How to do it...

1. To start, you will need to launch ArcGIS Pro and open the Arcade project you used in the previous recipe. This project should appear in your list of recently opened projects.

2. When the project opens, you should see the map of the City of Thomaston you were working with in the previous recipe. Close that map by clicking on the small **X** located in the tab at the top of the map view. This will reduce the computer's resources being used by ArcGIS Pro since you will not be working with that map in this recipe.

3. In the **Catalog** pane, right-click on the **City of Trippville** map and select **Open** from the menu that appears. This will open the map you will be using for this recipe. The map should look similar to the screenshot that follows. If not, use the **Trippville Labeling Streets** bookmark to zoom to this area:

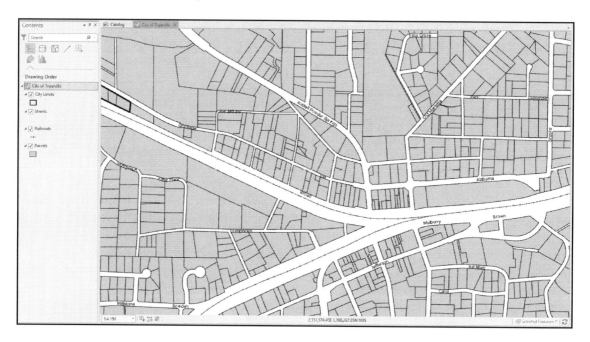

The newly opened Trippville map

Notice the streets already appear to be labeled with names. However, if you look closely, you should notice the names are not complete. They are missing the street type, such as road, avenue, or court. Let's see if you can figure out why that is happening.

4. Select the **Streets** layer in the **Contents** pane. Then click on the **Labeling** tab that appears in the ribbon.

5. Look at the value assigned to the **Field** option in the **Label Class** group and answer the questions:

> **Question**: What field is being used to label the Streets layer?

> **Answer**:

> **Question**: Is this a single field or an expression?

> **Answer**:

As you can see, the **Streets** layer is only using the **NAME** field to label the streets in the map with their name. While this single field would appear to contain the data needed to label the streets with their name, based on what you are seeing in the map, it is not the complete name. You need to examine the attribute table next to determine if there is another field that contains the street type information.

6. Right-click on the **Streets** layer in the **Contents** pane. Then select **Attribute Table** from the menu that appears. This will open the **Attribute Table** for the **Streets** layer, so you can examine it.
7. Locate the **NAME** field in the table. Then examine the values it contains.
8. Next, examine the other fields and see if you can determine one that contains the street type. Then answer the questions:

> **Question**: Is there a field in the **Attribute Table** that is used to store the street type?

> **Answer**:

> **Question**: If so, what is it?

> **Answer**:

After examining the table, you should have determined that the **TYPE** field is used to store the street type. It is not abnormal for the road name information to be broken down into separate fields. This is often true of the centerline data used as a geocoding source for E911/Emergency Response, address assignment, or general address location.

Now you know that in order to label each street with its full name, you will need to pull values from two separate fields. With that knowledge you can now create your expression.

9. Close the **Attribute Table** for the **Streets** layer. This will free up some screen real estate, so you can see more of the map.

10. If necessary, select the **Streets** layer in the **Contents** pane and click on the **Labeling** tab in the ribbon.

11. Click on the **Expression** button located next to the **Field** value in the **Label Class** group on the **Label** tab. This will open the **Label Class** pane, so you can build your expression.

12. In the **Label Class** pane, ensure your **Language** is set to **Arcade** using the drop-down arrow.

13. In the **Expression** area, you should already see the expression that is being used to label the streets based on values in the **NAME** field.

14. In the **Expression** area, add the following:

```
$feature.NAME+$feature.TYPE
```

15. Once you have completed the expression, click on the **Verify** button at the bottom right-hand side of the **Expression** area. It looks like a green check mark.

16. Once you validate your expression, it should say **the Expression is valid** in green lettering below the **Expression** area. Now click the **Apply** button to see how the expression you created labels the streets.

The expression you created is now indeed labeling the streets with both the name and type. However, if you look closely you will see that the two values are running together, as illustrated in the following diagram:

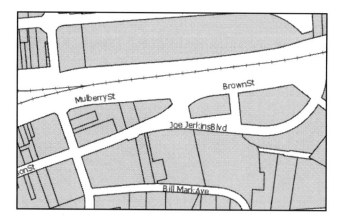

The space between the values is missing so that they are running together. You need to adjust your expression so that it adds the space between the two values.

17. Return your attention to the **Label Class** pane and your expression. To add a space between the values in the two fields, you will need to add a string representing the space. Click in the expression just after the + and type the following: " "+. There should be a space between the quotation marks. Your expression should now be:

```
$feature.NAME+" "+$feature.TYPE
```

18. Validate your expression once again. If it is valid, click the **Apply** button to see the results of your revised expression.

Arcade supports the use of several operators within its expressions. The operators perform basic logic functions in the expressions you create. Some of the common operators include:

- +: The plus sign adds two numbers together or concatenates two fields or strings
- –: This subtraction or minus sign subtracts one number from another
- ==: The double equals sign is the proper syntax for equals
- !=: The exclamation point with the equals sign means not equal to
- ++: The double plus signs increment values by one
- --: The double minus signs decrements the values by one

These are just a few of the operators you can use in Arcade. Go to `https:/ /developers.arcgis.com/arcade/guide/logic/` to see a complete list.

You should now see that a space exists between the name and the type, as illustrated in the following diagram:

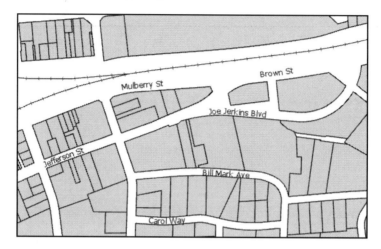

Congratulations on creating an Arcade expression! This is a very simple expression that concatenates the values in two fields together along with a string to create a single label. Let's take this to the next level and write another expression, which will change the color of the label based on the condition of the street. If you remember when you examined the attribute table for the **Streets** layer, there was a field that identified the condition of the road as either good, fair, or poor.

So, let's write a new expression, which will apply a green label to those streets in good condition, a black label to those in fair condition, and a red bold label to those in poor condition. You will start by defining two variables in your expression; one for the street name, which will use the expression you just created, and another for the condition.

19. Save your project before continuing.

20. In the **Label Class** pane, you will define a variable called name, which will use the expression you just created. In the **Expression** area, update your expression so it now reads:

```
var name=($feature.NAME +" "+$feature.TYPE)
```

21. Press the *Enter* key to start a new code line. Then define another variable which refers to the street condition in the **Condition** field. Type the following on the new code line you started:

```
var cond=($feature.Condition)
```

Your **Label Class** pane should now look like the following:

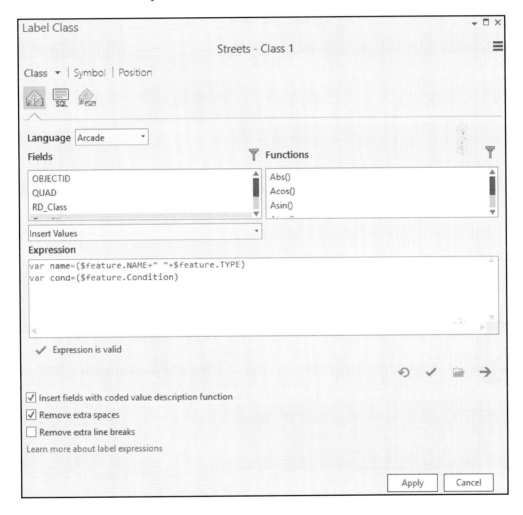

You have defined two variables in your expression now, **name** and **cond**. This allows you to use the variable in place of the full value the variable represents. This makes it easier for you to type and avoid syntax errors. Now it is time to add the logic that will evaluate the condition of each street and label it accordingly. You will use an `if` statement to do this, as you saw in the last expression you used in the previous recipe.

22. Return to the expression area within the **Label Class** pane and add the following code to your expression:

```
if (cond=="Good")
   {
   return "<CLR green='255'>"+name+"</CLR>"
   }
if (cond=="Fair")
   {
   return name
   }
else
   {
   return "<BOL><CLR red='255'>"+name+"</CLR></BOL>"
   }
```

23. Once you have finished typing the additional code into the expression, click the **Validate** button to ensure your syntax is correct.

As you type in each new line, you can use the **Validate** button to verify your syntax. The most common errors are missing quotation marks or brackets. Also, make sure to use double equals. If you have trouble writing the code, you can import the **Trippville Street Name Labels** with the **Logic Results.lxp** file located in `C:\Student\ArcGISProCookbook\Chapter11`.

24. If your expression is valid, click on the **Apply** button so you can see the results of your new expanded expression.

Once you apply your expression, you should see the labels in your map are now displayed in three colors—green, black, and red—as shown in the following screenshot:

This proves your expression is working. It is evaluating each street segment and displaying a label based on its condition and the parameters you defined for the label based on that condition.

25. Close the **Label Class** pane and save your project.

26. Close ArcGIS Pro.

You have now created two Arcade expressions for labeling streets with their names. The first expression you created was fairly basic. You concatenated two fields and added a space between the values to create a single label which displayed the full name of the streets. This is a very common use of an Arcade expression.

The second expression you created was much more complex. It included logic that determined how each label would appear in the map. Using `if` statements, your expression looked at the condition of each road segment and evaluated its condition, which was either good, fair, or poor. Based on that condition, it then rendered a label accordingly. The streets in good condition were labeled with green text. Those in fair condition were labeled with a black font. Lastly, those that were in bad condition were labeled with a bold red font.

Creating an Arcade symbology expressions

Arcade is not limited to use in labeling. You can also use it to control symbology. You may be thinking: why would you want to do that? ArcGIS Pro already has the ability to symbolize layers based on one or more fields of information, so that is a good question.

Arcade allows you to specify symbology based on values that do not exist in your database. It allows you to create symbology based on equations or functions. For example, you could have roads that have traffic count data and maximum designed traffic loads, but you want to symbolize the layers based on the current capacity—is it below, at, or over? There is no field identifying capacity. However, it can be determined by dividing the current traffic count by the design loads and multiplying by 100 to get the capacity percentage. Anything below 100 would be below capacity, anything at 100 would be at capacity, and anything above 100 would be over. Arcade allows you to build an expression that will do this. The best thing is that as the values change in the current traffic count or design traffic load data, the symbology is automatically updated and you only have two fields to maintain, not three or more.

In this recipe, you will symbolize the **Census Block Groups** for the Trippville area as either low, medium, or high population density. The density field does not exist, so you will use an Arcade expression to determine these values and then symbolize the **Block Groups** accordingly. This will require you to use logic expressions similar to those you used in the last recipe.

Getting ready

As with the previous recipe, you need to have completed all the previous recipes in this chapter and those in Chapter 1, *ArcGIS Pro Capabilities and Terminology*. This will ensure you have the required knowledge and skills needed to complete this one. You will also need to have ArcGIS Pro installed and access to a license. This recipe can be completed with any license level of ArcGIS Pro. The sample data also needs to be installed.

How to do it...

1. You will start this recipe by launching ArcGIS Pro and opening the Arcade project you worked with in the previous recipe. This project is located in `C:\Student\ArcGISProCookbook\Chapter11\Arcade`. The project should appear in your recently opened projects if you have been working through the entire chapter.

2. The project should open with the **City of Trippville** map shown in the view area. Close this map because you will be working with another one for this recipe.

3. In the **Catalog** pane, expand the **Maps** folder and right-click on the **Trippville Census Data** map. Select **Open** from the menu that appears. The new map should be displayed in the view area. It should contain four layers: **City Limits**, **Railroads**, **Parcels**, and **Census Blocks**.

4. In the **Contents** pane, select the **Census Blocks** from the list of layers. Then click on the **Appearance** tab in the ribbon.

5. Click on the drop-down arrow located below the **Symbology** button in the **Drawing** group on the **Appearance** tab. Select **Unique Values** from the list presented. This will open the **Symbology** pane.

6. In the **Symbology** pane, click on the set an expression button located to the right of the **Field** parameter, as illustrated in the following screenshot. This will open the **Expression Builder** pane:

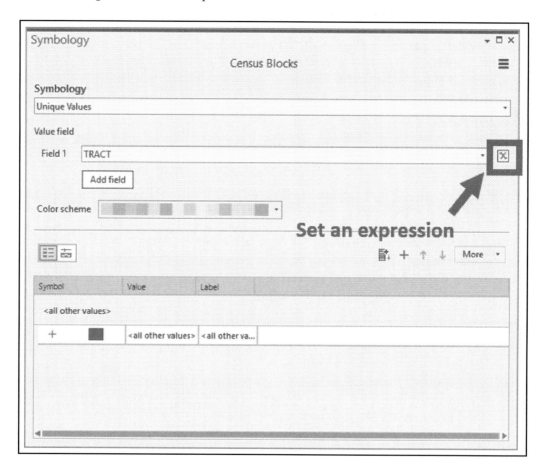

The **Expression Builder** pane should look very similar to the one you used to create labels. However, unlike labels, symbology only supports the Arcade language. This pane is divided into three basic sections or areas, as shown in the following screenshot:

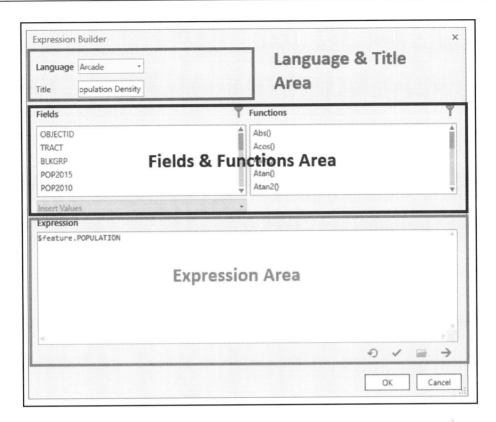

TIP

You can resize this pane to make it easier to work in. Move your mouse pointer to the edges of the pane. When your pointer becomes a double-headed arrow, you can then drag that edge of the pane in or out as desired.

The top area is the **Title** and **Language** area. Since Arcade is currently the only supported language, you do not need to worry about setting this option. The title is a name you give your expression. The fields and functions area allows you to pick fields and functions from the lists to add to your expression. This can help eliminate syntax errors. The bottom area is the **Expression** area where you build your expression as well as reset, validate, import, and export your expression. So let's start writing your expression.

7. At the top of the **Expression Builder** pane in the **Language** and **Title Area**, title your expression **Population Density**.

8. Now move to the **Expression** area in the pane to begin writing your expression. You will start by defining a variable that will calculate the population density. First delete the existing expression. Then type the following in its place:

```
var popden=($feature.POPULATION/$feature.SQMI);
```

This variable calculates the population density by dividing the total population of the **Census block** by its area in square miles. This will generate the population per square mile. Now you need to create the logic which will evaluate the value calculated by the variable to determine if the density is low, medium, or high. You will do this with an if/else statement.

9. Continue building your expression by adding the following code:

```
if (popden<=1335)
   {
   return "Low Density";
   }
else if (popden>1335&&popden<=1955)
   {
   return "Medium Density";
   }
else
   {
   return "High Density";
   }
```

The first line of your if statement evaluates whether the variable is less than or equal to 1335. If it is, then it returns a value of **Low Density**. If the variable value does not meet that criteria, it moves to the else if line. The else if line evaluates the variable to see if it is greater than 1335 or less than or equal to 1955. The double && signs in the expression act as the word *and*. So, the variable values must meet both operations. If the variable value does, then the expression returns Medium Density. Lastly, if the variable value does not meet any of the requirements in the if and else if lines, the expression returns High Density.

10. Verify you have not made any syntax errors by validating your expression. Click on the **Validate** button at the bottom of the expression area to do this. This button looks like a green check mark.

11. If your expression is valid, click the **OK** button. This will apply your expression and change the symbology for the layer. The **Census Block** layer should now display with the three categories you defined in your expression—Low, Medium, and High Density, as illustrated:

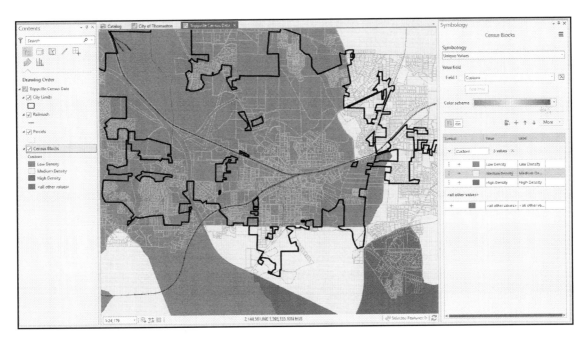

Results of Arcade symbology expression

The colors and scale of your map may be different, but the overall effect should be the same. You should see the three categories now shown in the **Contents** pane along with all other values. From this point you can make adjustments to the symbology as you would with any other layer. You can change the fill colors and patterns, change the order the values appear in within the list, and more. If you want to learn more about controlling symbology in ArcGIS Pro, we suggest you check out *Learning ArcGIS Pro* from Packt Publishing.

12. Feel free to make any adjustments you wish to the symbology assigned to the three values. Once you are done, close the **Symbology** pane.

13. Save your project and close ArcGIS Pro.

You have now created your first symbology expression using Arcade. As you have seen, a symbology expression is the same syntax-wise as a labeling expression, the difference being in how the results of the expression are displayed. With a symbology expression, the results change how the features within the layer appear in the map. With a labeling expression, the results are displayed as text within the map. The true power of these expressions is that they provide you with the ability to display different characteristics of your data by combining data, performing mathematical functions, and more. So you are not just limited to the exact data values.

Esri continues to expand the capabilities of the Arcade language with each new release of ArcGIS Pro. You have only touched the tip of the iceberg in terms of how you can use this expression language. Remember, it is supported not only in ArcGIS Pro but also in ArcGIS Online, ArcGIS Enterprise, and Esri SDKs and APIs.

12
Introducing ArcGIS Online

In this chapter, we will cover the following recipes:

- Logging into your ArcGIS Online account
- Creating a simple web map in ArcGIS Online
- Accessing ArcGIS Online content in ArcGIS Pro
- Accessing simple demographic data in ArcGIS Pro
- Using the ArcGIS Online Geoprocessing services

Introduction

ArcGIS Online is Esri's GIS cloud solution. It allows you and your organization to easily share data, maps, tools, and applications that can then be accessed via the internet. Prior to ArcGIS Online, you were required to have a dedicated GIS web server, such as ArcGIS Server, to provide web-based content to your users.

So, what is a cloud solution? The word Cloud is used a lot nowadays, but few really know what it is. Simply put, a cloud solution is one that leverages the internet to deliver a product. This can be in the form of hardware (servers), platforms (Windows, iOS, Linux), or software (Microsoft 365, Constant Contact, Salesforce).

ArcGIS Online is an example of **Software as a Solution (SaaS)**:

Example of an ArcGIS Online web portal

As a SaaS, ArcGIS Online provides the necessary tools to create interactive maps and apps, share and manage data, and integrate with other ArcGIS applications or other vendor solutions. ArcGIS Online also provides security that controls who can access your data. Like you own local network, ArcGIS Online requires users to log in to create, modify, or upload content. When you publish content in ArcGIS Online, you get to choose who you share it with. You can choose to share it with no one, which means only you can access it. You can opt to share it with the members of your organization, with part of a specific group, or you can choose to share content with everyone. This all assumes you are a Level 2 user. ArcGIS Online can even be integrated with your own local network security and logins.

ArcGIS Online supports two user levels, Level 1 and Level 2. Level 1 users are allowed to access and view content. So, they could view data shared via a web app with those in the organization or open a mobile application that allows them to view and query data. Level 1 users are not allowed to create, modify, upload, or share content. Those functions require you to be a Level 2 user.

Level 2 users are permitted much greater access to ArcGIS Online content than Level 1. Their access and capabilities are determined by the role assigned to their username. ArcGIS includes four basic user roles: viewer, user, publisher, and administrator. Each of these roles builds on the capabilities of the previous one. The view role limits the user to view only. So, they would be limited to the same basic access as a Level 1 user. The user role allows the user to edit features, add items, and share content. The publisher role allows users to publish hosted web maps as well as analyze the performance of layers in a web map. Administrators have the ability to manage other users, configure organizational settings, and manage ArcGIS Pro licenses. You can also create custom roles that mix and match the capabilities of the four primary roles. To learn more about the different ArcGIS Online user roles, go to `http://doc.arcgis.com/en/arcgis-online/reference/roles.htm`.

Doing things in ArcGIS Online costs credits. Most things that you do in ArcGIS Online cost some amount of credits. This includes storing data, hosting applications, and using ArcGIS Online services. Some things cost very few credits, such as storing data. It only costs about 1.2 credits per month per 1 GB of data stored in ArcGIS Online. Other functions cost more, such as geocoding or reporting. It costs 40 credits per 1,000 addresses you geocode. To learn more about credits and how they work, go to `http://doc.arcgis.com/en/arcgis-online/reference/credits.htm`. Credits are fairly cheap. You can get 1,000 credits for only $100.00.

Each license of ArcGIS Pro includes one Level 2 ArcGIS Online user and 100 credits. The ArcGIS Pro license level does not matter. If an organization (that is, business, agency, governmental unit) is the owner of the licenses, then they are combined. So if a City were to have three licenses of ArcGIS Pro, they would then get three level 2 users and 300 credits. These would be renewed each year, as long as the ArcGIS Pro licenses software maintenance is renewed.

There are some things that do not cost credits when using ArcGIS Online and its content. Here is a list of some of the things that do not cost ArcGIS Online credits:

- Making use of the Esri basemaps
- Uploading and downloading data
- Adding and using services from your own GIS server
- Simple viewing, querying, and printing of web maps by users

- Geocoding a single address
- Logging in to your account
- Managing your ArcGIS Online users or software licenses
- Viewing your organization's ArcGIS Online usage
- Configuring your ArcGIS Online account and organization

ArcGIS Pro is heavily integrated with ArcGIS Online. Within ArcGIS Pro, you can easily access a wealth of data, maps, and other services that expand the capabilities of your GIS. You will also find that much of the workflow between the two is very similar. This makes it much easier for users to shift back and forth between the two solutions.

In this chapter, you will get an opportunity to explore ArcGIS Online and see how it is integrated with ArcGIS Pro. You will start by exploring your access to ArcGIS Online. You will learn how to log in to your account and begin accessing content. Then, you will learn how to create a very simple web map using existing ArcGIS Online data. Next, you will explore ArcGIS Online's integration with ArcGIS Pro. You will learn how you bring data layers from ArcGIS Online into your own maps. Then, you will learn how to access demographic information from ArcGIS Online. Lastly, you will learn how to access some of the geoprocessing tools from ArcGIS Online.

Logging into your ArcGIS Online account

As mentioned previously, ArcGIS Online is a cloud-based solution. This means it is part of the web, so you access it just as you would any other web resource, using your web browser. This means you can access your ArcGIS Online account and content just about anywhere that you have an internet connection. It also means you can use a multitude of devices to access it. This includes not just your desktop computer or laptop, but also your smartphone or tablet.

In this recipe, you will learn how to log in and access your ArcGIS Online account. You will explore what resources might be available to you.

Getting ready

This recipe will require you to have an ArcGIS Online account and access to the internet. You will need to be a level 2 user. If you do not have an ArcGIS Online user login or do not want to use your organization's account to complete the recipes in this chapter, you can request a trial license from Esri, at `http://www.esri.com/arcgis/trial`.

You will also need a web browser that supports HTML 5 and JavaScript. This includes current versions of Chrome, Edge, Firefox, and Safari. Internet Explorer 11 or newer is also supported. Other browsers may also work but have not been tested by Esri.

You do not need to have completed any other recipes in this book to complete this one, nor do you need to have any GIS software installed.

How to do it...

1. Open your favorite web browser such as Chrome, Firefox, or Edge.
2. Go to www.arcgis.com. This is the web address for ArcGIS Online. When the site loads, it should look similar to this. Note that because ArcGIS Online is cloud-based, Esri often makes updates and changes:

My experience has shown that Chrome or Firefox tend to work better than Internet Explorer or Edge.

3. Click **Sign In**, located in the upper-right corner of the page near the Esri logo.
4. Enter your username and password in the indicated locations on the **Sign In** page. Then click the **SIGN IN** button. If desired, check the **Keep me signed in** box so you do not have to enter your login information each time:

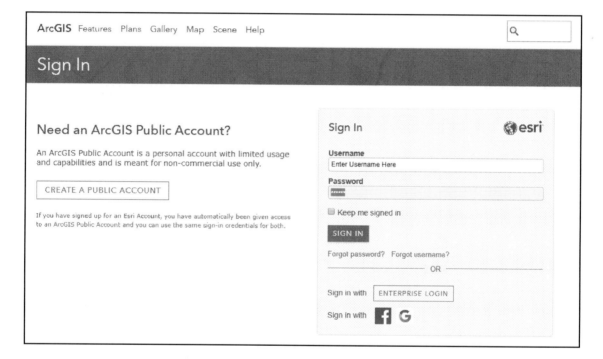

A couple of things to note on the Sign In page. First, ArcGIS Online also supports free public accounts. These accounts are limited on the functionality you can use. They only allow you to store up to 2 GB of data. They also have a limited ability to share content. Basically, you either share it with everybody or nobody.

Also note, you can integrate ArcGIS Online with your network login, or you can use your Facebook or Google login.

You are now logged in to your ArcGIS Online account. The page you see will depend on your user role. If you are an administrator, you are automatically taken to the **Organization** page. This lists all the existing ArcGIS Online users associated with your organization, along with their role:

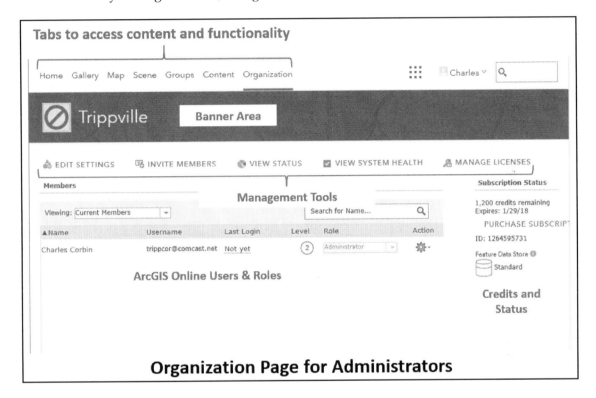

Organization Page for Administrators

If you are a publisher, user, or viewer, you are presented with your organization's home page. The home page, if it has been configured, will contain key content that you have access to. This might include web maps and applications, as shown here:

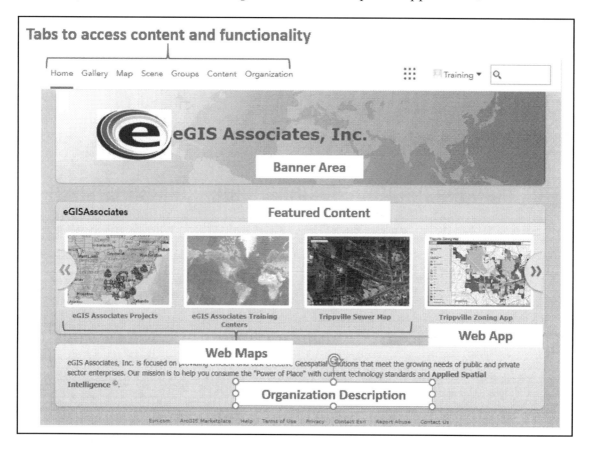

ArcGIS Online sample home page layout

5. Click the **Content** tab at the top of the page.
6. Take a moment to explore the **My Contents**, **My Favorites**, **My Groups**, and **My Organization** tabs. This will show you the content you have either created or that has been shared with you via groups or your organization.

If you have not used your ArcGIS Online account before, you may not have any content. So do not be concerned if you see nothing in your content tab.

You will now add a web imagery service to your ArcGIS Online account. Since this service is coming from another server, it will not cost you any credits.

7. Click the **My Content** tab.
8. Click **Add Item**, located in the upper-left corner under the **My Content** tab, and select **From Web**, as illustrated in the following screenshot:

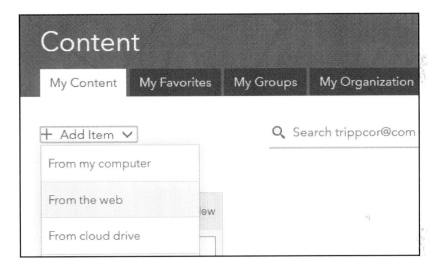

9. Ensure the **Type** is set to **ArcGIS Server web service**.
10. Type the following into the **URL**:
    https://services.nconemap.gov/secure/rest/services/Imagery/Orth oimagery_2017/ImageServer.
11. Set the **Title** to North Carolina Aerial Imagery.
12. Type the following in **Tags**, pressing the *Enter* key between each one: NC, Aerials, Imagery, and 2017.

13. Verify that your **Add an item from the web** window looks like the following, and click the **Add Item** button:

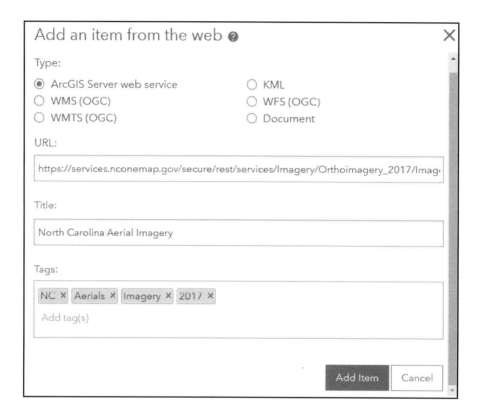

Once the new item has been added, you will see the **Properties** page for the new item. This allows you to see and configure properties associated with the items you add. Since you added this item using an existing web service, the properties are already configured based on the setting from the web server serving the image service.

14. Take a moment to review all the properties associated with the item you just added to your content.

15. Click the **Open in Map Viewer** button located on the right side of the page. This will allow you to view the service you just added to your ArcGIS Online content using the ArcGIS Online web viewer application.

Your web browser will now display the new **North Carolina Aerial Imagery** service you just added, as shown in the following screenshot. Later, you will learn more about the overall functionality of the ArcGIS Online Map Viewer. For now, you will just verify that your item was successfully added and is usable.

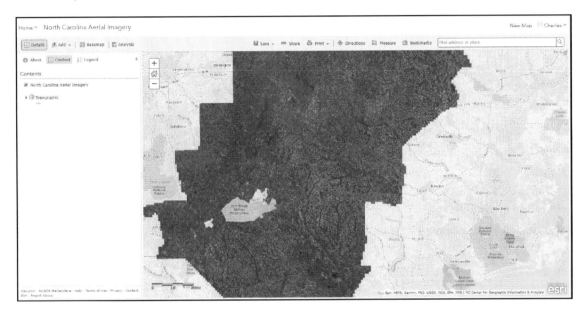

New ArcGIS Online web map with aerial imagery

16. Place your mouse pointer in the approximate center of the aerial imagery in the map and zoom in using your scroll wheel. Zoom in until you can see individual houses and roads. As you can see, this is some high-resolution photography.

17. Click the drop-down arrow located next to the **Home** button at the top-left of the page. Select **Content** from the menu that appears. This will take you back to the **Content** page.

    You should now see the new **North Carolina Aerial Imagery** service you added to your account. If you see it, you have successfully added content to your ArcGIS Online account.

18. Close your web browser.

You have now successfully logged in to your ArcGIS Online account. You not only accessed your account, but you also added content in the form of a web imagery service. You then viewed this service using the ArcGIS Online Map Viewer application.

Creating a simple web map in ArcGIS Online

Now that you know how to log in to your ArcGIS Online account and add some content, it is time to expand upon that skill and learn how to create a simple web map using publicly-available content. ArcGIS Online contains a wealth of data, provided not only by Esri but also by other users, that you are allowed to access and use freely. This sharing of information is one of the reasons ArcGIS Online can be a very valuable resource.

Creating a map in ArcGIS Online is very similar to creating one in ArcGIS Pro. First, you start a new map. Then, you select your basemap. Next, you start adding layers and configuring them. Then, you save your map. So, as you can see, the steps are very similar.

In this recipe, you will create a simple web map for the City of Trippville. This will include a couple of simple layers such as City Limits, Roads, and Natural Water Features.

Getting ready

This recipe requires that you have an ArcGIS Online account with at least a Publisher-level role assigned. You will also need internet access along with a web browser that supports HTML5 and JavaScript. You need to have completed the first recipe in this chapter to ensure you know how to access and log in to your ArcGIS Online account.

ArcGIS Pro is not required to complete this exercise.

How to do it...

1. Using the knowledge and skills you gained in the first recipe in this chapter, log in to your ArcGIS Online account using your web browser.
2. Click the **Map** tab at the top of the **ArcGIS Online** page you see. This will take you to the Map Viewer app.

    The Map Viewer app is not just to view existing data or maps. You also can create maps, edit data, share maps, and more. It is a very powerful tool. It is not unlike what you can do with a map or scene in ArcGIS Pro.

3. Click the **Basemap** button located on the top-left side of the **Map Viewer** interface. Select the **Streets** basemap.

4. Click the **Add** button located to the left of the **Basemap** button you just used. Select **Search for Layers** from the menu that appears, as illustrated in the following graphic:

5. Set the **In:** to **ArcGIS Online** using the drop-down arrow, as shown here:

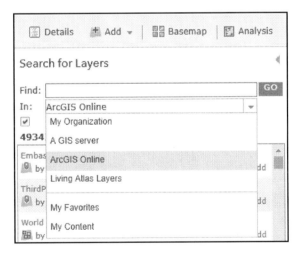

6. In the cell next to **Find**, type `Trippville` and press *Enter* or click the **GO** button. Several results should be returned by your search. Take a moment to scroll through the results to see all the information that has been published for the City of Trippville.

7. Scroll down until you see **Trippville_City_Limit published by Trippcor**, that is the book's author. Click the **Add** option to the right of the feature services.

8. Locate and add the **Trippville_Natwtr_Body** feature service and click the **Add** option. You can select a service published by anyone. Who published it is not important for this recipe.

9. Continue to repeat this process for the following layers:
   - Trippville_RW
   - Trippville_Railroad
   - Trippville_Parcels

10. After you have added all the required layers, click the **DONE ADDING LAYERS** button located at the bottom of the **Search for Layers** pane.

Your map should look similar the following screenshot. Like ArcGIS Pro and ArcMap, ArcGIS Online will assign random colors to your layers. So, your layers may look slightly different from this screenshot:

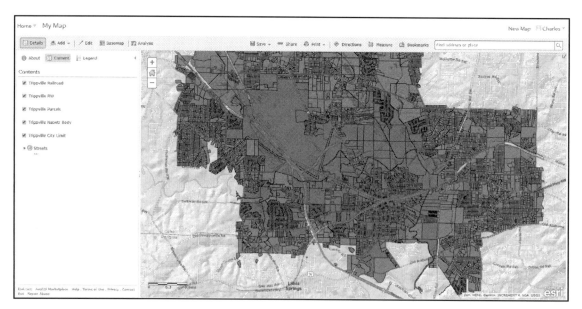

New Trippville web map created in ArcGIS Online

Just like in a Map in ArcGIS Pro, you now need to configure the layers in your web map. However, before we do that, you will save your map.

11. Click the **Save** button located near the top-middle of the **Map Viewer** app. Select the **Save As** option from the menu that appears, as illustrated here:

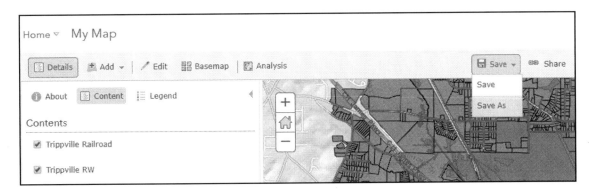

Saving a map in ArcGIS Online

12. Type the following values in the **Save Map** window that appears, and click **Save Map**:
   - **Title**: Trippville Basic Map.
   - **Tags**: Trippville, Map, City, Limits, Railroads, parcels, natural water (Press the *Enter* key between each tag).
   - **Summary**: This maps shows the overall boundary and basic features found in the City of Trippville.
   - **Save in folder**: Accept whatever value ArcGIS Online provides.

13. Verify that your **Save Map** window looks like the following screenshot, and click **Save Map**. Remember your **Save in folder** will be different:

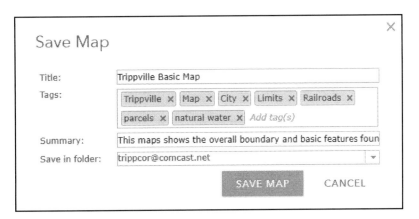

ArcGIS Online does not have an autosave. So, *remember to save early and often*.

14. Begin configuring your layers. You will start with the Trippville City Limit layer. Hover your mouse pointer over the layer in the **Contents** pane on the left side of the **Map Viewer**. Then select the Change Styles button, as illustrated in the following image. This will open the **Change Style** pane:

15. Ensure the **Choose an attribute to show** is set to **Show location only**.

16. Click the **Options** button located in the middle of the Location (single symbol) graphic under **Select drawing style**. This will take you to a pane that will allow you to adjust the symbology settings for the layer.

17. Click the word **Symbols** to open a window to adjust the symbology for this layer. In this case, you want to make the City Limits hollow with a thick black outline. This will allow you to see the area inside the City easily and identify the boundary.

18. Click the **Fill** tab at the top and then click **No color**, as illustrated in the following screenshot:

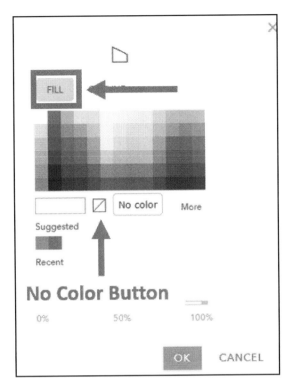

Adjusting the symbology in ArcGIS Online

19. Click the **Outline** tab located next to the **Fill** tab at the top of the window.
20. Select the black square located at the bottom of the second row. It should set the color code to #1A1A1A.
21. Set the **Line Width** to 4 PX.
22. Click **OK** to close the window.
23. Click **OK** again and then **Done** to apply all the adjustments you have made.
24. Place your mouse pointer on the **Trippville City Limit** layer and drag it to the top of the layer list so you can see it.

Like ArcGIS Pro and ArcMap, ArcGIS Online automatically places new layers in order based on their feature type. Points go to the top of the list. Lines go below points. Polygons go below lines, and raster go below polygons. You can change the draw order of the layers in your web map using the same process as in ArcGIS Pro. Simply drag and drop them into the order you desire.

25. Hover your mouse pointer over the **Trippville City Limit** layer again. This time, click **More Options**, as illustrated in the following graphic:

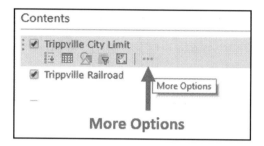

26. Select the **Rename** option from the menu that appears.
27. Rename the layer, `City Limits` and click **OK**. The name of the layer in the **Contents** pane should be changed to the new value you just typed.
28. Now change the symbology and rename the other layers, as indicated here:
    - **Trippville_Railroad**
        - Rename it to `Railroad`
        - Set **Color** to Medium Gray (#999999)
    - **Trippville_RW**
        - Rename it to `Road Rights of Way`
        - Set **Color** to Green, which is the 8th column in the 5th row (#38A800)
        - Set **Pattern** to **Dashed**
    - **Trippville_Parcels**
        - Rename it to `Parcels`
        - Set **Fill** to **No Color**
        - Set **Outline** as Dark Gray, which is the 2nd column in the 2nd row (#707070)
    - **Trippville_Natwtr_Body**
        - Rename it to `Lakes and Rivers`
        - Set **Fill** to Light Blue, which is the 10th column in the 4th row (#00A9E6)
        - Set **Outline** to Dark Blue, Which is the 11th column in the 5th row (#004DA8)

29. Click the **Legend** tab, located in the **Contents** pane, to see the results of the changes you have made to the symbology.

30. Verify that your **Map** looks like the following and then click the **Save** button to save your work:

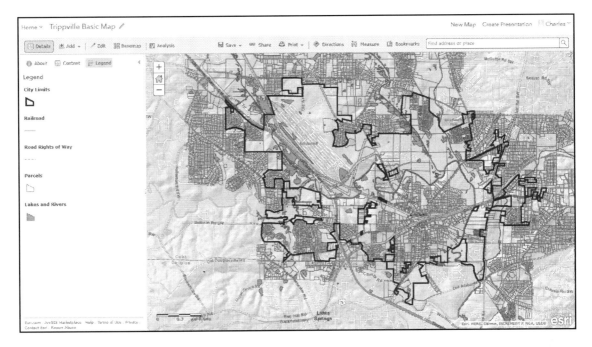

Trippville Basic Map results

You can also go to `http://arcg.is/1PKPLi` to compare your work with the results from the Author.

You have just created your very first web map in ArcGIS Online. You used existing data that others had already published for the City of Trippville. This is just a small sample of the data available in ArcGIS Online. You can find demographic information, aerial photos, terrain models, and more. It is a great place to start if you have no data.

31. Click the drop-down arrow located next to **Home** at the top of **Map Viewer** app. Select **Contents** from the menu that appears.

32. Take a moment to review your content.

 If you have not been using ArcGIS Online before completing the first recipe, you now have two items available in your content. One is the Web Map you just created, and the other is the Imagery Layer you added in the first recipe. As you continue with the rest of this chapter, your contents and the types of items will continue to grow.

33. Close your web browser.

Accessing ArcGIS Online content in ArcGIS Pro

You are not limited to the ArcGIS Online Map Viewer for accessing all the content available in ArcGIS Online. You can also access it from ArcGIS Pro, as well as ArcMap and other Esri applications. As a matter of fact, you have already been accessing ArcGIS Online content in the form of the basemaps that have been a part of every map and scene you have created. All of those are served by Esri through ArcGIS Online.

In this recipe, the Emergency Management Director has asked you to prepare a map that could be used in the event of an impending weather event. It will need to include weather radar information as well as weather warnings. This will need to overlay the GIS information the city already has so other ArcGIS Pro users can monitor weather events as they develop.

Getting ready

This recipe does not require that you have completed the previous recipes in this chapter, however, it is recommended to ensure you have some understanding of what ArcGIS Online is and how it works. You should have completed all the recipes in Chapter 1, *ArcGIS Pro Capabilities and Terminology,* or have equivalent experience using ArcGIS Pro before continuing with this recipe.

This recipe can be completed with all license levels of ArcGIS Pro. You must install the sample data before beginning this recipe.

How to do it...

1. Start ArcGIS Pro and open the `ArcGISOnline.aprx` project. This project is located in `C:\Student\ArcGISProCookbook\Chapter12\ArcGISOnline`. This project should open with the **Weather Response** map visible, as shown in the following screenshot. If not, open it from the **Catalog** pane using skills you have learned in past recipes.

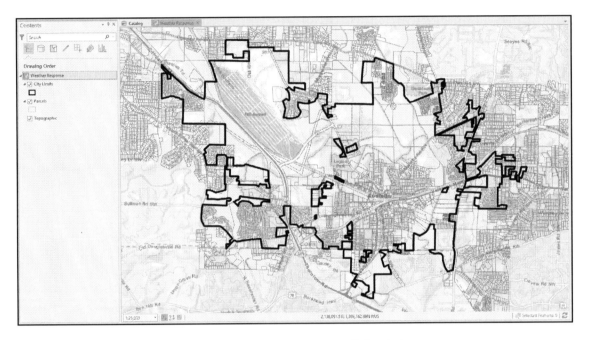

Weather Response map which should display when ArcGISOnline project is open

As you can see, this is a simple map that contains the City Limits and Parcels for the Trippville area. This information is coming from the same Trippville_GIS geodatabase you have used in past recipes. Now you will add some data layers from ArcGIS Online.

2. In the **Catalog** pane, click the **Portal** tab.

3. Now click the **All Portals** button. It looks like a simple cloud. It should be the third button from the left. This will allow you to access ArcGIS Online content that is being shared with all users.

4. In the **Search** cell, type `Weather`. This should return many listings for data in ArcGIS Online that you can access that has been tagged with the Weather keyword.

5. Select the **Recent Weather Radar Imagery Service**. Then right-click it and select **Add to Current Map**. This will add a layer to your map from ArcGIS online that shows the weather radar. Depending on the current weather around the Trippville area, this may show nothing or a lot of activity. This is a live feed from the **National Oceanic and Atmospheric Administration** (**NOAA**).

6. In the **Catalog** pane, locate the **NOAA NWS Warnings** and add it to your map using the same process as before. Again, this is a live feed from NOAA, so depending on the weather at the time you add this layer, it may also appear empty.

You have added two layers to your ArcGIS Pro map from ArcGIS Online. These two layers will provide basic weather information during a major weather event for the City of Trippville. These are national-level layers. Let's incorporate some more content that comes from other sources.

7. In the **Catalog** pane, change your search to `Georgia Weather`. Remember to press the *Enter* key when you type the new value.

8. Scroll down and locate the **NWS_Local_Storm_Reports** and add it to your map. This is a data feed that comes from the State of Georgia Emergency Management Agency. This will provide you with local information for the City of Trippville during a weather emergency.

9. Change your search to `Georgia Rivers and Streams` in the **Catalog** pane.

10. Scroll down and locate the **Rivers Streams Atlanta Region**. Add this data to your map, as you have with the other layers.

11. In the **Contents** pane, click the **List by Source** button then answer the following questions:

Question: What is the origin of each layer in the map?

Answer:

Question: Are all these layers being stored/hosted in ArcGIS Online?

Answer:

Your map now contains data from multiple sources. You have layers that reference your local Trippville_GIS geodatabase. You have several layers that are published to ArcGIS Online from multiple agencies including NOAA, GEMA, and the Atlanta Regional Commission. However, not all of these are stored directly in ArcGIS Online. The only layer that is actually stored in ArcGIS Online is the basemap. All the others are being published to ArcGIS Online via their own local GIS server.

ArcGIS Online provides the conduit to allow others to easily access the data. So, as you can see, ArcGIS Online provides a great resource for sharing information between multiple agencies and jurisdictions.

12. Explore some of the limits of the layers you added from ArcGIS Online. Click the **List by Drawing Order** button in the **Contents** pane.

13. Right-click the **SDEPUB.SDE.Rivers_Streams** layer and select **Properties** from the menu presented.

14. Click the **General** option in the left panel of the **Layer Properties** window.

15. Change the name to `Rivers & Streams`.

16. Click the **Metadata** option in the left panel. Review the **Metadata** and answer the following questions:

> **Question**: Who developed the data for this layer?
>
> **Answer**:

> **Question**: What was the original source from which the data was captured?
>
> **Answer**:

> **Question**: What was the date for the captured data?
>
> **Answer**:

As you can see, the metadata provides a wealth of information about the data in this layer. This is why it is important to create and maintain your metadata when you share that information with others. It allows them to know the who, what, when, why, and how of the data so the user can make educated choices about how to use the data.

Remember, the metadata for a feature class is edited via the Catalog View in ArcGIS Pro.

17. Feel free to explore other properties associated with this layer. Click **OK** when you are done.

18. Click the Symbol patch below the **River & Streams** layer, as illustrated in the following image, to open the **Symbology** pane:

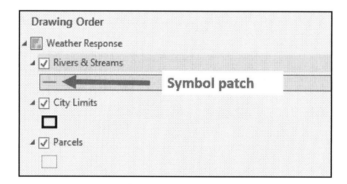

19. In the **Symbology** pane, ensure you are looking at the **Gallery** that provides you with a selection of preconfigured symbols.

20. Select the **Water (line)** symbol in the **ArcGIS 2D** style, as shown here, then close the **Symbology** pane:

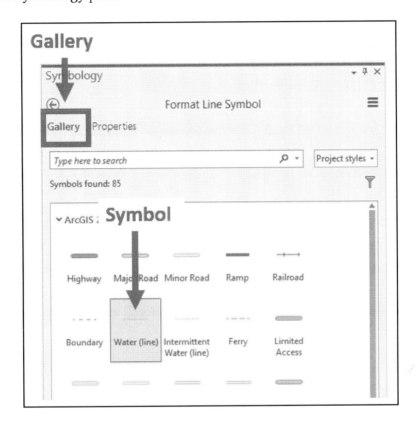

Gallery tab in the Symbology pane

21. Right-click the **NWS_Local_Storm_Reports** and select **Properties**.
22. Click the **General** option in the left pane and rename the layer `Local Storm Reports from GEMA`.
23. Click the **Metadata** and review the information there.
24. Review the other properties associated with the layer. Then click **OK** to close the **Properties** window.

25. In the **Contents** pane, expand the **Local Storm Reports from GEMA** layer. Then expand the **NWS Local Storm Reports Past 24 Hrs** group so you can see the associated symbology.

As you can now see, this layer's symbology is preconfigured as part of the service. You should have also noticed that the list of properties was much shorter than those available for the Rivers and Streams layer. This is because the Local Storm Reports from the GEMA layer is referencing an ArcGIS map service that is a type of raster service. As a user, you have a limited ability to change or adjust the display settings for an ArcGIS Map Service.

When you publish data to the web, be it through ArcGIS Online, ArcGIS Server, or ArcGIS Enterprise, you have to choose what type of service you will publish. The basic types of web services you can publish include Map, Feature, Geocoding, Geodatabase, Geometry, Geoprocessing, Image, and Network analysis services. Each of these has its own unique capabilities. For more information about all these different service types, go to `https:/` `/doc.arcgis.com/en/arcgis-online/reference/arcgis-server-` `services.htm`.

26. Feel free to examine the other layers you have added to your map. Once you are done, save your project.
27. Close ArcGIS Pro.

Accessing simple demographic data in ArcGIS Pro

Another useful integration between ArcGIS Pro and ArcGIS Online is the ability to access some simple demographic data that Esri publishes via their GeoEnrichment service. This data is accessed via the Infographics tool on the Map tab.

This tool presents the data as a series of graphs, tables, and reports. It can help you answer several questions about the area you are working in, such as:

- What is the average income level?
- What is the total population?
- How diverse is the population?
- What is the age demographic breakdown for the area?

The amount of information, level of detail, and scale available will depend on where you are working in the world. Esri maintains a large collection of demographic data, however it is not always 100% complete. To find out what data is available for a given region or area, go to `http://doc.arcgis.com/EN/ESRI-DEMOGRAPHICS/DATA/DATA.HTM`.

Using the Infographics tool does cost credits. So, each time you click in the map or scene while using the Infographics tool, you will use up a portion of a credit. This cost per use is very small. You will use up 10 credits per 1,000 views or clicks. So, each click only uses 0.01 credits. However, you should always keep this in mind when accessing ArcGIS Online-based functionality.

In this recipe you, will examine the Infographics tool. You will learn how to use and configure it to get the information you need.

Getting ready

You must have completed the other recipes in this chapter before starting this one. This will ensure that you have a stronger foundational understanding of ArcGIS Online and how it is linked to ArcGIS Pro. You will also need to ensure the sample data is installed before you continue.

This recipe, like the others in this chapter, will require you to have an ArcGIS Online user account. Any user level and role should allow you to complete this recipe. This recipe will use up some of your ArcGIS Online credits. The amount should be very small, under one credit in most cases.

How to do it...

1. Start ArcGIS Pro and open the `ArcGISOnline` project you used in the previous recipe. This project should be included in your list of recently opened projects.
2. Close the **Weather Response** map you worked with in the previous recipe by clicking the **X** in the tab with the map name at the top of the view.

It is recommended that you always close any map, scene, table, or pane you are not using. This should reduce the amount of computer resources ArcGIS Pro uses, which in turn should improve the performance of the application and reduce the possibility of crashes.

3. In the **Catalog** pane, expand the **Maps** folder so you can see its contents.

4. Right-click the **Demographics** map and select **Open**. Your map view area should now display the **Demographics** maps as shown here:

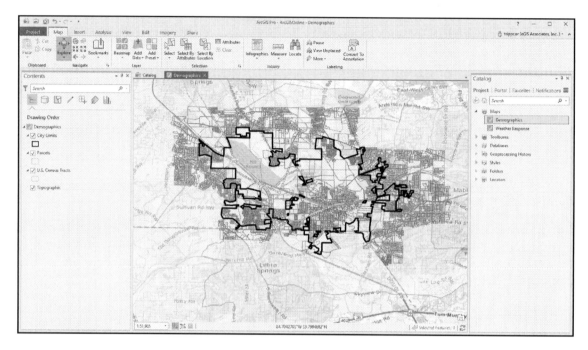

Demographics map which you should now have open

5. Review the layer list in the **Contents** pane.

As you can see, this map only contains four layers: City Limits, Parcels, US Census Tracts, and the basemap. You should be familiar with the City Limits and Parcels layers if you have worked through other recipes in this book. The US Census Tracts is a new layer you have not worked with. You will quickly examine its properties to become familiar with this new layer.

6. Right-click the **US Census Tracts** layer and select **Properties** from the menu that appears.

7. Click the **Metadata** option in the left panel of the **Layer Properties** window. Then answer the following questions:

Question: What years do these boundaries apply to?

Answer:

Question: Who created this data originally?

Answer:

Question: What does this layer represent?

Answer:

By looking at the metadata and answering the preceding questions, you should have gained a better understanding about this layer. You now know that this layer represents the US Census tract boundaries for the 50 states plus DC and Puerto Rico from 2010 to 2015. You also know it was originally created by the US Census Bureau. Knowing this can help you better determine how to use this information.

8. Close the **Layer Properties** window once you have answered the questions.
9. Right-click the **US Census Tracts** layer and select **Attribute table**.
10. Review the attribute table to see what information it contains. This provides you with even more insight into this new layer.
11. Close the attribute table when you are done reviewing it.

Much of the data retrieved by the Infographics tool in the United States starts with the US Census Bureau. Esri then extrapolates that information along with other sources to develop a more in-depth level of data that is useful in predicting growth, placement of new facilities, and more. Most countries have similar agencies that monitor population and other demographic makeup.

12. Right-click the **City Limits** layer in the **Contents** pane. Select **Zoom to Layer** from the menu that appears. Your map should zoom to show the full extent of the City Limits layer, as illustrated in the following screenshot:

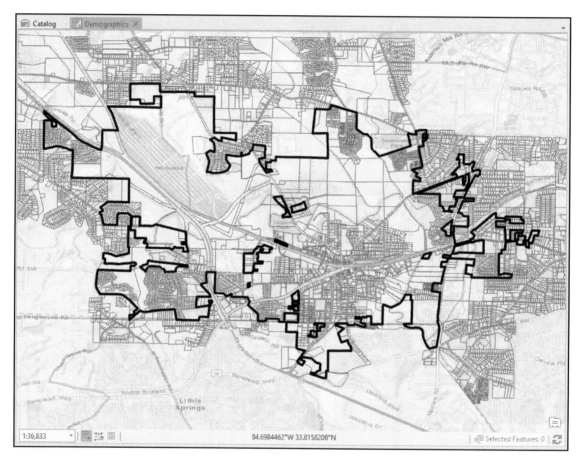

Map zoomed to City Limits layer

13. Activate the **Map** tab in the ribbon if needed.

   First, let's learn how to configure settings for the Infographics tool. This will help ensure the data you need to see is displayed.

14. Click the drop-down arrow located below the **Infographics** button and select **Configure Infographics**. This will open the **Configure Infographics** window, as shown here:

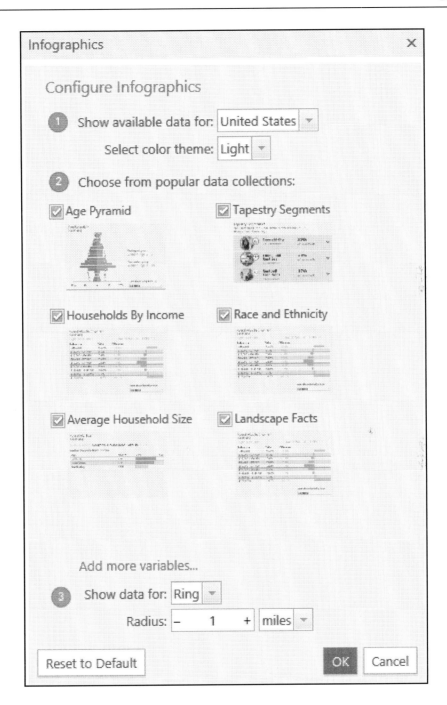

15. Take a moment to notice the basic options you can configure. First, you choose the country you want to explore. For this recipe, set it to **Show available data for: United States** using the drop-down arrow if needed.

16. If desired, you can change the color theme. The default is Light.

17. Notice the data collection that is available by default and answer the following question:

> **Question**: What are the six default data collections which are available with the tool?
>
> **Answer**:

The Infographics tool provides you with access to six different data collections by default. You can control which of these you see by clicking the check boxes to enable or disable those collections. You can also access settings and data by clicking **Add more variables**. This allows you to further refine the data you see presented in the Infographics tool.

18. You can control the area that the tool analyzes. Notice, by default, it is based off a ring distance to start. Click the drop-down for **Show data for:** to see what other options are available. Leave it set to **Ring**.

19. Click **OK** to close the **Configure Infographics** window.

Now you will put the tool into action.

20. Click the **Infographics** tool located on the **Map** tab in the **Inquiry** group.

21. Click at any point within the City Limits of Trippville. The **Infographics** window should then appear, as illustrated in the following screenshot. Your window may look different depending on how your tool is configured and if you have ever used it before.

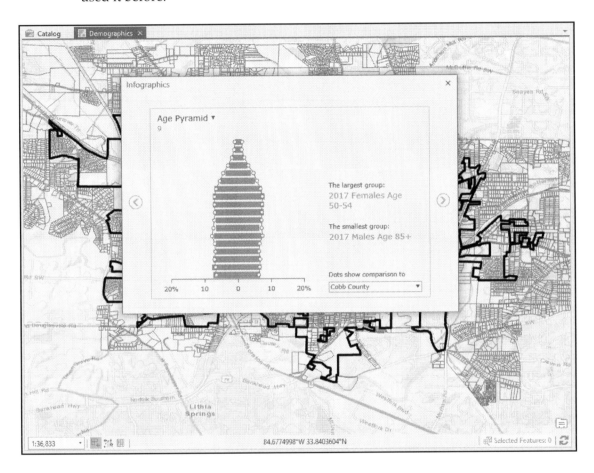

22. In the upper-left corner of the window, you should see a value with a drop-down arrow. This controls what is displayed in the window. If needed, click the drop-down arrow, as illustrated in the following image, and select **Age Pyramid**:

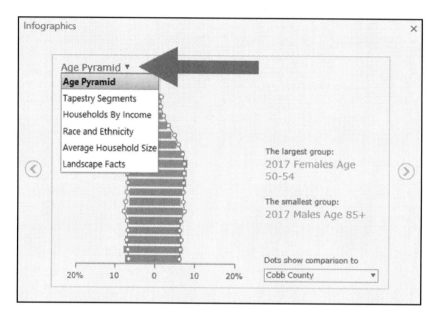

23. Ensure the **Dots show comparison to** option is set to **Cobb County** using the drop-down arrow. It is located in the lower-right corner of the **Infographics** window.

    Now, your **Infographics** window should look very similar to all the graphics you have seen so far. The Infographics tool can be configured to show different information. We will explore that later. For now, let's continue to examine what information is available out of the box with the default configuration.

24. Change the **Dots show comparison to** from **Cobb County** to **Georgia**. Notice how the graph changes.

25. Change it to the **United States** now and watch the graph to notice the changes.

    Each time you adjust the level at which the tool compares, the graph changes. The colored bars represent the data for the area you clicked. The line with the circles represents the values for the comparison (that is, Cobb County, Georgia, or United States). Now let's look at some other options.

26. Where you clicked the drop-down arrow to change the window to the **Age Pyramid**, click it again and select **Households by Income**. This will display a different graph that shows the percent of households within different income brackets and how the area you clicked compares to the larger area defined by the Bars show deviation from option in the lower-right corner.

You can also use the small arrows located on the right and left side of the Infographics window to change what data is displayed. This does the same as the drop-down menu in the upper-left corner.

27. Try some of the other data and comparison options.
28. Close the **Infographics** window once you are done exploring the data options that can be displayed.
29. Save your project.
30. If you are continuing to the next recipe, you may keep ArcGIS Pro open. If you are not, you may close it.

You have now seen how you can access very simple but informative demographic information using the Infographics tool. ArcGIS Pro allows you to customize this tool so you display the information you need to get the answers you are looking for, using the Infographics Configuration window. This is just a small subset of data that Esri has in its library. If you want access to more detailed and refined demographic data, you may want to investigate the ArcGIS Business Analyst (`http://www.esri.com/software/businessanalyst`) and Community Analyst (`http://www.esri.com/software/arcgis/community-analyst`).

Using the ArcGIS Online geoprocessing services

ArcGIS Online is more than just data and maps. It also contains powerful analysis or geoprocessing tools as well. These tools can allow you to perform analysis that would normally require you to have an extension, such as calculate service areas, determine watersheds, and create elevation profiles.

As mentioned, those types of analysis typically require an extension. For example, to calculate a service area, you would need the Network Analyst extension. However with ArcGIS Pro, you can access this functionality as a ready-to-use tool without an extension. These ready-to-use tools do use credits, and typically more credits than the Infographics tool. The amount of credits used by each tool is determined by a base level for the tool plus the additional options you select that add complexity to the analysis. For example, if you needed to calculate a service area based on a simple driving distance that would use less credits than one that was based on driving time, during a specified time period, that also took one-way streets and weight limits into account and avoided toll roads.

While these tools do use credits, they may still be a cheaper option than getting one of the Esri ArcGIS Extensions. The list price for an ArcGIS Extension is $2,500.00 for a single license of one extension, whereas the credits required for each analysis is a fraction of that number. So, unless you also need to create the data used in the analysis and maintain it, then ArcGIS Online tools may be a more sustainable financial option for you to consider.

In this recipe, you are working for a GIS Consulting company. You have been assigned a new client that is a concrete provider. They have several plants located throughout Georgia. They need you to calculate the service area for each plant based on an estimated one-hour drive time. That is the upper limit of time before the concrete in the delivery trucks start to become unusable.

Getting ready

It is recommended that you complete the other recipes in this chapter, along with those in Chapter 1, *ArcGIS Pro Capabilities and Terminology*, to ensure you have the needed foundational understanding of the topics and basic workflows used in this recipe. You will also need to ensure the sample data is installed before you continue, and you have an ArcGIS Online user account with permissions to use credits. You will also need internet access to complete this recipe.

This recipe will require you to use some of your ArcGIS online credits. It is estimated that this recipe should take about two credits or fewer to complete.

How to do it...

1. If you closed ArcGIS Pro when you completed the previous recipe, start ArcGIS Pro and open the `ArcGISOnline` project you used in the previous recipes in this chapter. This project should be included in your list of recently opened projects.

2. Close the **Demographics** map you were working with in the previous recipe, and open the **Corbin Concrete** map from the **Catalog** pane. The new map should open with a layer showing the locations of the seven concrete plants belonging to Corbin Concrete, as illustrated in the following screenshot:

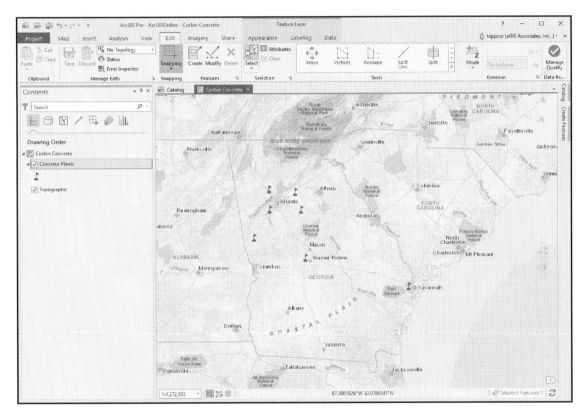

Map showing location of Corbin Concrete plants

Now that you can see the locations of the concrete plants, you need to calculate service areas for each plant based on a one-hour drive time. Traditionally, to do this you would need the Network Analyst extension and a road network dataset. Since this is a new client that has never used or had GIS, you do not have any of this data specifically for them. Luckily, with the ArcGIS Online ready-to-use tools, you do not need that. All you need is access to ArcGIS Online and a few credits to run the analysis.

3. Click the **Analysis** tab in the ribbon.
4. Click the **Ready to Use Tools** in the **Geoprocessing** group and select **Generate Service Areas**, as illustrated in the following graphic. This tool is accessing a geoprocessing service from ArcGIS Online:

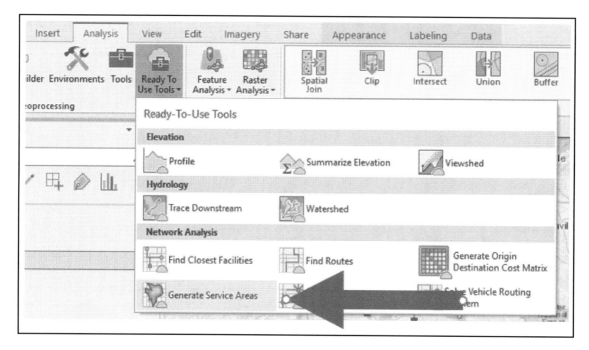

Accessing the ready to use Generate Service Areas tool

5. Set the **Facilities** to **Concrete Plants** using the drop-down arrow.
6. Set the **Break Values** to 1 by typing the number in to replace the default values.

7. Set the **Break Units** to **Hours** using the drop-down arrow.
8. Accept the default **Travel Mode** of `Custom`. By default, this mode assumes you are traveling by vehicle and will automatically avoid private roads, unpaved roads, and a few other types of traffic items. Later, you will investigate those settings and make adjustments.
9. Verify that your **GenerateServiceAreas** tool looks like the following and click **Run**:

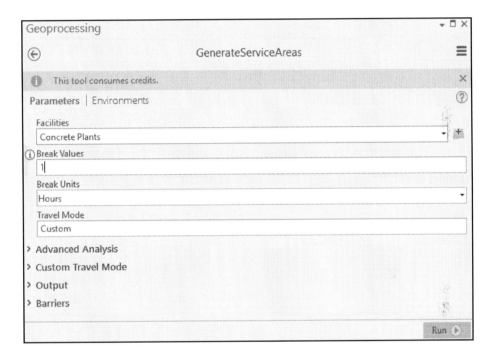

Depending on your internet connection speed and your computer specs, this tool may take several minutes to complete.

When the GenerateServiceAreas tool completes, a new layer will appear in your map. This new area shows the service area for each plant based on an estimated one-hour drive time, which should look something like the following screenshot:

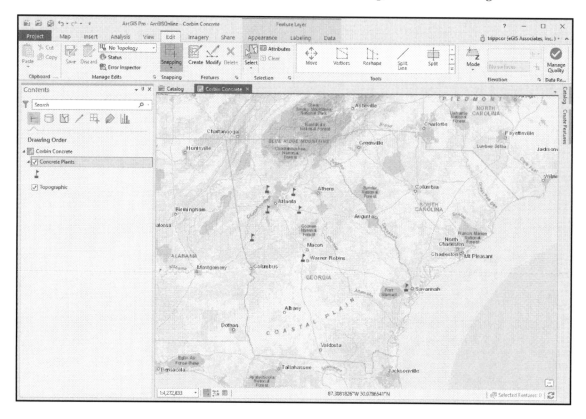

The client appreciates your efforts and thinks this is useful information. However, they now want to make a few adjustments to your analysis. Given that one hour is the maximum time for the concrete before it starts to become unusable, they want to build in a 15 minutes safety margin. So the new time will be 45 minutes instead of one hour. They also want to make sure the calculation avoids toll roads and restricted roads, as well as roads with height restrictions and weight restrictions. You will need to run the analysis again with the new parameters.

10. Right-click the **Service Areas** layer that was just added to your map and select **Remove** from the menu that appears.

11. In the **GenerateServiceAreas** tool, set the following parameters:
    - **Facilities**: **Concrete Plants**
    - **Break Values**: 45
    - **Break Units**: **Minutes**
    - **Travel Mode**: Custom

12. Expand the **Custom Travel Mode** options and enable the following restrictions:
    - **Avoid Carpool Roads**
    - **Avoid Express Lanes**
    - **Avoid Ferries**
    - **Avoid Gates**
    - **Avoid Private Roads**
    - **Avoid Toll Roads for Trucks**
    - **Driving a Truck**
    - **Height Restriction**
    - **Roads Under Construction Prohibited**
    - **Through Traffic Prohibited**
    - **Weight Restriction**

13. Accept the default values for all other parameters.

14. Once you have configured all the restrictions, click **Run**. Again, the tool may take several minutes to run due to the complexity of the analysis you are asking it to perform.

    Once again, a new layer will appear in your map. This represents the new service areas you just created with the shorter drive time and additional restrictions. To make the map and data easier to understand, you will now make some adjustments to the layer and its symbology.

15. Close the **Geoprocessing** pane.

16. Right-click the **Service Areas Layer** and select **Properties**.

17. Click the **General** option in the left panel of the window. Then rename the layer Plant Services Areas Based on 45 Minute Drive.

18. Click the **Appearance** tab in the ribbon.
19. Click the drop-down arrow below the **Symbology** button and select **Unique Values** from the options that appear. This will open the **Symbology** pane.
20. Set **Field 1** to **Facility: Name** using the drop-down arrow.
21. Set the **Color Scheme** to the **Basic Random Color Ramp** using the drop-down arrow.

When you click the drop-down arrow to see the list of available color ramps, if you look at the bottom of the list, you will see some options. One of them will display the name of each color ramp. You may need to enable that option to ensure you select the correct one.

22. In the grid located below where you selected the color ramp, change `Facility: Name` to `Plant ID`, as illustrated in the following screenshot:

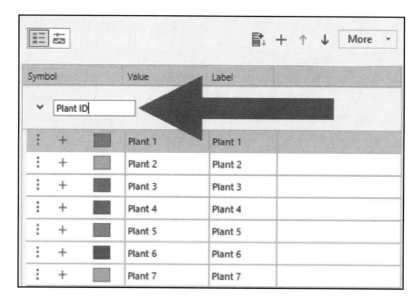

23. Close the **Symbology** pane.

24. Set the layer transparency to **40%** in the **Effects** group on the **Appearance** tab, as shown in the following screenshot. This will allow you to see the basemap underneath the service areas.

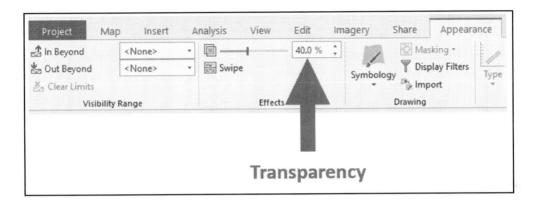

You have now created a map that shows the location of each concrete plant along with the associated service area for that plant. Now the dispatchers for Corbin Concrete will know what areas they can provide concrete to and which plant, or plants, will be the best choice to send the trucks from. You will use this map in a future recipe.

25. Save your project and close ArcGIS Pro.

13
Publishing Your Own Content to ArcGIS Online

In this chapter, we will cover the following recipes:

- Publishing shapefiles using your browser
- Creating a layer using a CSV file
- Publishing layer packages using ArcGIS Pro
- Publishing web layers using ArcGIS Pro
- Publishing 2D maps
- Sharing published content

Introduction

As you have seen if you completed the previous chapter, ArcGIS Online is an amazing resource. It provides access to a wealth of data and tools that can greatly enhance the abilities of your GIS. But, can you add your own data and maps to your content, or are you limited to the content that is already there?

ArcGIS Online does allow you to publish your own content. This can take many forms, including:

- Data files:
    - Shapefiles
    - Text files (TXT and CSV)
    - Spreadsheets

- PDF files
- Map packages
- Layer packages
- KML
- Styles
- And more…

- Web map and feature services:
  - Publish directly through ArcGIS Online
  - Connections to web maps from your own ArcGIS Server or Portal
- Web applications
- And more

For a full list of all the items you can add to your ArcGIS Online content, go to `https://doc.arcgis.com/en/arcgis-online/reference/supported-items.htm`.

Depending on the content you are attempting to publish, there are different methods you can use to publish it. Files can be directly uploaded to ArcGIS Online via your web browser. Maps and scenes can be published directly from ArcGIS Pro. The best method will depend on the content type, size, and desired capabilities. The number of credits you have can also influence the method.

In this chapter, you will begin to explore some of the ways you can publish your own content to ArcGIS Online. You will upload a shapefile and a CSV file to ArcGIS Online. You will then configure the ArcGIS Online options associated with the uploaded files. Next, you will publish a layer package from ArcGIS Pro to your ArcGIS Online content. From there, you will learn how to publish both an entire 2D map and 3D scene to ArcGIS Online. Lastly, you will explore simple methods for sharing some of the new content you have published.

Publishing shapefiles using your browser

ArcGIS Online can be used as a repository for GIS data and files. Putting these files up in ArcGIS Online allows you to access the information anywhere you have an internet connection, much like Google Drive or DropBox. It also allows you to use that data to create web maps and share them with others. This can greatly increase the overall flexibility of you GIS by making the data available whenever you need it, and not just when you are back in the office.

If you are going to upload and publish files to ArcGIS Online, some of them may need to be prepared or configured before you upload them. For example, a shapefile must be compressed into a single ZIP file before you are able to publish it to ArcGIS Online. This is because each shapefile actually consists of multiple files. If you remember from Chapter 2, *Creating and Storing Data*, a single shapefile will consist of a SHP, SHX, and DBF file at a minimum. Additional files such as a PRJ, SBN, and SBX might also exist. All of these files make up a single shapefile. So, it makes sense that in order to publish it to ArcGIS Online, you would need to compress all these files into a single ZIP file first.

The formatting required for a CSV or TXT file will depend on how you intend to use it in ArcGIS Online. If you just want to make the file available to download, then no formatting is required. However, if you want to map the data included in the file, then specific formatting is required. You will explore that in the following recipe.

In this recipe, you will upload a shapefile and CSV file to your ArcGIS Online content. You will start by zipping a shapefile which represents the city limits of Trippville. You will use that data later as a layer in a new web map you will create. Then, you will upload a CSV file containing natural wildlife view locations a friend has sent you.

Getting ready

This recipe will require you to have an ArcGIS Online account and access to the internet. You will need to be a level 2 user. If you do not have an ArcGIS Online user login, or do not wish to use your organization's account to complete the recipes in this chapter, you can request a trial license from Esri at http://www.esri.com/arcgis/trial.

You will also need a web browser that supports HTML 5 and JavaScript. This includes current versions of Chrome, Edge, Firefox, and Safari. Internet Explorer 11 or newer is also supported. Other browsers may also work but have not been tested by Esri.

It is recommended that you have completed all the recipes in Chapter 12, *Introducing ArcGIS Online*, before starting this recipe. This will ensure you have a strong foundational understanding of what ArcGIS Online is and how it integrates with ArcGIS Pro.

You also need to ensure you have installed the sample data before starting this exercise. This recipe will also use credits. It is estimated it will use less than 1 credit.

How to do it...

1. To get started, you will first need to create a ZIP file which contains the required files which form the city limit shapefile. Open `File Explorer`, or `Windows Explorer`, depending on what version of Microsoft Windows you are using. There should be a quick-start icon on your taskbar which resembles a file folder in a stand, as illustrated in the following screenshot:

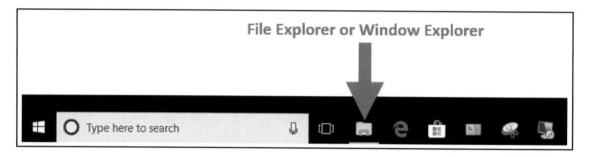

2. In the left panel of the File Explorer window, expand `This PC`, or `My Desktop`, depending on your version of Windows. From this point forward, we will assume you are running Windows 10.
3. Locate and select the `C:` drive, which is often labeled as OS or local drive.
4. In the right panel, scroll down and double-click on the `Student` folder.
5. Then, double-click on the `ArcGISProCookbook` folder.
6. Double-click again on the `Chapter13` folder, and then the `Files` folder.
7. You should now see a series of files within this folder. You will now select all those that make up the Trippville city limits shapefile. At the top of the right panel, click on **Name** to ensure you are sorting the files by name.
8. Select the `Trippville_City_Limits.cpg` file. Then, hold your *Shift* key down and select the `Trippville_City_Limits.shx` file. This should select all the files that make up the single Trippville city limits shapefile.

In order for a shapefile to be uploaded and work in ArcGIS Online, it must include the SHP, DBF, SHX, and PRJ files. Other files are also helpful but not required.

9. Once you have the files selected, right-click on any of the selected files. Then, go to **Send to** and **Compressed (zipped) folder** in the menu that appears, as illustrated in the following screenshot:

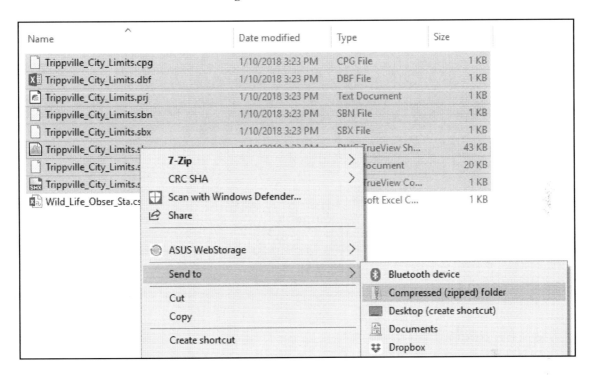

 If you have a ZIP utility you prefer to use, such as WinZip or 7-Zip, you can use it as well. The method demonstrated above will work for everyone without any additional software.

10. Name the new ZIP file `Trippville_City_Limits.zip`:

You have just completed the first process required to upload a shapefile to ArcGIS Online. Now, it is time to finish it by uploading the file to your content.

11. Open your web browser and log in to ArcGIS Online using the skills you learned in the previous chapter.

12. Click on the **My Content** tab.

13. Click on **Add Item** located in the upper-left corner below the **My Content** tab, and select **From my computer**, as illustrated in the following screenshot:

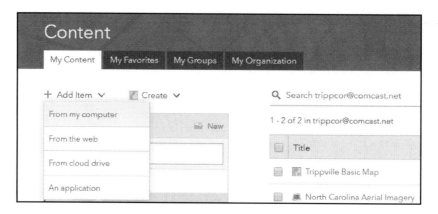

14. In the **Add an item from my computer** window under **File**, click the **Choose File** button as shown in the following screenshot:

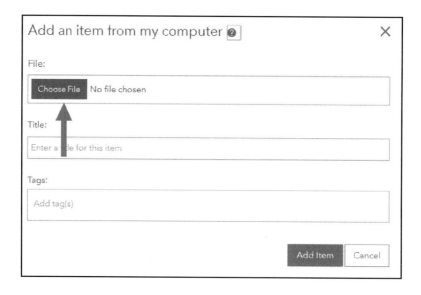

15. Using skills you have learned in previous recipes, navigate to C:\Student\ArcGISProCookbook\Chapter13\Files. Then, select the Trippville_City_Limits.zip file you just created, and click **Open**.

The **Add an item from my computer** window should change to indicate that the contents of the file you selected is a shapefile.

16. Ensure **Publish this file as a hosted layer** is enabled (adds a hosted-layer item with the same name).

This option not only adds the ZIP file to your content but will also create a hosted web layer. You can then use the web layer in web maps you create using ArcGIS Online, as well as in local maps you create with ArcGIS Pro. This does slightly increase the number of credits used, but by only a fraction.

17. Title the new item `Trippville City Limits`. If more than one person in your organization is also working through this recipe, or has done so in the past, add your name to the end of the title.

18. Add the following tags for the new item: `Trippville`, `City Limits`, `Boundary`, `Polygon`, and `Training`. Remember to press the *Enter* key for each tag.

19. Verify your **Add an item from my computer** window looks like the following, and click **Add Item**.

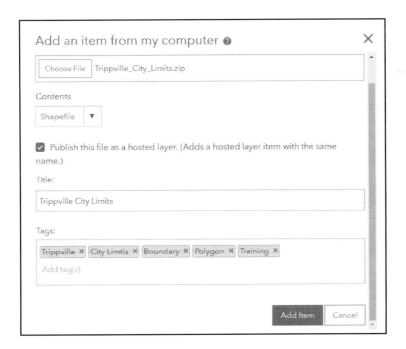

Once the file successfully uploads, you will be taken to a properties page. Here you can see the ArcGIS Online properties associated with the data you just uploaded to your content. It is important to ensure the information and settings for your content are correct and up-to-date. This forms the metadata which users will see to determine if this is the data they need. It also determines what capabilities the user will have when they use this data.

Now, you will update a few of the properties associated with the new file you just uploaded. You will start with the **Overview** and then move through the other levels, including **Data**, **Visualization**, **Usage**, and **Settings**.

20. Next to the **Thumbnail**, click on **Add a brief summary about this item**. This will allow you to provide a very short description about what this data is.
21. Type in the following summary: `This represents the City Limits for the City of Trippville`. Then click **Save**.
22. Under the **Thumbnail** and below the word **Description**, click on the **Add an in-depth description of this item**.
23. A robust text editing window will open allowing you to create a thorough description of this data. It can include pictures, links to other sites, and more. It is up to you how much detail you wish to provide. We will keep it simple for this new layer. Type in the following description: `This data represents the City Limits for the imaginary City of Trippville`. It was created as a shapefile using various sources of information, and adjusted to fit existing parcel data. This data is for training use only. Click **Save** once you are done typing the description.
24. Scroll down to the **Terms of Use**. This is where you can identify in-use restrictions, disclaimers, or other legal information you or your organization feels is required. Click on **Add any special restrictions**. This will open another text editing window. Type the following: `For training use only`, and click **Save**.

The **Overview** tab for the **Trippville City Limits** properties should now look like the following screenshot:

Properties of Trippville City Limits data in ArcGIS Online

25. Now, click on the **Data** tab located near the top of the page.

26. Here you can review and make changes to the attribute table for the city limits shapefile. You will not make any changes now; just take a quick moment to review it.

27. Click on the **Visualization** tab located next to the **Data** tab you just clicked on. This will allow you to view the data in a map. From here, you can set the default symbology which is used when this data is added to a map or scene. You will now make some changes to the default symbology.

28. In the left panel, click on the **Change Style** button.

If you don't remember which is the **Change Style** button, refer back to step 14 in the *Creating a simple web map in ArcGIS Online* recipe, in the previous chapter.

29. Click on the **OPTIONS** button located under item 2, **Select a drawing style** as illustrated in the following screenshot:

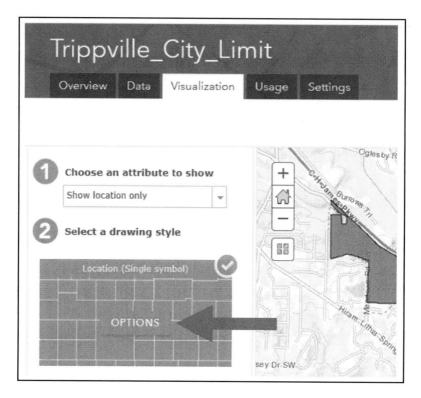

30. Click on the word Symbols to open the symbology settings window.
31. Using the skills you learned in the previous chapter, set the fill to **No Color**, the outline to **Black**, and the line width to 6 px. Then, click **OK**.
32. Verify your **Visualization** tab now looks like the following, and click **OK**.

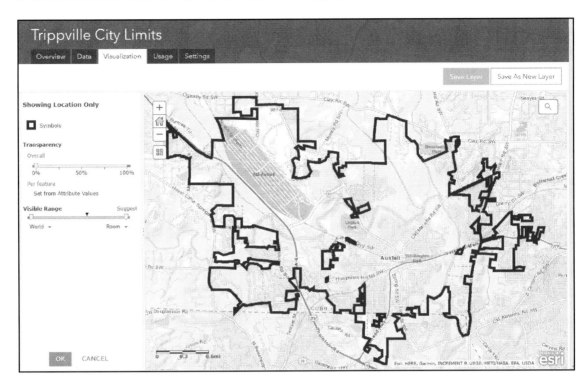

City limit data stored in ArcGIS Online shown in a web map using

33. After clicking **OK**, click **Done** to complete the symbology changes. Then click **Save Layer** to save the changes.

34. Click on the **Usage** tab at the top next to the **Visualization** tab. The **Usage** tab allows you to monitor how often and how much this particular item is being used.

35. Now, click on the **Settings** tab located next to the **Usage** tab.

36. The **Settings** tab allows you to configure various settings associated with the data you just uploaded. Take a moment to scroll through all the options available.

37. Feel free to make any adjustments you wish. When done, click on the **Content** tab located at the very top of the ArcGIS Online page.

Assuming you have not been creating ArcGIS Online content before starting this book, your content should now contain four items, as shown in the following screenshot:

The content of items you have published to ArcGIS Online

Notice there are two Trippville City Limits items. One is a feature layer. A feature layer is an item that can be added to maps or scenes as a layer. It was created from the shapefile you uploaded. The shapefile is the actual ZIP file you uploaded. That file can be downloaded from ArcGIS Online for local use similar to how you can download files from Google Drive or Dropbox.

38. If you are continuing to the next recipe, leave your browser open. Otherwise, you may close it.

Creating a layer using a CSV file

Now that you have uploaded a shapefile and created a feature layer based on the shapefile, let's look at a CSV file. You can upload a CSV or TXT file to your content just as you did the shapefile. Because it is a single file, there is no need to ZIP it before you upload it to your ArcGIS Online content.

When you add a CSV file to your content, it is typically used in one of two ways. The first is just to allow others to download the file or to use it as a standalone table. The file is not used to create a layer in a map or scene. In that case, you do not need to worry about formatting.

However, if you want to create a layer in a map or scene from the data in the CSV file, it will need to be formatted to support that operation. Here are the formatting requirements for a CSV file if you want to use it to create a layer. This also applies to a TXT file:

- The first line must contain column headers, not feature values
- The first line must include identifiers for two columns that will identify the location of the features
- Location column identifiers must be named:
  - Lat and Long
  - Latitude and Longitude
  - Longitude83, Latitude83
  - Longdecdeg, Latdecdeg
  - Long_dd, Latdd
  - Y, X
  - Ycenter, Xcenter
  - Xcenter, Ycenter
  - Point-y, Point-x
  - Point-x, Point-y
  - MGRS
  - USNG
  - Address
  - City
  - State
  - ZIP

In this recipe, you will upload a CSV file which contains information about wildlife observation points you got from a friend. He wants you to create a map showing where these locations are. Instead of uploading using the method you did with the shapefile, you will drag and drop it into a web map. Before you do that though, you will examine the CSV file to ensure it is properly formatted.

Getting ready

This recipe will require you to have an ArcGIS Online account and access to the internet. You will need to be a level 2 user. If you do not have an ArcGIS Online user login, or do not wish to use your organization's account to complete the recipes in this chapter, you can request a trial license from Esri at `http://www.esri.com/arcgis/trial`.

You will also need a web browser that supports HTML 5 and JavaScript. This includes current versions of Chrome, Edge, Firefox, and Safari. Internet Explorer 11 or newer is also supported. Other browsers may also work but have not been tested by Esri.

You will need to have completed the previous recipe before starting this one. It is also recommended that you have completed all the recipes in `Chapter 12`, *Introducing ArcGIS Online*, before starting this recipe. This will ensure you have a strong foundational understanding of what ArcGIS Online is and how it integrates with ArcGIS Pro.

You also need to ensure you have installed the sample data before starting this exercise. This recipe will also use credits. It is estimated it will use less than 1 credit.

How to do it...

1. First, you will examine the CSV file provided by your friend. Using skills you have learned in previous recipes, open `File Explorer` and navigate to `C:\Student\ArcGISProCookbook\Chapter13\Files`.

2. Right-click on the `Wild_Life_Obser_Sta.csv` file and select **Edit** from the menu that appears. This should open the file in Notepad, illustrated as follows:

```
Name,Latitude,Longitude,Condition,Bathroom
Willow creek,38.566,-106.626,Good,N
Fossil ridge,38.663,-106.621,Good,Y
Alder creek,38.51,-106.696,Poor,N
Bear Creek,38.597,-106.604,Fair,Y
Bear Gulch,38.422,-106.517,Poor,N
Rabit Hill,38.435,-106.521,Fair,N
Winchester Point,38.523,-106.701,Good,Y
```

3. Take a moment to review the contents of the CSV and compare it to the requirements listed at the start of the recipe. Then, answer the questions below.

> **Question**: Does the first row contain column names?
>
> **Answer**:
>
> **Question**: If so, what are the column names?
>
> **Answer**:
>
> **Question**: Does it contain location information with required column names?
>
> **Answer**:

After reviewing the information in the file, you will see that the first row does indeed contain column names which will be interpreted as field names by ArcGIS Online. It also does include location coordinates for each feature, along with required field names for those location values. So, this file is formatted correctly. You can use it to create a layer in a map or scene.

4. Close Notepad when you are done reviewing the information. If asked, do not save any changes or edits to this file. Leave `File Explorer` open.

5. If you closed your browser after completing the last recipe, open it and log in to your ArcGIS Online account.

6. Click on the **Map** tab at the top of the ArcGIS Online page.

7. Now, position `File Explorer` and ArcGIS Online on your screen so they are side by side, as illustrated in the following screenshot:

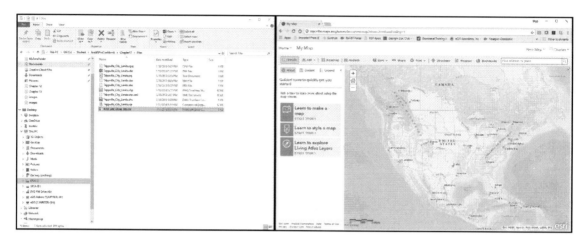

File Explorer and ArcGIS Online displayed side by side

8. Select the `Wild Life Obser Sta.csv` file in `File Explore`. Then, drag and drop it into ArcGIS Online in the map. If you have completed this operation successfully, points should appear in the map showing the location of the wildlife observation stations.

9. You have the option to configure the symbology for the new layer you just created. In this case, you will just accept the defaults determined by ArcGIS Online. So, click the **Done** button.

10. You need to save the map now. Click on the **Save** button and select **Save As** from the list that appears.

11. Title your map `Wild Life Observations Stations`. If others in your organization are also working through this book, or have, you may need to add your name to the end of the title to ensure it is unique.

12. Add the following tags: `Wild life`, `observation`, `locations`, and `training`.

13. Type in the following **Summary**: `Locations of wild life observation stations as identified by my friend`.

14. Verify your **Save Map** window looks like the following, and click **SAVE MAP**:

You have just created a new web map which contains a layer that was built from data contained in a CSV file. This map should look similar to the following graphic:

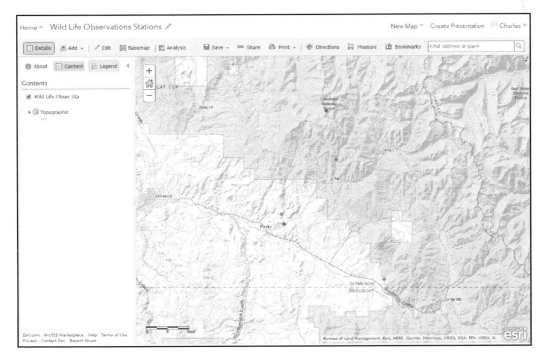

Results of adding CSV data to web map

This same exact process will also work for a TXT file. However, you may have created more than just a map with a layer. Let's explore your ArcGIS Online contents to see if you did create more content.

15. Click on the drop-down arrow located next to **Home** in the top-left side of ArcGIS Online. Select **Contents** from the list that appears.

16. Review your contents and answer the following questions.

> **Question**: Did the process you used to add the CSV file create multiple items in your contents?

> **Answer**:
>
> **Question**: What items did this process create?
>
> **Answer**:

Using the drag-and-drop process into a map only created the single web map, unlike the process you used for the shapefile which created multiple items. Because the data in the CSV file was for a friend and would only be used in the single map, it made sense to use the drag-and-drop method. If you knew you would be using that data again in other maps, it would have made more sense to use the same method you did with the shapefile.

17. Close your browser when you are done reviewing your contents.

Publishing layer packages using ArcGIS Pro

You have now experienced how you are able to publish files to ArcGIS Online. This includes GIS files such as shapefiles, and non-GIS files such as CSV files. So far, you have done this without using ArcGIS Pro. However, you can publish content to ArcGIS Online directly from ArcGIS Pro.

ArcGIS Pro can not only use content which has been published to ArcGIS Online, but it can also be used to author content. Similar to how you published the shapefile to ArcGIS Online, you can publish a layer from a map in ArcGIS Pro as a layer package. The layer package will contain all the layer property settings you configure in ArcGIS Pro, along with the data. The data referenced by the layer can be stored in various formats, including geodatabase feature classes, shapefiles, spreadsheets, and more. This is useful when you need to share information with someone that is not on your network or that does not have direct access to your GIS data.

In this recipe, you will publish a layer package from ArcGIS Pro to your ArcGIS Online content. In this case, the City of Trippville has hired a planning consultant to review their Zoning Ordinance and GIS data. The consultant does not have access to the City's network, so you will need to share that data with them using a layer package. The consultant does have an ArcGIS Online account, so this makes it easy to share with them.

Getting ready

As with previous recipes in this chapter, you need to have completed the recipes in Chapter 12, *Introducing ArcGIS Online*, as well as all previous ones in this chapter to ensure you have the foundational knowledge and skills needed to complete this one. You will also need to have ArcGIS Pro installed and a license assigned. Any license level will work to complete this recipe.

This recipe also requires that you have an ArcGIS Online account with at least a Publisher-level role assigned. You will also need internet access along with a web browser that supports HTML5 and JavaScript. You must install the sample data before beginning this recipe.

How to do it...

1. You will start by launching ArcGIS Pro and opening the `ArcGISOnlineContent` project. This project is located in the `C:\Student\ArcGISProCookbook\Chapter13\ArcGISOnlineContent` folder. When the project opens, you should see the **Zoning Map** open in the view, as illustrated in the following screenshot. If not, use the skills you have learned to open the map from the **Catalog** pane:

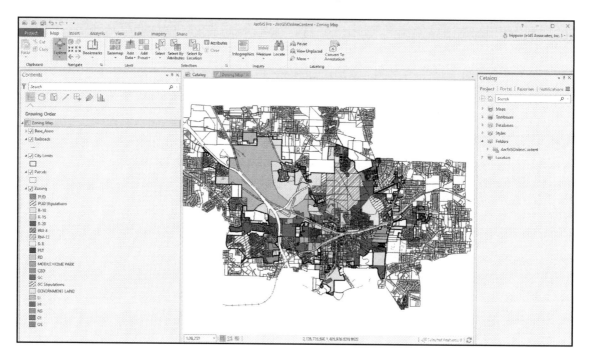

Trippville Zoning Map which should now be displayed

This map contains several layers. You only need to share one layer with the consultant. So, you will create a layer package and upload it to ArcGIS Online using a single tool.

2. Select the Zoning layer in the **Contents** pane.
3. Click on the **Share** tab in the ribbon.
4. Click on the **Layer** button in the **Package group** on the **Share** tab. This will open the **Sharing As A Layer Package** tool.

5. Under **Start Packaging**, ensure **Upload package to Online account** is enabled.
6. Set the **Name and Location** to `Trippville_Zoning` by typing that value into the cell. Make sure to include the underscore; spaces or other special characters are not allowed.
7. Accept the values that appear for the **Summary** and **Tags**. These were copied from the layers metadata.
8. Ensure none of the items under options are enabled. These do not apply to the data in this layer.
9. Under **Sharing Options**, ensure only **My Content** is selected. For now, you are not sharing this with anyone else. You will learn how to share in a later recipe.

10. Ensure your **Sharing As A Layer Package** tool is configured as shown in the following graphic. Then, click the **Analyze** button:

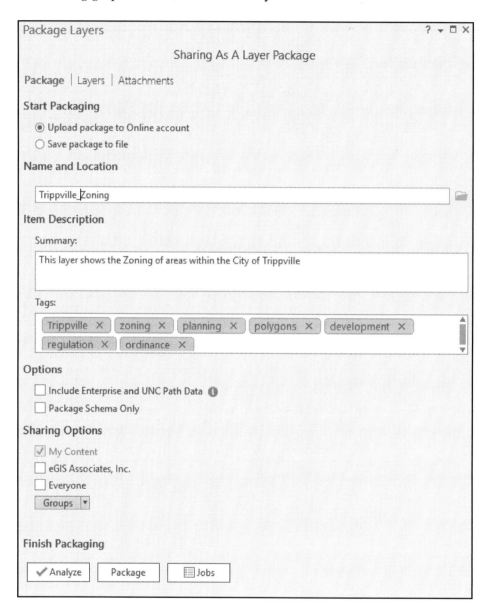

The **Analyze** button will review your settings and the layer to locate anything that might prevent the layer package from publishing successfully. The results will then be presented in the tool window. Any issues identified as errors must be fixed before packaging the layer. Messages should be reviewed, but you are not required to take action before packaging the layer. In this recipe, you should not get any errors or messages.

11. Once the analysis is complete and no errors are returned, click the **Package** button. This will create the layer package and upload it to your ArcGIS Online content.

12. Once the tool has run successfully, close it.

You could have also accessed this same tool by right-clicking on the layer in the **Contents** pane, then selecting **Share as Layer Package** from the menu that appears.

13. Now, to verify the tool actually uploaded the new layer package to your ArcGIS Online content, in the **Catalog** pane, click on the **Portal** tab located next to the **Project** tab.

14. Ensure **My Content** is the active resource. It should be the first button located just below the word **Project**. The icon resembles a cloud with a single person standing in front.

15. Review your ArcGIS Online content. You should see the content you created in previous recipes along with the new layer file that you just created.

If you do not see the Trippville_Zoning layer package you just created, you may need to refresh the pane. To refresh the pane, click on the three stacked bars in the upper-right corner and select Refresh from the menu that appears. With the Catalog pane selected, pressing the F5 key will also refresh the pane.

16. Notice the different icons associated with your content. Esri uses different icons to help you quickly identify different types of content.

17. Save your project and close ArcGIS Pro.

In this recipe, you learned how to successfully upload a new layer package to ArcGIS Pro. A layer package contains all the layer properties you configure in ArcGIS Pro, such as the symbology, labeling, elevation, transparency, definition query, and more, plus the actual data itself. All of that is compressed or zipped together in a single LPKX file and then uploaded to ArcGIS Online. Once there, it becomes part of your content, which you can share with others so they can download and use it in their own maps or scenes.

An important thing to remember with layer packages is that they are a copy of the data at the time the package was created. If changes are made to the data or layer properties after that, the layer package will need to be updated. Also, if you make changes to the data in the layer package, they will not be changed in the original source data either.

Publishing web layers using ArcGIS Pro

Publishing layer packages to ArcGIS Online is extremely useful if you need to share data with someone that needs to have access to the entire dataset and to work on a copy of the data. This allows them to run different scenarios, perform different analyses, and make changes to the data without actually impacting the data sharing through ArcGIS Online. What if you wanted to share a layer to ArcGIS Online that you wanted included in a web map, which users would access through the ArcGIS Online Web Map Viewer, or other custom web or mobile applications? A layer package would not allow that. What you need is a web layer.

Web layers allow you to publish a single layer so that it may be added to a web map. You add the layer using the same process you used in `Chapter 12`, *Introducing ArcGIS Online*, and the *Creating a simple web map in ArcGIS Online* recipe. Once added to a web map, you can then visualize it using the *Web Map Viewer* application or even incorporate it into your own custom web or mobile application.

There are seven different types of web layers you can create from ArcGIS Pro. These include: feature, tile, vector tile, map image, imagery, scene, and elevation. Web layers such as feature, tile, vector tile, map image, and imagery layers are created from 2D data. Scenes and elevation layers are created from 3D data. To learn more about these different types of web layers, go to `http://pro.arcgis.com/en/pro-app/help/sharing/overview/introduction-to-sharing-web-layers.htm`.

In this recipe, you will create a new web layer for the City of Trippville parcels. Several departments in the City are considering deploying GIS web applications. Most of these will need to include the parcel data, so it makes sense to create a new web layer. For this recipe, we will keep it simple and you will create it as a feature layer. This also uses the least amount of credits.

Getting ready

You must have completed the other recipes in this chapter along with those in Chapter 12, *Introducing ArcGIS Online*, before starting this one. This will ensure you have a strong foundational understanding of ArcGIS Online and how it is linked to ArcGIS Pro. You will also need to ensure the sample data is installed before you continue.

This recipe, like the others in this chapter, will require you to have an ArcGIS Online user account. User level 2 and the Publisher role are also required to complete this recipe. This recipe will use up some of your ArcGIS Online credits. The amount should be very small, under 1 credit in most cases.

How to do it...

1. You will start by launching ArcGIS Pro and opening the `ArcGISOnlineContent` project you used in the previous recipe. This project should be included in your list of recently opened projects.
2. The **Zoning Map** should still be open. If it is not, open it from the **Catalog** pane.
3. Notice this map contains the **Parcels** layer you need to upload to ArcGIS Online as a web layer. Select the **Parcels** layer and then right click on it.
4. Select **Share as a web layer** from the menu that appears. This option will be near the bottom of the menu.
5. Name the web layer you will create `Trippville_Parcels`. Remember that spaces and special characters are not allowed. Also, if you have others from your organization working through this book, or that have in the past, you may need to add your name to the end of the name for the web layer to ensure it is unique and does not already exist.
6. Verify the **Layer Type** is set to **Feature**. This is important. If you have it set to **Tile** or **Vector Tile**, you will use a lot of your ArcGIS Online credits.

7. Type in the following **Summary**: `This contains the parcel data for the City of Trippville and surrounding area. It was originally compiled by the county in which Trippville is located.`

8. Enter the following tags: `Trippville, parcels, polygons, property,` and `boundary`.

9. Under **Sharing Options**, select **My Content** and the name of your organization. This will not only allow you to access this data, but also all ArcGIS Online users in your organization.

10. Verify your **General** information looks like the graphic below. Then, click on the **Configuration** tab located at the top of the tool window.

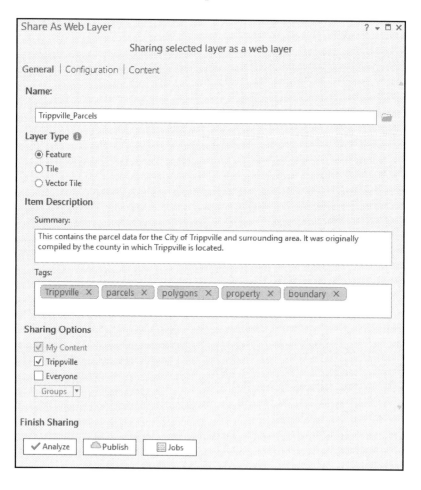

11. Under the **Operations** options, click on **Enable Sync**. This will allow the data to be downloaded to a device if they lose data connection.

12. Click on the **Analyze** button at the bottom of the tool. This will warn you of any issues before you attempt to publish the layer to ArcGIS Online.

13. If no errors are found, click **Publish**.

This might take several minutes to complete depending on your computer and internet speed. Do not be concerned if it does.

14. Once the tool completes successfully, close it.

15. Now to verify the **Parcels** web layer was successfully published to ArcGIS Online. In the **Catalog** pane, click on the **Portal** tab.

16. Review your contents. You should now have at least six items listed in your content, including the new feature layer you just created. If not, refresh the view. If the new web layer was successfully created, it should appear under **My Content** in your portal.

17. Notice that the icon next to the **Trippville_Parcels** web layer is different than the one for the **Trippville_Zoning** layer package. That is because they are two different types of data.

18. Save your project and close ArcGIS Pro.

You have just learned another way to publish a layer to ArcGIS Online. This time, you published it as a web layer that can be used in a web map, which you can view in the ArcGIS Web Map Viewer, or custom web or mobile applications you create.

Publishing 2D maps

Now that you know how to publish a layer as either a layer file or a web layer, is it possible to publish an entire map to ArcGIS Online? Well, of course you can. Just like a layer, you can publish a map as as map package or as as a web map.

Publishing a map as a map package uses the same basic procedure as publishing a layer package. It packages the entire map including layer properties and data into a single MAPX file. You can then upload that to ArcGIS Online, so others can download it just as they would a layer package. While certainly a valuable tool in your arsenal, it does have limited use. Publishing a web map offers much more flexibility.

A web map can be accessed and used multiple ways. You can add it to a project in ArcGIS Pro, or incorporate it into a web application so it can be used via a web browser and be part of a mobile application. Depending on the settings you configure, users might be able query, print, edit, and download the data using any or all of these access methods. All of this make web maps very versatile.

If you are going to publish a map from ArcGIS Pro as a web map, you need to ensure it is optimized to provide the greatest performance. In general, this means that simpler is better. You want to use simple symbology; basic line patterns, simple marker symbols, and generic polygon fills. Another thing you can do to improve performance is to apply scale ranges that turn on and off layers automatically as the user zooms in or out. Limit the use of labels; labels can greatly hinder the performance of a web map because they require a lot of processing to render. Limiting the number of layers to only those you absolutely need for the given map will also help it perform better. Each map should have a specific purpose. Make sure each layer in the map supports that primary purpose.

In this recipe, the Utility Superintendent has asked you to create a web map of the City of Trippville's sewer system. He is intending to deploy a new web and mobile application for the inspection and maintenance of this utility. He wants to display the current condition of the sewer lines in the map, so that, as the lines are inspected, the map will reflect the condition identified during the inspection.

Getting ready

Before you start this recipe, ensure you have completed all the previous recipes in this chapter and in Chapter 12, *Introducing ArcGIS Online*. This will ensure you have the foundational knowledge and skills required to complete this recipe.

To complete this recipe, you will need a level 2 ArcGIS Online user account with Publisher-level role permissions. You will also need an internet connection, a web browser which supports HTML 5 and JavaScript, and ArcGIS Pro. The sample data for the book must also be installed on your computer.

How to do it...

1. We will start by launching ArcGIS Pro and opening the project we used in the previous recipe, `ArcGISOnlineContent`. This project should be included in your list of recently opened projects.

2. The superintendent needs a map of the Trippville sewer system that shows the conditions of the sewer lines. The project already has a map which we will start with. Open the **Trippville Sewer Map** from the **Catalog** pane by right-clicking on it and selecting **Open**.

3. The new map should open in your view, containing the layers required by the superintendent, as illustrated in the following graphic. If the **Zoning Map** is still open, you can close it.

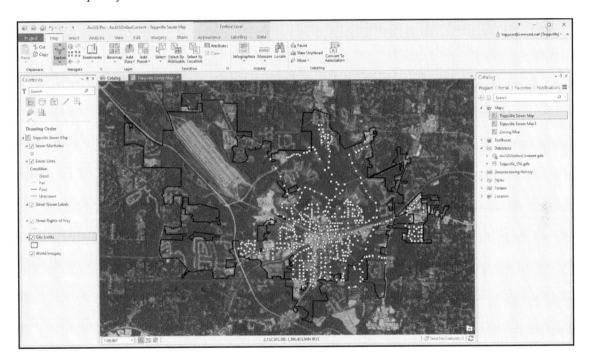

Trippville Sewer Map

This map will provide you with a head start. It already contains the required layers. They have been symbolized with simple symbols to ensure better performance via the web. The Sewer Lines layer is already symbolized based on the condition of each line. So, the basics have already been done. If you want to know more about how to create a map from the beginning, review, Chapter 1, *ArcGIS Pro Capabilities and Terminology*. You might also want to work through *Learning ArcGIS Pro* by Tripp Corbin from Packt Publishing as well. *Learning ArcGIS Pro* goes into great detail regarding the workflows required to create a map.

Now, you will configure some of the layers to provide better performance.

4. One of the first things you will do is limit the extents of the map to the City Limits of Trippville. This will allow users to click on the **Zoom Extents** button and be taken to the limits of the City. Right-click on the **Trippville Sewer Map** at the top of the **Contents** pane. Select **Properties** from the menu that appears.
5. In the left panel of the **Map Properties** window, select **Extent**.
6. Click on the radial button next to **Custom** extent. This should enable the **Calculate from option**.
7. Click on **Choose calculation type** and select **City Limits from the list** that is displayed.

The values for the top, bottom, left, and right should change. These values define the bounding limits used as the full extents of the map.

 By default, the extents of a map are equal to the largest layer in the map. This includes the basemap. So, if you make use of an Esri-provided basemap, the full extents for your map are equal to the entire world.

8. Click on the **Metadata** option in the left panel. Review the data contained here. As you can see, this has already been filled in for you. If this was a completely new map, you would need to fill this information out yourself before publishing the map to ArcGIS Online.
9. Click **OK** to close the **Map Properties** window.

10. Now, you will set the scale visibility for the **Sewer Manholes** layer. This will improve the overall performance of the map by only displaying this layer once you zoom in to a specific scale. You will start by zooming to the desired scale at which you want this layer to become visible. In the lower-left corner of the map view, locate the map scale, as shown in the following graphic:

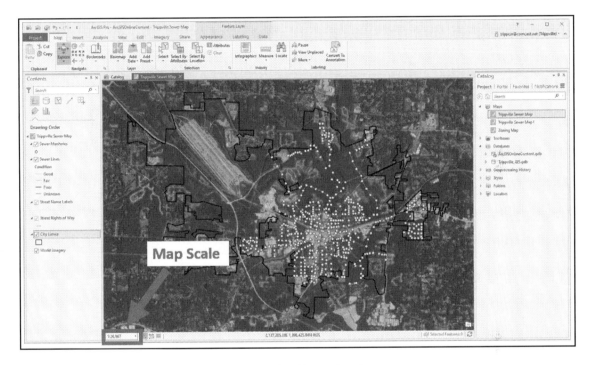

Map scale located in lower left corner of map view area

11. In that cell, type 1:4000, and press the *Enter* key. Your map will zoom to the scale you just entered. The area will be based on the center of your map view.

You can also type just 4000 and ArcGIS Pro will automatically add the 1: to the front. In future situations where you may want the map to be set to a scale where 1 unit equals so many different units, such as 1 inch equals 100 feet or 1 centimeter equals 5 kilometers, you can simply type that into this cell as well. ArcGIS Pro will automatically make the required conversions.

12. In the **Contents** pane, right-click on the Sewer Manholes layer and select **Properties** from the menu that appears.

13. In the left panel of the **Layer Properties** window, select the **General** option.

14. In the right panel of the window below where it says **Out beyond (minimum scale)**, click on the drop-down arrow and select **<Current>** from the list that appears. This should set the value to 1:4000.

15. Click **OK**. This will set it so that the Manhole layer does not become visible until you zoom in to a scale of 1:4000. This reduces the amount of data the computer must render when zoomed out beyond that scale. That improves the performance of the map.

16. Click on the **Full Extent** button located in the **Navigate** group on the **Map** tab in the ribbon. This will zoom your map to the extents of the map which you set earlier to match the City Limits layer.

17. Look at the map. The **Sewer Manholes** are no longer visible. That is because you have zoomed out beyond the 1:4000 scale.

18. Look at the box next to the Sewer Manholes layer. Notice it is grayed out and has a small rectangle below it. This indicates it has a scale visibility range assigned to the layer, and you are not zoomed to a scale that causes the layer to be visible. Now, answer the following question.

Question: What other layers appear to have scale visibility ranges assigned in this map?

Answer:

As you can see, several layers have scale visibility ranges assigned. This includes the **Street Name Labels** and the **Street Rights of Way**. The only ones that do not are the **Sewer Lines**, **City Limits**, and **World Imagery**.

19. Select the **Sewer Lines** layer in the **Contents** pane.

20. Click on the **Appearance** tab in the ribbon.

21. In the **Visibility** group on the **Appearance** tab, click on the drop-down arrow for **Out Beyond**, and select 1:4000 from the list that is presented. If you are still zoomed to the full extent, the **Sewer Lines** layer should no longer be visible in your map.

You have just assigned visibility scales to two layers within your map using two different methods. One was through the layer properties, and the other was using the **Appearance** tab in the ribbon. Both methods do the same thing. In the future, you can use whichever method works best for you.

You are almost ready to publish this map as a web map. You have verified the symbology is simple lines, points and polygons. You have enhanced the performance of the map by limiting the extents and applying scale visibility ranges. The next step is to verify all the layers have metadata, like you did for the map itself. While not necessarily required, it is a recommended best practice.

22. Using the skills you have learned, open the properties for each layer and verify the metadata has been filled out for each layer. You will need to close the properties window before you can open the one for the next layer. At least one layer is missing metadata information. Using the metadata from the other layers as a guide, complete the metadata for the layer or layers that are missing it.

23. Save your project.

24. Click on the **Share** tab in the ribbon.

25. Click on the **Web Map** button in the **Share As** group on the **Share** tab. This will open the **Sharing As A Web Map** tool.

26. Accept the **Default name** which should be **Trippville_Sewer_Map**. If others in your organization are also working through this book, or have, you may need to add your name to the end in order to make the name unique. Remember, spaces and special characters are not allowed.

27. Review the **Summary** and answer the following question.

Question: Where did the Summary come from?

Answer:

If you remember reviewing the **Trippville Sewer Map** properties, specifically, looking over the metadata, the summary in the tool should look familiar. It comes from the maps metadata. The same is true for the tags.

28. Under the Sharing Options, enable sharing with your organization. This will allow others in your organization to access the web map you are about to create.

29. Using the drop-down arrow, set the **Select a Configuration** option to **Copy all data: Editable**. This option will upload all the data referenced in the map to ArcGIS Online and publish it as feature layers, so the data can be edited using a web or mobile app in addition to ArcGIS Pro. This option also uses the least amount of credits.

The options available for configuration will depend on the source of the data referenced in the map. Because all your layers reference a file geodatabase, except for the basemap, you are presented with three options, all of which copy the data to ArcGIS Online. If your map contained data that referenced a web resource, you would be presented with different options. To learn more about all the configuration options you might encounter, go to `http://pro.arcgis.com/en/pro-app/help/sharing/overview/share-a-web-map.htm/`

30. Verify the **Map** options look like the following graphic, then click on the **Configuration** tab near the top of the tool window.

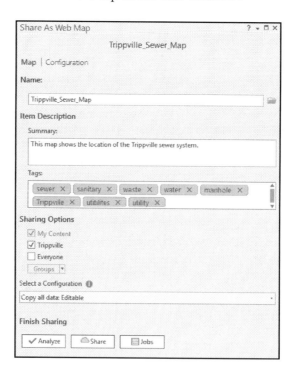

Sharing the Trippville sewer map as as web map using the Share As Web Map tool

31. In the window area located in the middle of the tool, select the **Trippville_Sewer_Map_WFL1** item.

32. The **Properties** option located above the window should now be available. Click on **Properties**.

33. Ensure the **Layer Type** is set to feature. If it is set to **Tile** or **Vector** tile, you selected the wrong configuration in step 29.

34. Click on the **Configuration** tab at the top next to the **General** tab.

35. Now, time to analyze your map to see if it contains anything which would prevent it from being published as a web map. Click the **Analyze** button at the bottom of the tool.

    When the analysis is complete, you should not see any errors. One thing you should know when publishing a web map to ArcGIS Online is it requires you to have a basemap. If you are using an Esri basemap, then your map must use the WGS84 Web Mercator Auxiliary Sphere coordinate system.

36. Click the **Share** button located at the bottom of the tool, next to the **Analyze** button. This will publish your map to ArcGIS Online.

37. Once the tool is successful, close it.

    You have successfully published your first web map to ArcGIS Online from ArcGIS Pro. As you have seen, there are many items you need to consider in order for it to be successfully published. Now, let's take a look at the new map you just published using the ArcGIS Online Web Map Viewer application.

38. Launch your web browser and go to `www.arcgis.com`.

39. Using the skills you have learned, sign in to your ArcGIS Online account.

40. Click on the **Content** tab near the top of ArcGIS Online, as you have done in previous recipes.

41. Examine your content. Assuming you have not used ArcGIS Online before starting this book, you should now have 11 items in your content. Three of those were created when you published the **Trippville Sewer Map** as a web map.

42. Click on the **Trippville_Sewer_Map** web map in your contents. This will take you to the properties of the web map you published.

43. Now to look at it in the **Map Viewer**. Click on the **Open in Map Viewer** button located on the right side of the page. The web map you created should now be open in the view, as shown in the following screenshot:

The Trippville sewer map displayed in ArcGIS Online as a web map

44. Place your mouse pointer over the approximate center of the City, and use your mouse wheel to zoom in until you start to see the sewer layers.

45. Feel free to navigate around your new map. When you are done, close your browser to exit ArcGIS Online.

46. Close ArcGIS Pro.

You have successfully published a web map from ArcGIS Pro to ArcGIS online. This map can now be used with those in your organization in many different ways. Users can log in to ArcGIS Online and open it in the **Map Viewer**, as you did. It can also be incorporated into custom web applications, which you will learn how to do in the next chapter.

Sharing published content

As you have seen, ArcGIS Online is a great repository of content, including maps and data. However, one of the strongest capabilities ArcGIS Online provides is the ability to share that content with others. Any content you add to ArcGIS Online can be shared so that others can also access and make use of it. That makes the content more dynamic and can greatly increase its value.

If you choose to share your content, you have three options for sharing it. First, you can share it only with yourself. That means you can access it anywhere you have a connection to ArcGIS Online, but no one else can. The next option is to share it with your organization. That allows that anyone with an ArcGIS Online user login from your organization will be able to access your content. Lastly, you can choose to share your content with specific groups. Groups can include specific users from your organization, and possibly those outside if allowed by your organization's ArcGIS Online administrator.

What users are allowed to do with the content that has been shared depends on three things: their user level, user role, and the settings for the content. Level 1 users will only have very limited capability, while level 2 users are allowed greater potential abilities. User roles are the next level which determine a user's ability to use the content. User levels and roles were discussed in more detail during the introduction to Chapter 12, *Introducing ArcGIS Online*. If you want to refresh your memory, you may want to review Chapter 12, *Introducing ArcGIS Online*.

The last thing that determines a user's capability is the settings for the content they can access. This is initially determined by what type of content it is. For example, the settings for a web map will be different than those for a feature layer. You saw some of these differences when you published these from ArcGIS Pro in previous recipes. Some possible optional settings you might allow are:

- Ability to download a copy of the data
- Enable editing
- Enable sync
- Prevent delete
- Allow Save As copy
- Allow tools and capabilities if used in an application

These are just a few of the possible settings options you might encounter. Typically, you configure these when you publish the content. However, you can adjust these settings as needed for any content you publish to ArcGIS Online via your browser and My Content.

But how do you actually share your content? It is actually very simple. As you have seen in previous recipes, when you publish content from ArcGIS Pro, you are able to select if you share the content with others or not. If you have already published your content, you can choose to share it or make changes to the share settings through your web browser and the ArcGIS Online portal.

In Chapter 12, *Introducing ArcGIS Online*, you created a basic map for the City of Trippville in ArcGIS Online. The purpose of this map was to create a template others could use as a starting point for creating their own web maps. In this recipe, you will adjust the sharing settings for the web map you created in Chapter 12, *Introducing ArcGIS Online*. In addition, you will review the settings for this web map to ensure all the capabilities that you believe will be needed are enabled.

Getting ready

Before you start this recipe, ensure you have completed all the previous recipes in this chapter and Chapter 12, *Introducing ArcGIS Online*. This will ensure the **Trippville Basic Map** you will need for this recipe exists, in addition to making sure you have the foundational knowledge and skills required to complete this recipe.

To complete this recipe, you will need a level 2 ArcGIS Online user account with Publisher-level role permissions. You will also need an internet connection, a web browser that supports HTML 5 and JavaScript, and ArcGIS Pro. The sample data for the book must also be installed on your computer.

How to do it...

1. We will start by launching your web browser and signing in to ArcGIS Online. So, launch your web browser and go to www.arcgis.com. Using the skills you have learned in previous recipes, sign in to your ArcGIS Online account.

2. Once you are logged in to your ArcGIS Online account, click on **Content** so you can see all your ArcGIS Online content. It should look similar to the following screenshot. Depending on how long you have been using ArcGIS Online, you may have more content.

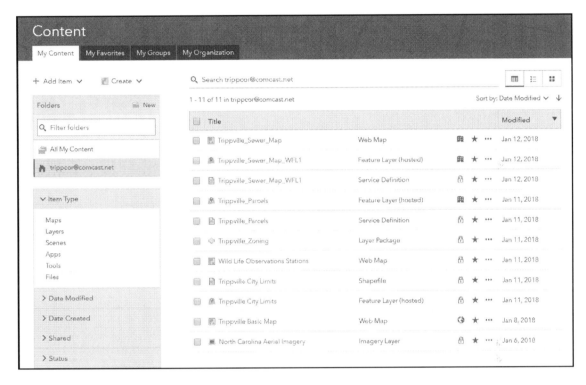

My Content page in ArcGIS Online

3. At the top center of the **Content** page is a search function. Search for the following value: `Trippville Basic Map`. This will filter your content so only items matching the search string are displayed.

4. Click on the **Trippville Basic Map** that is returned by your search. This will take you to the properties for this item. That is the starting point for sharing an item.

5. Before you share an item with others, it is a recommended best practice to complete the metadata associated with the item. So, you will do that now. Under **Description**, click on **Add an in-depth description of the item**. This will open a text editing box.

6. Scroll down to **Terms of Use** and click on the **Edit** button located to the right. This will also open a text edit box.

7. Type `For training` use only into the editing box, and click **Save**.

8. Now, click on the **Settings** tab located below the name of the web map, near the top.

9. Ensure that **Prevent this item from being accidentally deleted** is checked. Since you intend for this map to serve as the basis for other new web maps others might create, you do not want someone to accidentally delete it. Click the **Save** button.

10. Scroll down and review the other settings which are available. Accept the default settings.

11. Once you are done reviewing the available options, scroll back to the top and click on the **Overview** tab to return to the metadata.

12. Before you actually share the **Trippville Basic Map**, you want to create a group for those which will be allowed to create their own web maps in your organization. Click on the **Groups** tab located at the very top of the page. This will take you to the **Groups** page in ArcGIS Online.

13. Click on the **Create New Group** button to start the process of creating a new group.

14. Name the new group: `Map Makers`

15. Type the following **Summary**: `This group is for those within the organization which are allowed to create new web maps.`

16. Add the following tags: `Trippville`, `web maps`, `template`, `base layers`.

17. Set the remaining settings as indicated here:
    - Who can view this group? – people in the organization
    - Who can join this group? – only those invited by the group manager
    - Who can contribute content? – group members
    - What items in the group can its members update? - all items (group membership is limited to the organization)

18. Verify your **Create New Group** page looks like the following, and click **Create Group**:

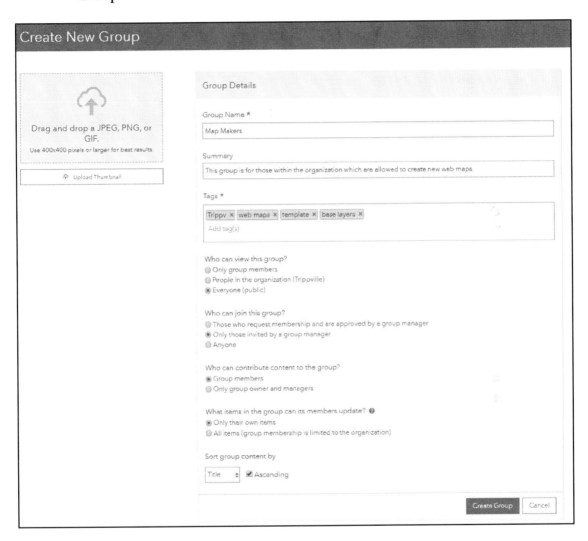

Creating a new Group page in ArcGIS Online

You can also add a custom icon/logo that will help others identify your group and its purpose. This must be a raster file including a GIF, PNG, and JPG file. The raster should be square and a minimum of 400 x 400 pixels.

19. You have just created a new group in your organization. Groups can be used to control who you share your content with. Edit the description for your new group using the skills you have learned to create descriptions for other items in ArcGIS Pro. Use the summary you created as a guide for creating your description.

20. Click on the **Content** tab at the very top of ArcGIS Online, located between **Groups and Organization**. This will take you back to your **Content** page.

21. Click on the **Trippville Basic Map** web map to return to its properties. Use the search tool if you need to in order to locate it.

22. Click on the **Share** button located on the right side. This will open the **Share** window.

23. Deselect the **Everyone (public)** and **Trippville** options. Enable the **These groups** option. Then, enable the **Map Makers** group you just created.

24. Verify your **Share** window looks like the following, and click **OK**:

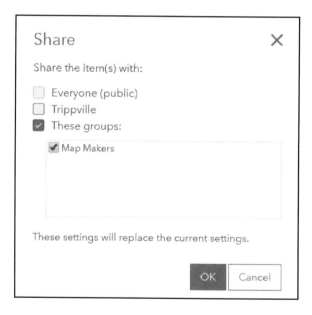

25. Click on the **Groups** tab at the top of ArcGIS Online.

26. Select the **Map Makers** group in the right panel of the page. This will open that group.

27. Click on the **Content** tab located under the group map. This will display all content which has been shared with the group.

28. Verify that you see the **Trippville Basic Map**, as shown in the following screenshot:

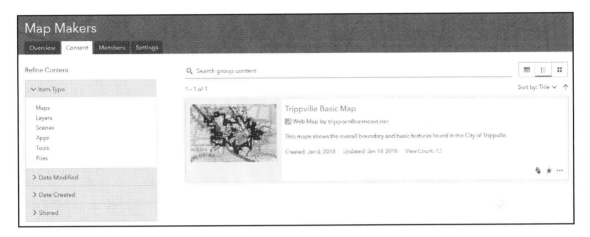

Map Makers group content in ArcGIS Online

29. You are done. It is just that easy. Now, close your web browser.
30. If ArcGIS Pro is still open from a previous recipe, make sure to close it as well. If asked if you want to save the open project, click **Yes**.

You have just shared content you created in a previous recipe with a new group you created within your organization. As you can see, it is very easy to share your content with others. You get to select specific content to share and have active control over who you share your content with. All this helps ensure your content is safe and secure. One thing to remember is that if you choose to share your content with everyone, that may mean everyone with access to ArcGIS Online, even if they are not part of your organization.

14

Creating Web Apps Using ArcGIS Online

In this chapter, we will cover the following recipes:

- Creating a simple web app using an Esri template
- Creating a custom application using Web AppBuilder
- Sharing your applications
- Embedding an ArcGIS Online map in a web page

Introduction

By now, you know that the combination of ArcGIS Pro and ArcGIS Online form a very powerful GIS solution for an organization. They allow you to maintain, analyze, and share GIS data with those inside and outside your organization, which in turn increases the effectiveness and flexibility of your GIS.

Data and maps are not the only thing ArcGIS Online allows you to share. You can also create and share web applications with ArcGIS Online. You may be thinking to yourself, *I am not a programmer. I have no idea how to create applications.* That is OK. With ArcGIS Online, you do not need to be a programmer to create quick but effective web applications which allow others to access the data and maps you have created. With just a little ArcGIS Online know-how, it is possible to create a web application similar to the one shown here in 5 to 10 minutes:

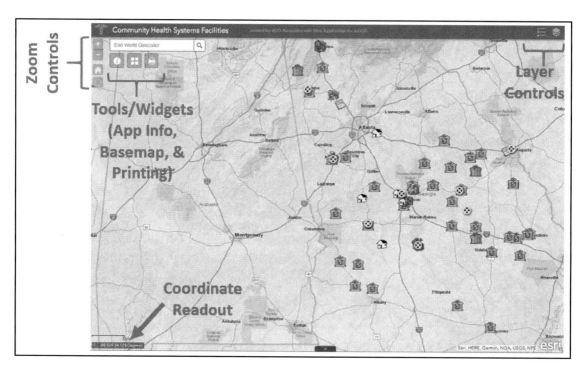

Sample web GIS app

ArcGIS Online provides at least two methods for creating web applications quickly and easily, even if you have no prior programming experience. The first is using one of the many predefined application templates Esri has created. The second is to use Esri's Web AppBuilder to create custom applications using a wizard. Either method allows you to create web applications or apps which users can then access via their favorite web browser to begin using your GIS content. This is a great way to extend your GIS to users that don't have access to or the skills to use ArcGIS Pro. You maintain and publish the data and maps, while the users do what they need to with the data via the web applications. They do not need to be a GIS guru. They have access to tools that allow them to use the GIS so they can do their jobs easier and better.

In this chapter, you will learn how to create some simple applications quickly and easily using both of these methods. Then, you will learn how you can share your applications with others, both inside and outside your organization. You will start by creating an application using one of the many Esri standard application templates. Then you will create a custom application using Web AppBuilder.

Creating a simple web app using an Esri template

Being able to publish your data and maps via a web app opens up a whole new level of use and accessibility that is not possible when sharing as simple web maps, feature services, or data downloads. A web application allows you to include functionalities provided by some of the tools you have in ArcGIS Pro. You can allow people to pan and zoom, query, print, edit, and more from within the application. This allows even those without GIS experience or software to become GIS users.

In the past, you had to have programming skills to create GIS web applications. That is no longer the case. Now, there are tools that allow anyone that has some basic GIS and computer skills to create their own GIS web applications. As mentioned in the introduction, ArcGIS Online includes several predefined web application templates that you can use to create your own application. Currently, you have access to over 20 application templates. These require little to no programming knowledge. All you do is plug in your maps and data, configure a few items, and off you go. Depending on the template you choose and the functionality you desire, you can have a web application up and running in under 5 minutes.

In this recipe, you will publish the map you created for Corbin Concrete in Chapter 12, *Introducing ArcGIS Online,* and publish it as a web application. The client wants a web application that will allow his dispatchers and sales teams to input the address where the concrete is to be delivered and to see which, if any, of their plants can provide the concrete.

Getting ready

This recipe will require you to have an ArcGIS Online account and access to the internet. You will need to be a level 2 user. If you do not have an ArcGIS Online user login or do not wish to use your organization's account to complete the recipes in this chapter, you can request a trial license from Esri at, `http://www.esri.com/arcgis/trial`.

You will also need a web browser that supports HTML 5 and JavaScript. These are current versions of Chrome, Edge, Firefox, and Safari. Internet Explorer 11 or newer is also supported. Other browsers may also work but have not been tested by Esri.

You must have completed all the recipes in `Chapter 12`, *Introducing ArcGIS Online*, and `Chapter 13`, *Publishing Your Own Content to ArcGIS Online*, before starting this recipe. This will ensure that you have the required maps and data along with a strong foundational understanding of what ArcGIS Online is and how it integrates with ArcGIS Pro.

You also need to ensure that you have installed the sample data before starting this exercise. This recipe will also use credits. It is estimated it that will use less than three credits.

How to do it...

1. You will start by launching ArcGIS Pro and opening the Corbin Concrete project located in `C:\Student\ArcGISProCookbook\Chapter14`. Using the skills you have learned in previous recipes, navigate to the `Chapter14` folder and open the `Corbin Concrete.aprx` project.

2. The project should open with a map, which looks familiar from `Chapter 12`, *Introducing ArcGIS Online*, as illustrated in the following screenshot. Before you are able to create a web app, you need to publish this to your ArcGIS Online content. The first step is to ensure the map and metadata are configured. Right-click on the **Corbin Concrete** map in the **Contents** pane. Select **Properties** from the menu that appears:

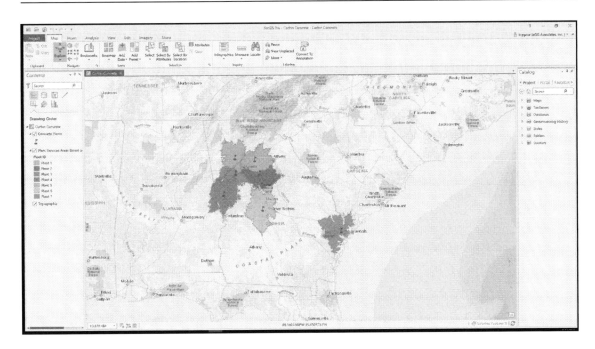

Corbin Concrete Map

3. Click on the **Extent** option in the left panel of the **Map Properties** window.

4. Ensure **Custom** extent is selected. If it is not, select it and set **Calculate from to Plant Service Areas Based on 45 Minute Drive**.

5. Click on the **Metadata** option in the left panel of the **Map Properties** window.

6. Using the knowledge and skills you learned in previous recipes, complete the metadata sections for the **Corbin Concrete** map. Click **OK** when done.

7. Click on the **Share** tab in the ribbon.

8. Click on the **Web Map** button located in the **Share As group** on the **Share** tab. This will launch the **Share As Web Map** tool.

9. Accept the default name, which should be `Corbin_Concrete`. If someone else in your organization is also working through this book, or if you have done so in the past, you may need to add your name to the end to ensure the name is unique.

10. Accept the values for **Summary and Tags**, which were pulled from the metadata for the map that you just entered.

11. Set your **Sharing Options** to **My Content** and your organization. They should be the top two options.

12. Set the **Select a Configuration** parameter to **Copy all data: Exploratory** using the dropdown. This option will allow users to view, query, and print the map. It does not allow them to edit the data.

13. Click the **Analysis** button. You should get a warning that says: Layer does not have a feature template set. Since you will not be editing the data contained in this map via a web application, this warning can be ignored.

14. Click the **Share** button to publish this map to your ArcGIS Online content.

15. When the tool completes successfully, close it.

16. Now you will verify that the **Corbin Concrete** map published to ArcGIS Online successfully. In the **Catalog** pane, click on the **Portal** tab near the top of the pane.

17. Look at the list of items available in your content. Verify that you see the Corbin_Concrete map you just published, as illustrated in the screenshot. Remember, you may need to refresh the pane to see it:

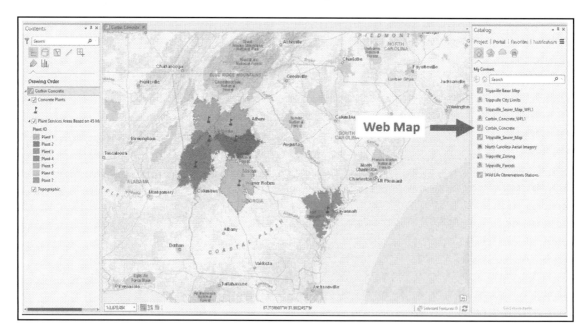

Corbin Concrete map successfully published to ArcGIS Online as shown in Portal tab

18. Once you have verified that the map published successfully to ArcGIS Online, save your project and close ArcGIS Pro.

19. Open your web browser and go to www.arcgis.com. Then sign in to your ArcGIS Online account, as you have done in previous recipes.

20. Click on the **Content** tab at the top of the page to view your ArcGIS Online content.

21. Locate and click on the **Corbin_Concrete** web map to open its property page.

Remember, when you publish a web map from ArcGIS Pro, it will often create multiple items in your ArcGIS Online content. This will frequently include a web map, service definition, and a feature layer. Make sure you click on the web map and not the feature layer or service definition.

22. Click on the **Open in Map Viewer** button on the right side of the page. This will open the web map in the ArcGIS Online viewer you have used in past recipes, as shown here:

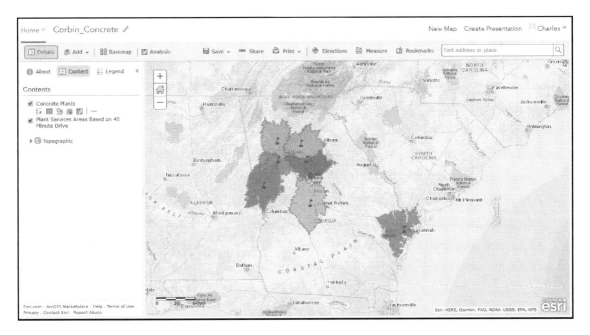

Corbin Concrete map viewed in ArcGIS Online Web Viewer

23. Click on the **Share** button located at the top of the map to open the **Share** window.

Notice that this window has several options. You can select who can view the map. Currently, it is just those within your organization. There is also a link to this map, which you can copy and email to someone you have shared the map with. If you share it with everyone, you can also post the map to your Facebook page and Twitter.

Under **Embed this map**, there are two options: **Embed in Website** and **Create a Web App**. **Embed in Website** is grayed out. You will learn more about that later.

24. Click on the **Create a Web App** button. This will allow you to begin the process of creating your own web GIS application.

25. The **Create a new web app** window will open. You should see three tabs across the top: **Configurable Apps**, **Web AppBuilder**, and **Operations Dashboard**, as illustrated in the following screenshot. Right now, you will focus on the **Configurable Apps** tab. Make sure **Show All** is selected from the options on the left side of the window:

ArcGIS Online App Template gallery

Configurable Apps are predefined application templates that include specific functionalities. You have limited configuration options to set up for each one of these. ArcGIS Online currently includes over 20 configurable template applications, including everything from simple map viewing to analysis and reporting. If you would like to learn more about the different available application templates, go to `http://doc.arcgis.com/en/arcgis-online/create-maps/ choose-configurable-app.htm`.

26. Click on the *Basic Viewer template* app. This will allow the dispatchers and sales team from Corbin Concrete to perform the functions they have asked for.

27. When you click on the **Basic Viewer template**, a new panel will appear on the right side of the **Create a New Web App** window, as shown in the screenshot. This new panel allows you to create a new web app, preview the web app so you can get an idea of what it will look like, and download the code for the app, so you can deploy it on your own web server. Click on the **Create Web App** button:

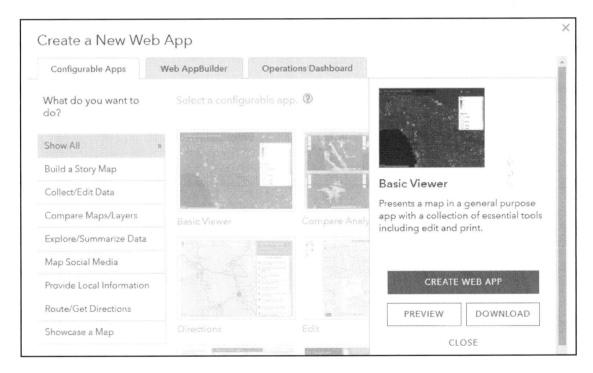

28. You will now configure some initial options for your new web application. Title your application `Corbin Concrete Plant Locations & Service Areas`.

29. Accept the tags and summary which were inherited from the web map.

30. Verify that your **Create a New Web App** window looks like the following and click **Done**. You may need to scroll down to see the **Done** button. Your **Save in folder** will be different as well:

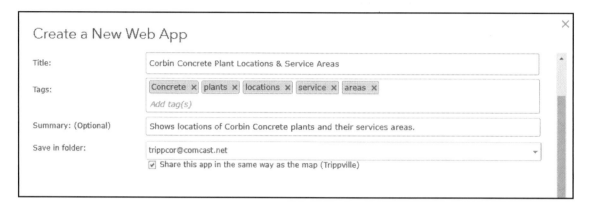

31. The web application configuration app will appear. You will now configure the functionality and appearance of your new web application. Under **Application title**, type: `Plant Locations`.

32. For the **Application subtitle**, type: `45 Minute Service Areas`.

33. Click in the **Details** window and type the following: `This application displays the Corbin Concrete plant locations and the service areas which are within a 45 minute drive time of each plant.` Users can enter an address in the search box at the top of the app to see if the address falls within a service area, and if so, which plant is closest to provide concrete to the entered address.

34. Click the **Save** button located under the web map. This will save your new application with the current settings you have configured.

Remember to save often. There is no autosave. If you lose internet connection or your browser locks up, all of your work will be lost.

35. Click on the **Theme** tab. This will allow you to configure the web application's appearance.

36. Set the **Header Color** to a light to medium gray. Try one of the last two options on the first row of the color palette.

37. Click the **Save** button to apply the color change. Feel free to adjust any of the other color settings as you see fit. Remember to click **Save** to see these changes applied in the preview area.

38. Below the color options are options for the layout. They control how and where the tools in the app are displayed. Try each of the options under **Choose a layout**. Remember to click on the **Save** button between each one to see what it looks like. Once you have reviewed all the options, select **Menu** bar and click **Save**.

You are almost done. There are just a few more configuration settings you need to set. Your application should now look very similar to the following:

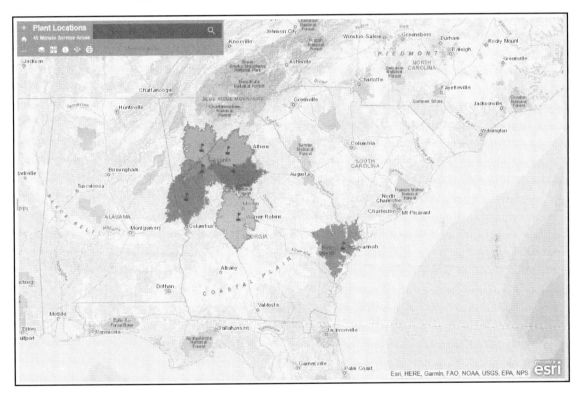

Draft web application for Corbin Concrete

Next, you will configure the functionality you wish to include in your new application:

39. Click on the **Options** tab to begin configuring the functionality.
40. Enable the **Display scale bar** on map. The sales team at Corbin Concrete have asked for this so they can roughly estimate the distance between the address they enter and the nearest plant.
41. Under toolbar options, enable the following options:

  - Basemap Gallery
  - Legend
  - Map Details
  - Measure Tool

42. Ensure all other toolbar options are disabled. You have just configured the tools that will be available in your web application.
43. Ensure **Display Editor** is disabled. You do not want dispatchers or the sales team editing data via this application.
44. Make sure the **Print** tool is enabled and click on **Add Legend to Output** to enable this option.
45. Scroll down and enable the **Add** toolbar labels feature. This will label each button in the application with its basic function. This will help non-GIS users more easily understand what the tools are.
46. Click the **Save** button to apply and save the changes you have made. Your application should now look like the following:

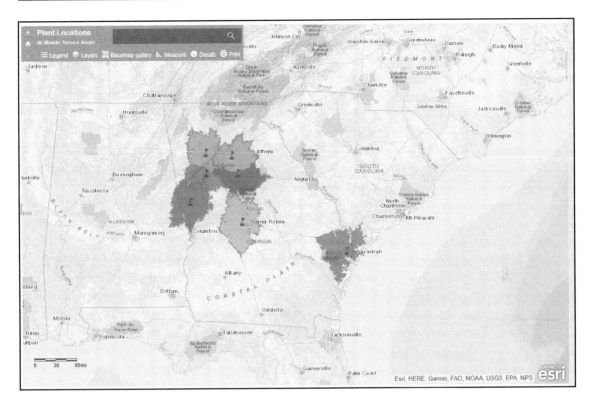

Plant location app you have been building

Lastly, for this application template, you will need to configure the **Search** options. This controls what the **Search** window at the top of the application is able to search for. By default, it uses the Esri World Geocoder service to pinpoint a location based on an address, coordinate, or common name. You can increase the search capability by allowing it to search the layers in your map and other data. You will configure it to allow the application to also search your services areas:

47. Click on the **Search** tab at the top of the page.
48. Notice the default settings. Click in the box next to the **Plant Service Areas Based on 45 Minute Drive**. This will allow the application to search that layer for specified values.
49. Now click **Edit**, located to the right of the layer name. This will allow you to configure how the search works for this layer.
50. Check **Enable Suggestions**. This will provide the user with possible matches as they type in values.
51. Set the **Maximum Suggestions** to 4 using the drop-down arrow.

52. Set the **Display field** to **Name** using the drop-down arrow.
53. Select **Name** as the **Search Fields** and click the **Save** button.
54. Save your application by clicking the **Save** button.
55. Now click **Launch** to see the application you just created. This will launch your new application in a new window within your browser, as shown in the following screenshot:

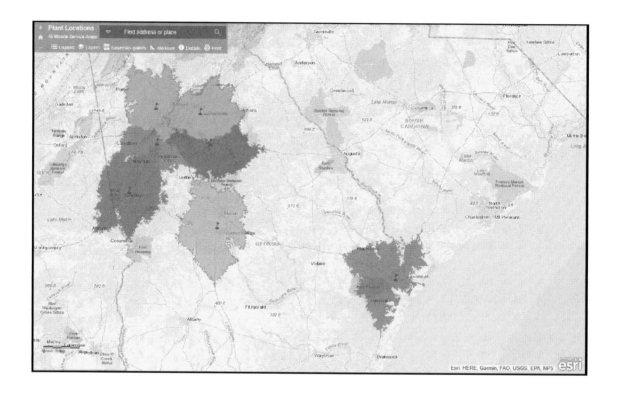

You have just successfully created your first GIS web application without any programming skills needed:

56. Now, let's take your new application for a test drive. Click in the **Search** tool where it says **Find address or place**. Type this value: 2712 Wilding Green Lane, Dacula GA. Notice as you type, your application is providing suggestions for possible matches to your search. Once you feel you see the correct match from the suggestions, select the suggestion. The map will automatically zoom in to the location you selected. At this scale it is hard to determine which specific plant serves this address, but because you can see a fill pattern you know immediately that this location is served by Corbin Concrete. So, this fullfills one of the requirements of Corbin Concrete.

57. Now, let's see if we can easily determine which plant serves this location. Click somewhere in the area around the address location. A pop-up window should appear in the map where you clicked, as illustrated in the screenshot. Review the contents of this pop-up window:

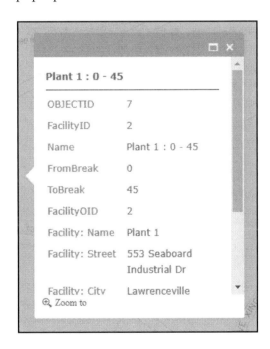

As you can see from the pop-up window, this location is served by **Plant 1**. So, you have met the other primary requirement for the application. Users can easily determine what plant serves an entered address:

58. Close the pop-up window once you are done reviewing its contents.
59. Examine some of the other tools within your new application. See what other functionalities users are able to access.
60. Once you are done examining your new application, close your web browser.

You have just created your first GIS web application, which allows users to locate a point in your map using an address or common name. That then allows users to determine if that location is in one of the service areas of a Corbin Concrete plant. However, that is not all users can do when using your web application. Users can also view the legend, turn layers on and off, change basemaps, measure lengths and areas, and print. You created this powerful and easy-to-use web application without having to write one line of code.

Creating a custom application with Web AppBuilder

You have just created your first GIS web application using one of Esri's customizable templates. While these are great and do result in some powerful apps, you may not find a template that does exactly what you need. This is where your other option for creating web apps comes in, Web AppBuilder.

Web AppBuilder allows you to create your own custom web app and to pick the tools you want to include. These tools are referred to as widgets. Web AppBuilder includes many base widgets which you can customize to suit your specific needs. This allows you much more flexibility when creating your own GIS web applications. If you do have programming skills, you can even create your own widgets which you can plug into Web AppBuilder for even more functionality and flexibility.

There are two versions of Web AppBuilder: **ArcGIS Online** and **Developer**. The ArcGIS Online version is embedded within ArcGIS Online. It does not require you to install any software locally or to have any programming skills. The Developer version is a bit more complex; it must be downloaded and installed locally. While you can use it like you do the ArcGIS Online version once installed, it allows you to create your own widgets or tools within the Web AppBuilder framework. If you want to download the Developers version of Web AppBuilder, go to `https://developers.arcgis.com/web-appbuilder/`. For the remainder of this recipe, we will focus on the ArcGIS Online version.

Corbin Concrete was very impressed with the web app you created for them in the previous recipe. It has really helped them see the value of GIS. This has given them another idea for a second application which will be used primarily by their sales team. They want a new app which has more capability. They want to be able to be able to draw in the app to show the location the concrete will be poured and be able to print it for the inside estimators. They also want the app to be able to locate the nearest plant to a location, as well as to be able to find any plant within a specified distance.

In this recipe, you will use Web AppBuilder to create a new web application which meets the needs of Corbin Concrete as outlined before. You will start with the existing Corbin Concrete web map you created in the previous recipe. You will then use Web AppBuilder to create and configure the new application with the required widgets as well as its general appearance.

Getting ready

To complete this recipe, you need to have completed `Chapters 12`, *Introducing ArcGIS Online*, and `Chapter 13`, *Creating Web Apps Using ArcGIS Online*, along with the previous recipe in this chapter. This will ensure you have the required data available and the understanding needed to complete this recipe. You will also require an ArcGIS Online account and access to the internet. You will need to be a level 2 user. If you already completed the required recipes, you should already meet these requirements.

You will also need a web browser that supports HTML 5 and JavaScript. These include current versions of Chrome, Edge, Firefox, and Safari. Internet Explorer 11 or newer is also supported. Other browsers may also work, but have not been tested by Esri.

This recipe will also use credits. It is estimated that it will use less than three credits.

How to do it...

1. The first thing you need to do is log in in to your ArcGIS Online account. So, launch your web browser and go to `www.arcgis.com`. Then sign in to your account as you have done in previous recipes.
2. Click on the **Content** tab at the top of the page to view your content.

3. In your content, click on the `Corbin_Concrete` web map. This should open the properties page for the web map, which you have seen in previous recipes, as shown in the following screenshot:

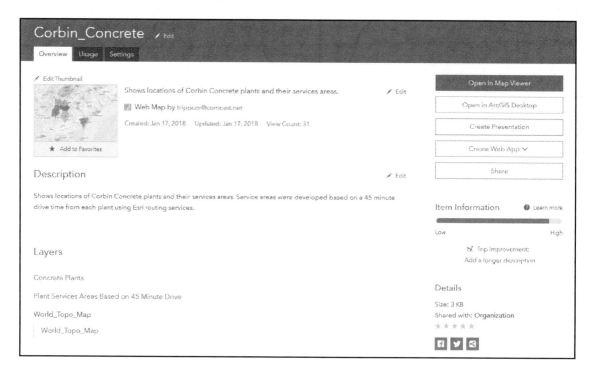

 Remember, there will be several items named `Corbin_Concrete`. You will have at least three: `Web Map`, `Feature Layer`, and `Service Definition`.

4. Click on the **Create Web App** button on the right and select **Using the Web AppBuilder from the list of options presented**, as illustrated in the following screenshot. This will allow you to start the process of creating a new web app:

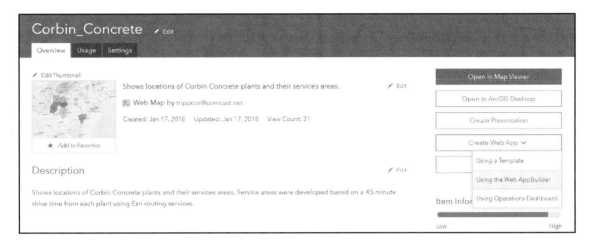

You can use a single web map in as many web apps as you need, there is no limit. So, a single web map may serve as the starting point for any number of web or even mobile apps you may deploy. You should always keep that in mind as you are designing and publishing your web maps. Remember, you also need to balance it with performance. The more data within a map, the slower it will perform.

5. Title your new web app *Corbin Concrete Sales Team App*.
6. Add the following tags to the list of existing ones: `sales`, `Web AppBuilder`, `draw`, and `find nearest`.
7. Type the following description: `This application was created for Corbin Concrete's sales team to allow them to locate the nearest concrete plant to a location and draw locations where concrete will be poured on-site.`

8. Verify that your **Create a New Web App** window looks like the following and click **OK**:

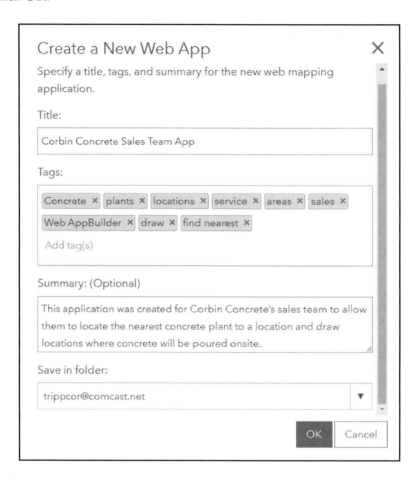

Once you click **OK**, Web AppBuilder will be automatically launched in your browser. As you can see, it is somewhat similar to the tools you used to configure your template application in the previous recipe. However, you have a lot more options available to you. You will start by configuring the general appearance of your application by selecting and configuring a theme.

9. As you can see, Web AppBuilder includes at least nine different themes you can choose from for creating your web application. Take a moment to select and review each one.

 Each theme is optimized to support specific functionalities. For example, the Billboard theme is designed to support simple tasks, such as printing or viewing data, whereas the Dashboard is designed to allow you to view multiple widgets at one time. To learn more about each of the themes available in the Web AppBuilder, go to `http://doc.arcgis.com/en/web-appbuilder/create-apps/themes-tab.htm`.

As you preview the web app on the right, it will update to give you an idea how your app will look and where the tools/widgets will be located. The style and layout options will also change.

10. Once you are done reviewing the themes, select the **Billboard Theme**. This creates an app that supports basic functionality, such as the functionality requested by Corbin Concrete.

11. Select a style color you prefer; any of the options will work. For the sake of future graphics, the author has selected the blue option.

12. For the **Layout**, select the second option, as illustrated in the screenshot. This will place the widgets you will add later in the upper-right corner of your new application:

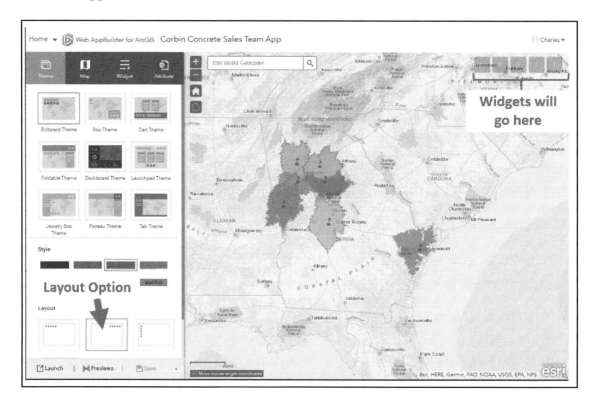

You will skip over the **Map** tab in this recipe since you already started with a specific web map. Now it is time to start adding the widgets you need to the application. Remember, widgets are configurable tools which provide the functionality to your application. As you can see in the **Preview** window, some widgets have automatically been added by default. This includes **Zoom Slider**, **Home** button, **My Location** button, **Scalebar**, and coordinate readout.

The **Zoom Slider** allows you to zoom in and out within the map. The **Home** button is similar to the **Full Extent** button in ArcGIS Pro. It will zoom you, to the full extent of the web map. The **My Location** button will automatically center the map where the application believes you are located. This is a great widget to include if the application will be used on mobile devices with GPS. It does not always work so well on computers in an office. This widget also requires an HTTPs connection.

13. Click on the **Widget** tab on the top-left side of **Web AppBuilder**. This is where you add and configure the widgets that will be in your application.

14. Notice that several are already highlighted. These correspond to the widgets that were included by default. Also notice the five gray squares located below the default widgets. These match the five gray squares located in the upper-right corner of the application preview.

15. Corbin Concrete has decided that they do not need an **Overview** map in this new application. This is one of the default widgets. You will now disable it. Move your mouse pointer to the **Overview** widget. When you do, two small icons will appear: one in the lower-right corner to configure the widget and one in the upper-right corner to hide it, as illustrated in the following diagram. Click on the Hide icon to disable this widget in your new application:

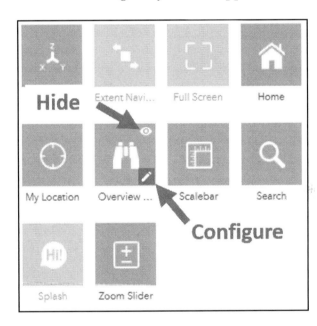

Once you click on the Hide icon, the widget should become grayed out. This indicates that you were successful in hiding the widget, so it will not appear in your application. To enable other default widgets in the future, simply reverse this process. Now, to add customizable widgets to your new application, we will start with a **Layer List** widget. This will allow users to turn layers in the map on or off:

16. In the left panel of **Web AppBuilder**, click on the first gray square labeled **Widget**, with the number one inside it. This will open the **Choose Widget** window.

The **Billboard Theme** you selected includes a large number of possible widgets which will work with this theme. This list will vary depending on the theme you have selected.

17. Click on the **Layer List** widget located in the middle row, as shown in the following diagram. Then click **OK** to configure the widget:

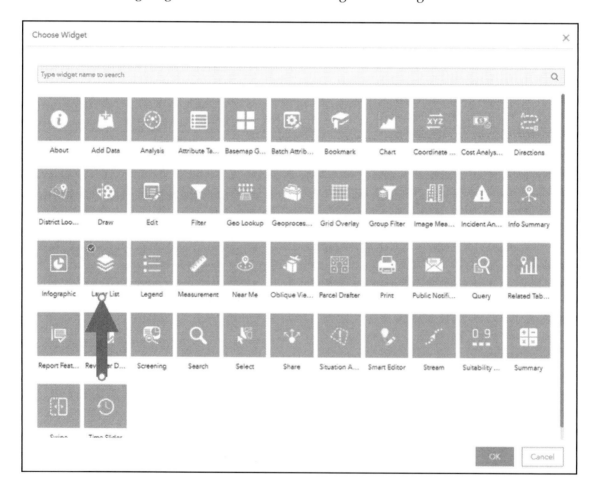

18. So, you can see that this widget includes several options. In general, you always want to keep things as simple as possible. Remember, your users will be sales people, not GIS experts. You will disable some of these options to reduce the complexity of the widget, so it only provides the capabilities that are needed. Disable the following options by clicking on the checkbox:
    - Transparency
    - Enable/Disable Pop-up
    - Move up/Move down
    - Description/Show item details/Download

19. Verify that your **Configure Layer List** looks like the following, and click **OK**:

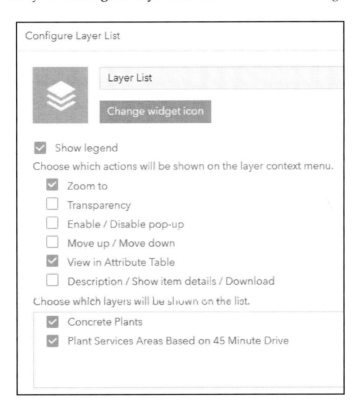

You should notice the **Layer List** widget now appears in the left panel of **Web AppBuilder**, as well as in the upper-right corner of the app in the preview area. This shows that you have successfully added your first widget. Now you will add a **Print** widget:

20. Before you add another widget, click on the **Save** tab at the bottom of **Web AppBuilder** to save the work you have done so far.

21. Click on the gray square now labeled as **Widget**, with a number one inside it. It should be located next to the **Layer List** widget you just added.

22. Select the **Print** widget from the gallery presented. It is on the same row as the **Layer List** widget. Once you have selected the widget, click **OK**.

23. Set the following values as indicated:
    - **Service URL**: Leave the default value.
    - **Default title**: Corbin Concrete Potential Project
    - **Default author**: Corbin Concrete Sales Team
    - **Default copyright**: Copyright Corbin Concrete. All rights reserved.
    - **Default format: PDF**
    - **Default layout: Letter ANSI A Portrait**

24. Verify that your **Configure Print** window looks like the following and click **OK**:

The **Print** widget has now been added to your application. Another capability that Corbin Concrete asked for was the ability to draw graphics in the map which would show the location where concrete would be poured for a project. You will next add the **Draw** widget which provides this functionality.

25. Make sure to save your application before you continue.
26. Again, click on one of the gray widget squares in the left panel.
27. Select the **Draw** widget from the gallery and click OK.
28. The **Configure Draw** window is not open. This widget has several options. Once again, you will simplify it. Since Corbin Concrete operates in the United States, you will remove all metric options from the widget. Move your mouse pointer to the **Actions** column for **Kilometers**. Several icons will appear. Click on the **Delete** icon, as illustrated in the following screenshot, to remove **Kilometers** from the list:

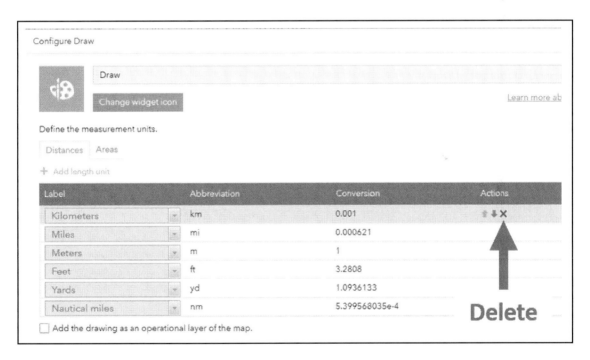

29. Repeat that process for **Meters** and **Nautical Miles**. You should be left with **Miles**, **Feet**, and **Yards**.

30. You have set the options for **Distances**. Now to do so for areas. Click on the **Areas** tab located just below the **Change** widget icon button.

31. You should now see a list of area measurement units. Remove all metric units using the same process you did to remove the distance units. Only Square miles, Acres, Square feet, and Square yards should remain.

32. Click **OK** once you have removed all the metric units from the list of **Areas**.

33. Save your app.

    You have just added your third widget to your application. The first three have been fairly simple. Now you will add a more complex widget, **Near Me**. This will allow the sales person to find the nearest plant to their location or where they click in the map.

34. Click on one of the gray widget squares again to open the **Choose Widget** window.

35. Select the **Near Me** widget from the gallery and click **OK**.

    When the **Configure Near Me** window opens, you should immediately notice, this widget is a lot more complicated than any of the previous widgets you have configured so far. This widget has five different tabs, each containing several parameters you will configure.

36. You will start with the **Search Source Settings**. Configure the parameters as indicated here:

- **Geocoder URL**: Accept the default provided automatically
- **Geocoder Name**: Accept the default provided automatically
- **Placeholder Text**: Enter Project Address
- **Country or Region Code(s)**: USA
- **Maximum Suggestions**: 6
- **Maximum Results**: 1
- **Zoom Scale**: 50,000
- **Min Scale**: 300,000
- **Radius**: 50,000

37. Verify that you have set the parameters correctly and click on the **Search Settings** tab.
38. Click on the **Set** button to the right of **Select search layers**. Click on the checkbox next to the **Concrete Plants** layer., then click **OK**.

You selected the **Concrete Plants** layer as the search layer since you wanted this widget to locate the nearest concrete plant to a given location.

39. Enable the **Set location** button. This will allow the user to click in the map to select a location from which to find the nearest plant.
40. Enable the **Set buffer** visibility. This will also allow the user to set the distance the tool will use to search and find the nearest plant.
41. Set the default buffer distance to 10.
42. Set the maximum buffer distance to 25.
43. Set the buffer distance units to **Miles**.
44. Limit the number of results to one.

45. Verify that your **Search Settings** match the following screenshot, then click **OK**. You do not need to configure the other tabs:

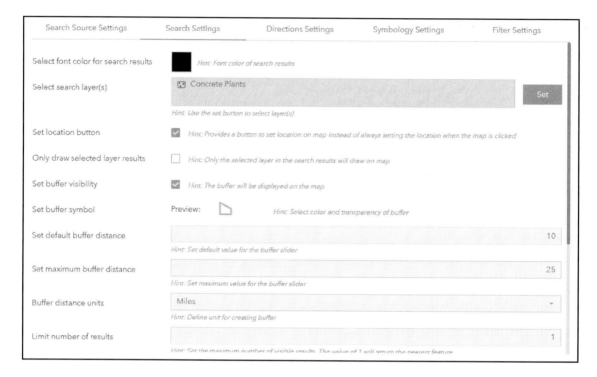

That is your fourth and final widget. This application should now contain all the functionalities requested by Corbin Concrete. Next, you will test your new application as well as preview how it looks on different devices:

46. Save your application before continuing.
47. Click on the **Previews** tab located at the bottom of the left panel in the **Web AppBuilder**.
48. You should see a list of different mobile devices in the left panel. This allows you to see how your application will look on the screen of those devices. Click on a few of the device options to see how your new application will look when used on them.

These previews are functional. So, you can test the tools and see how they will work on the screen of the device. This does not test them in the actual device environment, so it should not be used for, or be considered as, a debugging tool for the code. However, it will help you test the overall workflows for a given device.

49. Click the **Launch** tab at the bottom of the panel in **Web AppBuilder**. This will launch your new application in a new browser window on your computer.

50. Click on the **Layer List** tool located in the upper-right corner of your app. This will open the tool window.

51. Click on the checkbox next to **Plant Service Areas Based on 45 Minute Drive**, and watch what happens in the map.

52. The layer is no longer visible. Click on the checkbox again to turn the layer back on.

53. Using the **Zoom Slider** in the upper-left corner of the app or your mouse, zoom to the area where four of the services meet, as illustrated in the screenshot:

54. Now, you will test the **Near Me** tool to see if it locates the nearest plant to a location you click on the map. Click on the **Near Me** tool, which is in the upper-right corner of the app. It is the first tool in the row of tools you included in the application.

55. In the **Near Me** tool window, click on the **Locate on Map** button. It is located to the right of the Esri World Geocoder search cell.

56. Click in the map, at the location illustrated here, which is just to the north-east of **East Point**:

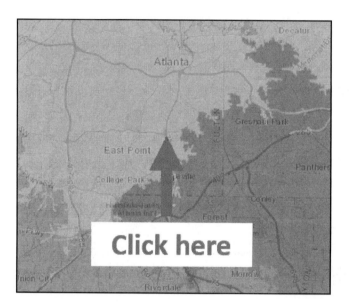

Once you click in the map, several things should happen. First, an address will appear in the Esri World Geocoding cell. Next, a circle should appear showing the search area, which defaults to 10 miles because that was the value you configured the widget to start with. Lastly, any results will appear in the tool window. If you click near the same location, shown in the screenshot, no results should appear. That means there is not a plant within 10 miles of this location. However, you have a distance slider within the tool which allows the user to increase or decrease that search distance.

57. Using the slider bar under **Show results within 10 Miles**, change the value to 15 Miles. This should display a result which indicates that **Plant 3** is the closest to the location you selected, as illustrated here, even though it is within the service area of several plants:

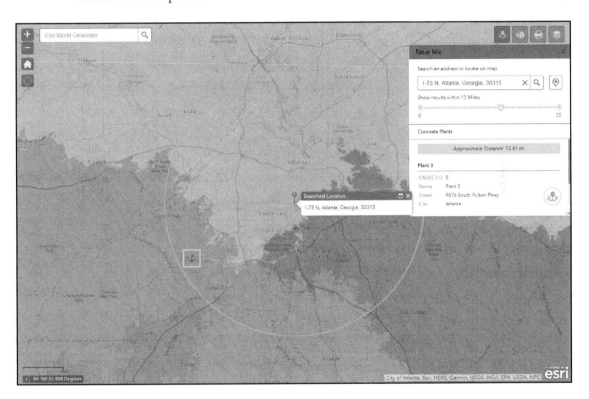

58. Close the **Near me** tool. Feel free to test the other tools if you desire.
59. Close your browser once you are done exploring your new application.

You have just created another web application. This time you used the Esri **Web AppBuilder** tool to create a custom application which includes just the tools your client, Corbin Concrete, requested. This allowed you to create a powerful but easy-to-use GIS web application. Again, you did this without needing to write one line of code.

Sharing your applications

You have created two very powerful GIS web applications. However, right now only you can access them. Just as you have to share web maps, feature services, and data files if you want others to be able to access them, you must do the same thing with your applications.

The process to share your applications is very similar to how you shared your other content. You have the same options in terms of who you can share them with: your organization, a group or groups, and everyone.

In this recipe, you will share the *Corbin Concrete Sales Team* app you just created so the employees of Corbin Concrete can access the application. They currently do not have an ArcGIS Online account or user logins, so you will share it with everyone. This will allow them to access the app without requiring a login.

Getting ready

You must have completed all previous recipes in this chapter as well as those in `Chapters 12`, *Introducing ArcGIS Online*, and `Chapter 13`, *Publishing Your Own Content to ArcGIS Online*, before starting this recipe. This recipe also requires that you have an ArcGIS Online account with at least a Publisher level role assigned. You will also need internet access along with a web browser that supports HTML5 and JavaScript.

How to do it...

1. The first step is to log in to your ArcGIS online account. Launch your web browser and go to `www.arcgis.com`. Sign in to your account.
2. Click on the **Content** tab at the top of ArcGIS Online to access your content.
3. Locate and click on the *Corbin Concrete Sales Team* app in your content. As you have experienced in previous recipes, this will take you to the properties for this application.

    As you did in previous recipes, you will need to complete the metadata for the application before you share it.

4. Click on **Add an in-depth description of the item**, located below **Description**. This will open a text editing window. Using the application summary which appears at the top of the page, and your previous experience, write a detailed description for the application, explaining its purpose, general functionality, that it was created with **Web AppBuilder**, and who it was created for. Make sure to click the **Save** button when you have completed your description.

5. Click **Edit**, located to the right of **Terms of Use**. Type the following into the text editing box that appears: **This application is intended as a training tool only**. No accuracy is guaranteed or implied. Click **Save** when done.

Now that you have completed the metadata associated with your application, you are ready to share it.

6. Click the **Share** button on the right side of ArcGIS Online. This will open the **Share** window.

7. Click in the checkbox next to **Everyone (public)**. This will allow anyone to access this application. Also, notice that your organization is automatically checked.

8. Verify that your **Share** window looks like the following, and click **OK** to apply the new setting and to close the **Share** window:

Once you click **OK**, another window will appear, as shown in the following screenshot, because the app references other items in your content. So, when you share the app, the same sharing setting must also apply to the content referenced in your web app. This means that you will also need to update the share settings for the **Corbin_Concrete** web map and feature layer. Luckily, ArcGIS Online makes this easy with the window that appeared:

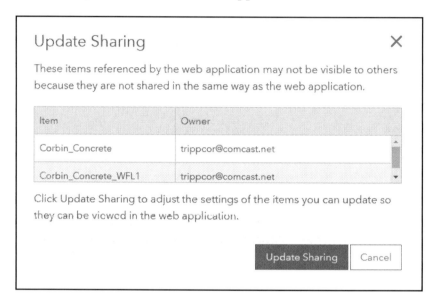

One thing to keep in mind when you update the sharing settings is that you are allowing others to access your content. So, make sure what you are sharing is appropriate for those you are sharing it with. You do not want to share sensitive information with everyone. Also, remember, that just because someone might be able to access it, what they can do with the content is also controlled by their role. If they do not have an ArcGIS Online user account, their ability to do more than just view, query, and print will be very limited.

9. Click the **Update Sharing** button in the window that appeared.
10. If you wish to test your share settings, scroll down in your browser until you see a URL on the right side. This is the web address for your application. You can click the **Copy** button located beside the address, then paste the URL into an email and send it to a friend or colleague. See if they are able to access the application you created.
11. Close your browser once you are done.

You are done. You have shared your web application so that others, both inside your organization and outside, are able to access it.

Embedding an ArcGIS Online web map in a web page

While creating web apps does allow you to create useful tools to expand the usefulness of your GIS, sometimes it might be overkill. Maybe you just want to create a map showing office locations and display it on your company website. Maybe you are planning a special event and just want to include a map to show the location of the event on the events website. You just don't need a web application.

ArcGIS Online also provides a way for you to easily embed a web map from your ArcGIS Online content into web page. Like creating a web app, it is pretty easy to do. It does help if you know a little about creating a web page for this to work smoothly, specifically, having a basic understanding of HTML, which is the basic language used to create web pages.

The **Planning Director for the City of Trippville** wants to show the City's **Zoning** map on the **Planning Departments** web page. He does not want a fancy app, he just wants a simple map that citizens can use to see the zoning classifications for areas within the City.

In this recipe, you will embed a new Zoning web map into an existing web page for the City of Trippville. You will start by creating a new web map using the Trippville Basic Map that you created in Chapter 12, *Introducing ArcGIS Online*. You will then add the zoning layer, which has already been published to the map, to create the new **Zoning Map**. Then you will share and embed the new map in the web page.

Getting ready

You must have completed the other recipes in this chapter, along with those in Chapter 12, *Introducing ArcGIS Online*, before starting this one. This will ensure that you have the required maps and data needed to complete this recipe.

You will also need an ArcGIS Online level 2 user account with Publisher role privileges. This recipe should not cost any credits to complete. If it does, it will be less than one.

How to do it...

1. First, you will need to log in to your ArcGIS Online account. Launch your web browser and go to `www.arcgis.com`. Then sign in to your account as you have done in previous recipes.

2. Click on the **Content** tab at the top of ArcGIS Online to access your content.

3. Scroll down through your content until you locate the Trippville Basic Map web map. Click on it to go to its **Properties** page.

4. Click on the **Open in Map Viewer** button on the right side. This will open the map in the ArcGIS Online Map Viewer application, as illustrated here:

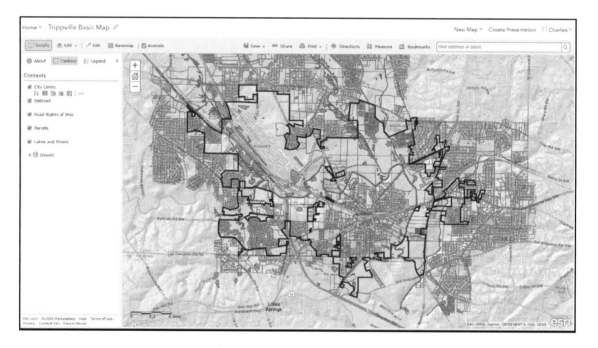

5. Click on the **Save** button located at the top of the map's viewing area. Select **Save As** from the list presented.

6. Title the new map `Trippville Zoning Map`.

7. Add any tags you feel are appropriate, such as `Zoning`.

8. Change the **Summary** to say: `This map displays the Zoning classifications for the City of Trippville`. Then click **Save Map**.

9. Click on the **Add** button and select **Search for Layers** from the list that appears.

10. Set the **In option** to **ArcGIS Online** using the drop-down arrow.

11. In the **Find cell**, type `Trippville Zoning` and click **GO**.

The new **Zoning Layer** should appear in your map, as illustrated here:

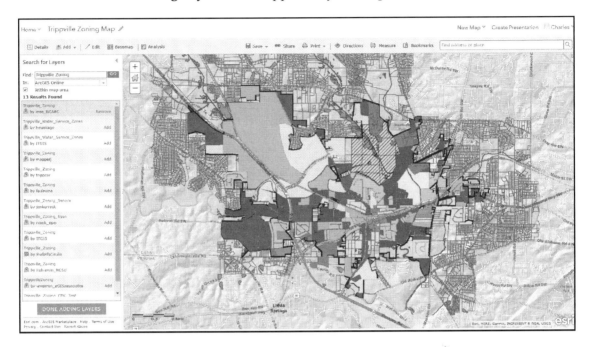

12. Click on **Done Adding Layers** to complete the process.
13. The **Trippville Zoning Layer** appears at the top of the layer list. It is blocking other layers. Select the layer in the **Content** and drag it so it is below the **Lakes and Rivers** layer.

You could have also clicked on the three dots in the menu below the layer and selected **Move Down** to change the position of the layer in the layer list.

14. Save your map by clicking on the **Save** button.

    Your web map should now look like the following screenshot. It should contain the **City Limits, Railroad, Road Rights of Way, Parcels, Lakes and Rivers**, and **Trippville Zoning** layers:

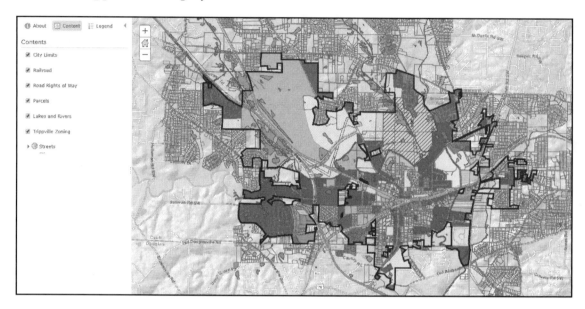

    You have now created the required map, which the **Planning Director** wants to display on the department's web page. Now it is time to share the new map and embed the code.

15. Click on the **Share** button at the top of the map view. This will open the **Share** window you have seen in previous recipes.

16. Because this map will be displayed on the City's public website, you will share it with everyone. Click in the checkbox next to **Everyone (public)**.

17. Another pop-up window will appear. Read the contents of the window and then click **OK** to close it.

18. Notice that since you selected everyone, the **Embed in Website** option is no longer grayed out. Click on the **Embed in Website** button.

19. Now you will configure the settings for how the map will appear on the website. Start by setting the width to 940 and the height to 600. Ensure that **Allow Responsive Sizing** is enabled. This will allow the size to automatically adjust for smaller screens.

20. For **Map Options**, enable the following options:
    - Zoom control
    - Home button
    - Legend

21. Choose whichever theme you like.

    Notice that as you make adjustments to the size and options, the HTML code located between the size and map options changes. ArcGIS Online is automatically creating and adjusting the HTML coding which will be required to embed the web map in your web page. You are now ready to embed the map into the department's web page:

22. Click the **Copy** button to the right of the HTML code in the **Embed in Website** window. This copies the HTML code to your clipboard, so you can paste it into your website.

23. Open your `File Explorer` and navigate to `C:\Student\ArcGISProCookbook\Chapter14`, using the skills you have learned in previous recipes.

24. You should see several files in this folder, including `Zoning.html`. That represents a web page you want to embed the map into. Double-click on that file to open it in a web browser; you can see it is a very simple web page.

25. Once you are done looking over the web page, return to `File Explorer`.

26. Right-click on the `Zoning.html` file and select **Open with** | **Notepad**, as illustrated in the following screenshot:

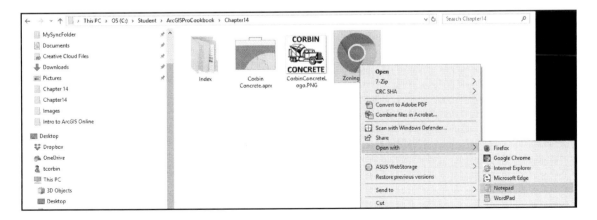

You can now see the HTML code used to create the web page you just viewed in your browser. As you can see, this is a very simple web page. Now you will embed your map into this page.

 HTML stands for **Hypertext Markup Language**. It is a fairly simple programming language used to create web pages. It uses a series of tags to identify and display content. For example, `<p>` indicates a paragraph, `<strong>` or `<b>` means display as bold font, and `<body>` indicates the main body of the code which is to be displayed in the web page. Each tag must be closed using the same starting tag with a slash, such as `</p>`.

27. Move your cursor in the page to just in front of where it says `<p> Please contact our Planning Director`, then press your *Enter* key to create a row between the two paragraphs.
28. Place your cursor in the row you just created and press your *Ctrl + V* keys together to paste the code from ArcGIS Online into the web page.

The code created by ArcGIS Online, based on your settings, should now appear in the web page code, as illustrated in the following screenshot. The ArcGIS Online code has been highlighted to make it easier to see:

```
<title>City of Trippville Zoning Map</title>
</head>
<body>

<p><strong>Welcome to the City of Trippville Zoning Map.</strong> This map
is maintained by the City's Planning Department. We make every effort to
ensure it is up to date.</p>
<style>.embed-container {position: relative; padding-bottom: 64%; height:
0; max-width: 100%;} .embed-container iframe, .embed-container object,
.embed-container iframe{position: absolute; top: 0; left: 0; width: 100%;
height: 100%;} small{position: absolute; z-index: 40; bottom: 0; margin-
bottom: -15px;}</style><div class="embed-container"><iframe width="940"
height="600" frameborder="0" scrolling="no" marginheight="0"
marginwidth="0" title="Trippville Zoning Map"
src="//trippville.maps.arcgis.com/apps/Embed/index.html?
webmap=3dcf67a83b1a4b49b14a37a720d907a7&amp;extent=-84.6978,33.7902,-
84.5819,33.8472&home=true&zoom=true&previewImage=false&scale=false&legend=t
rue&disable_scroll=false&theme=light"></iframe></div>
<p> Please contact our Planning Director, Nathaniel Keith at <a
href="mailto:nkeith@cityoftrippville.gov?subject=Zoning
Enquiry">nkeith@cityoftrippville.gov</a> if you have any questions.</p>

</body>
</html>
```

29. In the menu at the top of Notepad, click on **File**, and select **Save** to save the changes made to the web page code.

30. Return to your web browser, where you previewed the web page before you edited it. Press your *F5* key to refresh the page. You should now see the map you just embeded in the middle of the page.

31. Take a moment to explore the map on the page. Once you are done, close your web browser, file explorer, and Notepad.

You are done. You just successfully embedded a web map in a web page. As you just experienced, it is not hard and can add some great content to your website.

Other Books You May Enjoy

If you enjoyed this book, you may be interested in these other books by Packt:

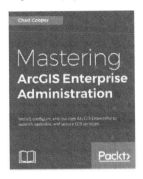

Mastering ArcGIS Enterprise Administration
Chad Cooper

ISBN: 978-1-78829-749-3

- Effectively install and configure ArcGIS Enterprise, including the enterprise geodatabase, ArcGIS Server, and Portal for ArcGIS
- Incorporate different methodologies to manage and publish services
- Utilize the security methods available in ArcGIS Enterprise
- Use Python and Python libraries from Esri to automate administrative tasks
- Identify the common pitfalls and errors to get your system back up and running quickly from an outage

Learning ArcGIS Pro
Tripp Corbin, GISP

ISBN: 978-1-78528-449-6

- Install ArcGIS Pro and assign Licenses to users in your organization
- Navigate and use the ArcGIS Pro ribbon interface to create maps and perform analysis
- Create and manage ArcGIS Pro GIS Projects
- Create 2D and 3D maps to visualize and analyze data
- Author map layouts using cartographic tools and best practices to show off the results of your analysis and maps
- Import existing map documents, scenes, and globes into your new ArcGIS Pro projects quickly
- Create standardized workflows using Tasks
- Automate analysis and processes using ModelBuilder and Python

Leave a review - let other readers know what you think

Please share your thoughts on this book with others by leaving a review on the site that you bought it from. If you purchased the book from Amazon, please leave us an honest review on this book's Amazon page. This is vital so that other potential readers can see and use your unbiased opinion to make purchasing decisions, we can understand what our customers think about our products, and our authors can see your feedback on the title that they have worked with Packt to create. It will only take a few minutes of your time, but is valuable to other potential customers, our authors, and Packt. Thank you!

Index

creating 397, 401, 403

C

CAD data
  adding, to map 81, 84, 86
central feature of geographic distribution
  finding 441, 442, 448
central feature
  reference link 442
Community Analyst
  reference link 581
composite relationship 149
Computer Aided Mass Appraisal (CAMA) 104
computer-aided drafting and design (CADD) 484
configuration keywords
  reference link 66
coordinate system
  changing, of map 305, 308, 310
  data, projecting 318, 322, 323, 325, 328, 330
  defining, for data 310, 313, 316, 317
  setting up, for map 299, 301, 304
  verifying, for an existing map 294, 296, 299
Copy Rows tool
  reference link 361
CSV file
  used, for creating layer 602, 603, 604, 606, 608
custom application
  creating, with Web AppBuilder 650, 651, 654,
    655, 659, 662, 665, 667

D

data
  editing, with map topology 278, 279, 282, 284,
    285, 288, 290
  enabling, to store Z coordinates 474, 475, 478,
    479, 480, 481, 482, 483
  querying, in joined table 120, 125
demographic data
  accessing, in ArcGIS Pro 572, 575, 578, 581
Developer version 650
Digital Elevation Model (DEM) 462
dispersion of data
  reference link 449

E

editing options
  configuring 159
Equator 292
Esri template
  used, for creating web app 637, 638, 641, 643,
    644, 647, 650
Excel spreadsheet
  importing, into ArcGIS Pro 367, 368, 371, 376,
    377, 378, 381

F

feature class 61
feature linked annotation
  about 140
  creating 140, 144, 145, 149
feature
  aligning 191, 196, 200
  calculating, Generate Near Table tool used 412,
    417, 419
  labeling, joined table used 113, 114, 119
  merging 185, 191
  reshaping 167, 173
  selecting, within specific distance 390, 395
  verifying, Near tool 404, 406, 407, 409, 411
FeatureID (FID) 63

G

Generate Near Table tool
  used, for calculating feature 411, 417, 419
geocoding addresses 90, 91, 97, 99
geodatabase feature class
  about 61
  multiple shapefiles, merging 346, 351, 352, 357
  shapefiles, converting 332, 337, 342, 344, 346
geodatabase topology
  creating 257, 258, 260, 262, 263, 266
  used, for validating spatial data 267, 269, 272
geodatabase
  creating 63, 72
geodatabases, types
  reference link 159
geographic dispersion of data
  calculating 449, 450, 453, 454, 456, 458